Openings

Openings

**A Memoir from the Women's Art Movement
New York City, 1970–1992**

Sabra Moore

newvillagePRESS

Published in the United States by
    New Village Press, New York, NY.
    bookorders@newvillagepress.net
    www.newvillagepress.net

New Village Press is a public-benefit, not-for-profit publishing division of Architects Designers Planners for Social Responsibility.

Printed in Korea

The printing papers used in this book are acid-free (Process Chlorine Free), and the binding is library quality.

Original paperback ISBN 9781613320181

Publication Date: 25 October 2016
First Edition

Library of Congress Cataloging-in-Publication Data

Names: Moore, Sabra, author.
Title: Openings : a memoir from the women's art movement, New York City
    1970-1992 / Sabra Moore.
Description: First edition. | New York, NY : New Village Press, 2016.
Identifiers: LCCN 2016015951 | ISBN 9781613320181 (paperback)
Subjects: LCSH: Moore, Sabra. | Artists--United States--Biography. | Women
    artists--United States--Biography. | Feminism and art--New York
    (State)--New York--History--20th century. | Art--Political aspects--New
    York (State)--New York--History--20th century. | New York
    (N.Y.)--Biography. | BISAC: ART / History / Contemporary (1945-). | SOCIAL
    SCIENCE / Feminism & Feminist Theory. | BIOGRAPHY & AUTOBIOGRAPHY /
    Personal Memoirs. | SOCIAL SCIENCE / Women's Studies.
Classification: LCC N6537.M6414 A2 2016 | DDC 704/.04209747109047--dc23
LC record available at https://lccn.loc.gov/2016015951

Front cover photograph: Sabra Moore, New York City 1985. Photo by Roger Mignon
Flap photograph: Sabra Moore, Abiquiú 2016. Photo by Roger Mignon
Frontispiece photograph: Frankie Buschke inside Printed Matter, *House Dress* installation,
                with Sabra Moore outside laughing, New York City 1984. Photo by Roger Mignon

Cover design by Lynne Elizabeth
Interior design and composition by Sabra Moore and Larry Van Dyke

I dedicate this book to my grandmothers,
Gladys Greer Parks and Caroline Lewis Moore, quilt makers and countrywomen,
and my great-grandmother, Lillie Parks, quilt maker, midwife, and healer.
My path spirals from their paths into new directions.

Acknowledgments

Writing *Openings* and assembling the images that form a parallel visual story has been as much a process as the living history that I recount. My spouse Roger Mignon shared in these experiences from his own vantage and also brought his camera to our actions and exhibitions. His photos form an important document of the period and I thank him for being there with me and for letting me use many of his pictures in this book. My friend Margaret Randall read chapters as I wrote them in starts and stops over seven years. Her enthusiasm gave me the courage to keep going, and her writer's eye caught many slips and omissions. Other friends were equally important readers. Lucy R. Lippard, who is also a participant in this narrative, and art historian Dr. Patricia Hills read the freshly finished manuscript. They are both part of the world I describe, so their comments made me feel I had written honestly; I appreciate their corrections of facts and spelling. Younger readers were also helpful. My fellow activist with the Española Farmers Market, Norma Navarro, and artist Cynthia Laureen Vogt both heartened me by finding these stories relevant to their own lives. I also appreciate the comments and solidarity of poets Joan Logghe and Marithelma Costa, writer Chellis Glendinning, and artists Marina Gutierrez, Iren Schio, and Bibi Lenĉek. Deirdre Lawrence, principal librarian at the Brooklyn Museum, encouraged me to organize my boxes of papers, photos, and ephemera in order to create an archive, now at Barnard College thanks to the determined efforts of independent curator Marina Urbach. This process, midway through writing the book, led me to go back and rewrite, adding details I had forgotten or not recorded in my journals.

I want to thank art historian Sharon Irish for suggesting I send the manuscript to New Village Press. I feel very fortunate to have found a kindred publisher who could appreciate the diverse aspects of this story and also the importance of its visualization. It has been a joy to work with New Village Press director Lynne Elizabeth to bring this book to the public. I also appreciate the kindness and expertise of Nikkol Brothers at Visions Photo Lab in Santa Fe for leading me through the process of converting the many slides and prints to digital format. Thank you to Ronald Christ for his friendship and for sharing advice based on his long experience as a translator and publisher. It has been exciting to pick up the many threads of conversation with the women whose art and actions fill this book. Thank you for your cooperation and willingness to loan photos and for the new stories we have traded. I also want to acknowledge my baby aunt Mary Jane Grigg, eight years my senior, who unexpectedly died this winter before she got to read this book, and send greetings into the ether to the many departed artists included in this narrative. One of the things we learned twenty years ago in our efforts to recover our art history was how quickly women's contributions and ideas can vanish. So I welcome the readers who will keep telling our stories and who will make new ones of their own.

Sabra working on a pastel, circa 1979, in her Warren Street studio in Brooklyn.

Table of Contents

Artists gathering at *Heresies* benefit exhibit, *Issues That Won't Go Away*, PPOW Gallery, 1987,
to read dedications honoring Lucy R. Lippard.

Staying Outside

Although our paths had often crossed at activist art organizations and demonstrations since the late 1960s, I first got to know Sabra Moore a decade later, when she joined the editorial collective of the Earthkeeping/Earthshaking: Feminism and Ecology issue of *Heresies* and was soon invited to be in the Mother Collective. By then, both of us had been working in feminist contexts for many years. We each came to New Mexico for the first time in 1972, and in the early 1990s our paths converged definitively when we both moved there. Now, we share a present as well as a past as active participants in our (very different) small New Mexican communities. True to form, Moore and her artist/woodworker husband, Roger Mignon, settled farther from Santa Fe and closer to the heart of northern New Mexico. Over several summers, they stayed in a shed just long enough for two tall people to stretch out in their sleeping bags while they worked on their adobe house and straw-bale studios on a mesa near Georgia O'Keeffe's White Place on a road often impassable in bad weather. They chose the light and space and vast views across an arroyo below Cerro Negro, where they coddle their chickens and cats and watch the passing mountain lions, coyotes, hawks, and eagles.

The collective that published *Heresies: A Feminist Publication on Art and Politics* (1977–1993) was a motley and evolving crew, although attempts at "diversity" never came quickly or easily. We took "the personal is political" seriously, but also realized that "the political is personal" was the equally important other side of the coin. Moore brings these together in *Openings*, which is the story not only of the too often forgotten grass roots of the feminist art movement but also of the author—her coming up in an East Texas union family, her hard-won college education, and her exhilarating and traumatic stint in the Peace Corps in Africa. Once she arrived in New York in 1966, her struggles to challenge and expand women's rights and her work in an abortion clinic and as a house painter were not the usual trajectory for an ambitious young artist. Feminist groups offered support and controversy. Consciousness raising is a form of storytelling, and our generation of feminists learned to understand our lives in the contexts of listening to others' stories. Among Moore's issues, and memories, is violence against women, which she knew firsthand. *Openings* is the story of personal and political battles along with disappointments and triumphs. I lived through some with her, heard about others over the years of our long friendship, and learned more from reading the book.

Moore brought to *Heresies* what she brings to this book—her unflagging commitment to working with others and to art for social justice. Her passions are contagious, and she has always reveled in collaboration despite its tribulations. The tidal wave of names that pervade the pages of *Openings* demonstrates the author's respect for her peers in the "cooperative world that we inhabited." In her art and in her activism, Moore has held firm to a straightforward class analysis of her own experiences in the New York art world, boldly tackling unspoken tabus. Americans don't like to think about class, much less talk about it. A rare instance of frank discussion of the subject occurred during the meetings of the collective editing the *Heresies* issue Mothers, Mags, and Movie Stars. We all vied to have roots in the working class. Moore was one of the few participants who had walked the talk, was proud of her family background, and made it a constant presence in her art. She has never bought into the race and class divisions of the dominant culture or the hierarchies that so virulently rule the art world. Her lived experience makes this book stand out among the still burgeoning literature on the feminist art movement.

The feminism and ecology issue of *Heresies* featured Mount St. Helen's erupting on the cover with a quasi-*National Geographic* border. It was a volcanic message about women artists' passionate commitment to protecting the environment. Coming from a rural background, Moore has always nurtured gardens—often embattled by social conflict, drought, and other threats—even in the cement canyons of New York City. Here in New Mexico, she is still combining art and community work. She has managed the Española Farmers' Market for sixteen years and made it a center not just for produce and producers, but for local arts. Her day jobs have been varied. During her years in New York, she did freelance photo research for books. In New Mexico, she has sewn for the Santa Fe Opera, run the Abiquiú recycling facility, and tutored Native American and Hispano children in after-school programs. She works with the local library and creates mosaic murals for elementary schools across northern New Mexico. And, of course, she makes her own art—colorful, layered, and simultaneously joyful and disturbing—often created from found materials cast off by nature and by others' lives.

This is the intuitive memoir of a charismatic outsider with many friends who has struggled all her life to create alternatives to the "art world of money and power." Moore makes it clear that it hasn't been easy, but whatever chaos life brings, she is in her studio and in the streets. And, somehow, she has also managed to produce this important book. In retrospect, it is not surprising. She has always incorporated stories—the backbone of culture—into her paintings and sculpture. The artist's book—xeroxed, collaged, and lovingly annotated—has long been one of her favorite mediums. This book's punning title (from exhibition openings to a broader sense of possibilities) suggests its layered offerings. For all her education and urban savvy, Moore has never forgotten her roots. Her East Texas background permeates her art and her social life. She bakes pies for potlucks and mourning households. She glories in the remains of ancient gardens on her land. A bottle tree welcomes visitors to the top of the mesa. Memory is a living force woven in and out of the present. She notes that she was raised to excel, but not "get a big head" in the process. This is an often painful and always generous book. Strength and vulnerability, friendship and betrayal, success and disappointment, and outrage and integrity are woven into a unique fabric. Moore often cites the quilt (her "grandmother's aesthetic") as a metaphor for her mission to restore context to art. A quote from a poem by Ho Chi Minh hangs on her studio wall: "After sorrow comes happiness." In New Mexico, her intimate attraction to the land merges with the Tewa petroglyphs in the arroyo below her home and the Hispano traditions surrounding her.

Among her subjects is violence against women, which includes the broader imposition of social powerlessness. The pain of not being taken seriously is familiar to most women of our generation, and Moore's exploration of its roots, its effects, and the triumphs of women who refused to tolerate it is inspiring. No artist wants to be ignored by the most prestigious galleries, museums, critics, and collectors. But, perhaps, activist artists are better equipped to deal with resistance to their chosen paths because they can gain strength from their independence from the commercial centers, their deeply held beliefs, their self-defined contexts, and the knowledge that, ultimately, their art is more important than that of many better-known artists.

This book brings back so many personal memories, and makes me (almost) wish that I'd kept a journal as Moore did—the source that gave birth to *Openings*. Many of us, of any age, will identify with her struggles and triumphs and see their impact in the broader world beyond art, where the art impulse is born. This book is not only a window into many forgotten histories but also a call to arms to the next generation of feminist artists. "We should stay outside and break up things" was the last line of Moore's contribution to the Earthkeeping issue of *Heresies*.

Lucy R. Lippard
Galisteo, Spring 2016

Activists with Women's Action Coalition (WAC) and Guerrilla Girls demonstrate against the opening of the Downtown Guggenheim, 1992.

Some Words of Caution

Sabra Moore begins her exciting narrative by explaining: "I didn't like the art world, and it didn't like me. I needed to make art, but I didn't know where that art could go. I was the wrong gender and the wrong class." Moore wastes no time in setting the stage for the dilemma most artists face: how to make art in a world that treats art as a market commodity and women artists as marginal at best. That dilemma is heightened by Moore's class and gender and laid bare by her keen perceptivity.

Moore's book is immeasurably enriched by the fact that it is not her story alone, but the braided stories of dozens of women artists in New York City during the 1970s and 1980s. New York City was the mecca, the city that beckoned emerging creative spirits, the place where everything seemed possible. Many of us were drawn to it, oblivious to the fact that what was readily available to the men always seemed denied to the women.

The women in Moore's world were doing brilliant and, in some cases, enduring work. Their concerns were those of all artists, plus some. Their gendered experience brought up questions previously relegated to their need to be taken seriously, or hidden in artistic genres long ascribed to "Anonymous." The museums weren't interested in showing them, nor were the important critics interested in reviewing what they were doing.

These women artists came from many different class and racial backgrounds, representing diverse experiences. They worked in a variety of mediums and styles. What linked them was a time, a city, and the courage to demand their place. Their collective solutions to the problem of easy dismissal were creative, courageous, sassy, and often brilliant. They were on the move, and *Openings* is their story, long waiting to be told. I say this is a cautionary tale because getting to know a time, a history, and a people too long ignored can ignite in readers an understanding and rage immensely useful to our lives today. Women artists are still vastly underrepresented in major museums.

I arrived in New York a decade before Moore, also a young woman and also from a provincial southwestern background. My New Mexico to her Texas. My need to make poetry to her need to make visual art. I landed, homeless, jobless, and relatively clueless among a group of painters just then breaking from anonymity—the abstract expressionists who were then making the great city their own. Perhaps, it is this experience, intimately shared although lived in subsequent decades, that makes this book so real to me, and so necessary. My New York world continues to shape me. And yet, looking back, I can still feel the leaden weight of misogyny and abuse that so crudely ruled and distorted the years I inhabited the city. Because I went on to Latin America at the end of 1961, it would take another decade for me to catch up with the feminist consciousness that empowered the women in *Openings*.

Walk-up flats and industrial lofts. Menial jobs that just covered rent and food and left the bulk of each day for the real work. Learning how to turn the Con Ed dials back, so as to pay as little as possible for light. Small artist-run galleries and thin self-published books. These were common realities for many New York City women artists. My own New York era predated the second wave of feminism by more than a decade. Too many of the women who yearned to write or paint or otherwise follow their creative dreams ended up denying their own creativity in lieu of the men's. They became artists' wives, mothers of their children, or itinerate "groupies" who promoted the men in more ways than I care to remember. Few of us survived.

Ten years later, when Moore arrived, women (at least those in the visual arts) were ready to do something about that cruel reality. They prioritized making art, but also organized, protested against the museums that refused to show them, and produced exciting publications and collective statements of purpose. In short, and against tremendous odds, many more survived.

Moore, with an intuitive recognition of the importance of that history, kept a journal, recorded the events, and preserved the invitations and flyers. Because she was at the center of an explosive world of emerging women artists, her relationships were deep and meaningful. She was part of the important *Heresies* collective. In this book, she recreates process as well as specific events and artworks. Her documentation of an era—filtered through the wisdom of time, her own astute analysis, and a wealth of personal stories—allowed her to write this pivotal book. That she is a consummate wordsmith as well as a marvelous visual artist, a talented book designer, and someone who cares about the women with whom she lived this history, shines on every page.

I want to say something about the personal stories. They are a big part of what makes this telling so valuable. Moore always understood that lives feed the work—especially lives that are vastly different from one another in terms of race, culture, and class. The marches and shows cannot be separated from what each woman brought to the work: their origins, relationships, and discussions; their memories and passion. Like one of the beautiful patchwork quilts of Moore's East Texas childhood, she juxtaposes the lives, ideas, art, and rebel energies in this magnificent offering that takes us back to a vibrant (and, I daresay, more transparent) time, and invites us to inhabit it through her powerful talent for recreating the stories and what they meant then and mean today.

The addition of more than nine hundred images, running in continuous frieze along the bottom of every page, plus two sixteen-page portfolios of full-page color images enrich this book immeasurably. This is the marriage of a necessary history and a publisher able and willing to produce it in all of its fullness. One brilliance has found its counterpart. Read this book and immerse yourself in the energy and innovation of a time, a place, and a people. But, as I've said, proceed with caution: you never know what discovering real history may do to the way you live and work today.

Margaret Randall
Albuquerque, Winter 2015

Sylvia Sleigh's portrait of Sabra Moore, called *My Ceres*, 1982.

Preface

Here was my dilemma: I didn't like the art world and it didn't like me. I needed to make art, but I didn't know where that art could go. I was the wrong gender and the wrong class. My father was a railroad man who organized for the union. He had been killed by a drunk driver when I was away from home, teaching as a Peace Corps volunteer in Guinea. When I left Africa the next year, I decided that I wouldn't return to Texas; I would move to New York City and become a painter.

Everyone had her own story, and each person felt like she was an outsider. For Emma it was race; for me, it was class; and Jackie and Ora thought you had to be an abstract expressionist and buy high gloss enamel paint at the hardware store and pee standing by the fireplace. And it felt useless to make art when the Vietnamese were dying.

The personal is political.

The women's art movement was a spontaneous movement for change by many individuals and not an orchestrated invention of a talented few. We came together because we needed each other, and we created forms, theories, organizations, shows, and actions out of that need. We also ricocheted apart, dropped out, and reunited. I was there. We were all there, but our history is now being written in the familiar terms that most of us have rejected—a few genius artists paving the way for others to follow. A door is opening and a few are being let inside. But some

1. Caroline Moore, *door stop doll* 2. Mimi Smith, *Knit Baby* 3. Zarina Hashmi, *woodcut* 4. Gris-gris, Guinea

of us thought we were redesigning and enlarging the whole building; others were for tearing the edifice down.

The political is personal.

This is how our emerging history is being written. In 1970, Judy Chicago changes her name and chooses to reclaim the primacy of her body by creating a series of paintings celebrating the vagina as a flower. A group of women studying in the Feminist Art Program at Fresno State College in California under the guidance of Judy Chicago and Miriam Schapiro decide to explore their feminist consciousness by creating *Woman House*, which personifies the body in which women are housed. Later, Schapiro appropriates the quilt and needlework patterns developed by anonymous women of all ethnicities and creates a series of collaged paintings based on these design forms. The rest of us hear about this, and the feminist art movement begins.

I am simplifying of course, and I also embrace and honor the two women that I have singled out. But I posit that at the same time that these visible events were being documented and discussed, other women artists were also meeting, talking, inventing, creating, or finding their private trajectories into the public sphere with quite different aims and visual forms. Our explorations were not as visible because we were not situated in the academy or allied with a more powerful male artist or writer. It is natural that the artists who come from the same social group as the writers, teachers, or critics of the time would be noticed first, and that is one of the reasons for the emphasis on white middle class feminism and its focus in art on the female body.

The actual art movement was more diverse, and I think it is time that we who participated speak for ourselves. We all cared about our vaginas, but some of us had other things to say first. I, for instance, needed to create a connection to the class I had left behind and chose to reconfigure the quilt making, sewing, and piecing of my grandmothers and to tell their painful

5. Malekeh Nayiny, *Mask* photograph 6. Emma Amos, *Will You Forget Me?* 7. Vivian E. Browne, *Benin Equestrian*

stories. Kazuko Miyamoto needed to make intricate ropes and nets based on the folk weaving from the Japanese countryside of her childhood. Vivian Browne needed to create veils and hidden words that cloaked paintings of trees and hinted at an American Indian heritage merged inside her African American identity. Ora Lerman needed to paint highly stylized still-life tableaux that explored her parents' Jewish diaspora from Europe to Kentucky. Are these art forms feminist? We think so.

There are many strands to the women's art movement, and the formal art we have created is only one part. It was a social movement for change and can be seen as the daughter of the civil rights movement and the anti-Vietnam War movement. It continued the intellectual work that was started by the anticolonialism struggles after World War II. It was a movement for equality with much discussion and tension about what we wanted to do with our power. Did we simply want women to have a place at the table formerly dominated by white men or did we want to change the role art played in society? If art validates a culture, who and what are being validated? Where should that art be placed? Who owns art? What is art?

8. Ora Lerman, *Make A Wish, If Birthday Boxes Only Bore...* 9. Sabra Moore, *House Dress/Gladys Story*

1

Where I/We Came In (Starting in 1970)

I am parading in front of the Metropolitan Museum of Art and carrying a sign that reads, "That's White of Hoving." Most of my fellow demonstrators are black artists and fellows; I am one of the few non-blacks and women on the line. We are protesting the exhibition *Harlem on My Mind*. The singer Nina Simone crosses the line and we all cry, "Don't go in! Don't go in!" but she does. The Hoving of my sign is Thomas Hoving, the director of the museum. A reporter notices me and asks, "Did you write that slogan?" I didn't, but I did help ghostwrite a manifesto for the Black Emergency Cultural Coalition, an organization of black artists founded by Benny Andrews, Henri Ghent, and Ed Taylor. I am a woman, remember, and this part of the story is a tortured love story. But it is my trajectory into the women's art movement.

It was 1966. I was freshly arrived in New York City from my Peace Corps stay in West Africa and I had decided to go to art school. A friend suggested the Brooklyn Museum Art School, and I arrived there armed with the colored pencil drawings I had made in Guinea. Gus Peck

1. Sabra Moore (all, colored pencil drawings, 1964–1966), *A Neighbor* 2. *Cows in the Yard* 3. *Forest near N'Zérékoré*

chaired the art school. "You are obviously talented," he said, steering me into the Saturday class rather than the full-time program. That's how I met my teacher, the man I shall call C, and that's how I came, four years later, to be protesting *Harlem on My Mind* and carrying the sign he made for me.

My first show was the group show, *Fifteen Artists*, curated at the Brooklyn Museum's Community Gallery in 1969 by Henri Ghent. At that time, there were black shows and white shows, though the white shows, which also were generally all-male shows, were simply called exhibits. Our show was reviewed in *ART Gallery Magazine* and my work was reproduced.[1] For years, based on that review, I would be invited into shows featuring African American women artists, and I would politely explain that I was the wrong color.

C was part of a group of black artists that revolved around the painters Romare Bearden, Benny Andrews, and Norman Lewis. I heard the men mention Emma Amos, Vivian Browne, and Faith Ringgold, and I came to know these women later. Once, as I was standing with Faith talking in the hall during a College Art Association and Women's Caucus for Art Conference, I spotted the painter Rick Mayhew, an old friend of C's, whom I hadn't seen for years. "Look, he's running away!" Faith said. Just as I had run away, just as C's friends had turned their backs and refused to help me when I tried to escape his violence.

Well, the women's movement happened for a reason, and our art and organizations developed out of necessity. When I ran away from C, when I saved my life, Janet Pfunder, an artist I had just met at a meeting of Women Artists in Revolution (WAR), invited me to stay in her loft on Lispenard Street until the danger had lessened. That's what the women's movement meant: an updated version of the Robert Frost line about family, "Home is the place where, when you have to go there/They have to take you in."[2]

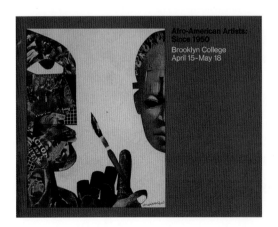  

4. Romare Bearden, *catalogue cover* 5. Driggs, *Rat cover*, 1/24/1968 6. Museum, *First Year Issue Magazine*, 1970

It was 1969. I was living with C and trying to find my way out, teaching English as a second language at Columbia University and an after-school children's art class at the Brooklyn Museum while also helping C build walls in our new Brooklyn loft on Pacific Street, trying to paint, and going to an endless series of demonstrations against the Vietnam War. I went to openings at an alternative venue called MUSEUM/A Project of Living Artists, and considered the possibilities for showing my artworks. "He may join a Selection Group and will, if selected, be able to exhibit his work," the brochure read in keeping with the concept of the one-man show. I made leaflets and graphics for the Fifth Avenue Vietnam Peace Parade Committee and *Liberation News Service* and a five-color silkscreen poster announcing the March on Washington that read "Imperialism Sucks," which the fledgling gay rights movement criticized in print. I visited my old Texas friend Jeff Shero, who had started the underground newspaper, the *Rat*. It was in an upstairs storefront on Fourteenth Street with a sign on the plate glass window of the former photostat business that had been altered to read, "Hot Rats." Jeff had been one of a group of friends who had gathered in Austin after John F. Kennedy's assassination in 1963. We students at the University of Texas had been waiting to hear President Kennedy speak in the afternoon, but he was killed that morning in Dallas. We spent the evening in a kind of walking vigil, wandering around campus and gathering in groups for comfort and outrage. I had not seen Jeff since I left Texas for my Peace Corps stay in Guinea. We walked over to the apartment of antiwar activist and Yippie[3] Jerry Rubin, and I showed him some of my pen and ink drawings. He asked me to make a cover for the *Rat*. The Chicago Eight[4] were on trial, so I made a red-and-white graphic drawing for the feature article with a giant screw poised above a screaming circular mouth. When multiple copies with my cover were displayed on the newsstands, C's friends expressed surprise. I also wrote an article about

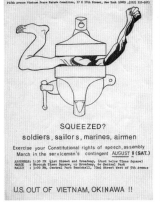   

7. Sabra Moore (all, 1969), *Antiwar flier* 8. Poster, *Imperialism Sucks* 9. *RAT* cover, 3/28/1969 10. Anonymous, *Flier*

the *Harlem on My Mind* demonstrations. The next year, the *Rat* became the *Liberated Rat* after being taken over by women in response to its rampant sexism.

I joined the Committee of Returned Volunteers (CRV), and we protested the war in Vietnam and Gulf Oil in Angola. I made more leaflets. We women formed a consciousness-raising group for the same reasons as the women of the *Liberated Rat*. Later, C would steal my phone list and call members of this group to threaten them over my decision to leave him.

The Vietnam War continued. We heard about the My Lai Massacre, and the Art Workers' Coalition organized a demonstration in front of the Museum of Modern Art, passing out color posters of the dead women and babies. I went and that's when I heard about WAR.

It is 1970, and Lucy R. Lippard has started visiting women artists' studios. "My preconceptions were jolted today," she notes, "I found that I could be moved more by content than by context."[5] She helps found the Ad Hoc Women Artists' Committee, which will protest the Whitney Biennial's exclusion of women. In 1970, Cecilia Vicuña is making *arte precario* in the Chile of Salvador Allende; Faith Ringgold is painting huge blood-soaked American flags; the women in the Feminist Art Program at Fresno State College are creating ironic posters of beauty queens; American soldiers in Vietnam are throwing the bloodied bodies of women into a ditch next to their slaughtered babies; Catalina Parra is learning about Dada and Fluxus in Germany; and I am running out the door of our loft with a kitten in my pocket while C is running back to the table to grab the gun that he has placed next to a letter addressed to me with straight pins stuck into my name. In 1970, Louise Bourgeois is making amorphous sculptures that combine vaginas, penises, and chrysalis forms; and her neighbor, Sylvia Sleigh, is lovingly painting the body hair onto her portrait of Phillip Golub; Jane Alpert is fleeing the police out the door of the *Liberated Rat* to disappear into the Weather Underground,[6] and the paper later prints a page saying, "You left

11. Art Workers' Coalition, *And Babies? And Babies* 12. Faith Ringgold, *The Flag Is Bleeding*

the water running"; Judy Chicago is making her first "cunt art" paintings; Glenna Park is raising three sons and making a quilt by sewing the laundry left on her bed into the bedspread, piece by piece; Mimi Smith is making string drawings of the furniture in her house; and Nancy Spero is in her loft, cutting out collaged images to combine with texts by Antonin Artaud.

The political is personal.

I still keep a poem by Ho Chi Minh on the wall in my studio. My first introduction to him was in Guinea. My African Italian neighbor had fought in the First Indochina War on the side of the French, and he showed me a propaganda booklet about the Vietnamese leader, which emphasized his great erudition. I backed into my opposition to the Vietnam War from my life in Guinea. I had a student there named Gobé, whose mother was Vietnamese. She ran a tiny rice shop in N'Zérékoré, one of the few functioning businesses along the empty dirt plaza. There was a framed photo of her and her African husband, newly married, smiling against the open sky. Gobé used to bring me animals from the forest: a civet kitten, an owl. I would try in vain to keep these wild creatures alive.

The Ho Chi Minh poem on my wall ends with, "What could be more natural? After sorrow comes happiness."

The summer of my escape from C was such a time, a blossoming. I started making abstracted pencil drawings of my new boyfriend, Arthur, and the color blue returned to my art, replacing red. I heard that C had gone to Mexico, so I moved back into my new apartment on Warren Street. I had quit my two jobs when I had disappeared into Janet's loft, but, somehow, you could live on very little money then.

I went to the meetings of WAR and also met women from the Connecticut Feminists in the Arts, who were in contact with the writer Anais Nin. WAR met in the same building as the

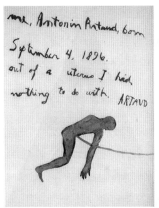  

13. Nancy Spero, *Artaud Painting—Me, Antonin Artaud, Born...* 14. Catalina Parra, *photo* 15. Sylvia Sleigh, *Philip Golub Reclining*

Art Workers' Coalition (AWC) and the Ad Hoc Women Artists' Committee (AHC). The abstract painter Joan Thorne attended meetings, as did the photographer Susan Kleckner, who had just started teaching at Pratt Institute. She and Janet Pfunder had become lovers. We three were close friends. Sara Saporta was also in our group, and she showed us an artwork she was making in the form of a chest of drawers, expanding my aesthetic framework for what constitutes sculpture. Her husband Carl was in a show at the Jewish Museum, and they invited all of us to visit them in upstate New York near Woodstock, where they wanted to start a commune at their farmhouse. Janet McDevitt would serve us hot tea in glasses with faceted patterns, adding a touch of elegance to the discussions. She and Jacqueline Skiles were making a video called *A Documentary Herstory of Women Artists in Revolution*. They filmed Faith Ringgold and me, among others. No men were allowed, and we laughed a lot as we planned our actions. We were soaking in courage from each other to take our own oppression seriously. In a public meeting at the Brooklyn Museum, one woman stood up to talk about sexism and all the men in the room laughed at this odd term. Their laughter carried a different meaning.

I have a leaflet from WAR proclaiming, "Museums are Sexist!" A series of masked eyes float across the page with a repeated mantra: "This is a woman looking at the world/This is a woman looking at men/This is a woman looking at women/This is a woman looking at you." After centuries of being watched, we wanted to turn the tables. Women used images of the female eye repeatedly as symbols of action. Look at the 1982 catalogue cover for the Women's Caucus for Art exhibitions, *Views by Women Artists*, with the pupil of a giant eye reflecting women's artworks. Or the logo for the 1990s organization Women's Action Coalition (WAC) with an eye surrounded by the slogan, "WAC is Watching/We Will Take Action." The Guerrilla Girls thoroughly masked their gaze while advertising themselves as watchdogs.

16. Sandra Lee-Phipps, *WAC demonstration* 17. Anonymous, *WAR leaflet* 18. Jacqueline Wray, *Views by Women Artists cover*

Another flier in tightly spaced type of various sizes read: "YOU TRUST YOUR MOTHER, BUT… Would You Let Her Run Your Museums and Cultural Institutions? The peaceful little WOMEN announce a new season."

WAR was taking aim at the Museum of Modern Art with a list of ten demands that would be repeated in various forms for the next fourteen years. The Black and Puerto Rican Committee of AWC expressed their support. "You say there is no quota system? You say a work of art is judged solely on artistic merit?" The first demand was: "1.a. An immediate M.O.M.A. [Museum of Modern Art] show of heretofore unknown women artists." The third demand read: "3.c. Contemporary black women artists exhibition."

I was still unpeeling the layers of C's presence from my life, gradually arranging my studio to suit my own tastes in the Warren Street brownstone where I now lived. I started working with oil paints again, giving up the acrylics C had insisted I use. At first, I tried to make my painting area like a carpentry shop in the same way C's studio had been arranged. He had been the first person to encourage me to have my own studio, and I still had his workspace as a model in my mind. He had taken the front half of our loft on Pacific Street for his painting area, installed his saws and tools, and painted the walls black. He cast his shaped paintings in layers of epoxy and made a ventilated area for this purpose. We moved there from our loft on Greenwich Street in Manhattan one freezing winter evening; my cold-shocked houseplants lying limp on the floor after I had brought them inside from the white van. The loft was in rough condition, and we worked together for months to create our living and work spaces while I would squeeze time to go over to the Fifth Avenue Vietnam Peace Parade Committee or go to the university to teach. We were on the top floor, overlooking the train yards on Pacific Street. The area was even more isolated than Greenwich Street had been. There was an interior corridor from our floor that led to a small

19. WAR leaflet, 1970 20. Anonymous, *button 21.* Call for demonstration 22. Kate Millett reading

carriage house enclosed within the courtyard of the factory building. You could look down on the skylights of the lower floors from this room. I moved my studio into the carriage house, creating a separate space for myself. I abandoned that hard-won studio when I left C.

My new apartment was the parlor floor of an 1840 Greek Revival building with high ceilings and graceful woodwork. The previous owners had extended the floor by opening up the backyard windows like doorways and building a kitchen and sitting area. This extension was narrow, only about six feet wide, and sunny like a porch. I cooked and ate there, reserving most of the parlor as my studio. I had left most of my clothes and other items on Pacific Street when I fled C's violence, but I still had many mementos from our relationship. One day, I took all of C's letters and postcards into my kitchen, reading each letter and then burning it in the sink where I usually washed dishes. One was a postcard from Mexico with a girl steering a canoe whose long brown hair and cropped bangs looked like mine. But rereading a letter sent to me in England ("There is no you, only me") gave me the courage to ignite the rest, even the ones I loved.

Susan Kleckner knew the writer and sculptor Kate Millett. We women were all reading books on feminism and art, trying to reeducate ourselves. Kate's book, *Sexual Politics*, had just come out and her portrait painted by Alice Neel was on the cover of *Time* magazine. This publicity led to her being outed as a lesbian before she had the opportunity to reveal her orientation to her mother. Visibility has its price. Kate later created a series of painful autobiographical installations. One shows her realistic life-sized severed head inside a cage. I went to another exhibit at the Women's Interart Center in 1972. A mannequin is seated amidst rows of empty folding chairs with a single hanging lightbulb illuminating her fixed smile. We viewers were forced to peer at this installation through bars, making us voyeurs of her discomfort. I left and went

  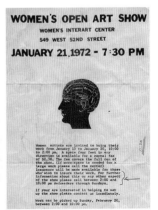

23. Kate Millett, *Madhouse* 24. Anonymous, *Pratt Faculty Exhibition flier* 25. Anonymous, *Women's Interart Center flier*

upstairs, finding relief by watching two white ships floating along the dirty Hudson River in the late afternoon light.

I have a dream-like memory of another meeting from this period: encountering Valerie Solanas at the door passing out a broadside she had printed called *SCUM (Society for Cutting Up Men)*. She was the person who later attacked and shot the artist Andy Warhol. When Warhol recovered, Alice Neel painted him nude above the waist, revealing the terrible scar.

Someone in WAR heard about Women's Services, an abortion clinic that was opening under the sponsorship of Judson Memorial Church and the Clergy Consultation Service on Abortion. The law had just changed to legalize abortion in New York and Colorado, but abortion was still criminalized in the rest of the country. The clinic wanted to hire feminists who had had illegal abortions to work as counselors and paraprofessional doctor's assistants. I qualified. They would pay $50 a day. I went for an interview and Janet's neighbor, the painter Georgia Matsumoto, also went.

I am standing beside a doctor and he is inserting a series of dilators into a patient's cervix, gradually increasing the diameter of the instrument. I manage to keep watching though I want to avert my gaze. This is a test and I have passed. I have switched roles. In Guinea, I was the woman on the table. I was the woman who borrowed the bus fare to travel alone to Kankan because I happened to read in an old *Life* magazine that abortion was legal in Czechoslovakia and the doctor there was Czech. He agreed to help. As I was being wheeled into surgery, a Vietnamese doctor came over and proclaimed, "See, she's American and I'm Vietnamese and we're friends." I tried wanly to acknowledge this ideal. I was the woman who left the village celebration the next day to crouch behind a tree and pass huge clots of blood from my incomplete abortion. My housemate and fellow Peace Corps volunteer, Sally, saved my life two weeks later when she

26. Lamidi Fakeye, *Sabra next to carved doors, Ibadan* 27. Demonstration, Guinea 28. Traore Sekou, *Niamou drawing*

heard me hemorrhaging in the next room and rushed me to the hospital. I was making morning coffee in our kitchen when the blood started pouring from my body. I had simply lain across the bed, silent and confused from loss of blood, unable to call out.

When I worked at the clinic, I learned that a pregnancy of fourteen weeks is the most dangerous period for an abortion. The Czech doctor had left a fragment of placenta, which later caused my hemorrhaging, but hadn't warned me of the danger. Later, I learned to recognize the clean sound of the surgical instrument scraping the muscular wall of the uterus as an indication that no placental attachment remained, and I was vigilant with my patients to listen for that signal of safety. I had not chosen to become pregnant, and my women friends had tried to help me with herbal remedies before I took the bus to Kankan in desperation. I had visited the nun who ran a women's clinic in my town of N'Zérékoré, trying to confirm the pregnancy. She insisted that she couldn't tell, warning me not to harm myself. I never alerted the Peace Corps in Conakry; they would have sent me home in disgrace. Sally and I lived near two French women in our teachers' neighborhood. We called them *les deux* Nicoles since they were both named Nicole—one was heavy and the other small, and they were lovers as we later came to understand. *La grande* (the large) Nicole had sat with Sally and me as I soaked my feet in cold water and took quinine. Later, we three sat again as I drank vast quantities of an herbal concoction Guerzé[7] women used. It had taken us weeks to negotiate for those leaves. It was *la grande* Nicole who drove me to the hospital when Sally ran for help.

The month I became pregnant, *la petite* (the small) Nicole died in childbirth from eclampsia. Sally, *la grande* Nicole, and I had sat with her in the steamy hospital room as she lapsed into unconsciousness from her repeated convulsions. She kept muttering through her coma about all the zeros on the recent tests that her students took. "Zero, zero, zero, bebé, bebé, bebé."

 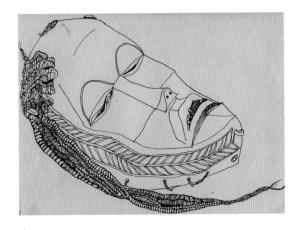 

29. Sabra Moore (all, ink drawings, 1964–1966), *Ibeji drawing* 30. Mask drawing 31. *Ibeji drawing*

We took turns with cold cloths on her forehead. That was all the medicine or treatment we had available at the hospital; the sole doctor had returned to Europe and only nurses remained on staff. A Polish doctor arrived at the hospital just one week before I hemorrhaged and was able to save my life with an emergency dilation and curettage without anesthesia. I kept begging him to stop. *La petite* Nicole was still unconscious when her African French daughter, Guenola, was born, a calm and beautiful infant. The medicine to treat eclampsia arrived across the nearby Liberian border a day too late to save *la petite* Nicole's life. She was stuffed with creosote leaves and buried in a pale pink dress in the local cemetery—the smell of creosote pervades my memory as I think of her funeral. *La grande* Nicole wrote *la petite* Nicole's parents in southern France, informing them of their daughter's death and the unexpected birth of a granddaughter. Months later, they replied, asking for custody of Guenola. "What will the neighbors think if we don't raise our granddaughter?"

I doubt that the Clergy Consultation Service on Abortion had foreseen the dynamics of hiring feminists who had endured illegal abortions to staff the new clinic alongside male doctors, none of whom had participated in consciousness-raising let alone criticism/self-criticism.[8] Suddenly, the doctors were being required to speak gently to a woman in crisis and be assisted by a group of newly trained paraprofessionals, each with a passionate identification with the patient on the table before them. The counselors were women and the patients were women, but, with the exception of one, all of the doctors were men. Only the law was new.

I hand you vignettes. The counselor Susan Murdock, who has just opened her own karate dojo, lines up with other women to block the clinic doors from the assault of a crazed man who wants to baptize the fetuses. Dr. June Fine, the only woman doctor, is pregnant with her first planned child, whom she will name Hampton after the assassinated Black Panther, Fred

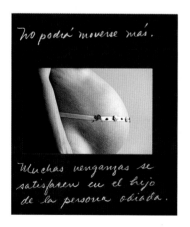 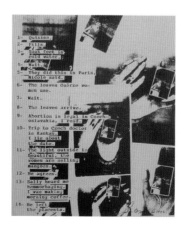 

32. Marta Maria Perez, *To Conceive* 33. Sabra Moore, *Choice Histories page art* 34. Kazuko, *Heresies Women's Pages*

Hampton. One of our patients arrives pregnant by a married right-to-life senator from Utah and has come in secret. A twelve-year-old from Florida refuses her abortion because she is insulted that her mother thinks she's too young to have a child. Her mother had been a teenager herself when she had started having children and now she works making tires in a factory. The next day, they both return. One of the doctors believes that abortion should be painful to expiate guilt. Another doctor flies in weekly from St. Louis and sweats profusely as he performs the abortions. One doctor, Dr. William Walden, gives a completely painless abortion—he is the only one who has figured out an effective method for numbing the cervix. We all start seeing him for our own medical care. At the Christmas banquet, the director thinks it's clever to place the instruments of abortion in the food, so we counselors carefully remove all the implements, wash them, wrap them, and put them away before sitting down to eat. No one wants the hams he has presented as gifts. I decide to not eat meat and abstain for the next five years.

The director who tried to give us Christmas hams was Dr. Hale Harvey. He had performed safe abortions in Louisiana before the law changed. He trained us counselors to be paraprofessionals who stayed with the patient through all the phases of the abortion, including birth control counseling and assisting the doctor at the procedure. We were supposed to ask each woman her reason for wanting an abortion. Once during my training, I forgot to ask this question. Dr. Harvey whispered, "Don't forget the moral justification." It turned out, however, that he was a doctor of philosophy only, and he left the clinic shortly after this revelation. The Clergy Consultation Service on Abortion hired a new director who was a medical doctor, Dr. Bernard Nathanson. At about this same time, the clinic administration started trying to limit the time we counselors spent with each patient, having decided that the issues with abortion had been

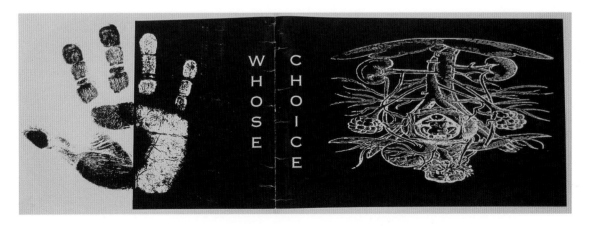

35. REPOHistory, *Choice Histories catalogue cover*

primarily problems of access and were now resolved through the existence of a legal medical facility for a full year.

I worked evenings three nights a week, starting at four in the afternoon. The clinic was in a tidy brownstone on the Upper East Side. At midnight, I hurried along the empty blocks to reach the subway for home, my mind filled with the troubled stories of each patient and images of the tiny translucent fetuses. We counselors now possessed a swelling stream of other women's needs. We began to feel that we were standing between the patient and the doctor, and started meeting together to figure out strategies for our situation. Tears and anger punctuated these discussions. We fantasized a clinic where all aspects of women's sexuality—natural childbirth, abortion, birth control, menopause, and child care—could be addressed and where pleasure and trust could play a role. We fantasized a clinic run by feminists. Then we returned to the situation at hand. We wrote up a series of six demands in the form of a four-page *Staff Proposal* presented to the clinic board. The first item stated, "Abortion is Not Purely a Physical Problem," and analyzed the types of women who came to the clinic and the diversity of their needs. We gave examples:

> Two weeks ago, a young woman bank teller from the Bronx came here after unsuccessfully trying to abort herself with an enema tube and a coat hanger. When asked why, she said she had only vaguely heard abortion was legal. She works in the Chemical Bank around the corner. . . . Many women expect to be punished by sterility, depression or frigidity. . . . Older women often feel embarrassed. . . . Some women really wanted the baby and were . . . too poor to have a child.

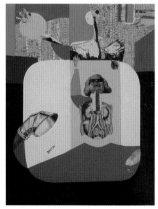

36. Suzanne Opton, *Four Women* 37. Sabra Moore, *Make It New (L.N.S.)* 38. Mimi Smith, *Don't Turn Back the Clock*

We had tried to get the worst doctors fired—the ones who made racist or sexist remarks to the patients in our presence, the doctor who raised his hand in greeting and said, "How," when introduced to a Native American woman, or the one who insisted that the speculum was "no bigger" than the penis that had impregnated the woman. Most of the doctors were rushing. They had a financial incentive—they were paid by the number of abortions performed during each shift. We were demanding participation in clinic policies that directly affected women. The clinic administration's deadening response resulted quickly in our formation of a new group, the Temporary Committee to Get Us a Union. Our meetings and proposals had attracted attention, and some of us were being harassed. Michele Clark, one of the receptionists, had just been fired for insubordination. Michele was a poet; she wrote us a long letter:

> Then I was informed that I was to be answering phones upstairs . . . instead of downstairs as I'd always done on weekends. Now, there's quite a big difference in these jobs: at reception . . . one gets to see all the patients, talk with their relatives, in general, one is somewhat involved with the work of the clinic and the women.

She had become upset at the news of her new assignment and had walked outside to talk to a friend—this was the excuse for her abrupt dismissal. She was also accused of "knitting while doing reception," which she admitted. The Temporary Committee to Get Us a Union met and wrote up more demands: "two weeks of severance pay for Michele, . . . a consistent system of warnings . . . [and] an end to over scheduling in the form of no more than four patients per assistant." We contacted the Local 1199 Drug and Hospital Union, reasoning that negotiating a

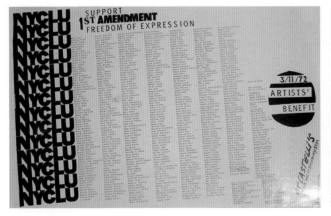  

39. NYCLU Artists' Benefit poster 40. Sabra Moore, *Women Act Now (L.N.S.)* 41. FLAGS leaflet

job description would preserve birth control counseling, enforce the four-patient limit per work shift, and give us job security while organizing. The union sent out a sturdy and grounded officer, Vivian Goia, to help us; once we started signing union cards, our activities were protected.

Local 1199 was the only union at the time with an art gallery as part of its Bread and Roses Cultural Project, a program echoing the cultural slogan of birth control pioneer Emma Goldman. The filmmaker Donna Deitch heard about our activism and came over to my apartment to film one of our meetings as part of a documentary. Dr. June Fine was meeting with us and brought infant Hampton to the filming, who napped on my bed throughout our earnest discussions, narrowly missing being hit by a falling klieg light. It took us a year to sign up enough counselors for an election, weathering the accusations of being materialistic, selfish, unthinking agitators. During this time, the clinic started hiring nurses whom we trained to do our same job, splitting the union vote between the newly hired nurses and us paraprofessionals. Even with a divided vote, we won. I became a delegate for Local 1199. The Clergy Consultation Service on Abortion considered us mercenaries for wanting a union contract, never understanding the intensity of our commitment to other women or our need to influence how legal abortion was handled.

A few months after our union victory, I quit the clinic and became a housepainter. Georgia Matsumoto quit too. We worked together as housepainters for the next seven years. Years later, after the clinic closed and reopened as a runaway shop staffed by volunteer counselors, the director Dr. Bernard Nathanson had a change of heart. He narrated a video called *The Silent Scream* in which a fetus is manipulated on film to look like it is recoiling from the suction instrument. He had decided, in retrospect, that abortion was murder. This is the same man who would not listen to our complaints about the doctors.

42. Sabra in Warren Street garden and Saskia cat in studio window 43. Pearl Street Studio

I was trying to paint again, working in a very cloaked fashion on abstract images that held hidden personal meaning. I went to see indigenous art at the American Museum of Natural History, peering into the ostrich egg that Bushmen artists had used to carry their paint pigments or memorizing the form of a Northwest Coast Indian wooden cage layered with carved fish floating inside the grid. I read Kuo Hsi on landscape painting. I visited Joan Thorne, a fellow activist from WAR, in her studio and went to shows of Joan Mitchell, Louise Nevelson, Charles Burchfield, Pat Steir, and the Symbolists. I bought a book on Tantric art. "A woman generally can't obtain a state of Buddhahood unless she reincarnates as a man." I ventured cautiously to the Brooklyn Museum of Art, meeting Georgia for a show on Navajo blankets. Those weavers were guided by Spider Woman regardless of gender. Another day, I was trying to analyze a dream with my therapist Corinna when I blurted out, "How can I sit here talking about my vagina when they're dropping mines in Haiphong Harbor?" Nixon suddenly went to China and was greeted by the People's Liberation Army. I read Simone De Beauvoir's *Prime of Life* and felt glad to be myself, not her. Walking home along Court Street, I passed a huge graffiti on a wall near my apartment proclaiming, "Pygmies Eat Elephant Placenta." Another afternoon, I visited Georgia at her loft. Heading back to the subway, I passed a newsstand and spied the headline, "Supreme Court OKs Abortions." I ran back to find Georgia, astonished at the level of my emotion, feeling vindicated for my suffering in Guinea and our struggles at the clinic. It was January 1973.

While I had been holding the hand of a stranger, helping her through her abortion, other women had been out on the street, looking through the museum doors and picketing, demanding inclusion of women artists in exhibitions. Some had been going inside the building and performing discreet symbolic actions, such as leaving clean Tampaxes inscribed "50% Women" in unsettling locations. In 1973, artists with Women in the Arts (WIA) became tired of waiting for the

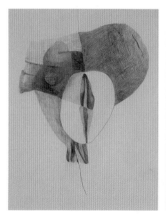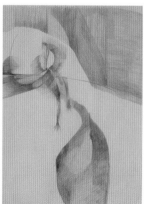

44., 45., 46., 47. Sabra Moore, pencil drawings, 1970, *Untitled* (all)

museums to develop a women's show and decided to create their own museum show. At first, they wanted an open show that would include all five hundred members, but they compromised on a curated show chosen by a committee of three WIA members: Sylvia Sleigh, Ce Roser, and Pat Passlof; two art critics: Betsy Baker and Linda Nochlin; and the museum curator: Laura Adler. *Women Choose Women* was shown at the New York Cultural Center, a museum-in-passing as it turned out, but at least a museum.

    Women Choose Women didn't include everyone of course. It is interesting that artists such as Alice Neel, Betty Parsons, or Joan Mitchell needed this show, but almost no woman was famous in 1973 except within the artists' circles. I remember picketing the Museum of Modern Art in 1984, handing out leaflets. A man angrily returned my leaflet. "They had a Louise Bourgeois show!" Of course, they also had a Picasso show, a Matisse show, a Max Ernst show, etc., but the existence of one woman's show made our protest mute for the indignant passerby. The real impact of *Women Choose Women* was the simple existence of works by so many women artists in one place.

    Lucy R. Lippard wrote an essay for the *Women Choose Women* catalogue and offered some tentative ideas about female content or form: "a uniform density, or overall texture, often sensuously tactile and repetitive to the point of obsession; the preponderance of circular forms and central focus . . . layers or strata, an indefinable looseness or flexibility of handling."[9] Sylvia Sleigh later told me that she had to fight for the integrity of this essay. She had solicited Lucy to write for the catalogue on the promise that her writing would not be altered. When she had looked over the layouts, it was clear that Lucy's essay had been edited, so Sylvia had sat there until the full text was restored. This same scenario would be repeated, to opposite effect, when the feminist A.I.R. Gallery asked Sylvia's husband, the art critic Lawrence Alloway, to write

 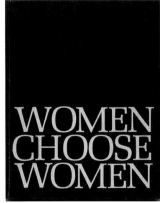

48. Artists protest Whitney Bicentennial, 1976 (Cynthia Mailman is in center with beret) 49. *Women Chose Women* cover

an essay for an exhibition. The artists did not like the results because Lawrence excluded some and praised others. When they asked him to make changes, Sylvia left the gallery and the essay went unpublished.

I was on a frugal sabbatical, collecting unemployment after quitting my clinic job, when *Women Choose Women* opened. I had not shown my work since leaving C for fear of his reappearance. I went to see this show, hoping to find some point of identity and feeling absurdly left out. My heart quickened at a small painted wooden house on fire by Vija Celmins.

The Vietnam peace pact had just been signed in Paris. This same year, Salvador Allende would be overthrown in Chile and thousands slaughtered with American complicity. Nixon would shortly depart from office in disgrace. Inside the museum, the artists looked at their bodies or swam into luxuriant abstraction. Only two of the paintings alluded to politics: one of May Stevens's personified penises, which she called *Big Daddies*, and a Faith Ringgold painting of a Black Power postage stamp.

The day Richard Nixon resigned from office, I was on the Upper West Side, painting an apartment and listening to WBAI Radio. They played the reggae tune, "The Bigger They Come, The Harder They Fall" over and over, and I danced alone, taking breaks from rolling paint to dance again and again.

Georgia and I advertised our house painting services with the phrase, "Your apartment painted with care & attention by women artists." We occupied a hybridized position—we were artists, but not quite working class. A housepainter is a fly on the wall, working while people live their lives around you. This work heightened my class awareness. I had grown up with an absurd conflict between my parents: Daddy would accuse Mother of being uppity because she had a

50. Georgia Matsumoto, *Untitled engraving* 51. Sylvia Sleigh, *Working At Home* 52. May Stevens, *Big Daddy With Hats*

college degree. It took me years to realize that he had paid for her education with his job on the railroad so that she could become a schoolteacher.

When I worked on the *Heresies's* Mothers, Mags & Movie Stars issue in 1983, each member of that magazine collective took her turn around the table to describe her family's class history. One pattern we noted was that the mother was usually the one who moved up in class, often by becoming a teacher. My family had followed that pattern, but my father's bitterness came from a separate source. Daddy had been an organizer for the Brotherhood of Locomotive Engineers and Trainmen. Our first trips outside of Texas were for strikes; we went to St. Louis and to New Orleans for strikes and we frequently traveled to Pine Bluff to meet with a union friend called Mr. Tom. We stayed with Cajuns in New Orleans—that memory is always accompanied by a strong coffee smell and by a feeling of exhilaration and power. Daddy liked to call us his "boys"; this was considered a compliment. The men at the rail yard were often surprised to meet my sister and me when we went with Mother to pick him up after his shift on the train. He ran for head of the union in Texas when I was about ten, but was defeated by a man he considered a crook. That incident ended his union activism. My sister Nancy and I used to iron and starch his work clothes. I remember the moment when he started wearing a suit to drive to work rather than his crisp overalls. Even as a child, I recognized shame.

Neither Georgia nor I had a car, so we often carried our ladders and brushes on the subway. It was an art to get into the subway doors with a six-foot ladder and a big woven tool bag before the doors closed. Once when we both exited, a stranger followed and kicked me from behind, furious, I assume, at these visible signs of our craft. Another time, I was carrying a ladder alone across the Brooklyn Bridge, returning home from Manhattan. Two older women in dresses ran after me to express admiration. No one seemed to be neutral.

53. Christine and Frank Moore at the Red River bridge with sister Nancy 54. Lillie Parks's morning star quilt on clothesline

We never were good at estimating the hours for a job, but we were true to our word about care and attention, painting as the hourly wage we hoped to earn decreased. Once, we painted all the chairs in the Theatre de Lys in Greenwich Village, working at night so the paint would dry before the next evening's performance. Georgia's boyfriend, Bob Berg, was a jazz musician, and he came and played the piano while we worked. We would start side by side in the center of a row and then move out, each of us painting thirteen chairs.

Georgia grew up in Minnesota. Her family had moved there from California just in time to avoid the internment camp where her other relatives were sent during World War II. There were few Asians in that Nordic community and her family tried to fit into the dominant culture. When she was in high school, Georgia had drawn a self-portrait, but then realized that she needed to erase and flatten her facial features to depict her own image. She went to Yale School of Art, but lived surreptitiously in her painting studio to make ends meet. Each morning, she would hide her bedding. Once, she ran into her teacher, Al Held, and he asked her what she was painting now. "Apartments," she replied. We were loading our ladders and paint bags into a taxi one evening when a fan of Yoko Ono blocked the car, insisting that Georgia was the famous artist.

I have kept journals since 1964, and it is interesting to look back and see what I wrote and what I omitted. The years at the clinic are mostly filled with dream analysis. During the period when I am trying to leave C, I am silent about the events, but recorded my awakening dreams. I had repeated dreams about a furry gorilla-like animal and I defended myself from this creature. One morning, I realized that this animal was my vital self, trying to free me, and I embraced her. C was away teaching in Poughkeepsie, so I was alone in the loft. That day, I played the Beatles album, *Abbey Road*, all afternoon, and I was finally able to cry for my father's death. He was killed

55. Ruth Gray, *Monkeys in Moonlight* 56. Linda Peer, *Avalokiteszara… with Kaposi's Sarcoma* 57. Guerrilla Girls card

in the fall of 1965 while I was living in N'Zérékoré, a few months before *la petite* Nicole's death and my abortion. The next day, I packed and tried to leave C.

I was never a Guerrilla Girl and the origin of their disguise had nothing to do with my dream figure, but they adopted the same animal as their mask for speaking witty truth to power. In New Mexico, my friend Pat D'Andrea amplified her voice in support of environmental causes by appearing as a full-suited Grace the Gorilla years before the emergence of the New York simian persona. What is it about this animal that makes women feel safe and powerful? The sculptor Linda Peer thinks the Guerrilla Girls chose this mask in part because a woman wouldn't be attractive wearing a gorilla face and as a play on the role of a revolutionary guerrilla.

In my family, we always talked about our dreams. My mother and her mother both believed that they dreamed about true things and would act upon them. When my grandmother, Mother Gladys, dreamed that she visited me in my Warren Street apartment, she told Mother how relaxed she felt to know what my place looked like. Mother always knew when Daddy was injured on the train. If my grandmother dreamed you were coming to visit, she would prepare for your arrival.

I traveled to New Mexico in the summer of 1972 right after I quit my job at the clinic. In that journal, I recorded everything, not simply dreams. I drew the rock and cloud shapes and made notes about the colors. And I returned to drawing with colored pencils like I had done in West Africa. I wrote to a friend, telling her that I planned to move to New Mexico, but it took me twenty years to do so.

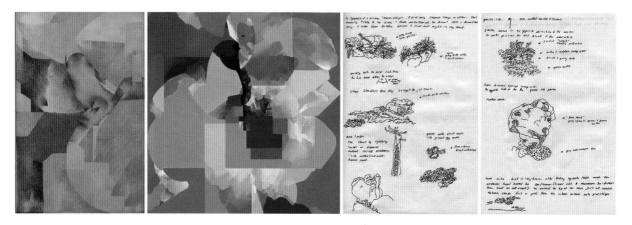

58. Sabra Moore, *From Bandelier* 59. Sabra Moore, *Untitled* 60–61. journal pages, Book #48

2

Everyone Wants to Open a Gallery

I was walking along Atlantic Avenue in Brooklyn, a street flanked by low nineteenth-century red and yellow buildings. The street ends at the East River. You can stand at the intersection of Atlantic Avenue and Court Street and imagine running down the grassy hill—now covered by asphalt—to greet the ships docked at its base. Across the river, the silver towers of Manhattan crowd together, but the Brooklyn side is open and sunny. Near this intersection, there is a man-hole that serves as an entrance to a brick-lined passageway—a defunct underground railroad that runs beneath Atlantic Avenue. This is not the entry to the subway, which startled me the first time I took the train. I had pictured the subway as a sort of gleaming tube, but then discovered that it was simply a grimy train in a long tunnel.

Standing at that intersection, I ran into Roger Erickson, an artist I had known from my days teaching children at the Brooklyn Museum. Roger made collages with images loosely taped to paper and published an occasional magazine called the *5-Cent Cigar.* He told me about a

1. Anonymous, *poster* 2. Drewann Rodney and Sabra Moore install logo in Atlantic Gallery window
3. Drewann Rodney, *gallery poster*

new artists' cooperative gallery, Atlantic Gallery, forming on Atlantic Avenue, and invited me to a meeting.

Artists-run galleries were sprouting all over the city. Everyone had the idea of forming his or her own venue and bypassing a dealer system that seemed inherently unfair. People wanted to control the distribution and presentation of their art. Some galleries were exclusively for women artists (A.I.R. Gallery and SOHO20 Gallery, which were later joined by Ceres and Central Hall), but women were in all the artists-run galleries and often formed a majority. Other galleries had an artistic focus (Prince Street was a realist gallery; 112 Mercer showed political art), but most cooperatives were eclectic and reflected the changing tastes of the members. We were beginning to see ourselves as workers or producers. People were talking about an artists' union and an artist's contract to ensure copyright and the French legal concept of *droits morals* (moral rights) to protect the integrity of the artwork.

In the seventies, it was possible to rent cheap storefronts and live in cheap lofts. The artists-run gallery movement couldn't have happened without the booming war economy and the exodus of manufacturing jobs that made space available. A small core of artists had started meeting in a former hardware supply store on Atlantic Avenue to found Atlantic Gallery. I joined that group; the gallery opened in 1974. The store's massive oak counters and cabinets were still in the space, and its basement was populated with big metal pumps for filling containers with kerosene or other fuels. Our landlord, Lou Shaloub, was one of the merchants on that street. He rented three stores to cooperative galleries nestled among Middle Eastern restaurants and specialty grocery stores, hoping our galleries would attract diners. He wanted to sell the oak fixtures to us, but none of us could afford his prices. The oak cabinets ended up in the dump.

4. Kate Correa, *Untitled* 5. Malekeh Nayiny, *Untitled* 6. Rebecca Leonard, *Seeraubel-Jenny (Pirate Jenny)*

Our group was wildly eclectic, ranging from artists connected to the Brooklyn Museum or Pratt Institute to a photographer who wanted his son to inherit his gallery membership. Most of us lived in Brooklyn near the gallery and liked the idea of showing our art in the neighborhood. Ruth Gray, for instance, lived in a brownstone facing the river in Brooklyn Heights. She made large paintings of rumpled beds that hinted of the night's occupants. Her boyfriend, Jess, was a television cameraman and former husband of the political activist and writer Grace Paley. Barbara Spiller, who lived a few blocks from the gallery, made expressive nude self-portraits. Frances Buschke and her partner at the time, Kate Correa, also lived nearby. They were collaborators who made exquisite collaged paintings using earth pigments and other found natural materials. We became lifelong friends. Another founding member, Drewann Rodney, lived near Sheepshead Bay; she made graphic drawings of patterned roadways, reflecting her training as a designer. She and I struggled with painting the red logo she had designed onto the gallery plate glass windows.

But not every member based her work in Brooklyn. The masked and cloaked figures in the altered photographs of Malekeh Nayiny, an Iranian-born artist, reflected her dual cultural identity.

My new neighbor on Warren Street, Jackie Clipsham, joined the gallery later. She was a potter who taught ceramics at the Brooklyn Museum Art School and knew about my struggles to leave C. She had been an activist in the Congress of Racial Equality (CORE) and later transferred her experience in the civil rights movement into fighting for people with disabilities based on her own small stature. She had been born with disproportionate dwarfism. When Jackie saw my *ibeji* dolls from Nigeria, she discovered that the proportions of her body, seen as deformity in this country, were idealized in African art. During the period when I was in hiding from C, Jackie alerted me to the vacancy of a rent-controlled apartment on the parlor floor of the building where she lived and managed to reserve my place there. I had hastily rented an empty floor in an

7. Emily Barnett, *Life and Art in the Studio* 8. David Cole, *Artists-Owned Spaces flier*

industrial building near the Fulton Fish Market and moved my paintings there while C was away at his weekly two-day teaching job at Vassar College. I foolishly waited at our loft to announce my departure in person. I had imagined that I could renovate the raw industrial space on my own, but was relieved when Jackie found the apartment for me.

Another founding gallery member, Roger Mignon, had studied with Phillip Pearlstein at Pratt and painted nudes in realistic settings. He once painted a life-sized nude self-portrait wearing only his eyeglasses, "in solidarity with my models." He took one of the heavy metal pumps that the landlord had abandoned in the basement and used it as a painted object in several of his artworks in later years. He and I both came from union families—his father was an Italian immigrant who organized for the communications workers; his mother's parents had fled the last Czarist pogram against Jews in the Ukraine. We were members of the construction committee and spent hours over many months discussing the designs for gallery desks and moveable walls. We became easy friends; it was the first time I had simply enjoyed companionship with a man who attracted me without acting on my attraction. One day, he kept calling to arrange an excursion to the lumberyard; we couldn't decide on the timing for our trip. Finally, he called back and invited me to dinner. That date launched a life pattern of building things together that has united us since that our first construction project, through the renovation of a loft and, later, the building of our straw-bale studio and adobe house here in New Mexico. We got married in the late eighties, but that is another story.

Brooklyn was still considered the "other" side of the river from the core art center in Manhattan. Some of us had lived in SoHo or Tribeca before it gentrified and had moved to Brooklyn for cheaper rent and quieter neighborhoods. When C and I lived on Greenwich Street in Tribeca, developers tore down the two blocks of nineteenth-century buildings between our place

9. Drewann Rodney, *Mass/Maine* 10. Stephanie Rauschenbusch, *Breakfast With Cezanne*
11. Roger Mignon, *Waiting for a Phone Call*

and the river. Further downtown, workers were digging a huge hole for the construction of the World Trade Center. The site was ringed with lights, and C and I would walk down at night to watch as the machines cut deeper. The vacant lots were forlorn, with an occasional street of shuttered brownstones left standing. That spring, I threw sunflower seeds into the rubble-strewn lots. When the sunflowers bloomed, other plants sprouted with them. I discovered that the men working at the few remaining green markets on the street had also been throwing seeds into the rubble. One evening, I was cooking supper and glanced towards the windows. A truck driver, who had just finished his delivery to the produce market below, was standing on top of his cab, looking into our place, curious about the only lit windows along the darkened street. We moved the next winter to Pacific Street in Brooklyn.

The galleries and the artists' neighborhoods were extensions of one another, and each had its local character. In the artists' buildings, people formed lasting friendships based on shared struggles. Kazuko Miyamoto, an early member of A.I.R. Gallery, told me this story: She had moved into a loft on Hester Street with her boyfriend. The minimalist artist, Sol Lewitt, lived in the same building. Kazuko knew of his work from her studies at the Art Students League of New York, but had never met him. One day, there was a fire in the building, and all the artists-tenants ended up standing together outside. Sol started talking to Kazuko, and then asked her to help him on one of his artworks. His penciled grid drawings were designed to be rendered by others on a much larger scale for public installation. Thirty years later, Kazuko was still working for Sol and saw their collaboration as a support for her own sculpture.

We artists lived illegally in the lofts of Manhattan and Brooklyn—lofts were zoned for commercial use only. An ethos of concealment was part of that life. We didn't wash the windows, for instance. We concealed our beds and kitchens. The bedroom in our Pacific Street loft was

12. Kazuko, *Woman in Blue Blanket* 13. Pearl Street Studio 14. Judith Fox, *Person who is a woman and old, leaning*

built behind a black painting wall; one of C's paintings served as a hidden doorway that we would remove each night. In our Greenwich Street loft, C once created another doorway by cutting through an adjoining wall into the floor of the vacant building next door; we used that space for storage. No one noticed. Roger and I opened up five windows in the brick wall of our sixth-floor Pearl Street loft in Dumbo (Down Under Manhattan Bridge Overpass); it was months before the landlord bothered to look up and see the new windows. There was an inverse relationship between the living and workspace—the workspace dominated.

The construction of the gallery spaces followed the same ideas; we built them ourselves. But the galleries were visible. Renovating the space was the starting point for most cooperatives. Barbara Zucker describes building A.I.R. Gallery: "I remember Patsy Norvell and Laura James knew about carpentry, so we lined up and were taught to build walls and lay floors. Someone else learned basic electrical work and a few members worked on that. It was a good time, with all those bodies and minds building one loft."[1]

Like the design for A.I.R. Gallery, we created two rooms at Atlantic Gallery so that two artists could show concurrently and each artist could exhibit on a yearly basis. One artist forgot she was painting from a scaffold and stepped off the edge while we were building, but we all survived the construction. The building didn't survive quite as well. We women in the gallery decided to piece a brightly colored banner that we hung from the flagpole mounted on the brick parapet. As the wind whipped from the river, the powerful cloth lifted and took part of the parapet with it, landing on the roof. We repaired both.

Atlantic Gallery had two big sunny plate glass windows with a huge potted rubber tree installed behind one. Painter Cynthia Mailman, a member of SOHO20 Gallery and friend of Roger's from his Pratt days, once scolded me for allowing plants in the gallery windows rather than

15. Artists-collaborators for Atlantic Gallery banner, *The Phoenix* photograph 16. Ruth Gray, *Untitled Polaroid*

featuring only art. We members took turns sitting for our shows at the desk Roger and I had built. The room was bisected at various locations by our so-called moveable walls. It took four strong people to move one wall, so we tended to keep a set arrangement. I was sitting at the desk one afternoon when a homeless man wandered in, muttering to himself. Transients often came to our galleries; one man attended every opening at any conceivable location, enjoying the food and the art, occasionally being invited to exhibit his Ivory soap carvings. But as this man walked around the gallery, I slowly overheard the content of his mutterings: an obsessive rambling about violence. I was alone and watched him circle the room, finally realizing that he couldn't find his way out. I stood behind the open front door and as he circled again, I beckoned him into the doorway, locking the door behind him.

A few years later, Atlantic Gallery moved to a building on West Broadway in Manhattan. The building that had housed the gallery in Brooklyn became a store again, selling prosthetic devices instead of art. We had the entire second floor in the West Broadway site with a wall of plate glass windows and a separate stairway going directly up to the gallery. This time, we built a permanent dividing wall that did not have to be moved. I pieced another banner for the new location—a long, skinny one with plenty of flaps for air currents. We hung it above the second-floor fire escape. It must have looked good as it waved across the gallery face; someone stole it after only ten days on display. We posted leaflets about the banner's disappearance, but it was never found.

A year after my return from Guinea, I was awarded a Fulbright fellowship to study African art at the Centre for West African Studies at the University of Birmingham in England. I left my paintings and colored pencil drawings with C for safekeeping. A few months into the fellowship, he demanded I return and threatened to destroy my artworks. I returned. It's hard to think about

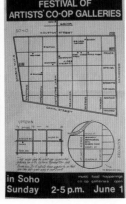

17. Roger Mignon, *Atlantic Gallery moves to W. Broadway* 18. Anonymous, *Flier* 19. Roger Mignon photograph, *Exhibit at Atlantic*

my truncated education; I have seldom mentioned it. But I think the work in the cooperative gallery and in the women's movement provided me with the university I had abandoned.

Some artists saw the cooperative gallery as a means to move into the dealer system and others saw it as an opportunity to explore ideas and create shows free of commercial imperative. I am in the latter camp. I was in Atlantic Gallery for eight years—through two locations and five one-person shows.

I think we all make work for someone in particular to see. I make art for my grandmothers, for the people I knew in Guinea, and for my peers, who are mostly women. Some members of this mythical audience of my heart might not like my work, and many are dead, but that is not the point. I feel the connections.

When I lived in Guinea, I experienced art in context. Art was everywhere: some of the houses had painted patterns; the wooden spoons had etched designs; there was a rich ceremonial life with music and dancing; and people would sing to me on the road. It was also my first time to live in a country free of racism. It took me a while to recognize that cultural absence in which difference is simply that. The summer I was twenty-two, I traveled alone down the coast of West Africa to Nigeria, up across the Sahara Desert to Ouagadougou, and then back to Guinea via the Ivory Coast. To start my journey, I went very early to a dirt lot in N'Zérékoré where trucks gather and waited with others to secure passage. I was able to book first class passage in a truck loaded with palm nuts for delivery to Monrovia, which meant a passenger seat in the cab next to the driver. By the end of my trip, I could identify most people's tribal origin by the patterns of their facial scars and tattoos or the print on their cotton robes.

I met Lamidi Fakeye that summer, taking the advice of other Peace Corps volunteers and going to visit his workshop in Ibadan, Nigeria. Lamidi was a fifth generation traditional carver.

20. Sally Brody, *Show poster* 21. Roger Mignon photograph, *Atlantic opens on West Broadway* 22. Rich Samuelson, *Exhibit poster*

Even though he had converted to Islam as a young man, his art remained rooted in the Yoruba pantheon. He carved the house posts for the first government after independence, but that patronage evaporated with Nigeria's shifting politics. He took me to see the doors he had carved for the Catholic church with its panels of Yoruba figures reinterpreting the story of Christ, and mailed me photos of his work when I returned to N'Zérékoré. Years later, I was able to return these photos to him for his biography during one of his many visits to Roger's and my loft on Pearl Street. Africans I met often saw physical traits simply as descriptions; this ease used to startle me. "When I met Sabra, she was thin like pencil!" Lamidi once told Roger, "We felt sorry for her. Now, she is a real woman!" "Listen to my friend's voice, like a bell!" he would add.

One time, my housemate Joan Bancroft and I took a short trip to the Fouta Djallon region north of N'Zérékoré. As a courtesy, we stopped at the provincial governor's house in Labé. They insisted that we spend the night. Madame Thieu, the governor's wife, gave me a fine indigo *pagne* (a wrap worn as a skirt) and got her tailor to quickly sew the traditional blouse, a tight-fitting top with a wide ruffle at the waist. She brought me the outfit to try on and then promptly returned to inspect the effect. She deftly produced two large handkerchiefs and stuffed them down my blouse, making my bustline more presentable. Then, we all sat down to eat from the rounded bowl of rice and fiery peanut sauce.

I had bought some woven cloth and indigo pagnes when I was in Nigeria and showed them to friends after my return to N'Zérékoré. Then, I stored them in a metal trunk that my parents had shipped from Texas. The trunk was filled with clean sanitary napkins, which I never used, preferring Tampax. Evidently, Daddy had purchased this ample store on his own, not knowing my preference, and removed them from their boxes, neatly stacking them to conserve space. One afternoon, someone stole the locked trunk. I reported the theft, hoping to retrieve

23. Lamidi Fakeye, *Carving* 24. OSPAAAL, *Solidarity/Zimbabwe* 25. Sabra Moore, *drawing* 26. Lamidi Fakeye, *Carvings*

the Nigerian cloth. Weeks later, a policeman bicycled to my school to report the recovery of the trunk. It had been found thrown out in the forest. I went to the police station and there was the opened trunk, filled only with clean wet sanitary pads. *"Qu'est ce ca?"* ("What is this?") the officer asked. I paused. *"Du coton,"* ("Cotton") I replied.

The Greek merchant in town, Thanos Mengrelis, had asked me to make drawings of Guerzé masks and gris-gris objects for a book he was writing. I would go to his house in the center of town and sit inside a shady courtyard with bougainvillea flowers in profuse bloom. He would bring out masks and other ritual objects for me to draw, and then offer me cake and tea. His refrigerator was filled with eggs, an unthinkable display of wealth in an economy where one egg cost fifty cents at the market. His collection of art was also suspect; a few years earlier, Ahmed Sékou Touré's government had conducted a demystification campaign and burned masks in the town center. Other masks were stored in a vacant house. For the Guerzé, these masks were deities—the wood was infused with spiritual power before carving. I sat there and drew. I drew over one hundred objects—masks of all varieties, woven cages for carrying chickens, and hunters' shirts embellished with magical pouches. I felt saturated with this iconography. Since I was in the Peace Corps, I refused to be paid, somehow thinking the drawings would be returned to me when his book was published. I kept thirty. Thanos kept all the others.

A plane came to N'Zérékoré every Thursday and landed if the weather was clear. The landing strip was located near Mount Nimba, a loaf-shaped mountain of iron thick with trees. That fall, it happened that my father died on a Thursday. I was at home cooking when a stranger bicycled to my house carrying a letter that had arrived with the plane. It simply said that I had to return immediately to the United States. Four hours and a thousand miles later I was in the capital city of Conakry and learned that my father had been killed, but by then I couldn't cry.

27. Sabra Moore, *Niamou drawing* 28. Sabra Moore, *Mask drawing* 29. Sabra Moore, *Two Niamou drawings*

I was wearing the indigo dress I had bought that summer in Nigeria and carrying a canvas bag with a book, some tangerines, and a black gourd from the rainforest as gifts for my family. Henry Norman, the Peace Corps director who had written the pithy note, was traveling with me. As the plane landed in New York City, I threw up. Most of my luggage was confiscated by customs. My mother was waiting for me in Texas. Daddy had been crushed in the accident, and my family had arranged with the funeral home for his face to be rebuilt, wanting me to be able to see my father again. When I went with Mother to the funeral home, she hurled herself onto his corpse in the casket and I stood there, only able to recognize his hands. I returned to Guinea two weeks later, feeling like I was taking the bus home. It was five years before I was able to cry—that day I spent listening over and over to *Abbey Road* and decided to leave C.

I dream that I am standing in front of my parents' house. Daddy's green pickup is parked in the driveway with the passenger door ajar. I rush over. He is sitting with his legs partly out of the truck; his pink heart is beating weakly through translucent skin and I try to save him, but he dies.

I returned to live in the United States a year after Daddy's death. I considered staying in West Africa; it was the place I had felt most at ease. But I wanted to find something in my own culture as the basis for my artwork. I didn't want to be an expatriate drawing my inspiration solely from Africa without something to add of my own. I decided to live in a city. I knew two people in New York and only one person in San Francisco. I chose New York.

I had experienced art in context once before I lived In Guinea, standing around the bed with my kinfolk, talking about the quilts the women were making. People would tell stories connected to the reused fabric or give an opinion on a color or a border. Every woman in that East Texas community could sew or quilt; some were better at it than others, but everyone understood the context.

30. Sabra walking to school truck, N'Zérékoré 31. Lillie Parks's crazy quilt on Gladys Parks's clothesline

I was taught to sew as a child, beginning with doll clothes. Those patterns were printed all on one sheet of tissue paper, which you cut around. My sister and I had quilts for our dolls and for our bed. I made all my own clothes until I was eighteen, and could create a dress pattern from looking at a magazine photo. Mother and I collaborated on many complex sewing projects; we once reupholstered the front car seat in naugahyde. When I moved to New York, I had put this skill aside.

Both of my grandmothers were quilt makers. My mother's mother, Gladys Greer Parks, made her own quilts and also quilted for her mother-in-law, Lillie, who died when I was fifteen. Daddy's mother, Caroline Lewis Moore, was less skilled as a quilter, but made other things— doorstop dolls out of bottles and gourds, and stuffed dogs. She could crochet and tat. She was a gardener and singer. She was also set apart by two experiences. Her father was a carpetbagger who fought for the Union during the Civil War. She married three times; her second husband was murdered by her first. My grandfather Harry was her third husband. They lived in a spare plank farmhouse that her father had built. I often visit that vanished place in dreams, and when I awake, I can smell the wet sandy yard and the musty wood of the walls.

Grandmother Caroline died in 1977 under hard circumstances. She had already lost her farm; her children had forced her to move into town when Harry died ten years earlier. Caroline had chronic heart problems, but her two remaining children, Henry and Opal, had more serious health issues. They were both diagnosed with lung cancer. That year, my aunt and uncle abruptly moved Grandmother into a nursing home, throwing most of her household items into the street. I flew down to see her and tried to help her reclaim her little house. She wouldn't let me help. "You be my granddaughter and I'll be your grandmother," she told me. Shortly after my failed visit,

32. Caroline and Harry Moore in their yard 33. Sole remaining quilt of Gladys's mother 34. Sabra Moore, *4/TELLS #2*

Henry and Opal died from lung cancer within two weeks of each other; Caroline died a few days later. I went again to Texas for her funeral.

I dream that I am walking down an outdoor stairway in the city. Grandmother is sitting on the steps and I hurry to her side and kneel down to touch her face. She is dying. I say, "Remember your garden."

I tried to make a painting for her shortly after her death. I made a pink painting with a circular image, replicating her method of planting flowers within circles framed by the sand-colored earth. But the abstract painting on canvas didn't adequately express my feelings. It took me years of working with other women artists in our movements, creating shows and projects, to translate these insights and needs into the visual forms I was seeking.

35. Caroline Bryant (center) during her second marriage, circa 1910 36. Grandfather Harry Moore (left) with mules

3

We Must Have Theory & Practice & Many Meetings

Sylvia Sleigh told me about going to her first meeting of the Ad Hoc Women Artists' Committee (AHWAC): "Everyone whom I had been trying to avoid for years was there!" May Stevens and I have been having a discussion about founders and followers: was the women's art movement linear, with our own newly minted First Mothers, followed by everyone else? Was it like the clever sperm that penetrated the egg and started the ball rolling or like the egg herself, dividing, subdividing, and multiplying? That explosion of cells was the uncontrollable part. Or was it like Sylvia's meeting, with a discreet circle of women who already knew each other finally deciding to act?

Barbara Zucker and Sue Williams founded A.I.R. Gallery and then had to learn how to "relinquish our initial roles." People now associate other artists with A.I.R. Gallery—Nancy Spero, Howardena Pindell, and Sara Dienes, to name a few. Mary Beth Edelson, Joyce Kozloff, Lucy Lippard, Betsy Hess, and seventeen others founded *Heresies*. Lucy Lippard also helped found Political Art Documentation/Distribution (PAD/D) and AHWAC. May Stevens and Sylvia Sleigh

1. Tomie Arai and others, *Wall of Respect for Women*, New York City, 1974 2. Jerri Allyn, Arlene Raven, and friends, *Greetings 1985*

were among the founders of SOHO20 Gallery. No one can quite agree on who founded Women's Action Coalition (WAC) because several small groups were meeting at the same time. Jerri Allyn helped found two performance groups, The Waitresses and Sisters of Survival. Miriam Schapiro came to New York to found the Feminist Art Institute (FAI), but Nancy Azara ended up running that women's school. Ann Sutherland Harris and Judy Brodsky helped found the Women's Caucus for Art (WCA) when a group of women art historians felt excluded from the College Art Association (CAA). The WCA always had a dual identity with the local chapters, centers of activism by artists, and the national organization run by academics who focused on the yearly conferences. Cynthia Navaretta founded *Women Artists News* (*WAN*), and Ellen Lubell founded another magazine, *Womanart*. Faith Ringgold cofounded "Where We At" Black Women's Artists and AHWAC. Martha Wilson founded Franklin Furnace, and Christy Rupp helped found ABC No Rio. Josely Carvalho and Kathie Brown helped found Central Hall Gallery; Josely directed the Silkscreen Project that made leaflets and political banners. Carol Hamoy and Carol Grabel helped found Ceres Gallery. Tomie Arai didn't found anything, but she directed the Cityarts Workshop's mural projects. I'm not sure who wants to claim founding Guerrilla Girls or the action group Pests, but people know their names. Somehow, we all found each other.

Except for the galleries, many of these groups and magazines are now defunct, but they played their roles as we were figuring out what to do and how to reclaim our history and how to make a new history.

Saigon fell to the North Vietnamese Army and National Liberation Front (NLF) in 1975. After years of protest, the Vietnamese resolved their own struggle in one dramatic summer. Mao Tse-Tung died the following year. I had once dreamed of Mao as my grandmother Caroline; she died the year after his death. It's odd now to think about Mao's Cultural Revolution, which proved

3. ABC No Rio: The First Five Years. 4. Greetings from the NYC/WCA, 1981 (*WCA Newsletter*), montage by Sabra Moore

so disastrous for the Chinese. We women adapted a version of his critique/self-critique in our consciousness-raising groups without clearly understanding its original context.

I had been backing my way into activism again by reading the women's art magazines. *WAN* regularly reported on the activities of the WCA and also did feature articles on women artists. If you read *WAN*, most women seemed to be realist painters working with autobiographical themes, a description that excluded my work. *Heresies*, the feminist journal of art and politics, had just published its first issue in 1977. I subscribed to *Heresies* and to the West Coast journal *Chrysalis*, which focused on performance art. *Signs: Journal of Women in Culture and Society*, edited by Catharine Stimpson, was another interesting magazine. I still use Catharine's phrase when I describe my spare photocopier artists' books. She called them "minimalist novels."

I made a shelf in my studio for the women's art journals, keeping a phantom dialogue with this community by reading. I wrote out a long list of the various objects my grandmothers made, thinking of writing an article for the *Heresies's* issue on Women's Traditional Art, but it never went past the list. Jackie Wray later told me how Miriam Schapiro would get the other artists on that issue to cut out images for her to collage, causing Jackie to end her participation with *Heresies*.

One day, I received a pink card in the mail from the Center for Feminist Art Historical Studies, signed by Ruth Iskin, Lucy Lippard, and Arlene Raven: "If you consider yourself a feminist, would you respond by using one 8 ½" x 11" page to share your ideas about what feminist art is or could be." I recently found my heavily marked draft for a reply I never sent: "I start with my body. Men start with their bodies too, but it is a different body. My body is smooth and plain. It is a little girl's body. I am told, 'everything is inside.' I am told not to touch, look, etc. That's the 'different-in-the-future' part, but the 'inside' is always there. I go around with sticks, making doodle bugs come out of holes, pulling bag worms out of bags, emptying everyone out, or building up

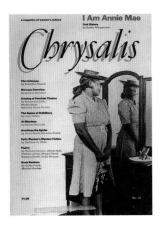  

5. *Chrysalis* issue #10 cover, 1980 6. *Chrysalis* issue #3 cover, 1977 7. Amy Zerner, *A Woman's Web (Is Never Done)*, 1979

homes for lady bugs, homes for brown bees, taking out of containers or putting into containers. I am told breasts will grow, eggs are inside, your period will come. I don't think little boys are told 'your sperms will come'. . . . All of this gives me as a female a very different time sense."

Tom Boutis and Theresa Schwartz visited my studio from Landmark Gallery, looking carefully at my new collages replete with fragments from Africa and cutouts of birds. "You want to know what happens next." "Yes." "Nothing. We have nothing to offer you. We like to go around looking at work to get an idea of what people are doing." As he was leaving, Tom noticed my *Imperialism Sucks* poster hung on the wall. "So you were involved in that too? All the best people were." On Susan Kaprov's advice, I took collages over to show curators at the Museum of Modern Art and the Brooklyn Museum, collecting only comments and snippets of advice.

Daddy kept appearing in my dreams as a ghoul. His funeral haunted me; I felt like he was trapped inside that double steel casket and couldn't get back into the earth. I decided to try to free him with a farewell ceremony of my own invention. I cut little strips of colored paper symbolizing different aspects of Daddy's life—his union activism and work on the trains, his childhood on the farm, his sense of adventure, his cowboy outfits, his singing, and the pain of his accident. One Sunday, I set up a little shrine in my Warren Street kitchen next to the white sink where I had burned the letters from C. I now had access from the kitchen to the garden below, which I entered by climbing out the window behind my stove and down a ladder. Jackie had rented the garden to me, and I was growing vegetables. I set out a sage candle and incense next to Daddy's photo and his paper symbols, and burned the papers in a red bowl, one by one—my sweetest memories of his character and sorrow for his suffering going up in thin smoke. Then, I threw the ashes out the kitchen window, letting them float free onto the garden below. Since this ceremony, he has appeared as himself in my dreams, usually he wears a hat.

8. Sabra Moore, *Rio Grande as Viewed from Alamo Canyon*... 9. Sabra working on pastel, circa 1979

My brother-in-law had bought one of my small paintings as a surprise birthday gift for Nancy. When I went to Texas to visit my family, Mother and I drove over to visit her. *Forest Picture* was hanging in her living room over the gerbil cage, turned on its side. Without thinking, I took it from the wall and started to readjust the hanging wire so it would hang upright as I had painted it. "Can't I turn it the way I want it?" Nancy said. "No." I insisted. Mother sat on the couch silent with disapproval. We drove down to the country to visit my grandparents. Mother Gladys talked about Grandma and Grandpa Greer, who had raised her after her mother died. "Her hair was black. Papa's hair was black. They were part Choctaw, part Scotch, but they weren't dark skinned." I quote Colette in my journal. "I belong to a country I have abandoned."[1]

I was still doing house painting and working independently while looking around for other kinds of work. I applied for a Kennedy Center's Changing Education through the Arts (CETA) job along with hundreds of other artists. Only a few got work. I got hired to paint some walls in Claes Oldenburg's studio. When the carpenters left in the early afternoon, I went around carefully looking at all the soft sculpture. There were two vastly oversized stuffed electric light switches; I touched both at once and then put away my tools and left for the day. All the machines in his loft worked smoothly; even the imposing elevator doors opened and closed with a soft sound.

Richard Waller called me from the Brooklyn Museum to invite me into a show. The Community Gallery, site of my first group show, was celebrating its tenth anniversary with an exhibit of ten artists, *The First Ten*. I showed pictures I called *window paintings* with cloud-like forms emerging in and out of square openings in the center of each image. A reviewer at the opening thought they weren't really abstract because of the window shapes, but I felt they were. Another man came over to me after he had noticed my birthplace listed on the wall labels. He was a musician from Oklahoma, and we talked about the red dirt in Texas and Oklahoma. "Also

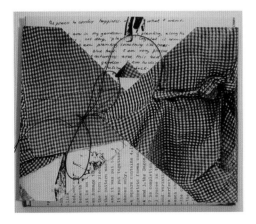   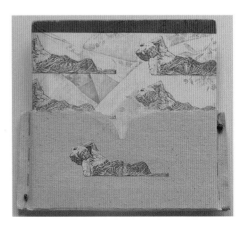

10. Sabra Moore, *notes, notes*, 1980 11. Sabra Moore, *Flower* (top), *Wash & Iron* (below) 12. Sabra Moore, *Gladys Sad Box*

in Vietnam," he added. A lawyer was there whose apartment I had painted. He was interested in buying a painting, and I told him about the Artist's Reserved Rights Transfer and Sale Agreement developed by the American Civil Liberties Union. In addition to guaranteeing copyright, it provided for moral rights for the artwork—the artwork couldn't be altered without the permission of the artist. He was reluctant. "Why not a simple bill of sale?" Roger introduced me to Laura Shechter, a realist painter of jewel-like interiors; he knew her husband from working in commercial art. She was going to WCA meetings and encouraged me to come. She talked about the collaboration between art historians and artists. At the edge of the crowd, I spied C, leaning against a wall, watching me. He had returned to teach at the Brooklyn Museum Art School. We didn't speak.

I had been visiting with Marilyn Dalumer from my old Committee of Returned Volunteers (CRV) consciousness-raising group. "We knew your life was chaotic. We knew you were in despair. You were often late to meetings." "I had to fight to go to the group. C took the list of names and was threatening to kill the members. I don't think I let people know about this."

I dream that I look out into the backyard of my family's house and see a woman lying horizontally, bound to a cross, choking at the neck. I call the police, but the police say, "This is not the sort of emergency where we come out and help."

Laura was referring to the participation of art historian Ann Sutherland Harris in the WCA meetings. Ann was working with Linda Nochlin on the survey show and book, *Women Artists: 1550–1950.* It's easy to forget now that in 1978, people thought there had been almost no women artists in the past except for the anonymous crafts women. We were like orphans with no historical references. Growing up, I had only heard of Georgia O'Keeffe, Mary Cassatt, and Grandma Moses. When Ann and Linda started researching this show, many of the early artworks were stored in museum basements and some were attributed to men. They talked about the

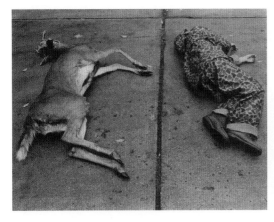

13. Chris Millon, *Death Drawings: Hunting in Suburbs* 14. Pat Ralph, *Flying High* 15. Selina Trieff, *Pink Bird on Her Shoulder*

dust. Thanks to these two historians, you can now find monographs and postcards for Artemisia Gentileschi, Sofonisba Anguissola, and other artists whose names I love to pronounce.

Remember that when God created the world in seven days and made Adam and Eve, Adam then named all the animals and claimed dominion over them. When the Europeans came to this continent, they immediately renamed everything in sight. Language is a powerful tool of control, and some of our hardest battles have been over words. If you are not named, you do not exist.

Art historian Alessandra Comini was talking about the erotic content in the patterning of Gustav Klimt's paintings. I had come to my first WCA meeting, hoping to reestablish my commonality with other women artists. Here was a roomful of potential coworkers who could address issues of art, power, context, and money. Corinne Robbins showed slides of contemporary women's art. Instead of simply comparing my work to the art of the past, it made sense to look at the work of my fellow artists. I felt exhilarated. I thought of Jane Helen Levy's poetic response to Marge Piercy. "I don't have anything to say." "Yes, you do. You just don't have anyone to say it to."

Ora Lerman was president of the New York City/WCA (NYC/WCA) when I first started attending meetings. She and I became close friends. Her artwork fit into the descriptions from *WAN*—highly toned, realistic still-life paintings bordered by a pithy autobiographical text. Ora had been an abstract expressionist painter, but then went to Japan on a Fulbright scholarship and had been influenced by Japanese woodcuts. Through the feminist movement, she began to work with images from her immigrant Jewish family and started to incorporate toys and mannequins like the ones she remembered from her father's department store in Kentucky. She was a member of Prince Street Gallery along with several fellow WCA activists, including the watercolorist Marion Lerner-Levine and painters Selina Trieff and Tomar Levine. I was particularly drawn to

16. Sylvia Sleigh, *Selina Trieff* 17. Sabra (left) and Nancy Hagin (right) at a NYC/WCA meeting, 1980 18. Nancy Hagin, *Early April*

Selina's work. She paints herself, often in a clown costume or in a setting with goats, as obsessively as Frida Kahlo, but without Frida's emphasis on suffering. The exuberance of the studio Selina shared with painter Bob Henry belied the melancholy of her paintings. Their daughter's two fanciful hand-built dollhouses dominated their living space and gave the room a theatrical quality.

The NYC/WCA met in a changing venue of artist's studios, giving a double layer to each meeting. There was usually a panel or a talk followed by a discussion. We women always had food at our meetings and we would spend time afterwards looking at the host's artwork in her studio. One meeting was at Sylvia Sleigh's studio. Sylvia was always dressed in extravagant clothing and elaborate make-up, and her house was filled with paintings of male nudes reclining against cloth as intricately patterned as Klimt's. The jeweler Gloria Orenstein was speaking about ornamentation that evening, describing its function as a personal attribute rather than a symbol of power or status. Her intricately crafted necklace echoed that ideal. At another venue, we debated femaleness in art. Did it exist? I thought of Mother Gladys and how she would describe the fabric of a childhood dress—the way it felt to the touch, the shape of the collar; her sense of detail had shaped my way of looking at things.

Alice Neel came to talk at a meeting. She stood there in her sturdy shoes and advised us to live long lives. Success comes late to women, she said, and it's best to keep healthy. She told us about being in a show with Mary Cassatt; Alice's father had worked for the railroad and Mary's brother had owned one. One time, she painted a bishop or high-ranking cleric. Some of her friends had imagined that Alice would disapprove of this bastion of the church, but no, she loved painting his gorgeous dress.

My vegetable garden was flourishing despite the cutworms eating the zucchinis and threatening the dipper gourds. I would climb down my ladder from the kitchen window to draw

19. Alice Neel being filmed, 1976 20. Bibi Lenĉek, Ora Lerman at NYC/WCA 21. Sylvia Sleigh, *Aphrodite: Annie Shaver-Crandell*

the big sunflowers with petals unfolding like cowlicks. I had brought back ponderosa pine seeds from New Mexico that I managed to sprout, improbable green needles bulging out of three small pots. I had another show at Atlantic Gallery, including my first attempt at making a painting about Grandmother Caroline's garden. Harold Olejarz reviewed my work for *Arts Magazine*, comparing my color clouds to Symbolist paintings. My landlord, Bob Marcheski, an interior designer, sold a large painting for me to one of his design clients at a Wall Street firm, insisting that my artwork was "corporately saleable," contradicting my deepest instincts. Susan Kaprov thought I should take slides to her occasional Fifty-Seventh Street dealer, Terry Dintenfass. "Tell her that your paintings have been compared to the Symbolists and that you have sold to corporate firms. But don't expect too much from her; she makes all her money from artists' estates."

My old Peace Corps friend Maggie Rodgers had a house share for the summer in Amagansett and invited us to spend a weekend at the beach. The painter Anita Steckel also shared that house. I liked her collages of big nude women floating languorously over the tops of skyscrapers and considered her a well-known artist. She was in a group show on Fifty-Seventh Street, but the dealer wouldn't give her a solo show. "I went to Razor Gallery, an artists' cooperative. I had the work; it's like digestion, you must show it."

I worked for several months on a WCA committee chaired by Naomi Teppich, researching statistics. We each followed one particular art magazine and counted the number of times women artists were reviewed or featured. It wasn't too demanding to find these numbers since they were so slight. Women were usually mentioned in separate articles featuring women only. There were very few monographs. Women were often excluded when a writer was analyzing a trend or movement. Male artists of color shared in the same lack of attention that beset women of every ethnicity.

22. Anita Steckel, *Giant Woman on Empire State* 23., 24. Muriel Castanis, exhibit cards (both), *Spirit of Liberty*

This dearth of coverage didn't imply acquiescence to the modest gains women artists had made in exhibiting in galleries or museums. "Does Feminism Conflict with Artistic Standards?" art critic Hilton Kramer pondered in the title of his review of a group show that included women artists.[2] According to Kramer, commercial galleries had "flung open their doors" to women and the results weren't pretty. I wrote him a letter newly armed with statistics: "If it were a show of 30 men, would it be a 'Man's Show'? If you disliked 20 of the works . . ., would it make you wonder, 'Can men be good artists? Has flinging open the door to men lowered the standards of art? Should they be sent back to the carburetor?'" A review by Vivien Raynor the following year was even more vitriolic: "So-called liberation may have increased the number of working women artists tenfold, but it hasn't done much for art beyond widening the choice of clichés. The odds are 10 to one that a fair-size group show by women will be heavy on female genital images; at least one of the participants will be 'the eternal child,' and the best work in all probability will be the least feminist."[3]

In 1987, Josely Carvalho and I curated *Connections Project/Conexus*, a collaborative exhibition between women artists in Brazil and the United States. The writer and fellow WCA activist, Susan Gill, was commissioned to interview us for Vasari's Diary, a monthly column in *ARTnews*. Months passed, and then Susan told us that the article had been killed. The magazine had just done a feature article on another woman artist and couldn't follow so quickly with more commentary focusing on women.

Women, of course, long for information about or by other women artists and writers. I recently wrote to a number of friends from this period, asking them about their involvement in the women's art movement. They consistently misinterpreted one question: "Please name five women who mattered to you most from the women's art movement and tell me why." Most artists

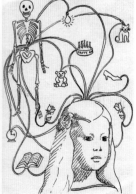

25. Nancy Deffenbach, *For Frida* 26. Linda Peer, *Woman on a Couch* 27. Linda Peer, *Installation at Windows 462*

chose to list women from the past that had mattered to them. Sylvia Sleigh listed her first mother-in-law, Margaret Greenwood, "a very beautiful actress who can be seen in early films, who told me about the sufferings of the suffragists in England." Linda Peer included "Mother Teresa, Inger Christensen, the Danish woman poet who wrote *Alphabet*, and Hildegard van Bingen, the medieval mystic, composer, and artist." May Stevens listed Artemisia Gentileschi, Kathe Kollwitz, and Mary Cassatt. Selina Trieff mentioned Kathe Kollwitz, Frida Kahlo, Grace Hartigan, Alice Neel, and Mary Frank because "all of these women used images that had meaning to me." Joyce Kozloff named Linda Nochlin for her "critical writing, not only *Why Have There Been No Great Women Artists?* but also work on European orientalism and the objectification of women in western painting," Frida Kahlo, and Amy Goldin, "who was struggling to find a methodology to discussing the decorative arts, folk, and outsider art, utilitarian arts." She also liked *History*, a novel by Elsa Morante on the "tragedy of war through the life of a poor woman in Rome."

When I was in college at the University of Texas, my studies were in Plan II, a liberal arts honors program focusing on great books. Later, I could recall reading only one novel by a woman writer among a packed syllabus, Virginia Woolf's *The Waves,* and having not a single female professor. So, for about ten years, I read only novels by women simply to catch up. But it was not all theory. When the sculptor Linda Peer married her first husband, they were traveling in Italy and made their vows of love by placing their hands on a book of Giotto's frescoes. Linda was one of the first people I met through *Heresies*. She was uncompromising and brave in her opinions—and she was an apprentice stonemason at the Cathedral of St. John the Divine. That endeared her to me.

I traveled to Europe for the first time when I left Guinea at the end of my two-year assignment. Fellow volunteer Carol Zeitz and I decided to spend a few weeks in Europe before flying

28. Joyce Kozloff, *Vestibul, Amtrak Station, Wilmington, DE* 29. Janet Goldner, *studio with Malian-influenced sculptures*

back to the United States. We both had our Peace Corps readjustment allowances and felt flush with money. We flew to Paris, but the city seemed gray and cold after the golden sunlight of the tropics. I felt physically deprived of trees, smells, music, sound, and air. We kept running into symbols of colonialism—African objects in the museums and Egyptian obelisks in the plazas. We kept moving south: first to Italy and finally finding a sense of ease in Greece. Unlike people who grew up in cities with museums, I had an arbitrary art education—a Kandinsky exhibit in San Antonio when I was in college and occasional visits to the Dallas Art Museum. Now, I was seeing the entire Italian Renaissance for the first time in person. I found it bloody and daunting until I discovered the clarity of Giotto and Masaccio.

Lucy Lippard called me. I had sent a letter with a proposal for a *Heresies* issue on feminism and ecology. "I found your ideas very exciting," she said, and invited me to work on that issue collective. Lucy outlined the process. The editorial collective would meet weekly, discuss the ideas for the issues, solicit contributions, and make selections, and then design and paste-up the magazine. "There's no guarantee that your article will be published simply because you are part of the collective." I decided to try.

The WCA clung to its academic root and structured its meetings formally around panels and events, but *Heresies* had a different ethos. It was a collective, militantly open and egalitarian in theory. I must have needed the atmosphere of both; I worked with *Heresies* for twelve years and the WCA for about eight. Each editor ended up, after a very extended period, helping to produce a ninety-six-page book crammed full of stories and articles within a passionately designed format. Every inch of that magazine had been argued, traded, weighed, and then physically assembled by the issue collective, which would meet weekly for the duration. In the case of the Feminism and Ecology issue, we met for two and a half years. Mount St. Helens had

30. Phyllis Janto, *Shadow House, Light House, Long House* 31. Merle Temkin, *Merle's Daytime: Sundial*

exploded during our deliberations, so we put the volcano on the cover. People died, had babies, split up, left town, had shows, came out, published books, and lost and gained jobs, our lives interspersed between these meetings and the inevitable arrival of more poetry or another photo or article to read. I could never be objective about its look or quality because each magazine represented such a triumph of endurance and struggle.

We had a two-tiered structure: the Mother Collective, which selected the topics for each issue and did the fundraising and organizing of events, and the Issue Collectives, which were made up of the editors of each issue and usually included some members of the Mother Collective plus anyone interested in working on that topic. No editor was paid. We only had a few part-time paid staff members, and they were usually also members of the Mother Collective—a mistake, as we later learned. We worked by consensus, which often translated as delay. The Democrats have nothing on *Heresies* for a quiet filibuster.

People tended to keep their ties to *Heresies* long after their activism ended; we never had a structure for eliminating anyone, so our masthead simply grew with the years. We newer collective members would occasionally meet with the associates, every previous member of the Mother Collective. I remember one meeting in which Miriam Schapiro was criticizing us, complaining that the magazine had gone downhill in quality. We were seated in a circle, so we took out all the previous issues, placed them in the center, and asked people to choose their favorites. All the covers were chosen except for the plain red first issue. That was how it was; we could never decide or discriminate. It was our strength and our burden.

When I started working on the Feminism and Ecology issue in 1979, several issue collectives were meeting simultaneously, but each year, the production slowed. The magazine was theoretically a quarterly, and people would subscribe for four issues no matter how long they

32. Heresies issue #1 cover 33. Marion Lerner Levine, *The Ghost's Cup* 34. Donna Henes, *Vernal Equinox ceremony*

took to be delivered. We produced twenty-seven magazines over about sixteen years, so there are really twenty-seven different views of *Heresies*. We were mostly visual artists with a fair sprinkling of writers and poets and one anthropologist; all of us were political activists. Many of the visual artists also used words or performance in their artwork; some lectured on art or taught; the writers usually wrote about art. And here we come again to the importance of naming things. Through the magazine, we named ideas, people, trends, and activism—though that was not our goal. The naming often came late anyway due to our erratic production. In the late eighties, some of us wanted to change the ninety-six-page book format and make a broadside or a magazine that could be sold in grocery stores or produced more quickly. But others fiercely resisted changing anything. When *Ms. Magazine* folded as a glossy magazine and then reappeared in a new format, the new *Ms.* mimicked the visually packed look of *Heresies*. We had unintentionally become an institution.

Heresies rented a small white office on an upper floor of a building on the corner of Lafayette and Spring Streets. In the seventies, there were few galleries in SoHo, so the walk down Spring Street could be lonely. Just impressions now as I think back about walking into the office that first afternoon. A bright room with big windows facing downtown was filled with a large table. The painter Harmony Hammond might have been there, her hair very short and blond, along with the filmmaker Su Friedrich working quietly pasting up pages at another table. Sue Heinemann, efficient, nervous, and full of reliable ideas, and Lucy Lippard, with her rapid energy that would focus a conversation, were also at work. Sue worked as a copy editor for her day job. Lyn Blumenthal, a fellow Feminism and Ecology editor, was working on a documentary video project at the time, interviewing well-known artists and writers. When she transcribed her interview with Lucy,

35. Janet Culbertson, *Shelter Island Trees at Night* 36. Harmony Hammond, *Sneak*

the text was much longer than the others even though the interview was for the same length of time. Lucy packs words and thoughts into a very dense space.

I knew almost no one at *Heresies* when I went for the first meeting of the Feminism and Ecology issue. We sat around a table, each person introducing herself and talking about her ideas. We hoped to redefine the traditional dichotomy of woman/earth versus man/technology. Some women mentioned the autonomy that women farmers might feel or the fact than many botanical illustrators had been women. Many of us were gardeners. Were women artists making earthworks that were different in kind from their male peers? We were sitting within the physical radius of Three Mile Island's near meltdown and wanted to address issues of radiation and food. The scope of our ambitions echoed James Baldwin, whom I had been reading. "If there is no moral question, there is no reason to write. I'm an old-fashioned writer and despite the odds, I want to change the world."[4]

Was Ana Mendieta at our first meeting? She worked with us on the Feminism and Ecology issue. I picture her in a poncho, very pretty and slightly aloof. Of course, she supported the idea of a volcano on the cover. The painter Ellen Lanyon had recently moved from Chicago into a loft in the same building as Lucy Lippard ("It is easy to be famous in Chicago"). After the publication of the Feminism and Ecology issue, Ellen gave each of us a print she had made of a dissected erupting volcano inside a drinking glass. She was briefly on the Mother Collective, but quit. "I should really have been in the first group with May Stevens, Joyce Kozloff, Ida Applebroog, Joan Snyder, Miriam Schapiro, and Mary Beth Edelson."

Feminism and Ecology was the thirteenth issue, and, by chance, we ended up with thirteen editors. Sandy Gellis was in our group, and my friend Linda Peer. Sandy impressed me by purchasing a posthole digger for an earthwork she was making. It was, after all, the ecology

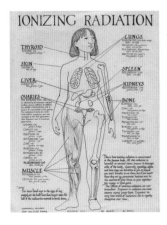  

37. Anonymous, *leaflet* 38. Science for the People, *Three Mile Island Disaster* 39. Ana Mendieta, *Silueta Series*

issue. I went to her show at 55 Mercer Gallery with all the beautiful earth samples sent by friends in distant places displayed in plastic bags around the walls. Her show was paired with Mimi Smith's shed-sized paper houses ornamented with handwritten texts. Sandy's marriage dissolved during our deliberations. The separating couple simply built a wall dividing their loft in two, each remaining at home. Sandy and Jane Logemann spent months interviewing scientists and artists to produce a much distilled article that could be squeezed into the issue ("Does intuition play a part in your work?" "Do art and science interact with each other?").

The painters Elizabeth Riley, Shirley Fuerst, and Cora Cohen attended meetings for a time, but only Shirley stayed. The other editors were artists as well. Phyllis Janto was a wood carver who spent summers in Maine with her blind husband, a painter; she gave Sylvia Sleigh a Maine coon kitten that Sylvia painted in her homage to the Hudson River. Phyllis later joined Atlantic Gallery just as I was leaving the cooperative. Merle Temkin was newly arrived from California; Lucy knew Merle's faceted sculpture made from mirrors and had invited her to come by. The longtime environmental activist and painter Janet Culbertson worked on this issue, as did Sarah Jenkins, a photographer and partner of performance artist Donna Henes. For years, Donna performed a standing-eggs-on-end ceremony during the spring equinox in the open courtyards of the World Trade Center, co-opting the phallic energy of those twin buildings with row upon row of erect eggs lining the rails and walkways.

Some members of the Feminism and Ecology issue attended the Women and Life on Earth conference in 1980 at Amherst College, working furiously over a snowy three-day weekend on a collaborative installation for that event. I went. I describe the weekend as "midway between a camping trip and a slumber party among half-strangers." There were sixteen artists trying to create an installation within three rooms. Kathy Grove, Chris Costan, and Ellen Rumm—artist

40. Jenkins photograph, Donna Henes's *Spring Equinox celebration*, World Trade Center, 1980
41. Ann Marie Rousseau, *Women's Pentagon Action*

friends from Chicago—attended. Kathy and Chris worked with the collective for many years after this conference. We all brought materials as starting points. I brought dried plants from my
garden, dying morning glory vines red and Jerusalem artichoke stalks blue, savoring their tangy
flavors as they heated in a hot dye bath on my kitchen stove. Ellen Rumm brought a forty-pound
box of paprika and someone else brought cumin. The radio journalist Celeste Wesson came with
bales of straw, and others contributed barbed wire, bits of prom dresses, and colored chalk.
Someone thought to bring rolls of white paper. Most of us didn't know each other, so there was
a lot of theory and talk as we sat down in an empty gallery space with our disparate collection of materials and tried to create a collaborative installation. The straw kept getting moved
around, and the mass of dyed vines pushed this way and that. Ellen poured her paprika on the
floor to form patterns, but none of us were sand painters. Nan Becker was among the recent
graduates from Yale School of Art in attendance. She started writing on the walls in the room
that we called the "bad" room, representing current social conditions. The paprika ended up in
the sunny "visionary" room, and the straw became a changing nest for the middle room of "passage." Celeste took out her tape recorder as we talked about our lives and ideas in a series of
marathon monologues that got more intertwined as the weekend progressed. The artwork grew
and then contracted in fits and starts, interspersed with opulent meals prepared by the conference organizers. Nothing was really resolved; the installation stopped changing simply when the
weekend ended.

The following weekend, we returned for the conference, but the atmosphere of heady
interaction had cooled. Some conference participants identified themselves as environmental
artists, unlike the makers of our installation. It was my first encounter with Helene Aylon, who
asserted that nature made her art, not her. She achieved this by pouring thick amounts of oil on

42. Discussion at *Women & Life* on Earth installation, Celeste Wesson (center) next to Sabra and Chris Costan (right)
43. Sabra working

large canvases and allowing the oil to dry and form a skin over the pooled oil, bulging out like a pregnancy. Various well-known artist-friends would then puncture the skin, creating a painting-as-performance piece. This denial of agency bothered me. What about gardens? Gardens are fabricated. Are gardens nature or art? Calling a garden an artwork seemed to diminish its potency as a producer of food and flowers and as an activity whose anonymous and culturally diverse aesthetics belong to everyone.

The Brooklyn journalist Eileen Blair organized a show at Profile Gallery in the elegant lobby of an old hotel near the Hudson River. Eileen hoped to become a dealer and this show was the ephemeral inauguration of that desire. I was invited to participate and many of my new friends from the Feminism and Ecology issue came. Elizabeth Riley, a tall, intense woman who made sculpture by pulling apart dresses and reconfiguring them, had just visited my studio. She was separating from her lawyer husband and facing the challenge of earning her own living for the first time. She said that she liked the structure of my paintings and could see faces in the cloud shapes, which most people didn't notice. But she thought my color looked like "Woolworth store color"; she had grown up among the pale tones of Connecticut. I had been observing the color from many recent shows and felt in good company with my preferences—Rufino Tamayo's watermelons, the frescos of Pompeii, the idiosyncratic shapes and forms of Arthur Dove, Frida Kahlo giving bloody birth to herself, and Northwest Coast transformation masks.

One day, I was walking back from a house painting job and stopped into a shop in Brooklyn called Friendship Store Limited. The owner recognized me. She had once purchased my *Imperialism Sucks* poster, but her former husband kept the poster after their divorce. I brought her another print and shyly told her that my price had increased by five dollars. She gladly paid me, and added two Chinese soaps wrapped like a gift.

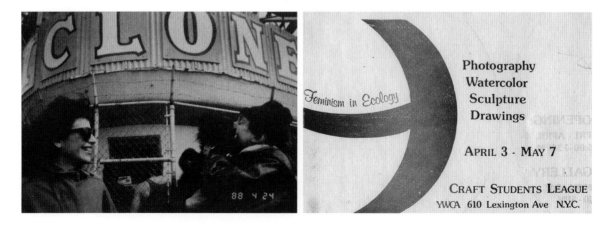

44. Lyn Blumenthal at Coney Island 45. Invitation, *Feminism in Ecology*, Craft Students League

Ana Mendieta was showing a film about the earthworks she called *siluetas*, and many of us went. Ana would go privately to a site in the country and create a depression in the earth with her body, ignite the perimeter by sprinkling gunpowder, and photograph her outline going up in flames. "I work abstractly, but the pieces have content," she said, understating the implications of her imagery. Some months into our meetings, artists on the Feminism and Ecology issue were invited to organize a group show. I forget who designed the invitation, but only the name of *Heresies* was printed without any of the artists' names. Ana got very angry and refused to participate. "I respect myself!"

Our meetings could become contentious. "I've never been as reactive as I've been in this group," Lyn Blumenthal said during one of our criticism/self-criticism sessions. We were nearing completion of the delicate process of making final selections for the Feminism and Ecology issue. "The conflicts are political, but they're seen in terms of personalities," I countered. "But it's also a difference in taste," Ellen Lanyon said, noting the obvious range in our ages, family background, and artistic prominence. "I think everyone has learned from each other and made changes."

Other editorial collectives were also meeting. May, Harmony, and Lucy were working on the topic of propaganda for the ninth issue, Women Organized/Women Divided. May was one of the founders of *Heresies*, but she was no longer active on the main collective. She often lectured about women's art. Dressed in black, her hair clipped back in the front, firm, quiet, delicate, unyielding, May managed to recruit many new artists to work on *Heresies* even as her own participation waned. She had introduced me to Vivian Browne at one of the WCA panels, and I saw Vivian again at *Heresies*. She was writing an article about her visit to the People's Republic of China for the eighth issue, Third World Women—the only issue published without the participation of

46. Leaflet, *Racism Is the Issue* 47. Michele Godwin, *Heresies #15* cover 48. *Heresies* issue #9 cover

an editor from the core collective. The editors for the third issue, Lesbian Art and Artists, had all been lesbians (Harmony and Su represented the collective), but there were no women of color from the collective to participate in Third World Women; everyone was white. When the issue was published, Sue Heinemann hosted a dinner party at her loft for members of both the Third World Women issue and the Mother Collective and proposed afterwards that the collective simply invite all the Third World Women editors to join *Heresies*. Including that entire editorial group would have made the core collective multicultural and avoided the issue of tokenism that later arose. But Sue was in the minority at the time and nothing changed. Vivian and May later recruited the young painter Michele Godwin to make drawings for the cover of the second issue on race, Racism Is the Issue, the fifteenth issue. Vivian would never agree to join the Mother Collective after the dinner debacle, but Michele did. At one point, thanks to Michele and Ellen, we ranged in age from eighteen to sixty.

Three of us from the Feminism and Ecology issue now live in the southwest: Linda Peer in Utah and Lucy Lippard and me in New Mexico. Harmony Hammond and May Stevens are in New Mexico as well. Two members are dead: Lyn Blumenthal and Ana Mendieta.

But let us go back to 1979. That year, Ora Lerman asked me to run for president of the NYC/WCA, not that there were other candidates. I was recruited, like Michele. After I agreed, I had a vivid dream.

I dream I am making food for a huge group of people, outside, in an open field. Ora is there, and she takes off in a tiny silver plane, leaving me.

49. Ora Lerman, *Who Are We? Where Are We Going?* 50. Helen Aylon, *Earth Ambulance*

4

We Organize Shows, Create Actions & Ephemeral Institutions

A friend once told me, "I wish we could sign up for the advanced course." Tired of constantly having to start at the beginning with the Women's Caucus for Art (WCA) meetings, she meant. Because new people kept coming to meetings, the same issues would arise. How do you get into a gallery? Where can you show your work? Are there any job openings? How do you get reviewed? How can you get a dealer to visit your studio? Do you want to see my work? Some of us had already reached conclusions about those questions and wanted to talk about other issues. Why should it matter that women and/or minorities have been excluded? What is different about our multiple visions? Do we want to be part of the current gallery system? Who is our audience? Who else has been excluded from looking at or participating in art? What can we do to change things?

Another version of the beginner course, as asked by writer Betsy Hess: "Why does every issue of *Heresies* have to include woman-the-gatherer, man-the-hunter and woman-the-peacemaker, man-the-warrior?"

1. Camille Billops 2. *Printed Matter* opening (l), Sylvia Sleigh, Bibi Lenĉek, Linda Peer, Marithelma Costa, and Fabio Salvatore 3. Lenora Champagne, *Manna*

One answer was to create an alternative vision through exhibitions, conferences, actions, and organizations. Sometimes, our organizations replicated the institutions that excluded us. They became a kind of theater, where women assumed roles of power within these places. But some of our organizations and events evolved into models radically different from the dominant marketplace for art.

The New York City Women's Caucus for Art (NYC/WCA) had a board of directors and officers; I became its third president. It was part of the National Women's Caucus for Art, whose main function seemed to be organizing a conference to coincide with the annual meetings of the College Art Association (CAA). There were around five hundred members of the New York City chapter by the late seventies. Some were activists, others came to an occasional panel, and others simply attended the annual conference.

The local board functioned a little like the *Heresies* Mother Collective: we planned meetings and events. Several women on that board were teachers; others were artists. Kathy Schnapper, who was improbably writing a book on Picasso, produced our monthly newsletter. Annie Shaver-Crandell taught art history at Lehman College and also made quilts, reversing the accepted pattern by machine stitching the hand-pieced tops. Bibi Lenĉek made pastel paintings of interiors that hinted at erotic encounters. As a child, she had emigrated from Italy with her Slovenian parents, both professors. Her paternal grandfather was a revered Slovenian poet. Bibi's husband at the time was Tak Inagaki, a producer for Japanese television. Jackie Wray had been active with the Women's Interart Center. I recognized her Texas accent; she had grown up in Fort Worth, daughter of a newspaperman. Ora Lerman hadn't really flown away in her silver plane; she was still active on the board after relinquishing the position of president. And many others participated—Sharon Gilbert, who made photocopier artists' books on political issues; the sculptor

4. Tak Inagaki crew filming Sharon Gilbert installing art 5. Bibi Lenĉek, *Domestic Scenes: A Cup of Cocoa*

and teacher Linda Cunningham, who later lived with performance artist Betsy Damon; and the painter Jacqueline Gourevitch, a close friend of Ora. Jacqueline would later be awarded a studio residency at the World Trade Center the year before its 2001 collapse. She had planned to work on a series of cloud paintings from her high perch in the Twin Towers, but the distant street grid drew her instead, which is all that remains from those collapsed towers now.

The WCA membership was predominately white, so we decided—without announcing this as policy—that all our panels would include minority artists as speakers. We stuck to that decision. Remember that race, the topic for *Heresies's* eighth issue (Third World Women), had to be readdressed as racism in its fifteenth issue (Racism Is the Issue). If you do not start as an integrated group from the beginning, it is very hard to diversify later. People already feel left out. Women's Action Coalition (WAC) repeated this same mistake in the early nineties, and while everyone was debating what to do, I invited the Caribbean-born performance artist Lorraine O'Grady to cochair a meeting with me. Why wait and debate when you can act?

The CAA/WCA conference was an occasion for many artists' groups to organize events; I had inherited the responsibility to host the upcoming conference scheduled for 1982 in New York City. We had slightly over a year to organize. Art historians were the ones training students to look at the world's art, and it was still a highly skewed version with white male artists at the core. That limited vision reminded me of my first look at a map when I arrived in Guinea. I had trouble recognizing the familiar world until I realized that the United States wasn't in its usual place at the center. I wasn't interested in being an academic, so I was an odd choice to coordinate the caucus events, but there I was.

We met one evening in Ora's loft to brainstorm ideas for a series of exhibitions, sitting among her immaculate still-life paintings of dolls. (Some artists might consider dolls frivolous,

6., 7, 8. NYC/WCA board meeting, (left to right) Sharon Gilbert, Joan Turken, Ora Lerman, Jacqueline Wray, Turken, and Sabra

but Ora rendered them as icons, giving everyday objects the weight of allegory.) We started fantasizing about exhibits. Vivian Browne suggested a show exclusively of black women artists, and we pictured tracing the influence of Africa in American art. Another woman mentioned the historic Armory Show, and we imagined a show of all nations, tracing not only the influence of African and Native American cultures, but of all immigrants, "for justice and for aesthetic discovery." Someone talked about the art historians in our meetings. "This would never be possible for a group of male artists—it would be a blood bath. But we women have needed role models, we have needed our history, and we have turned to historians to write art criticism." "Everyone has forgotten that art is for healing," Audrey Flack insisted, thinking perhaps of her own still-life paintings with Marilyn Monroe treated as a goddess. "But I think people still make art for that reason," I countered. "No, everyone wants a gallery."

Even though we had begun to work on the plans for the conference, we still held our usual series of local panels. Linda Cunningham was organizing a panel on "Greatness: A Re-Evaluation" for a related group, the Coalition of Women's Art Organizations (CWAO). I was invited to speak along with the performance artist Lorraine O'Grady, the editor of *Signs* Catharine Stimpson, the painter Joan Semmel, and others. This was my first time participating on a panel, and I wanted to use this forum to make the aesthetic tastes of my grandmothers visible. I was interested in the ways they used decoration to soften the hardships of ordinary life, and I brought some objects to represent their point of view—Caroline's sunbonnet and a photo that she had framed by smoothing aluminum foil behind the snapshot of her and her third husband, Harry. Showing these objects generated an immediate reaction. "We should not romanticize the past and place domestic arts and quilts on the level of art." Lorraine insisted. "Greatness is a religious concept for a secular age." Joan thought I was elevating a sunbonnet to the level

9. Ora Lerman, *Which Side of the Door of Dreams Do We Enter?* 10. Faith Ringgold, *Doll Kit* 11. Ora Lerman, *Sea Light Strokes Me*

of transcendent images in painting. "I'm not comparing Grandmother's bonnet to a painting by Rubens. I'm not presenting these as objects of art. I am saying that being able to make things serves as a basis for looking at other levels of art, and when this is absent, people may feel intimidated." Catharine summed up our debate. "There are three arguments brewing: do we really want to democratize art objects? Is there a woman's art? Is there greatness?"

I dream I am preparing food for a meeting, walking into the room carrying a clear glass pitcher of translucent water.

My annual solo show was opening at Atlantic Gallery in December of 1980. I was trying to move beyond abstraction and incorporate my dreams and memories directly into the art works, using shadowy images from Guinea in a series of collaged paintings on paper, and incorporating photos and excerpts from my journals into my first artist's book, *notes notes*. I had dreamed about a snake and was struggling to recreate this dream on a big gessoed panel; I could feel the tugging sensation as I pulled the blue snake out of my left eye and woke with the tingle of the dream's residue on my face. Friends kept visiting my studio. I talked to fellow gallery member, Judy Fox, about my unfashionable love of color. "What's wrong with being pretty? I think women like pretty things. To worry about your color sense is to deny a basic part of yourself." For the show announcement, Roger took a photo of me posed joyously next to *Picture from Dream-Blue Snake, Snake-in-the-Eye* with the same hands-on-hips gesture of the Nigerian ibeji doll I kept near me in the studio.

Ruth Ann Applehoff came to my show and started talking to me about an idea for an exhibit on women and nature that she was proposing for the lobby of the Women's Bank. I went over to meet her at the Whitney Museum of American Art where she worked as a curator. She told me that, after going to her first WCA meeting, she had come back into work the next day

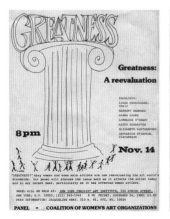  

12. Flier for CWAO "Greatness" panel, 1980 13. Roger Mignon photograph, *Sabra's 1981 exhibit card* 14. Nigerian ibeji doll

excited about meeting so many women artists. The director got angry and said, "It isn't professional to know artists." She heard Lucy Lippard speaking at another meeting and asked her if
she thought it was unethical for curators to know artists. "How could I work like I do if I didn't
know artists?" Lucy replied.

*I dream I am flying, my arms outstretched, soaring and gliding and dipping, not simply
swimming through viscous water.*

I called Faith Ringgold to invite her to participate in another of our WCA panels, this one
called, "The American Quilt: An Innovative Art Form." "I used to know you in the sixties. Whatever
happened to you?" I was surprised that she remembered me; I had blocked out that period of
my life and imagined that others had forgotten as well. I told her about C's violence. "I had to
start again. I needed to be back in ordinary life, not art-world life." Some of the rifts were closing.

There were four of us on the quilt-making panel, including the writer Pat Mainardi; Faith
and I, who both worked with ideas derived from sewing; and Susan Hoffman, who showed her
quilts as cloth-tapestries at Kornblee Gallery. I wanted to talk about form and jumped in with
the assertion that women invented the art form of *colláge* through piecing. Quilts are flat and
patterned, but are meant to lie on the bed and to provide warmth for the sleeper. Their design
implies the body in the same way that Navajo blankets are intended for the human figure. Both
are now viewed like paintings, but they are not simply decorative. Ora joined the conversation.
"Carl Andre reclaimed the floor as an art space, maybe the bed is next." Pat quoted a biased
catalogue essay for a Smithsonian show on pieced quilts that described sewing as tedious. "I
consider the quilting a meditative period, like drawing," Susan said. "Unlike carpentry or painting, both of which require patience, sewing is considered tedious," I complained, noting that
geometric designs were often described as "tough" and appliqué was seen as "pretty" based

15. Bibi Lenĉek (photograph, both), WCA panel on quilts, Ringgold (left), Taylor, and Manairdi 16. Hoffman and Sabra holding quilt

on the same gender-biased logic. Faith had recently recruited her mother to make clothes for her life-sized cloth doll sculptures. When she showed these dolls on college campuses, drama students sometimes animated the figures, adding an element of ritual. "I don't know why more people don't make dolls." My grandmothers reused clothing to piece their quilt tops; we would recognize the reconfigured scraps of our donated clothes and tell stories, so the quilts became memory banks within the family. Pat countered that the "best quilts" were made from new materials, but we three outnumbered her in this opinion, preferring materials with associations from a previous use.

Cynthia Navaretta, the editor of *Women's Artists News*, went to the panel on quilts and reviewed it in her journal. She asked me to review the project organized by Charlotte Robinson, *The Artist and the Quilt*, for her magazine. I made some artist friends angry by disliking the project because of the division between quilt makers and artists. The show was billed as the "first quilts as art." The artists who made the most successful quilts were the two women who also came from that family tradition—Faith Ringgold and the San Antonio-based artist Marilyn Lanfear. Marilyn later told me that she felt like she had to make a quilt that would please both the museum and her aunt. She made a finely sewn white quilt that unbuttoned into two sections, called *A Quilt Is a Cover*, alluding to her impending divorce. Others simply used ideas for paintings transposed onto cloth, the inverse of creating an image through physically adding parts. I started dreaming in code about my grandmothers' quilts.

I dream that I am holding an oversized book printed in sepia, slowly turning each page and looking carefully at the paintings made by my women relatives who have come before me.

Susan Kaprov was working on an impressive series of color Xerox photos for an installation in the lobby of the Brooklyn Museum. She lived nearby in Brooklyn Heights; I met her at one

  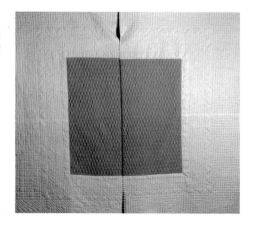

17. Faith Ringgold, *Echoes of Harlem*, 1980 18. *Women Artists News* cover 19. Marilyn Lanfear, *A Quilt Is a Cover*

of our first Atlantic Gallery shows. Tall, thin, and blond, she looked like a fashion model. "Did you ever do that?" she asked me. "I couldn't stand the way they were always touching and adjusting my clothes." Susan was a frequent nude model for Sylvia Sleigh. She had a friend with a color copier and would go sit on his machine after hours to create vaginal images masked by the patterning in her large-scale grids. Roger and I helped her mount the Xerox photos on aluminum panels. Each panel was joined to form a quilt-like wall, and we spent a day working with museum personnel to install the photos. I loved the atmosphere of many people working together on one woman's artwork and came home exhilarated with a sense of possibility.

A few weeks later, several of us went to San Francisco for the February 1981 WCA Conference armed with our complex concept for a series of shows called *Views by Women Artists* for the conference the following year in New York. We had combined many of the ideas from the brainstorming at Ora's loft into one proposal with multiple points of view. WCA founder and printmaker Judy Brodsky felt these ideas were "getting out of hand," but Ora disagreed: "That's one person's opinion. I like the way you are—you are multifaceted." Linda Cunningham introduced me to artists from other cities as the "very good, very democratic, low-key president of the NYC/WCA who has board meetings I enjoy." "What do you do, Sabra? I've always wondered," she asked. "I paint apartments." My reply was met with silence.

An old Peace Corps friend, Dan Clark, was living near San Francisco in Jenner, and I traveled up the coast to visit him. He also chose to paint houses for his living despite his college degrees. The beauty of his place perched above dramatic cliffs facing the Pacific Ocean jolted me back into our days in Guinea as volunteers in rain forest towns. I longed for the saturation of light and the feathery trees emerging from the morning fogs. I felt dissatisfied. "I want my artwork to get louder and clearer in a singing way," I wrote, "and better. Maybe I should just start

 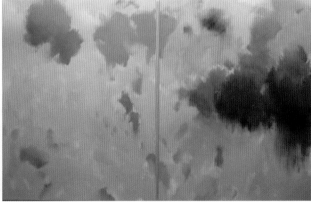

20. Susan Kaprov, *Precambrian Waltz*, Port Authority Technical Center 21. Jacqueline Gourevitch, *Cloud Painting #101*

assuming that I do communicate, that everything communicates, but that not every communication is acknowledged."

Ora and I traveled to Boston together later that spring to see the Turner exhibition. On the train, she told me about visiting Georgia O'Keeffe in Abiquiu. Many women artists had tried to visit that famous painter only to be rebuffed, but Ora had succeeded. She had brought a magazine with photos of a chrysalis as a gift. O'Keeffe reacted to the images: "Oh, how awful!"

The Feminism and Ecology collective had been meeting all spring at the same time we had been organizing the shows for *Views by Women Artists*. The *Heresies* issue was nearing completion just as many members of the editorial collective were leaving town for the summer. I was staying. I had just started my first photo-research job for Tree Communications on a book on Japanese art that was part of a sumptuous Time/Life series. Susan Kaprov had worked as a photo researcher and helped me find this project. It was a physical adjustment, sitting in an office looking through beautiful art books, clipping pictures and taking notes, after my daily regiment of moving up and down ladders and stretching my body to roll paint on apartment walls. At first, I ached from the stasis, but I loved doing research. One afternoon, I was reading a book on the Heian period of art. The author notes, "Women came to play an increasingly important part in this elegant, refined court life . . . the feminine influence of the court encouraged the tendency to over-refinement and sentimentality."[1] This softened aesthetic was quickly corrected by the two hundred years of samurai-dominated warfare that followed.

In the evenings, I often went over to the *Heresies's* office to work on the Feminism and Ecology issue. We had been making selections of the articles and images throughout the spring, but we had also chosen to create one or two articles to include people we wanted to feature. Sarah Jenkins and I went over to the Brooklyn neighborhood of Bedford-Stuyvesant to interview

22. Diana Mara Henry, *photo* (type design by Sabra) 23. *Heresies* issue #13 cover 24. Ellen Lanyon, *Mount St. Helens*

and photograph Hattie Carthan, the founder of the Magnolia Earth Tree Center. The center was the offshoot of Hattie's campaign to save one venerable magnolia tree in her struggling African American neighborhood, which led to the founding of the Magnolia Earth Tree Center ten years later and planting 1,500 trees. "All these articles are about women being radicalized—each doesn't see it until it happens to her," Lucy summarized. "Or Doris Lessing's idea that every part affects every other part," I added.

We all agreed to put Mount St. Helens on the cover and to make visual headlines that incorporated images. Sandy Gellis designed the cover to mimic the yellow-bordered *National Geographic* magazine. I set to work making ornately collaged headlines. Sue Heinemann, Cindy Carr, Amy Sillman, Su Friedrich, and I worked off and on throughout the summer designing and pasting up the magazine. We got the pages ready for press with all of us pleased with how it looked. Sue told me, "When Sandy Gellis saw it, she thought it looked very different from the other issues. *Heresies* had gotten a certain 'look,' and it was nice to see that image changed. Amy Sillman felt this issue leads you more visually into the writing." But other newly returned editors had a different reaction. Merle Temkin was so offended by my ornate headline for *Environmental Sculpture* that she wanted the photo of her minimalist sculpture removed. Cecilia Vicuña had expected for her poem to be handwritten. Linda Peer thought the Chinese characters in her article were too pale. Ellen Lanyon felt she could have made a better design for some of the pages. We had accidentally dropped a paragraph off of Michelle Stuart's article. Lucy thought some of the design looked fussy. I kept a grim list of their comments. "Don't worry," Ellen insisted, "we weren't there." "It isn't enough to feel. I did the job in the absence of someone better qualified who wasn't there." The issue got back from press in October. Hattie Carthan loved it; the writer Florence Falk loved it. We had featured her article on the anti-nuclear martyr Karen Silkwood.

  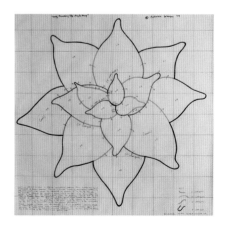

25. Judy Simonian, *Wall Exposure No. 1* (type design by Sabra) 26. Hattie Carthan (type design by Ellen Lanyon)
27. Patricia Johanson, *Leaf Fountain / 3/8 Phyllotaxy*

Sarah Jenkins told me, "At first, I didn't like the issue. I have had to let myself get into it." Despite our differences, we had a party. Linda Peer and I walked back home together over the Brooklyn Bridge from Manhattan in the warm rain.

I ran into Lucy in December. "You probably don't want to hear this, but you will be receiving a letter inviting you into the *Heresies* collective." I was meeting at Sylvia Sleigh's house regularly for organizing *Views by Women Artists*, and bought her husband, the art critic Lawrence Alloway, a copy of the Feminism and Ecology issue. He commented on the volcano cover. "I know *Heresies* thinks holes in the ground are women." He criticized what he saw as irrationality in several articles, and I heatedly defended the magazine.

I dream that volcanoes are sprouting throughout the city. I walk past a volcano in the center of the street, looking worn out, with cars speeding along on either side.

Lucy was working with painter Jerry Kearns for a PAD/D conference to coincide with the CAA events scheduled for February 1982. Things were starting to unravel in Central America with Ronald Reagan's assistance, so artists were thinking politically again. Linda Cunningham was selecting panels with Judith Stein for our parallel WCA/CAA conference, Women & Art in Society. I had been working the entire year with the committee, coordinating *Views by Women Artists* while also meeting with the Feminism and Ecology issue and doing my photo research job. Months afterwards, when I tried to file away the papers from this process, I had to lay down on my studio floor, dizzy from memories of the strange little side effects that had come with my activism. My landlord saw an opportunity to evict me from my rent-controlled apartment and rummaged through my trash for the thrown out envelopes addressed to the WCA/NYC at my home. At the hearing with the Rent Control Bureau, he presented these torn envelopes as evidence. "She has

 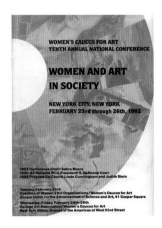 

28. Jacqueline Wray, *Views invitation* 29. Poster, *Women and Art in Society*, 1982 30. Sharon Gilbert, *Waste*

violated her lease by running an art organization out of her apartment." He was right about the art organization.

The NYC/WCA board had sent out a call for *Views by Women Artists* and held an open meeting right after Ora, Linda, and I returned from meeting with the National WCA president, De Renne Coerr, at the San Francisco conference. We got back a plethora of ideas, and selected twelve proposals from a mix of artists, critics, writers, and professional curators. Others kept coming in as people learned about the project, swelling the selection to sixteen exhibitions. We stopped at that number. This was an artists-organized event, so the rules reflected our sense of fairness. There was no submission fee, only an acceptance fee. Any woman could submit work to any of the sixteen shows, but she could only exhibit in one show. If her work were selected by more than one curator, the artist chose the show. An artist-curator could not exhibit her artwork in her own project.

Many of the shows organized by artists reflected their aesthetic commitments. Faith Ringgold proposed the open and unpredictable *Wild Art Show*. The realist painter Sylvia Sleigh curated a realist painting show. Sharon Gilbert organized an overtly political show, *The Future Is Ours*. I was ahead of myself with *Pieced Work*, focusing on artwork that employed my grandmothers' piecing techniques months before I chose to do this in my own work. The watercolorist Marion Lerner-Levine proposed a watercolor show; sculptor Marjorie Strider proposed a sculpture show. You get the idea. There were two group retrospectives; video artist Ann-Sargent Wooster selected a showing of historic videos and Eunice Golden, who painted erotic nudes, curated *Sexuality in Art*.

As the listings grew, people would call to fill in the gaps. Cora Cohen, briefly of the Feminism and Ecology issue collective, called. "I looked over the proposals. I should have known, in

31. Donna Henes, *Invitation, Wild Art Show, 1982* 32. Linda Cunningham, sculpture, *Like Time, Like Light...*

a women's show like this, that artists would be more interested in sewing than painting." "But *Pieced Work* is the only show with sewing," I countered. Cora wanted, "abstract art, with brush on canvas." "Well, send us a proposal." Emily Sorkin's *Abstract Substance and Meaning* was the result.

Curators and critics also organized shows. Lucy Lippard cocurated *Working Women/ Working Artists/Working Together* with sculptor Candace Hill-Montgomery at the Bread & Roses Gallery of Local 1199, my old clinic union. Candace was well known for the subtle symbolism in her installations; she once installed a full-sized yacht in a littered backyard lot in the South Bronx as a symbol of possibility. Ruth Ann Appelhof organized *Nature as Image & Metaphor*, the offspring of the women and nature show we had been discussing. She was deluged with entries and calls. "The number of calls made me feel how little attention women artists receive," she said. Her exhibit was the only show at a regular gallery, Greene Space, and the only venue where a painting was stolen, a large painting at that. We also accepted the proposals of Ellen Lubell, editor of *Womanart (Women Artists: Self-Images)*, independent curator Susan Sollins (*New Sculpture: Icon and Environment*), and writer Corrine Robins (*Sculptors Drawings*). In the catalogue introduction to *Views by Women Artists*, I wrote, "Art is supposed to be neutral to distinctions among its makers. We are uneasy about acknowledging differences in this country. . . . Vermeer's wife had eleven children."[2] I described the series of exhibits as "reality shows. They are one time/this time."

We had anticipated support from the National WCA. Starting in April, I wrote De Renne with a report about our organizing efforts, asking which parts of the conference her group would be organizing and what kind of financial support we could expect. After receiving no reply to three letters, I mailed the next via registered mail, as I would when I wrote to my pugnacious

33. Maureen Connor, *Count Orgaz Comes Again* 34. Lorna Simpson, *Untitled* 35. Eileen Spikol, *Shades of Venus*

landlord, and I also wrote to Ruth Weisberg in California. "De Renne seems to be in bad way," Ruth replied, "others report a total absence of activity and an alarming lack of funds." De Renne finally answered my letters in mid-July. We had figured out by then that we were on our own. She had photocopied my most recent letter and densely scribbled notes in the margins, highlighting a message in the upper corner with blue ink: "Let's always say 'Conference' (and not use the word 'convention'—it sounds so beer drinking)."

After we selected the sixteen shows, the curators and artists set to work purely on faith. We had no money and no exhibition spaces when we started out in the spring. Within ten months of continuous meetings, we had found all the spaces and raised thirty thousand dollars. Lawrence Alloway later told me that a museum would have taken two years to organize such a project with a paid staff. We had done it from our hearts in one exhausting year.

Sylvia Sleigh had been an organizer for *Women Choose Women*, the last big survey show over ten years earlier. She came to the first open call meeting and raised her hand to volunteer. The next day, she wrote me a two-page letter in red ink, summarizing her ideas for the shows. "I so much enjoyed the meeting, and found it most stimulating. The more I think about it, the better it seemed." She joined our Exhibition Committee. Lawrence was already in the early stages of the paralysis that took his life. It simplified things for Sylvia for us to meet in the parlor of her brownstone on West Twentieth Street. We formed a committee of seven women and met weekly. We would sit on the couch underneath *The Turkish Bath*, her remake of a painting by Ingres, with naked male art critics substituting for the sumptuous women in the older version. Lawrence was posed reclining nude next to John Perreault, Scott Burton, Carter Ratcliff, and her model Paul Rosano. We could count on one hand the male art critics favorable to women artists, and many were included in this painting. Sylvia's house, like the homes of most artists, was filled

36. NYC/WCA board, Sylvia Sleigh in *Views* T-shirt next to Linda Cunningham and Bibi Lenček 37. Sylvia Sleigh, *The Turkish Bath*

with her own artworks. This had not always been the case. Many of the artists in Lawrence's critical books and essays were modernists; he had coined the word "Pop Art." Sylvia's work was profoundly romantic and realistic. He had not wanted her to hang her paintings when they first settled in New York City. One evening, the famous abstract expressionist painter, Barnett Newman, was visiting. "Sylvia, you should hang your paintings in the living room! Maybe a dealer or critic would see them." She hung her paintings after those comments.

Sylvia asked to paint my portrait shortly after we met. I would learn the details of her life history as I sat for her in the months after finishing the work of our committee. She had painted a series of portraits of women's artists, but for some reason, she placed my portrait in a separate category and called it *My Ceres*. She called my spouse, Roger, the prince regent. While painting, she would cheerfully recount the harsh details of her childhood abandonment by her mother or describe her efforts to earn a living as dressmaker or various hurts and struggles—all without the slightest self-pity. I would listen and try to sit still.

We would make lists each week of all possible exhibition spaces—galleries, building lobbies, industrial spaces, and artist-run venues. Everyone would bring suggestions. Then, we would divide up the week's lists and try to obtain the spaces. When we succeeded, we would figure out the best show for an available space, checking off the sixteen shows one by one. *Pieced Work* ended up in the lobby of 26 Federal Plaza, site of *Tilted Arc*, the much-disputed sculpture by Richard Serra. True to its name, the sculpture was set diagonally across the entrance to the building; you had to walk around it at an odd angle to enter the lobby. After the fifth time circling this low steel wall while carrying artwork, I was ready with the office workers to remove the impediment.

38. Anne Pitrone (with Nancy Cheng), *The Revolutionary Scale: Masks for the Office*

At the last minute, Linda Cunningham found a space for Sollin's sculpture show in the beautiful old McGraw-Hill Building on Forty-Second Street, which was undergoing renovation, but she had to arrange to clean and paint the space. We also added an open artists' books show as a national exhibition, and placed it in the US Customs Building near the Brooklyn Bridge. You passed through an ornate doorway flanked by giant statues of mythical women and crossed a shiny marble floor to reach the glass cases where the books were displayed.

There were a few false starts. Parsons School of Design had agreed to schedule Sylvia's *Realist Painting* show, but at the last minute, decided to give their own faculty the exposure during the CAA conference. Sylvia wrote to the school that she was "shocked at your [the school's] disorderly handing of the application." Pace University had agreed to donate their gallery space, but this time, it was a *Views by Women Artists* curator who backed out. Corrine Robins decided the gallery was too small.

Once we had found all sixteen spaces, we had to figure out how to get the visitors to all the openings, which we had scheduled for two evenings during the WCA conference. The shows were all over the city: at Westbeth, the artists' housing near Greenwich Village, downtown near the bridges, on Wall Street, uptown on Forty-Second Street, and in SoHo. There were over 450 participating artists who would want to go see all the shows; we would need some kind of special transportation. Bibi Lenĉek was on our committee, submitting detailed descriptions of each exhibition space she negotiated. Her husband, Tak Inagaki, chartered small buses from Queens for his Japanese television company. I called him for a referral. He called back and offered to organize the buses. On the two opening nights, Japanese "bus girls" would come into the exhibits holding signs, "Bus Leaving." The gallery goers would board the bus and travel to the next venue.

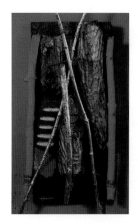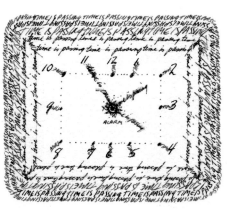

39. Nancy Azara, *Blue Ritual* 40. Mimi Smith, *Travel Clock* 41. Howardena Pindell, *India (Lakshmi)*

Another committee member was Jacqueline Wray, a painter and designer, who volunteered to design the catalogue—72 pages, 16 essays, and 140 photos all typeset and pasted up by hand. The New York State Council on the Arts (NYSCA), impressed by our "ambitious and well-organized" project, had funded our catalogue; its grant helped us gain legitimacy for more funding. I only learned later how angry Jackie had become from the pressure to finish the *Views by Women Artists* catalogue in time for the openings. She sent me a card: "And I am really clear that you know I will do my best to get the mechanicals to the printer as soon as possible—I am also clear that you're upset at the curators who have been being like they have been being, etc. . . . Sorry I don't have your good qualities of being positive about what volunteers will do when it comes to deadlines. You are a very special and unusual person." She also designed the two posters that announced the exhibits and listed over 120 additional support shows with women artists throughout the city. Jackie got all the work done in time; we had the catalogues available at the shows. We named every single artist, every curator, every volunteer, and every funding source—everyone. She designed the cover with the emblem of an eye; its iris contained fragments of the artworks from the shows. Months passed and we started speaking again.

Of course, the curators weren't paid. None of us were paid. We were women after all, and we expected a lot from each other. Faith Ringgold was in my *Pieced Work* show; I needed a photograph from her and other details about the artwork she was bringing. She needed information from me about her catalogue essay for *The Wild Art Show*. She wrote me in exasperation in early January, "I am just overwhelmed with the work I have to do. . . . I tried to reach you, but *you cannot be reached*, and I don't want to make it a habit of calling Roger. Even when I call your job, you do not reply. I know you are busy, but it is very frustrating to know that you cannot reach the person who has the answers you need. So I just figure things out for myself and hope that

42. Mierle Laderman Ukeles, *Walls of Stress/Bowls of Devotion...* 43. Elyse Taylor, *Ingrid* (*Pieced Work* show)

you will understand." The editors at Tree Communications were exasperated with me as well. I almost lost my job from the escalating phone calls at work as the February openings approached and an embarrassing stack of urgent messages mounted on the receptionist's desk for all to see. It took months to be offered a second project.

We had accepted Gylbert Coker's proposal for a sculpture show, called variously *Figure/ Personality* or *Sculpture: The Figure*. Her title appeared on all the early lists of exhibits, but in October, just before the prospectus was sent out to artists, she withdrew. "I have given serious thought to this business of not paying the curator for services rendered, and quite frankly, I cannot live with it. . . . Let it be clear that I would love to do my exhibition. The Lever House space is perfect for sculpture and the way I envision it, it would be sensational . . . , but I will not do it for free."

Organizing the support shows was an intense project itself. Volunteers sent letters to every commercial, alternative, or artists-run gallery listed in New York City gallery guides, asking each gallery to show artworks by women during the conference. The responses were predictably varied. The artists-run spaces easily arranged for a woman's show, but the more commercially established galleries often cited scheduling problems as an explanation for the dearth of women in their venues. The director of Pace Gallery wrote to complain that the Philadelphia/WCA had never returned a Lee Krasner drawing loaned for an exhibit at the Women's Building in 1976, deflecting attention from their inability to arrange a show. I wrote Judith Stein in Philadelphia, and she tracked down the drawing. It wasn't missing at all; Judith Brodsky was able to confirm its delivery to Krasner years earlier. Other dealers wanted to assure us that they showed women artists and sent listings for these shows, regardless of the date. The archivist for OK Harris Gallery sent the dates for the two women's shows scheduled in 1982, but added a postscript

44. Marina Gutierrez, *Mut with Stars* (detail) 45. Bibi Lenĉek, *TV Couple* 46. Nancy Spero, *exhibit card*

assuring us that "works by women can always be seen in the back gallery." Pam Adler Gallery sent a listing for a show by Charles Clough slated appropriately for February. I wrote back. "Is Charles Clough a woman artist? The name can be deceptive." Adler responded with a handwritten note. "Charles Clough is a man."

As January approached, De Renne reemerged, sending memorandums to all the chapter chairs with incomplete calendars for the events. Kathy Schapper was organizing a publications table and she wrote me. "Perhaps we should have a conference call with De Renne just to pacify her. It's so frustrating to see your excellent efforts sabotaged. . . . There are some very capable people on the various committees—it is a credit to the approach you have towards leadership." At the end of January, less than a month before the conference, De Renne sent two hefty *Conference Planning Workbooks* to Bea Kreloff and me to help us organize the events we had almost completed.

We printed five thousand catalogues. We had figured that 450 artists would each get ten, the artists' friends would buy one, the curators would want several, etc. After the shows, we organizers were left with boxes of catalogues stored in our kitchens, our closets, our lofts, and our studios. Gradually, people brought them to my place. When Annie Shaver-Crandell became the next president of the NYC/WCA, she drove over and deposited her entire set of boxes of the "wretched catalogues" in our loft. "I hope Roger can use them for insulation." At the time, I did not understand what this meant. When I was leaving New York to move to New Mexico in 1996, I still had over thirty boxes of *Views by Women Artists* stored above our darkroom. I was determined not to dump them on the street. I called the National WCA offices and offered to ship them for free. They declined. Then, I called the bookstore at the National Museum of Women in the Arts, and also received a "no." Finally, I wrote to Hacker Art Books with the same offer.

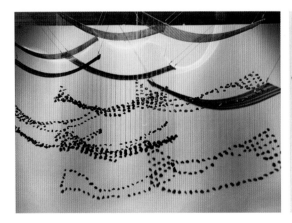  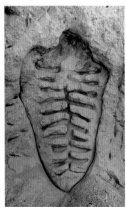

47. Pamela McCormick, *Suspended Stone* 48. Tania Kravath, *T-shirt* 49. Ana Mendieta, *Itiba Cahubaba*

Mr. Hacker called, delighted, and took the lot, which he has sold. *Views by Women Artists* is now reselling on the Internet for fifteen dollars a copy.

Tania Kravath designed a T-shirt emblazoned with the words, "Women Artists Take Over New York City." In our hearts, we did momentarily capture the New York City art world, though only we seemed to know about the coup. "Can 450 women artists, 51 percent of the world population and 50 percent of the New York art world (for the month of February [1982] only) be ignored?" I asked art critic John Perreault in a letter on March 6, trying to break the silence. The answered seemed to be "yes"; the daily press ignored the event. We failed to get any coverage in the art magazines. Lawrence wrote an essay for the *Village Voice* on March 30 with the headline, "Where Were You the Week of the 23rd?" analyzing the lack of coverage. Lawrence, a former editor for *Artforum*, had his own explanation: "The cachet for art critics is either the dealer system or radicalism—the women's art movement falls outside of those two categories."

The women's press came through under duress. Elsa Honig Fine had offered to print essays from all sixteen curators in an issue of the *Woman's Art Journal* (*WAJ*) featuring *Views by Women Artists*, but balked at publishing the essay by Candace Hill-Montgomery, accusing her of writing in "Black English." "I told her it did not conform to our style," she wrote in a letter to Lucy Lippard, adding, "I am quite familiar with Black English, having taught at Knoxville College, one of the oldest Black colleges in the South, for five years." She included a copy of her book, *The Afro-American Artist: A Search for Identity*. Candace accused Elsa of censorship; Lucy withdrew her essay in solidarity. We debated how to respond. In order to support Candace, we would all need to make the same protest, and no one would be published. I wrote Elsa. "I know you have certain 'rules' for language which you feel unable to bend, but I think these articles represent a sensitive issue of trust between white and black women that cannot be overlooked." We proposed the

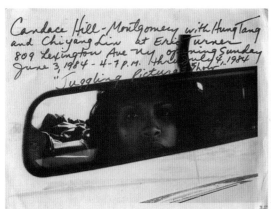  

50. Candace Hill-Montgomery, *Juggling Picture Show* 51. May Stevens, *Ordinary-Extraordinary* 52. *WAJ cover*

compromise of her issuing an editorial statement relinquishing responsibility for the content and style of our articles. We had a membership of five hundred; I added a warning. "The New York Advisory Board is meeting Wednesday night. If Candace's ideas are excluded in the *WAJ* as a part of *Views by Women Artists*, we will have to take some sort of public stance. I wanted you to know that we would do this." Lawrence told us later that Elsa had called him for advice after receiving my letter. He told her that she would have to "swallow it" and "print the lot." She published the essays without further editing, noting in her introduction that some essays, "for example, 'Introduction' and 'Working Women' do not conform to our usual style . . . and are printed here in the spirit of inclusion and diversity."[3]

We celebrated the birth of two babies after working on *Views by Women Artists*, Bibi's boy, Nikko, and Sharon's girl, Elena, born the same year, and one litter of tortoiseshell kittens, born to my red cat Saskia and sired by a cat belonging to a friend of Bibi. And there was one death. Linda Cunningham had invited May Stevens to moderate "The First Ten Years: Mapping," the opening panel at the WCA conference. I was a panelist. Her son had committed suicide a few weeks earlier by jumping from the George Washington Bridge, but May kept her word and spoke at the conference.

I got to know May better while preparing for her panel. Despite her recent tragedy, we mostly talked about politics and art. "Some people would say that if you're concerned about reaching people, you should make art as simple as possible." I responded, "I feel, let a thousand flowers bloom. Everyone cannot like you. I want to say what I have to say." May agreed. "I feel very much as you do."

I was permanently inoculated by my experience with *Views by Women Artists* from ever pressuring curators or dealers to show my artwork. We organizers were on the receiving end of

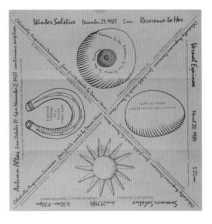

53. Flier, *A to Z, An Intensive Workshop*, Jeri Allyn, May Stevens, Holly Zox 54. Donna Henes, *Reverence to Her* performance flier

so much intensity and need. It was a bit like the Christmas lights on the small house trailers here in New Mexico—with an inverse relationship between the size of the house and the number of lights and decorations. Some artists thought we had power, but we only had the power of our collective work and will.

I dream that I am standing in Texas, in the full, sweet sun, just me, warmed in the clear daylight, standing alone.

I stopped acting as NYC/WCA president the summer after *Views by Women Artists.* I wrote a note to the board after our meeting in May:

> In the beginning, when I agreed to do this (President), I felt like it would be a way to talk with other artists and writers about our common situation. . . . I approached these two years from my perspective as an artist, with the problems that bother me—namely, what is the work *for*, who sees it. . . . I also felt (feel) the Caucus is too white, too middle class, and we made a tiny inroad into that. . . . I think we've enjoyed each other. I'm always touched, when I've had a meeting at my place, to discover that the dishes have been placed in the sink.

We had a panel on "Women & Art in the Forties" for the last meeting I chaired, listening to the stories of women painters and muralists from a period of activism and inclusion for women artists. Helen Phillips, Dorothy Dehner, and Frances Avery were among the speakers—most were married to male artists whose names are still familiar. Ora presented me with a potted prickly euphorbia at the end of the evening that grew to over seven feet before I moved from New York City. I welcomed Annie Shaver-Crandell as the new president; then, I took a break from the

55. NYC/WCA board, Bibi Lenĉek is holding Baby Nikko next to Joan Watts. 56. May Stevens, *Soho Women Artists*

WCA, not imagining how easily friends can become enemies. But I had discovered that I liked organizing shows. They were tangible—like our artworks, like a magazine.

The WCA had money left over, and Annie used some of those funds to duplicate the installation slides from the sixteen shows. She brought me a huge batch of duplicates to keep, all unlabeled. Annie was an art historian, and she started giving lectures on *Views by Women Artists*. I kept overhearing comments urging "old leaders" to "retire" and to not "hang out on the board." The National WCA invited me to become a vice president, but I wasn't interested in that sort of structure divorced from creative work. I was still a member of the local board, like Ora, and we continued to help organize panels. Later, Christine Havice wrote a history of the WCA and completely omitted our activism, crediting the events of the 1982 conference to National WCA President De Renne Coerr.

Roger and I were working on companion shows for Atlantic Gallery scheduled for the winter following *Views by Women Artists*. He was painting two wall-sized canvases with political allusions. One was filled with beautifully rendered sharks that wouldn't be able to coexist together in their natural ocean environment. The other included multiple figures of Roger, all wielding big sticks like a tribe of cave men quadruplets. It was called *Grunk*; he titled the shark painting *Oh Grandma...* in reference to Little Red Riding Hood and her grandmother's big teeth. I finally felt able to make a show about the painful events relating to Grandmother and my aunt Opal and was accumulating the materials I needed. Curating *Pieced Work* had strengthened me. My strategy was to color Xerox many personally resonant items and compose large-scale photocopier "quilts" and paintings. I already had letters from Caroline and Opal, Grandmother's sunbonnets, a church fan, aprons, and her doorstop doll, but I needed some photos that my cousin had inherited when Opal died. I typed my cousin a letter, requesting copies of four photos. Weeks

57. Roger Mignon, *Oh Grandma...* 58. Sabra Moore, *Caroline's Songbook (My Version)*, color Xerox cover

passed with no response, and I decided to try a different tactic. I purchased a card illustrated with a songbird and sent a handwritten note. She mailed a box filled with old photos to my sister in Texas. Nancy mailed it to me. Mother and Nancy had looked through the photos, all unfamiliar ones—including Caroline as a young woman, many photos showing her second husband Chester Bryant who was murdered in 1910, and other snapshots and tintypes. The four pictures I had requested were not included, but I was still delighted with this trove. "Why would you want these pictures?" Mother asked. "We never knew her at that age." "But I am interested in my grand-mother as a young woman." "Chester Bryant is not a relative of ours. He doesn't have anything to do with our family."

There was a big anti-nuclear protest in June, and many artists were making puppets and banners. Roger got oversized photostats made at the advertising agency where he worked. I mounted the giant cutout figure of the multiarmed goddess Shiva on Styrofoam and strung various implements of peace and war along ropes emanating from her arms—fish, arm, leaf, bread, and paint brushes on one side; bombs and explosions on the other. We marched under the slogan "Dis-Arm the War Makers/Arm for Life." We were walking up to the demonstration, and I was carrying the multiarmed goddess cutout and all her implements tightly wrapped as a package when we were stopped by reporters from WNET who were impatient for us to untwine. I felt grumpy to be asked, but Roger and one of the newsmen took both ends of the ropes and unspooled the goddess and danced while I talked. Then, we proceeded to join the eighty thousand others and paraded alongside the many heartfelt slogans. We walked with a group of women from the WCA. Bread and Puppet Theater was there in force with puppets of the River and Woods; Roger had often helped make giant puppets with them at their home base in Vermont and Maine.

59. *Dangerous Works* flier 60. Sylvia Sleigh, *My Ceres (Sabra Moore)* 61. Gladys Parks, *String quilt*

I was still going over to Sylvia's to pose for my portrait. After painting, we would visit with Lawrence, who was now homebound in his wheelchair. We started talking about the concept of the artist-as-genius—the artist as an expert who made objects that others couldn't make. Lawrence insisted that this was a post-World War II phenomenon, arising out of the advent of mass production as the dominant ethos. "But not in the rural South. My grandmother still quilts." "But yours is a minority experience." Lawrence felt people could now express eccentricity by the products they chose to buy. "But that is a passive choice; it's not the same as providing for yourself by making things," I countered. "The craft tradition is in the past. Mass production has given us the life we have grown to expect."

Tree Communications hired me for another photo editing project, finally deciding to overlook my many distractions at work while organizing *Views by Women Artists*. I started researching materials for a book on the Fertile Crescent and, for the first time, I had a signed contract. I had been hesitant about researching art from the regional heart of the patriarchy, but I quickly found tantalizing evidence of a matriarchal core. "We find the word 'freedom' used for the first time in man's recorded history; the word is *amaryi*, which . . . means literally, 'return to the mother.' However, we still do not know why this figure of speech came to be used for 'freedom.'"[4] I finished a month's work developing an outline. Then, we traveled to New Mexico and went again to archaeological sites and a ceremonial dance at Isleta Pueblo. I had a light heart because of my book contract. Kate Correa was taking care of my cats on Warren Street. One day, she saw a cascade of white flakes flying past the back windows. My landlord Bob Marcheski was throwing rock salt onto the zucchinis in my garden, one of many attempts to drive me out of my rent-controlled apartment by attacking the plants I nurtured. I had been there during the first attack. I was working in my studio when I heard sounds of demolition outside my kitchen. Two men were

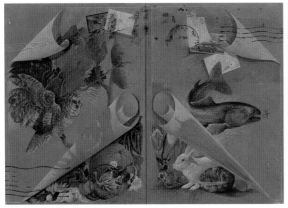  

62. Ellen Lanyon, *Chromes: II Autumn, III Spring* (detail) 63. *Heresies* flier. 64. Cecilia Vicuña, *Con cón, Chile*

tearing down my neighbor Jackie's potting shed and throwing the broken bits of wood and glass directly onto my growing vegetables. I threw open the window and started climbing down the ladder to the garden. Shamed, the workmen helped me remove the debris. When we came back, things had changed with Tree Communications as well. My book project had been unexpectedly cancelled.

I was now meeting regularly with *Heresies* Mother Collective and had started working with the editorial collective for the eighteenth issue, Mothers, Mags & Movie Stars, our meditation on class. The *Heresies's* office had moved from Spring Street to the Cable Building on Broadway. We had four staff members. Three were on the main collective—Sue Heinemann, who ably managed the production, and the artists, Sandra de Sando and Kay Kenny. The office manager and poet, Patricia Spears Jones, opted to simply work on staff and not join the collective, but she was an editor on Mothers, Mags & Movie Stars. Cecilia Vicuña, a Chilean poet and artist, was also working on that issue collective and on the Mother Collective. She had joined after working on Racism Is the Issue. New members would be invited after each issue, so our membership and concerns were always in flux. Cecilia had a wonderful presence as a reader. I remember hearing her quietly recite a poem in Spanish based on the archaic pottery of Chile. The translator who followed in English stumbled in unintended embarrassment over the erotic imagery. Cecilia made delicate sculptures out of sticks, feathers, bones, and string that she called *arte precario*. In an exhibit at Exit Art, many of these sculptures were strewn across a wide bed of sand with no traces of their placement—as if Cecilia had hovered in the air during their installation. But my favorites from that show were small shrines next to street water hydrants, paying homage to a life source that most of us took for granted.

65. Sue Heinemann, *Keep Out*. 66. Carr, Champagne, and Jones, *Women in Research* 67. Emma Amos, *Diagonal Diver*

A lot of women who worked on Mothers, Mags & Movie Stars, or on the companion is-sue, Satire, stayed with the main collective for many years—painter and professor Emma Amos; Brazilian printmaker Josely Carvalho; Lenora Champagne, a performance artist originally from New Orleans; and Holly Zox, an intense young artist from Ohio with closely cropped hair who was proud of her lesbian identity. One of Holly's small sculptures, purchased at a *Heresies* benefit, is hanging in my studio—a wooden cutout of a crouching wolf with a silver chain around its neck and the text, "Catch Me If You Can."

A few of us were Southerners. Patricia Jones came from Arkansas and designed a page on mammies for the Mothers, Mags & Movie Stars issue, one of many black artists who have made artworks about that ambivalent figure. She collaborated on a theater performance entitled *Women in Research* with two other Southern refugees, Lenora Champagne and Cindy Carr. The performance is about three women who move from their hometowns to Manhattan. Cindy later wrote the acclaimed book, *Our Town: A Heartland Lynching, A Haunted Town and the Hidden History of Race in America.*

Our production facilities improved during Mothers, Mags & Movie Stars; Su Friedrich and Cindy Carr had pasted up many of the early issues of *Heresies*, working patiently with X-Acto knives and rubber cement as others met and talked in our crowded office. The situation changed after the artist Kathie Browne joined our editorial collective. Kathie owned a typography business on Fourteenth Street and Broadway with hot wax machines, glass table tops for laying out the pages, Xerox machines, and the luxury of instant type corrections. We all moved over to her shop to work on weekends and evenings when it was time to paste up and design this issue.

Heresies was having a benefit exhibit at Frank Marino Gallery, and Sue Heinemann and I were designated to hang the show. We would hang one room and then Frank would come around

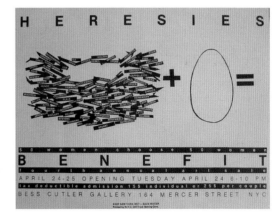

68. *Heresies* Benefit, Frank Marino Gallery with K. Webster, Carr, and Jones. 69. *Heresies* Benefit poster, Bess Cutler Gallery

and rearrange the works. That evening, I had to crawl out of the bathtub, unable to stand upright with my sore back. I noted how Frank noticed which works attracted commercial attention. He would ask me how he could contact those artists.

Most of our shows at *Heresies* were benefits with varying degrees of financial success. One year, Louise Bourgeois contributed a small white marble sculpture of a house that was so smooth we all longed to touch it. Michelle Stuart bought it. Any of us would have also enjoyed owning one of Michelle's fine artist's books thick with scrubbed earth. We were each other's best art patrons—trading works, arranging to pay on time, or buying outright if the price was reachable. One year, we decided to have a second board of women with wealth or influence who might help us raise money. We gave the potential board members a wonderful dinner with food we had each prepared. But we could never figure out how to get these women to take the next step and support the magazine.

The performance artist Vanalyne Green had just moved to New York City from California. I invited Patricia and Vanalyne over for supper. "Your house is really Southern," Patricia said. "It's like my aunt's place." We started telling stories about growing up in Southern evangelical churches and getting saved. "I was around twelve, sitting on the mourners' bench. All the kids were getting saved. I was waiting for a sign from God. It didn't come." So, Patricia had left and became an Episcopalian. I added my story. I was thirteen at church camp. Everyone was jumping up, getting saved, witnessing for Christ. I went outside and prayed for a sign. It didn't come. I ran off crying, convinced that God wasn't there. Vanalyne's story also involved a sign. Her parents were alcoholics and she had become friendly with a Christian couple. She had placed her hand on a white Bible. "When I lift my hand, the handprint will be gold," she had told herself. It wasn't, but she decided to get saved anyway. "It worked for two years."

70. Linda Peer, *I Make Myself* 71. *Protective Devices* poster 72. Vanalyne Green, *Trick or Drink* (still photo)

Sylvia and I went to an opening for her neighbor, Louise Bourgeois, enjoying her witty woman/house combination prints and her sculptures sprouting with unruly penis forms. Sylvia told me about an old conflict between Lawrence and Louise's husband, Robert Goldwater, both art critics. Lawrence liked the paintings of Barnet Newman and Robert liked the works of Rothko. The two men had a running argument about whose art ideas had come first. Once, Sylvia gave a dinner party at their brownstone. "One group was on one floor and the other on another." Eventually, the two men stopped speaking over this impasse. I stopped to visit with Lawrence after the opening, telling him how much I liked eccentricity in art. "How long have you felt this?" "For a long time." "Before or after you read Lucy Lippard's 'Eccentric Abstraction'?" But I hadn't read that essay.

I had gone to see Thalia Doukas in the spring and arranged for a group show at the window installation venue, Windows on White, called *Protective Devices*. It was scheduled to open near Christmas, a couple of months before my show at Atlantic Gallery, and I set about contacting artists whose work I admired. I had a rubber stamp made with the title and designed a flier with a photocopier image of an ornate woolen glove. Each artist would create a small artwork suitable for window display and page art for a photocopier artists' book catalogue. Sylvia was participating with a drawing of a breastplate. Many artists made works with masks or clothes worn like armor. But some used only their bodies. Linda Peer made a small artist's book about transforming her body through bodybuilding, handwriting the title, *I make myself!*. I envisioned the protection of home and made a color Xerox book of my vanished childhood house in Commerce; different views of that beloved abode floated out from the book's spine like wings. Thalia sent me a note. "*Protection* can be supplied by large pieces of furniture. Even the heaviest of these types

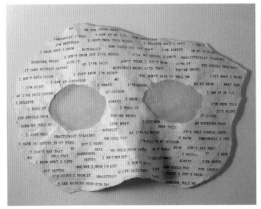  

73. Sharon Gilbert, *Mask of Opinion* 74. Hannah Wilke, *And I Played/& I stayed 'Til Heaven* 75. Sylvia Sleigh, *Lorica for Athena*

of objects can be made to glide or roll across most floors. In calmer situations, the application of a sofa, futon, piano, etc. can disarm, clearing the air for possible dialogue."

Hannah Wilke came to visit me and delivered her piece for the show. "You gave us a good assignment!" She stood in my studio complaining bitterly about her lack of proper acknowledgement from art critics, *Heresies*, the women's movement, Art Workers' Coalition, and others. I kept trying to change the subject and show her my work. But her piece was wonderful—a photograph of herself hugging her mother in the kitchen, with the words . . .*And I Played/And I Stayed/Till Heaven*. She told me about a bird flying into her loft shortly after her mother had died of cancer, which comforted her by its unexpected appearance. Hannah was well known for her vulva-shaped sculptures formed out of chewing gum or clay that she arranged into patterns and for her theatrical nude self-portraits. She had a quality of childish play in her work that contrasted with her stunning figure. In the *Views by Women Artists* catalogue, Hannah is pictured seated nude on the floor with her legs splayed and an odd assortment of penis-shaped objects and guns strewn about the room. Only women with shapely bodies seemed to make this sort of performance/photography.

Since a window show is always open, we celebrated the first day of the exhibit outside on the street followed by food in a little café nearby. Chris Costan told me, "I have complete confidence in you now. The first time could have simply been luck. You have very good ideas."

I was still working feverishly to finish the pieces for the Atlantic Gallery exhibit. All the works were related and told in fragments the conflicted story of Caroline and her daughter, Opal. I printed many color Xeroxes from Grandmother's clothing and Opal's letters and kept cutting, rearranging, and joining the pieces or heat-transferring fragments onto painted paper with an electric iron. I often keep my journal open as I work. One night, I noted that the emerging works felt like

76. Sabra Moore (both), *Caroline Had a Beautiful Garden/Swept Dirt/She Planted...* 77. *House Book*

"a whole thing, with all the ambiguities of a being separate from me." I kept altering the forms, eliminating rectangles, and working with fragile materials by choice to explore this painful episode. Sylvia understood my methods of construction. "They're not painted; they're composed." The key kimono-shaped painting was based on the dream I had had after failing to rescue Grandmother and move her back into her house. "Remember your garden," I had said as she died in my dream. I remembered her garden for her by combining images of her and Opal with photos and drawings from Africa, printing the same text I had used on the pink painting made shortly after her death. *Caroline had a beautiful garden/swept dirt/she planted flowers in circles/like they do in Africa.* I translated the elements of quilt making into these new works—repeated patterns, sewing, using resonant materials, and printing out words that only intimates would know.

On the evening of the opening, I felt alone and exposed even though Roger's companion show was also opening and the gallery was crammed with our friends. I had written a statement that alluded to the conflicts between my aunt and grandmother, ending in their deaths two weeks apart. Linda Peer said, "I think this show is a tremendous step into artistic maturity." Despite the encouraging comments, I had an intense letdown of energy afterwards.

At the last minute, I decided to go for a day to the WCA conference in Philadelphia, taking the train. Our Atlantic Gallery shows were still up. I brought copies of the *Protective Devices* photocopier catalogue, which had ended a few weeks earlier. I went around to shows and events that afternoon with Vivian Browne, keeping my tender feelings at bay under a cloud of jokes and laughter. "I can't take you anywhere!" Vivian teased. We ran into Suzanne Lacy, and I gave her a *Protective Devices* catalogue. "I almost sent work to that show." We saw Faith Ringgold, fresh from a panel on women and power. "Well, you're powerful too." But I felt the opposite. Then, joined by Nancy Azara and Catherine Allen, we all went to the banquet. Wilhelmina Cole Holladay

78. Sabra Moore (all), *Pieced for Opal* 79. *Caroline's Songbook (My Version)* 80. *Pieced for Caroline*

was giving a talk about her collection of women's art and her plans for a new women's museum in Washington, DC. She explained how "God inspires man to make art" to the suppressed laughter of a roomful of women artists. Someone stood up and asked if the proposed museum would make a commitment to show feminist and contemporary women's art, not simply her collection of historic paintings by women. That would be the prerogative of a future nameless curator, she asserted. Later, I saw the art historian Ann Sutherland Harris. Ann had seen my show at Atlantic Gallery and added my name to her mental list of artists for an exhibition idea called "Mourning Works." She wanted to buy a painting, but couldn't let her husband know. "He wants to buy art for investment only."

Shortly after returning home, I learned that my neighbor, Jackie, had agreed to be bought out from her rent-controlled apartment and that I would lose access to my fine vegetable garden.

I decided to leave Atlantic Gallery; Roger was staying. My abrupt departure spawned reactions. One of our last house painting clients when Georgia and I were still working together was a self-taught artist named Calvin Towle, who lived near my Warren Street apartment. Calvin admired the painter Vincent Van Gogh and wanted Georgia and me to recreate Van Gogh's bright yellow and brown color scheme in painting his tiny bedroom and hall. We became friendly. Calvin told stories from his mixed-blood Mohawk uncle. When he had farmed with horses or mules, he said, the uncle stopped work at sundown so the animals could rest. But when farming became mechanized, he never got to stop before midnight. Calvin would visit the Atlantic Gallery exhibits. When he learned that I had left the gallery, he called me. Would I give him my paintbrushes, he asked, assuming that quitting that co-op gallery meant giving up on making art.

Sandy de Sando and Kay Kenny had arranged with curator Marcia Tucker for the *Heresies* collective to have a show at the New Museum, paired with a photography exhibition by

81. Installation, *Classified: Big Pages from the Heresies Collective*, The New Museum

En Foco. It was the last show at the New School venue before the museum moved to Broadway. We were divided, as usual, about how to approach this show, but decided on making a series of twelve oversized wall pages, 8´ x 10´ each, based on the ideas we were exploring for our issue on class. We called the show *Classified: Big Pages from the Heresies Collective*. Somehow, our title never got into the catalogue. Some women had wanted to have a group show of their individual works at the museum rather than create an exhibit collaboratively in a manner reminiscent of our magazine. I suspect the later splits in our collective stem in part from this exhibit.

I dream that I am in Lucy's loft. I go and sit in the street window with my legs dangling outside. I ask Sandy de Sando to pull back on my arms to keep me from falling, but instead she starts to push me out the window, saying, "I can't help myself."

We started brainstorming about ideas for *Classified*—the arrangement of rooms in our childhood homes, how people dress, class mobility, Cinderella, movie stars, paper dolls, media images, our mothers, and Mother Mary. We also planned a series of performances during the exhibit, and divided into small collaborative groups to work on specific pages. Sue, Holly, Nicky Lindeman, and I decided to collaborate on a double page for *Dream "Kitschen"*. I remembered how Mother would cut out cloth fruits and iron them on with starch for the summer kitchen curtains. I found an actual window, printed text on the glass, and added a small curtain to make it reminiscent of the window over Mother Gladys' sink. Lenora used that window in her performance, projecting slides onto its glass while wearing a pig mask and waiting for toast to rise up out of the toaster like a holy sign. Holly and Nicky arranged shelves and tables with resonant objects and collaged magazine photos onto the wall. Sue had saved the X-ray from a recent medical test, and placed this X-ray of her spine over an ironing board and lit it from below, creating a starry dot pattern glittering through her backbones. During one of our many critiques, Patricia said that

82. Heinemann, Lindeman, Moore, and Zox, *Dream Kitschen* 83. Lenora Champagne performance with window

"the *Kitschen* is the center; it pulls people in. I don't know why it's so strong—maybe because of its messiness—not the messiness associated with male violence." Lenora felt like the *Kitschen* had an "unfinished quality connected to life as it goes on."

Lucy described the process of developing the show in a catalogue statement: "The show is a visual version of our upcoming issue, *Mothers, Mags & Movie Stars*. . . . Our meetings took on the double aspect of sewing circle and study group. Most of our anecdotes centered on images, clothes, objects, spaces."[5] A few women made individual works. Lyn Hughes made an elaborate game board about social mobility while Kay Kenny made a piece about Cinderella. Sandy made a life-sized mannequin of Mary with Mother Anne. Two groups worked with ideas about our mothers. Vanalyne, Patricia, and Holly made a gridded page with media images of famous women or stars alternating with written texts. I made a double-page hybrid collaboration called *A Roomful of Mothers* in which members of the collective gave me photos of their mothers to use. I collaged silhouetted photos of our mothers into a folded-out room plan. It was a challenge to see if our mothers could fit together in this simulated space as we daughters managed to sit together each week. Vanalyne, who had made performance art about her difficult relationship with an alcoholic parent, said, "It's interesting to see my mother depicted in a way different from how I would handle it." We had handwritten our class stories, which I color-Xeroxed, layered with ghostly fabrics, and then pieced into a quilt format. I worked up to the last minute on these ten-foot pages, rushing into the museum an hour before the opening. Nicky had left a message on my answering machine, "Your ass is grass." But Nicky, Holly, and Lucy were there when I bolted in, nervously sweeping near the empty space where we quickly hung my works. "They're different from everything else in the room. The show needed this," someone said. "They're homey," I said. Certainly, they filled up the big blank space on the wall.

84. Sabra Moore (all), *A Roomful of Mothers* 85. *Gladys Apron #5* 86. *A Roomful of Mothers* (detail)

Lenora Champagne, Vanalyne Green, Jessica Hagedorn, and Laurie Carlos gave performances in front of the assembled pages. Vanalyne's piece had nudity, and the male museum guards would alert each other and rush in to gawk during the salient moments.

Vanalyne urged us to have a critique of the show. She felt that the differences between the artworks reflected our various responses to the collective process. "Some people can't work collectively," Sue observed. "Then how come they're in the collective?" Lucy asked. Patricia, who had always kept a distance from the group, told us we had pushed her into "feeling part." "Many people find the works incomplete and hard to understand," Kay and Sandy insisted. Patricia countered, "I have heard the opposite; that the show is rich and complex. It's like throwing back to the culture the images that have been given to us."

Lucy had invited me to participate in a show she was curating at Ohio State University, *All's Fair: Love & War in New Feminist Art*. She had decided to include only artists who had never been in one of her many feminist exhibitions. Art movers came by to pick up my work; it was a wonderful contrast to my usual packing and hauling experiences. She had selected *Caroline Had a Beautiful Garden. . .* from the Atlantic Gallery show and my photocopier artist's book *Caroline's Songbook—My Version*. The show opened at the same time that we were finishing our wall pages for *Classified*. My old college roommate, Helena Schlamm, was living in Columbus and got to see the show. "I was so glad your work was about an actual person," she wrote. Lucy explained her concept for the show: "The range of style and content should make clear, yet again, that feminist art is not a monolith, nor a temporary 'movement,' to be swept away when its market potential is exhausted, but a way of life, a state of mind, a political commitment to other women."[6]

I went "raffle-boarding" with other collective members during the *Classified* show dressed appropriately in a handmade double-cardboard sandwich board and standing on the street corner

 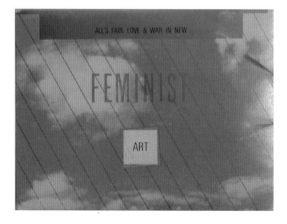 

87. Sabra with Heresies raffle board 88. *All's Fair: Love & War in New Feminist Art* 89. Marina Gutierrez, book page, *Race*

trying to raise money for *Heresies* by selling raffle tickets. A big show of the paintings of Frida Kahlo paired with photographs by Tina Modotti opened downtown, and many of us women artists went to see it—our first real introduction to this iconic artist. "Why can't art be as personal and specific as a novel by Alice Walker?" I wrote in my journal.

I dream that I am riding an escalator, carrying brushes and three colors of paints, with a copy of The Artist's Handbook *tucked under my arm. Sue Heinemann passes me riding in the opposite direction and I holler over to her, "I paint whenever I can."*

Another group was organizing a huge show at the Terminal, a defunct industrial building with interior courtyards and intricate spaces located in a warehouse district of Brooklyn. *Heresies* was invited to move *Classified* there, but the collective couldn't agree, so the show wasn't hung. I went to the opening. Artists had filled every available corner of that cavernous place with a variety of shows, but what I remember is Marina Gutierrez's sculpture of paper clothes hanging quietly on a line. When I called later to invite Marina into one of my shows, she said, "Do I know you?" and I explained seeing this piece in Brooklyn.

I participated in *Artists' Library*, one of the exhibits at Terminal, by making *House Book*, another exploration of my childhood house. Each page revealed a changing sequence of multiple pages visible through cutouts where the house had been. I brought this book to show Lawrence and Sylvia when I posed again for my portrait. "It's one of the best examples of nonlinear progression that I have seen," he said. Lawrence had often mentioned the idea of editing an art magazine with me; he liked the diaristic style of my press releases. "We should meet about it—seriously; I'd rather work with you than Donald Kuspit." Kathy Schnapper was visiting Sylvia, and we all started talking about *Overlay*, Lucy's new book about artists' responses to archaic cultures. Only he and I had gotten around to reading her book. Lawrence had written a book on land

90. Mother Gladys in bed 91. Sabra Moore, *Gladys Place (laser transfer curtain lifts to her clothesline)*

art—he considered it the same subject. I liked Lucy's book and said so. "Maybe we shouldn't do a magazine together," Lawrence responded.

I traveled again to Texas, bringing slides from the exhibit at Atlantic Gallery to show Mother and Nancy, risking their outrage about my exposure of family conflicts. Nancy said, "I still haven't dealt with my feelings about Grandmother." We talked about Caroline. "Some of Daddy's people in the hills of Oklahoma had enough Indian blood to get government money," Mother said. "Isn't Mother Gladys also part Indian?" "Yes, Papa's mother, Grandma Greer, was Indian. We're a little of everything." I brought the unfinished rag rug that Mother Gladys had shown me how to make. When Mother and I went down to the country to visit my grandparents, she kept rummaging through drawers, pulling out scraps of cloth to send back with me.

The year of 1983 ended with an erotic spirit. A group of women were organizing *Carnival Knowledge*, a show on sexuality, at the alternative art and performance space, Franklin Furnace, the brainchild of performance artist Martha Wilson. The Furnace hosted all kinds of events in its long narrow building on Franklin Street around the corner from Printed Matter, Inc. and the Feminist Art Institute. You entered it like a shotgun house and worked your way through a maze of bookcases and exhibition rooms. Martha's crowded, glassed-in office always reminded me of the dispatcher's room for the railroad, a hub where workers got their assignments for the next train. Martha often performed in the guise of her persona, Nancy Reagan, her gleaming red hair and voluptuous figure a tantalizing alter ego for the anorexic First Lady, giving everyone a sense of zany political possibility.

Mercifully, I only participated in *Carnival Knowledge* with artwork. One of the *Carnival* organizers was Anne Pitrone, who also published articles in *Heresies*. She was a writer and artist whose unsparing descriptions of working class life bordered on being transgressive. The poster

92. Sisters of Survival, *Shovel Defense* 93. *Carnival Knowledge* (both) flier 94. *Working Woman's Wheel of Misfortune*

for the exhibit included a photo of the organizers posing topless with pornographic film stars. Who said feminists lacked a sense of humor? One day, years later, Anne called me for advice about artist deductions on her taxes. I used to run into her at various events, but I hadn't seen her in a long time. I couldn't really help her with advice either since Anne had disappeared into a much higher tax bracket. Her day job as a toy designer had mushroomed into a lucrative career and pushed her outside of our artists' circle.

I had been having dreams about Daddy and about men breaking into my rooms. I was after all, losing my garden to a harassing landlord. Often in these dreams, it seemed that Daddy hadn't actually died, but had been living a separate life somewhere else during those nineteen years since his car wreck. One of the artworks I made for *Carnival Knowledge* was about my father's little black gun, which he had kept in the bedroom dresser drawer. I called it *Daddy's Gun*. My parents didn't seem to realize that I would play with this gun and handle the beautiful silver and copper bullets, and then carefully replace them in the drawer. I made a replacement gun out of wrapped cloth and gesso and placed it in a small wooden box, and then made a little sewn gessoed book the same size as the box-drawer with paintings of the gun and the pithy story of my modest childhood transgression.

95. Sabra Moore, end page, *Making* 96. Sabra Moore (both), *Daddy's Gun* (box) 97. *Daddy's Gun* (book)

5

It's 1984

There was a vacant lot under the Manhattan Bridge flanked by the stone buttresses of the bridge. Across the street from this lot, Roger lived in a red brick building shaped at an angle to accommodate the bridge. I would walk to his loft under the shadow of this vast structure with the cars and trains rumbling above me. The cobblestones made an uneven surface for my feet. I never wanted to linger en route to the door, walking quickly past another fenced lot to enter the building. Visitors often rang his bell without letting their finger off the button until he had thrown the key down to them or hurried to reach the door. He was on the sixth floor. It took time. This neighborhood now has an acronym, Dumbo (Down Under Manhattan Bridge Overpass). An aura of fashion and danger has made it a popular address, but in 1984, Pearl Street was simply that, an industrial place that the factories had vacated, a street where artists managed to live.

Roger was one of the first artists to move into the Pearl Street building, which he did shortly after his graduation from Pratt Institute. The sixth floor had been a knitting mill, and two

1. Roger Mignon, *Roger and Sabra under the Manhattan Bridge in Dumbo* 2. *5 & Dime Artists' Holiday Store*

artist-couples divided the space and renovated it to create two rough living areas after vacuuming up vast amounts of needles and lint. Those relationships spiraled apart and new people moved into the building, but Roger remained. I moved there the year after my landlord sold the Warren Street building.

People used to comment on our telephone message: "What is that noise? It sounds like an ocean." The wash of traffic over the Manhattan Bridge was an ocean of industrial sound. Once when I was sitting on the couch during a rainstorm, a ball of lightning came into the room and shimmered for an electric moment, then exited.

The lot across the street kept changing. There was a metal shed just beyond the shadows of the bridge formerly used as a storage building by the bridge workers and later as a shelter for a homeless couple who would come and go pushing a bulging shopping cart. Then, the city tore down the shed. The lot would fill, then empty, then refill with trash. For a brief period, filmmakers found the site. No one seemed to realize that our building was occupied. It was fully occupied by artists except for Paul Watson, the Jamaican die cutter who fabricated machines from steel on the fifth floor a few feet below our loft. We woke one night to the sound of machine gun fire, a prop for filming, but my sleepy brain refused to believe that the actors were simply playing at violence. Another afternoon, elegantly dressed models set up a table amidst the trash and were photographed enjoying their dinner. A rock star was filmed flanked by muscle men with drums strapped to their backs. They crouched before her as she pounded these human drums—the stone arches framing a staged brutality. And once, there was a fair with miniature Irish ponies.

One day, we ran into a neighbor, Scott Miller, loading his car with artwork. "Come see the *Times Square Show!*" he announced. This exhibition was in a derelict building on Forty-Second

3. *Artists Call, events* 4. Roger Mignon, *Doorway* 5. *Todas Las Americas*, poetry 6. *Nicaraguan Painters*

Street that had been taken over temporarily by artists. Art had blossomed as a form of collective speech, and many groups were organizing idea-oriented shows in unusual locations or as serial exhibits in multiple places similar to *Views by Women Artists*.

It was 1984 in more ways than one. The Sandinista Revolution had triumphed in Nicaragua in 1979, but the Reagan administration was trying to undermine the new government by covertly funding their enemies, the Contras. In Guatemala, the Mayas were being massacred with American military aid. Many artists and activists had been going to Nicaragua or El Salvador to show solidarity with the revolution there, often traveling with the support group, Ventana. Central American poetry, images, and history kept intruding into our consciousness. Even in the Earthkeeping/Earthshaking: Feminism and Ecology issue, *Heresies* published an interview by Margaret Randall with Daisy Zamora, the vice minister of culture under the Sandinistas, who described her life as a guerrilla fighter and poet—an interview that was ecological only in that Zamora had been fighting outdoors.[1] Of course, in Managua, there had been an earthquake. [2] Now, the public was finally beginning to acknowledge what our government was doing. A broad coalition of artists and intellectuals were organizing *Artists Call Against U.S. Intervention in Central America* (*Artists Call*), a national series of shows, actions, and performances in response to these events. Many of the artist-organizers had been involved in Art Workers' Coalition and Public Art Documentation/Distribution (PAD/D), including Lucy Lippard, May Stevens, and Rudolf Baranik, May's husband. Rudolf had experienced war first hand and not solely as a soldier. He was born in Lithuania and had escaped the massacre that befell his entire family because he had happened to be in the United States. He was attending college in Chicago when the Nazis invaded his town and killed the Jewish half of the population with the enthusiastic participation of their Christian neighbors.

7. *Artists Call* flier with Claes Oldenburg graphic 8. *Reconstructed Codex*, opening pages 9. Flier, *Reconstruction Project*

Since *Views by Women Artists*, I had chosen to focus on my own work and organize wom-
en's shows independently, paddling and keeping my head above the wrenching in-fighting at the
local New York City Women's Caucus for Art (WCA). I was in the midst of reading books written
during the Spanish conquest of the Americas. One was by the third bishop of the Yucatan, Diego
de Landa, the seminal scholar for Maya studies and also the person who destroyed the codices
in 1562. He described that auto-da-fe plainly and without apology: "We found a great number
of these books . . . and since they contained nothing but superstitions and falsehoods of the
devil, we burned them all, which they [the Maya] took most grievously, and which gave them great
pain."[3] Only four Maya codices survived this conflagration.

How could a person who appreciated a culture choose to destroy it? This historical event
felt current to me; I experienced it in my own cloaked family history. We hold in our bodies and
in our genes the marks of conquest. Women are often victims of rape during wars or partners
in love during times of change and bear the new generations of culturally mixed descendants.
I felt women artists were the ones to explore this subject by recreating, on our own terms, one
of the four surviving codices. We could symbolically renew a codex and, in the process, educate
ourselves. I proposed *Reconstruction Project* to the organizing committee for *Artists Call* and was
accepted for an exhibit at Artists' Space, an alternative gallery on Spring Street.

I chose the *Dresden Codex*, named after the European city where it now resides, as the
book to reconstruct. The accordion-shaped codex unfolds to thirteen feet; ours had the same
dimensions. The original pages were eight by three inches and made out of bark paper with a
gesso ground. I replicated that format by preparing forty sheets of heavy watercolor paper with
a traditional gesso of rabbit skin glue and whiting. My friends from Atlantic Gallery, Kate Correa

Reconstructed Codex in sewn page sequence: 10. Frances Buschke 11. Nancy Spero 12. Liliana Porter

and Frankie Buschke, came over to help me gesso, heating the glue in my kitchen and spreading the papers across the studio floor to dry.

I invited nineteen women to work with me in creating *Reconstructed Codex*; Kate and Frankie were among the first to accept. The artists in this project were a cross-section from our various groups. Sharon Gilbert had helped organize *Views by Women Artists*. I found Marina Gutierrez through her clothesline sculpture at the Arsenal. Helen Oji had been on one of the WCA panels. Emma Amos, Kathy Grove, Linda Peer, Chris Costan, Josely Carvalho, and Holly Zox all worked with *Heresies*. Nancy Spero and Kazuko were founders of A.I.R. Gallery. I met potter Camille Billops through Vivian Browne. Camille has a theatrical presence; her eyes heavily outlined like an ancient Egyptian. She and her husband still maintain the Hatch-Billops Collection that archives works by artists of color and images of race and racism. As the artists accepted, I sent them two of our prepared pages. Helen Oji told me, "When I got the papers, they were so beautiful. You didn't need to do anything more."

Some artists refused. Michelle Stuart, who had worked in Mexico, wrote, "I must decline. I am much too close to the Maya to work on this project nor do I agree with it being even partially destroyed."

All the artists lived in New York City except two Native American artists whose work I knew through *Heresies*—Colleen Cutschall from North Dakota and Jaune Quick-To-See Smith who lived in New Mexico. Others had also been published in *Heresies*—Liliana Porter, painter and printmaker originally from Argentina, and Catalina Parra, another exile from the Pinochet regime like Cecilia Vicuña. Catalina's aunt, Violeta, revived folk singing in Chile and her father is the Chilean poet Nicanor Parra. Virginia Jaramillo completed the group; she is a papermaker

Reconstructed Codex in sewn page sequence: 13. Josely Carvalho 14. Virginia Jaramillo 15. Emma Amos

who works purely in color and form. Her friend Liliana teased her at the opening: "She forgot to make the painting!"

Some of us met at my studio and developed a book list on the Mayas, focusing on the earliest sources. I had discovered the magnificent epic poem, the *Popol Vuh*, and Sharon Gilbert found a symphony by Alban Berg based on the same poem. We wanted the installation at Artists' Space to be vibrant. The book would be displayed on a turquoise stand in the center of the room that Roger was building, but we needed to make artworks for the walls. Most Native American cultures have directional colors—red (east), black (west), white (north), and yellow (south). We each selected a directional color and made a painting in one color, seven feet high by three feet, with five artists for each color.

This was a reconstruction of ideas and images, not a reproduction from an original, and the pages and paintings took many forms. Some women took a formal approach, responding to the shapes of the glyphs. Holly used glyphs paired with a text about her Jewish grandmother. Colleen mimicked her Lakota culture's quillwork by painting in short lines to create a pointillist eagle centered above the "rain god" tabloid on the left and the "death god" tabloid on the right. She explained, "You see the self-appointed god of Native cultures is the symbol of the eagle, a symbol of US nationalism, which has no other important value to the majority of Americans other than for its monetary value." Frankie responded to the fiery destruction itself by assembling layers of blackened and burned papers. Like Rudolf, Frankie's parents had narrowly escaped the Holocaust in Germany by immigrating to California. And Sharon made two white pages annotated like a song and based on the *Popol Vuh*. Of course, there was an exploding volcano painted by Helen Oji.

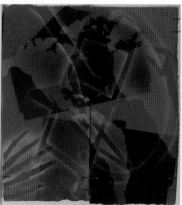

16. Installation, yellow and red walls 17. *Reconstructed Codex* pages continue: Kathy Grove 18. Sewn *Codex* on platform

I chose the color yellow, which is a color that is associated with a Maya death deity, and struggled to balance that concept by adding cutouts of babies in my family. Marina was also working with that color by making rubbings. "I knew I was on the right track when I saw your work," Liliana later told me. "I realized how European I am. It was very difficult for me to work on this page. You can see how much I had to erase on the back."

Jaune called from New Mexico just before she mailed her artworks: "I have been working full time on this project since I received your papers. I feel very deeply about this and made two banners that are very political and may hurt people, [and they are] about how Native American art has been taken from people and placed in museums where Native people can't see it."

Ten of us met again at my studio just before we installed the show to arrange the pages in sequence and sew the book together. The gallery installation was dominated by the purity of color; five same-colored paintings were hung on each wall, saturating the room. The book was laid flat and the viewer had to approach to appreciate its complexity. The Berg symphony whispered its musical transcription from inside the turquoise stand. At the opening, Kazuko's three-year-old son was just tall enough to see the pages at nose height, but he managed to distinguish his mother's artwork—a miniature black felt hat filled with straw—from the others. I made corn bread for the opening, which I had left in a covered basket at the gallery earlier that same day. When I came back for the party, a thin line of crumbs led from the half-empty basket.

Our show was one of fifty-nine events, poetry, exhibits, films, and performances for *Artists Call* during that cold January and the months following. It was impossible to see everything, but Roger and I went around to several exhibits and performances, often handing out the flier I had made for *Reconstruction Project*, bristling with photocopied feathers. We went to see the street of banners that Rudolf had organized and walked later in a procession from Forty-Seventh

19. Roger Mignon (both) Installation, red wall, *Reconstruction Project* 20. Installation, black wall, *Reconstruction Project*

Street downtown to Judson Memorial Church where each person carried the name of a murdered or disappeared person from the Americas. The giant white birds from Bread & Puppet Theater flanked our march. As we reached the church, we read the name and released a white balloon and then went inside to see the impressive series of group shows assembled there. I hadn't been to Judson Memorial since they had switched sides and opposed our union organizing at the abortion clinic they sponsored. My favorite show was *Latin American Mail Art* organized by Josely Carvalho. An Argentinean artist wrote on her decorated card, "We want to blossom too."

I recently retrieved the oversized *Artists Call* poster from a box in my studio where it was tightly curled. Claes Oldenburg designed the poster, which depicts a big banana being tugged off its pedestal against a field of pumpkin yellow. *Artists Call* had the same uphill fight for publicity that *Views by Women Artists* had encountered—it was hard to topple the big bananas that govern what gets noticed in the art world. Consciousness-raising was a part of organizing these content-driven events, and the organizers wanted word to spread. *Reconstruction Project*, however, got noticed in many ways. Sue Heinemann was writing an article about *Artists Call* for *In These Times* and told Rudolf that she could not include everyone: "For instance, I'm not writing about Sabra and *Reconstruction Project*." Rudolf offered to cut a couple of lines so our show could be mentioned. Grace Glueck from the *New York Times* reviewed only three shows from the mass event, including ours, singling out Frankie's "charred-looking tablets," Colleen's "intricate composition of two Mayan gods . . . that cleverly suggests bead work," and Holly's "poem about a Jewish grandmother (honest!)."[4] I was delighted despite Glueck's bizarre reading of the actions of Bishop de Landa, who, Glueck wrote, "campaigned against such unnerving Mayan customs as the sacrifice of children."[5] I called Lucy to get her reaction to the review: "It made me so mad that I could barely read it. First, it only happened because I called Grace and said, 'Aren't you

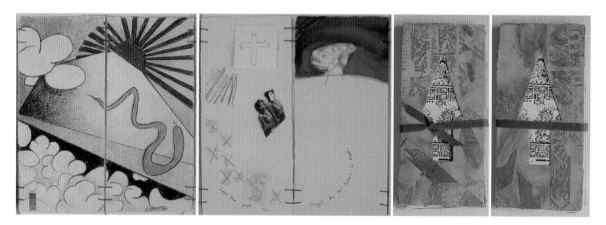

Reconstructed Codex pages continue: 21. Camille Billops 22. Linda Peer 23. Front and back gessoed covers

going to write about *Artists Call* or at least go to the installations?' She didn't mention [in her article] that there were thirty-five galleries; she didn't mention the children's show." The response of Valerie Smith at Artists' Space was more positive: "It's so wonderful this show is getting so much play." Many people were suggesting that we travel the installation.

Before we sewed the pages, I made direct same-size color Xerox copies of each page to use as the mechanical for a photocopier version of the *Reconstructed Codex*. I set to making a labor-intensive edition of thirty books, folded like the original, with gessoed covers opening onto an introduction to the project. We had prepared the pages by scoring and tearing so that each page had a variable deckled edge, and now these edges had to be cut out by hand. I cut an arrow-shaped opening into each gessoed cover, mimicking the doorways at the ruins in Uxmal. Liliana thought these openings made the covers look phallic.

I was having trouble making the folds in the edition work when I suddenly got a call from Mother about my grandparents. Mother Gladys and Daddy Chess had been staying near her house in Dallas for the past two months in a nursing home called Serenity Haven that was anything but serene. I had opposed this move, but Mother had been convinced that the doctors in Dallas could find a treatment for the persistent pain of Mother Gladys's shingles. My grandfather had come with her, refusing to be separated after sixty-six years of marriage, but he hated the place: "Gal, they've put me in the penitentiary . . . I didn't want to be set down in a mess of concrete." Her pain hadn't lessened despite the numerous drugs, and her disorientation had increased. She started having seizures and stopped recognizing many people who visited her. I called her; she was expecting me. "My granddaughter is going to call," she had told people. I told her I would come down and see her. "Can you afford it?" she asked twice. The family had decided to send them both back to Clarksville in an ambulance, returning them to their familiar

24. Roger Mignon, *Sabra with Gladys & Chester on porch* 25. Sabra Moore, *Generate*, page from artist's book

surroundings. *Reconstruction Project* was about to close, but Roger, Frankie, and Kate offered to take the show down in my absence so that I could go.

Mother's family had a different cultural background from Daddy's. She had grown up on a two-hundred-acre farm run by her grandmother, Lillie Parks. Lillie's husband had died when their children were teenagers, so she ran the farm alone. Each of the five children farmed the land collectively with their mother on forty-acre parcels, but their big cotton fields along Red River echoed the plantation system and added to the complex racial and social identity I was seeking to unravel. Lillie had married her cousin, a family tradition, but after she became a midwife and healer, she started to observe that each of her children had physical oddities that she attributed to inbreeding. She banned first-cousin marriages for her children. Daddy Chess met Mother Gladys when she arrived with her grandparents as sharecroppers from North Carolina. He helped them move from Arkansas to the farm, and they fell in love on the ride back. They were married the following year. My mother was the first-born: "Granny told me that all their babies had been born with blond hair, but my hair was black because of the Indian blood from Mother Gladys."

I flew with my nose pressed to the window of the plane, savoring the changing land and making drawings from my perch in the air, noting the emerging rivers and the brown fields dotted with green woods. Mother met me, and we drove immediately down to Clarksville to see Mother Gladys in the nursing home there. She was still confused: "It's frightening how much I've forgotten." She told me how often she had dreamed about me. "I told them, 'I've got to eat; my granddaughter is coming.'" My uncle and aunt came with other kin to my grandparents' house, and we all crowded into the small kitchen to cook familiar foods and bring Gladys and Chester home for supper. "Will I spend the night here?" she asked. "No, not yet." She couldn't recognize her yard, but she recognized the inside of the house, imprinted from years of living in the same

26. Sabra Moore, *Generate*, page from artist's book 27. Sabra sitting with Mother Gladys in living room

rooms. We settled together on the couch after eating, and she started to talk about piecing quilts with her sister-in-law, Bertha. One time, they were both piecing a quilt top and Gladys went out to feed their yellow cow Queenie, who was pastured next to the house. She picked up a pile of hay and a big king snake was inside. "Bertha heard me screaming and came running with the hoe. We killed the snake, but I couldn't piece the rest of the day. I kept feeling the snake in my hands."

Mother and I argued. She was upset that her youngest grandson wanted to be a musician. "It's no kind of life," she said. "But what about me? I'm an artist." Mother now had a boyfriend named Larry, and we were all happy for her new situation—the first real relationship since my father had died nineteen years earlier. She had expected Mother Gladys to disapprove perhaps because of the turmoil when she had eloped with Daddy at age eighteen. My parents always insisted that they eloped because of Daddy's carpetbagger blood, but I had my doubts. Mother had come down to visit with Larry some months earlier before the recent health crisis. Mother Gladys met him at the door and shouted with joy. "I have been praying that Christine would find someone!" Mother had left the country culture years ago to become a teacher in Dallas, and she was happy with her choices, seeing her life as an improvement over her parents' situation. It dismayed her that I was returning to our rural roots as a source for my artwork and that I was acknowledging our family's racial complexity. When I left, Daddy Chess said to me, "Do you think we'll milk a cow together again?"

Reconstructed Codex was still awaiting my return, and I finished the edition, distributing nineteen to the artists and saving ten for other venues. Roger and I went on a trip to Mexico City and the Yucatan to see the pyramids that had filled my imagination during my immersion in *Reconstruction Project*. I filled an entire journal with drawings from Teotihuacan, Uxmal, Tulum, Chichen Itza, and Isla Mujeres. "I think happiness is human," I wrote in my book after looking at

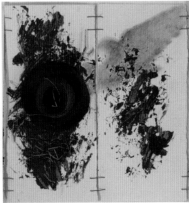

Reconstructed Codex in sewn page sequence: 28. Helen Oji 29. Kazuko 30. Marina Gutierrez

paintings of rain gods frolicking on Maya pots. "The absence of happiness or jokes in art often means power and aggression. Power is always serious." We went to Frida Kahlo's electric blue house. I loved her proliferation of objects—dolls, plates, *recuerdos*, flowers, revolutionary posters, paintings, and glass cases with her journals and papers labeled with symbols, not words. It reminded me of a comment about my own studio from one of Roger's fellow painters: "Only a woman could paint in such an environment." I cried when I stood in Frida's bedroom with the mirror above her bed and one of her body casts lying across the mattress. "It felt like confronting the world with the strength of her fragility." As we left the house, I spied a wall of postcards and went over to buy some, but all the postcards were of Diego Rivera's paintings and none were of Frida's work. I made notes of all the birds, the changing colors in the sky, the horizontal landscape in the Yucatan with the pyramids piercing the trees like mountains, the floating rocks in the *cenotes* near Uxmal, and the elaborate offerings of tiny pots beside the dark lake in the cave at Balamchanche. In Merida, I dreamed about Mother Gladys. It felt like an actual visit to her. "She is much stronger," I wrote, "as if she has come out of a serious ill period and is reorganizing her awareness." When we returned to New York, I learned that my grandmother had improved and that her mental confusion had been mostly caused by the pain medications.

I was ready to work again in my studio and started looking for venues for new projects. I proposed a window installation for SOHO20 Gallery, and they liked the idea so much that they decided to use the windows for their own members. Sharon Gilbert, Bibi Lenĉek, and I had been developing a show called *Latitudes of Time* scheduled for the City Gallery at Columbus Circle. I started making a clothes line sculpture with the leftover cutout houses from *House Book*, echoing Marina's concept.

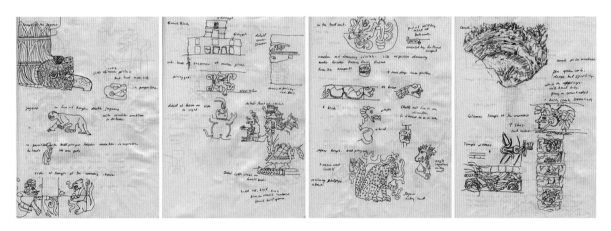

31. Sabra Moore, Journal #37 drawings (all), *Chichen Itza temples* 32. *Tulum* 33. *Chichen Itza* 34. *Chichen Itza cenote*

An action was brewing that spring—one that proved pivotal for others and me. Betsy Damon came to our WCA board meeting to talk about an upcoming show at the Museum of Modern Art (MoMA). The museum had been closed for almost a year for renovations, and the opening show, *An International Survey of Recent Painting and Sculpture*, was scheduled for June 14. Only 14 artists out of 165 were women. As the word got out, anger rose. We had been protesting the unequal treatment of women and minority artists for fourteen years and seemed to have gained about one representative for each year of protest. Betsy asked the WCA to help organize a demonstration, and we agreed.

Betsy was best known for her performance as the *7000 Year Old Woman*. She would appear on the street with her skin and hair painted white and gradually attach, then detach, 420 small bags filled with sixty pounds of colored flour. Su Friedrich photographed these performances, and her images were stunning. Betsy stands alone in a circle on an ordinary street, a ritual figure surrounded by ambivalent crowds. The dissonance gives the scene power. Her persona reminded me of the hunters I had seen in Guinea, their shirts adorned with medicine bags. I later learned that Betsy had probably seen these shirts while visiting Nigeria.

Betsy proposed that women converge on MoMA, carrying rocks and flowers. I think she envisioned building a shrine there, but I envisioned the police, watching hundreds of women with rocks marching to the glassed-in museum entrance. So we modified the design of the demonstration. I can't remember who thought of Flag Day, but June 14 was Flag Day and someone came up with the idea of "Wave on Flag Day." Betsy and Annie Shaver-Crandell wanted us to model our dress on the suffragists and wear yellow and white. Instead of rocks, I suggested that we all bring show cards, and then we decided to pin those on yellow sashes or suspenders. We three became coordinators, but there was a ready crowd ahead of us, pushing the event forward.

 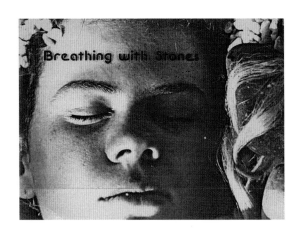 

35. Su Friedrich photo, Betsy Damon as *7,000 Year-Old Woman* 36. Damon, *Meditation/Chant* 37. *Let MoMA Know* flier

The *Heresies* Collective, the Women's Interart Center, and the New York Feminist Art Institute were cosponsors, but the WCA board remained the think tank.

And we were thinking fast. Someone acquired the elegant little aluminum badge that MoMA planned to distribute—a thin rectangular pin divided in the center by a horizontal line that read: "The Museum of Modern Art/OPENS." Was it Ora Lerman's idea to copy this pin? We were all talking at once. We decided to add a line below: "OPENS/But Not To Women Artists." We managed to find the money to pull this off, substituting silver cardboard for the aluminum and taping a safety pin on the back. On the day of the demonstration, we were passing the subversive badges out to all the marchers, but the museum curators and staff kept asking the guards to collect handfuls and bring them inside.

We were fighting, but the sides could shift. Even within our organizing group, we couldn't agree on a slogan. I proposed "Let MoMA Know"; Betsy and Annie wanted "Women's Visibility Event"; and we had already printed the phrase, "The Museum Opens, But Not to Women Artists." We made posters; other people made posters. There was no official poster or slogan except in retrospect. We used all of them.

There were three demands: that the museum display women's work from their permanent collection, that it feature women in loan exhibitions, and that it establish a policy for acquiring artwork by women. We prepared a two-page alphabetical listing of four hundred prominent women artists from the past decade. This list became an organizing tool for the march. I called Mary Beth Edelson to see if she was coming. She said that no one she knew was coming. I told her about the list. "Is my name on it?" "Yes." She came. We talked about the march in our weekly *Heresies* meeting. Lucy had demonstrated at the Whitney in the seventies; she was coming. "We kept yelling, 'Let us in!'" Holly Zox was cool to the idea of putting her energies into such a

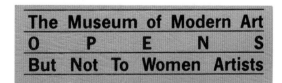

38. *MoMA Opens* demonstration flier 39. *But Not To Women Artists* badge 40. *Let MoMA Know* demonstration flier

protest: "The museums are elitist." "Yes, but they legitimize culture," I argued. "We need to do this for the issue of fairness and to change how people perceive culture."

On the day of the march, hundreds of women poured into the street in front of the museum wearing yellow sashes emblazoned with names of women artists or bristling with colored show cards. Some of us had met to assemble ribbons that we wore like overgrown suspenders trailing below our knees, defying Virginia Wolf's admonition against wearing medals. We bedecked our ribbons in the images of our collective achievements, usurping the prerogative of the museum to decide which artists were worthy of attention. Some carried signs. Others had printed the names of artists from many countries and women from the past to wear on sashes across their breasts. Ora appeared wearing a sunbonnet. Patricia Jones held a sign that read, "MoMA Doesn't Always Know Best." We hugged. We shouted slogans: "You don't have to have a penis to be a genius!" and "MoMA! Where's Mama?" I had stayed up the night before finishing the *Model MoMA*, a small painted wooden replica of the museum with an opening in the top. I had already trespassed in the model's interior galleries, printing wax transfers of petroglyphs and mirror slogans including "Can MoMA Contain Us?" along its yellow walls. Marchers could write their names on strips of paper and place them inside, becoming symbolically included. Roger helped me glue the sides, and I constructed a stretcher out of driftwood so that we could parade with the *Model MoMA* as the names were added. Ora and Lenora met me to help carry the model, but the driftwood pole broke and the little museum crashed to the sidewalk, spilling its contents. Sando de Sando later said, "You fell apart in front of everyone when your *Model MoMA* fell apart." But Ora and Lenora helped me push the sides back together, and we sat it on the sidewalk on top of a yellow-checkered cloth. It filled with names there.

41. Carol Bruns photograph of MoMA protest (both), Joyce Kozloff holds *MoMA Dearest* sign 42. Unidentified man crossing street

Some people had read the flier and came prepared with bags of printed names. "Help fill the *Model M.o.M.M.A.* with names and images of women artists. Make the *Model* contain us," the flier had read. Others scribbled their names on the cards and narrow strips of paper I had brought. Some stuffed show cards or envelopes lined with names, keeping their promise to friends in other cities to include them. The *Model MoMA* was bulging by the end of the march, unkempt with its heterogeneous offerings, though we couldn't carry it into the museum.

This time, the press noticed that we had been left out and converged in force. Betsy attributed it to her publicist, Vera. After all, "Visibility" was her slogan of choice. She and Annie had written a press release, listing themselves as organizers with Annie as spokeswoman, omitting my name. I had assumed we would be anonymous behind the groups. I glimpsed them giving interviews to reporters while I stood on the line with the *Model MoMA*, receiving names. The journalists, however, moved around among the marchers, talking with many of us and not simply with Annie and Betsy. A reporter from *Newsweek*, interviewing Linda Cunningham and me, confided that she had problems with sexism at *Newsweek* as well.

The Guerrilla Girls trace this show to their founding: "In 1985, a band of feminist artists founded the Guerrilla Girls in the wake of Kynaston McShine's remark that any artist who wasn't in this international survey at the Museum of Modern Art should 'rethink HIS career.'"[6] The mass demonstrations by women artists during the show have been replaced in the Guerrilla Girls's history by their own lone band of activists.

Women kept leafleting MoMA throughout the show. Annie and Betsy went on the talk circuit. I tried to discuss my feelings of betrayal with them by arguing that "a *Visibility* event in which the organizer who structured the event creatively (me) isn't visible." I pointed to the way

43. Sabra and Linda Cunningham in action 44. *WAN* cover 45. Clarissa Sligh photo, Frankie Bushke and banner

the march was described in the New York Day By Day column of the *New York Times* to emphasize my contribution to its design:

> "MoMA opens, but not to women artists," read one banner. Several people marched wearing necklaces of invitations to art exhibitions by women. A miniature model of the Museum of Modern Art stood on the sidewalk on West 53rd Street, filled with the names of hundreds of female artists.[7]

We agreed to collaborate on writing an upcoming article in *Women's Artists News*; Betsy teased me that I should start wearing a "visibility cloak." Once again, Annie delivered artifacts to my studio: the yellow ribbons with show cards attached.

Lucy had invited me to do an installation for the months of July and August for the windows at Printed Matter, Inc. "I know you have this problem with Roger, but I'd love for you to do the installation. Go speak with Alice Weiner." There was a problem with Roger—he had found a lump under his chin when he was trimming his beard. It proved to be a benign fetal cyst, and he was scheduled for surgery to remove it. I also kept hearing news about my grandparents. Mother had, at last, decided that her parents needed to move back into their home. Daddy Chess got his old car in working order, but as they were preparing to move, Mother Gladys refused to leave. "I'm sicker than Chester thinks. I like my room here. I have two friends and a closet for my dresses. He thinks if we go home, things will be the way they were before. He's wrong." I went to see Alice Weiner and arranged for the art installation. The struggles with Mother Gladys's frailty had started to weave their way into the artworks I was planning. I wrote a text for one of the two kimono-shaped *House Dress* works I had in mind.

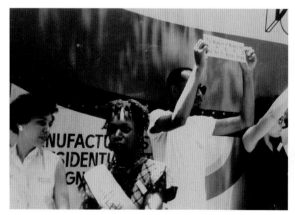 

46. Bruns photo, male supporter holding sign 47. Lucy Lippard & May Stevens walking together, Sligh photo

She loves her room. It's a pretty room, not like the one she has at home, she says. When her daughter took her home, she looked for her summer dresses. "Where do I keep my summer dresses?" she said. "Usually you move them into the hall closet for winter, then back into the chifforobe in the spring, but this year, you were sick." She recognized her housedresses, but not the dress-up ones. "Do I like this dress?" she asked. She prefers her housedresses that button up in the front, with round collars and pockets. At the nursing home, she has two best friends, one is white, one is black. In her old age, she's forgotten the rules.

SOHO20 Gallery called as well, scheduling an installation for their windows for August. I set to work. I started making two window-sized artworks for the Printed Matter, Inc. windows. They had to be double-sided since the windows opened into the artists' bookstore and visitors would be able to view both sides. Both were paper works shaped like large kimonos. One was solid with the text I had written printed on the inside and images on the street side. The other was composed of many small house patterns sewn to form the same kimono shape with pithy details from Gladys's life printed across one side of each little house. "She has a picture of Jesus walking on the water above the bathtub," one house read. "She controls the distribution of her quilts," read another.

I was writing to Mother Gladys frequently. She had my aunt Mary Jane read my letters aloud to both of them. I struggled to write a press release for *House Dress/Gladys Story* installation that my grandparents would also appreciate, crediting Mother Gladys's quilts as an inspiration for my artworks. I was still in the middle of making these pieces when Roger went to the hospital for surgery. He came back to stay at my apartment while he recovered—I was still living on Warren Street. Linda Peer came to visit. She saw *House Dress* in progress. "It's not sculpture," she said. "I didn't say it was."

48. Sabra Moore (both), *House Dress/Gladys Story* 49. *Sixteen Houses* (detail) 50. Roger Mignon, *Sabra at window show*

I dream I am walking with Roger and Daddy Chess on a dirt road. We come to a cross-roads. Daddy Chess has his old car and drives off with me into a field filled with birds of all kinds and sizes, leaving Roger on the road. I make him slow down so he won't hit any birds. Then we swerve back onto the road and I run to find Roger, still walking.

I added a personal manifesto to the wooden frame of one dress: "Make Visible Indigenous Culture Starts At Home." I was scheduled to install the two *House Dress* works the next morning. Roger and I went out for the first time since his surgery to eat Chinese food, and later that night, I started sewing the last house patterns as he slept. He woke as his face started to swell. I kept sewing, insisting he simply apply ice and go back to sleep, but his face kept swelling and we had to drop everything and rush off to the emergency room for an antidote to the allergic reaction. The next day, I installed *House Dress/Gladys Story*. When my grandparents received the announcement, Daddy Chess called me from the nursing home and said, "Gal, you're raising her name up in New York City!"

I planned to celebrate the two window installations with one "mid-window" opening in early August, giving me time to finish the works for SOHO20 Gallery. This second installation was called *Selling the Bed*, which was related to the loss of a wooden bed I had loved as a child. My parents sold this bed in trade for a modern gray Formica bedroom suite when I was about eight years old. The day before the man came to pick up the old bed, I made little drawings of its headboard and footboard and kept them as talismans, perplexing my parents. For the installation, I drew the bed from memory on a seven-foot-high piece of gessoed watercolor paper, cut out the bed drawing, and then sewed it back into the cutout shape and painted it. Mother used to make white organdy curtains for all the windows, and I hung small organdy curtains across the top of the painting, echoing her curtains and the ones in Frida Kahlo's paintings. I paired this

51. Sabra Moore, *Sixteen Houses* 52. Roger Mignon (both) *Interior, Printed Matter* 53. *Moore Installation*, SOHO20 window

work in the companion window with four tiny beds flanking a large text work that mirrored the size of the painted bed. One bed was made from twigs, one from feathers, one from bark, and one from paper.

Roger helped me install the two cutout paper beds in the windows at SOHO20 Gallery, and then we returned the next day to photograph. Sometimes, the street can offer unintended contrasts with the art on the other side of the glass. A homeless woman younger than me occupied the sidewalk space adjacent to my installation; her exposed bed inside a cardboard box was far more challenging than any artwork. She got up to move. "Please don't move on account of us," I said. "We are just photographing my window installation." "Oh, it's time for me to go across the street," she insisted in a cultivated voice. We both smiled politely at each other as if the situation were normal.

One of the editors from Tree Communications, Henry Weincek, wrote me a long letter: "Your art is so personal that it's difficult to praise it to your face. 'Thank you for having such vivid memories' is the awkward phrase that would come out." There was a flurry of interest in buying the *Gladys Story* works at Printed Matter, Inc.; Alice Weiner offered to handle the details. "It's very nice the way you considered the inside," Alice said. "I'm not surprised that someone with money would want to buy it." "That's nice of you," I replied. "No, it isn't; it's true. It's really beautiful. It's one of our best windows." "Of course, I love hearing that, but it's difficult to respond." "Now, don't let it go to your head." "That's exactly what my mother would say."

The year of 1984 was one of bloody determination—no cause was left unattended. Roger and I were each working on new artworks for *Art Against Apartheid*, a series of shows planned for the fall. He was drawing a black-and-white skeleton, and I was painting a large cutout of the map of Africa called *Africa is 3X the Size of the United States*. I was trying to visually incorporate

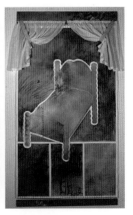

54. Roger Mignon, *Sabra & homeless woman at installation* 55. Sabra Moore (both), *Gesso Bed* 56. *Selling the Bed*

Roger's observation that money is more important that labor. Once again, I interrupted this process to fly to Texas. Mother Gladys's health had deteriorated, and Mother called to ask me to come down for her birthday in late August. Daddy Chess had been taking her home for small visits with the connivance of a nurse. They had lunch at home on his birthday. "We ate potted meat," he said. Another time, they had tea. He wanted both of them to be home when I arrived for her party.

I plunged into the essential world of my childhood. Mother and I drove down to Clarksville and took my grandparents to their house. I planned to stay after the party for three days so they could be at home. Mother Gladys was too ill for them to stay at home alone. We put her to bed in her room, and I went outside to pick up the spoiled pears under the old tree and rake the yard. "Sabra . . . I . . . want . . . to . . . tell . . . you . . . that . . . I . . . love . . . you . . . very . . . much . . . with . . . all . . . my . . . nasty . . . heart." Daddy Chess came into the room to visit. "She's a heifer, but I wouldn't take a million dollars for her." He talked about Mother. "James Chester [Mother's brother] liked to sew doll clothes and piece quilts. He liked to stay with Gladys. Christine liked to go everywhere with me. She should have been the boy and he the girl." Jewell, Mother Gladys's half niece, came to visit, and we sat together beside her bed to talk. Her grandmother was an enrolled Cherokee; we called her Aunt Hazel. She was both my step-great-grandmother and great aunt. She had married Mother Gladys's father, Lon, after they were both widowed. "Sabra, did you ever marry? Do you have children?" "No." Then we both sat there in silence. I wanted to photograph the quilts, but I was afraid my kinfolk would find this odd. "No one would think it was funny. Everyone is pleased that you honored her with your show," Mother said. So I pulled the quilts out of the closet and the trunk and photographed them one by one, hanging them on her clothesline.

57. Sabra Moore, *Gladys Place (view under curtain)* 58. Gladys Parks's quilt hanging on clothesline

Mother loved teaching and had opened a private school after she retired. After the birthday party, she had to return to Dallas for her school, leaving me alone with my grandparents. She was angry that I was encouraging them to stay home for a few days. Mother Gladys felt her anxiety. "Chester, do you think we'll live through the night?" "Sure, Gal. We'll live." We did, settling down into conversation. Her speech had become more fluid in familiar surroundings. She started remembering when she had married Chester. "Granny Parks was anxious that we marry so young because, at that time, you didn't have to go to war if you were married. Now, I think Chester would be too old." They lived in his mother's house that first year of marriage, and then he sold the cotton crop and went to town to buy the furniture that they still used, loading everything into a big wagon to haul back to the farm. "She was a good housekeeper. It's funny, when her mind went, how quickly all of that left." I took them back to the nursing home the next day. "Do you think you and Roger will ever get married?" "We might."

Nancy Spero had made a red-and-black text collage emblazoned with "The Year of the South African Woman" as the poster for *Art Against Apartheid*. I barely finished my large Africa-shaped painting and brought it to my assigned space at 22 Wooster Street. I was ushered into a basement gallery and grabbed a broom to sweep down the cobwebs from the wall. The organizers had really found every possible usable location for these shows. "It's perfect, having an apartheid show in this environment," a man tried to explain, "a beautiful gallery upstairs and a dark basement below." As I was struggling to hang my piece, an artist entered wearing a poncho and hurried to help me. "Hold it from the edge—it's still wet!" I protested as he placed a thumb over the oil-painted surface. "Finger-prints are good! I discovered a long time ago that the work that looks too finished looks dead." That's how I met sculptor Willie Birch, partner at the time to Marina Gutierrez. Willie didn't spare a moment to tell me that he had been disappointed with the

 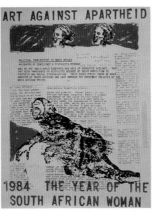  

Art Against Apartheid protest fliers (all), 59. *Artists' Meeting* 60. Nancy Spero, *poster* 61. *Mandela Birthday* 62. *Street Action*

artworks in *Reconstruction Project*. "I thought the concept was incredible. I read it when Marina got the letters. There were people dying to see that show, but when I saw it, that was it!" "You didn't like the book?" "The book was good, and the concept!"

I dream that Roger and I are walking around after a nuclear holocaust. I am carrying paintings.

We all went to Vivian Browne's show at SOHO20 Gallery that fall with Ora arriving by bicycle, Emma standing around chatting next to her husband Bobby, and Camille talking about how she used to wear a painted clothespin in her hair. But mostly, Vivian's friends noticed that she had eliminated the veils from her new paintings. For many years, Vivian had floated a translucent material over her painted surfaces, deliberately muting the clarity of the image. Her new paintings had an embedded handwritten text that you could scarcely discern among a landscape of trees, but the veils were gone. Vivian was a close friend of May Stevens, who also used text in her work, but May's texts were usually printed. May later started using handwritten words in a series of paintings she made about the drowning of Rosa Luxemburg. Like Vivian's texts, it was almost impossible to read these words; they were evocative, but not explicit. Vivian always felt that May had adapted this concept from her paintings without acknowledging her as a source.

Mierle Laderman Ukeles called and asked me to invite fifteen women to participate in *Touch Sanitation*, her performance work honoring sanitation workers. Only Josely Carvalho and Kathy Grove showed up out of the people I invited, but the street was crowded with union members and other participants. Mierle's magnificent mirrored garbage truck was parked nearby so that passersby and sanitation workers could reflect each other as trash was collected and hauled away. "Why is necessary work—service work—so often invisible? Is there room in a democracy for everyone to be respected?" Mierle asked. She had installed a wooden porch on

63. Becket Logan, Emma Amos with *X Flag* 64. Vivian Browne, *Versitile Source* (detail) 65. Camille Billops dancing

the sidewalk in front of the Ronald Feldman Gallery. It looked like a scaffold, but it was meant to recreate a suburban matron's porch. We were asked to walk over to the porch and thank the sanitation workers for cleaning up after the world. Our action was meant to symbolically erase the insults that these workers often endured, but it felt awkward. Josely left before the handshake; she felt that well-known political figures were being called up first. I stayed, thinking about my father's indignation. Ana Mendieta was walking up the street and rushed over to greet us. I thought she was still at her artist's residency in Rome. She lived with Carl Andre, her spouse, in a high-rise building on Broadway, but she was now trying to reclaim her old apartment that she had sublet. It was the last time I saw Ana.

In October, I skipped an appearance on the panel about the impact of our demonstration against MoMA, "Now MoMA Knows," at A.I.R. Gallery, keeping my word to read poetry with Marithelma at Marymount Manhattan College the same evening. I still was disgusted by the competitiveness that surfaced during the march, but I sent a statement for Betsy or Annie to read in my absence. We had affected each other by our march, but it was unclear if we had also affected museum policy. The response in the established art magazines seemed ambivalent; the arguments about poor quality or relevance had long been the excuse for the absence of women's art in museums, and Gerard Marzorati seemed to be recycling some of these ideas. He had written a review in *Art News* analyzing Kynaston McShine's concept of art "of the moment" and using our demonstration as a contrast to the incisiveness of the curator's selections. He faulted us for omitting Cindy Sherman and Barbara Kruger from our list of artists even though Kruger was on our list. "The women outside the museum didn't care whether Kynaston's show was of the moment; they just wanted more women painters and sculptors represented."[8] I used the statement I gave to Annie and Betsy to respond: "The recent review of *An International Survey*

66. NYC/WCA board on the occasion of Annie Shaver-Crandall's final meeting as president 67. The group five minutes later

of Painting and Sculpture by Gerald Marzorati is using our demonstration as a counterpoint to announce that the period of democratization in the arts is over."

Roger and I had been going to poetry readings with Marithelma and her husband Fabio Salvatore that fall, stopping one evening to hear Allen Ginsberg read with Nicanor Parra, Catalina's father. Fabio was a fellow member of Atlantic Gallery; Marithelma was briefly a Spanish teacher for Roger, Kate, Frankie, and me, but she despaired of our progress. She and I often performed together at public readings of her poetry with English following Spanish. She liked to call me her alter ego.

A.I.R. Gallery hosted a subsequent panel on feminism that was chaired by Lucy and entirely composed of women associated with *Heresies*. This time, I appeared and was grateful for the presence of performance artist Jeri Allyn, who carried us through the rough spots of conversation. *Heresies* moved again. We downsized from the Cable Building, and the excess files that wouldn't fit into our new modest office were parceled out to Ellen, Lucy, Sue, and me. And we had another benefit exhibit, *Earth, Air, Fire, Water*, at Bernice Steinbaum Gallery, which had artists whispering that each successive show netted less money.

In January of 1985, Ronald Reagan issued his second annual State of the Union address and PAD/D started to organize a counter-assessment called *State of the Mind/State of the Arts*. Josely Carvalho and Kathie Browne offered Central Hall for one of the exhibits, and we all began working on pieces about reproductive rights for *Choice Works*. We were meeting weekly anyway, still working on the *Heresies's* Mothers, Mags & Movie Stars issue, so the show was simply an extension of our constant association.

68. *Speaking Volumes* card 69. Roger Mignon, Marithelma Costa reading poetry 70. *Earth/Air/Fire/Water* show card

1. Sabra Moore, *House Dress/Gladys Story*, part of window installation, *Printed Matter*, 1984

2. Great-grandmother Lillie Parks's crazy quilt, circa 1950s, recycled cloth, embroidery

3. Sabra Moore, *Pieced for Caroline & Harry,* photocopier images created in Xerox machine

4. Faith Ringgold, *Echoes of Harlem*, acrylic on canvas, 1980

5. Diana Kurz, *Children (An Artist's Response to the Holocaust)*, series related to her Viennese kin

6. Sylvia Sleigh, *Working at Home*, oil on canvas, 1969

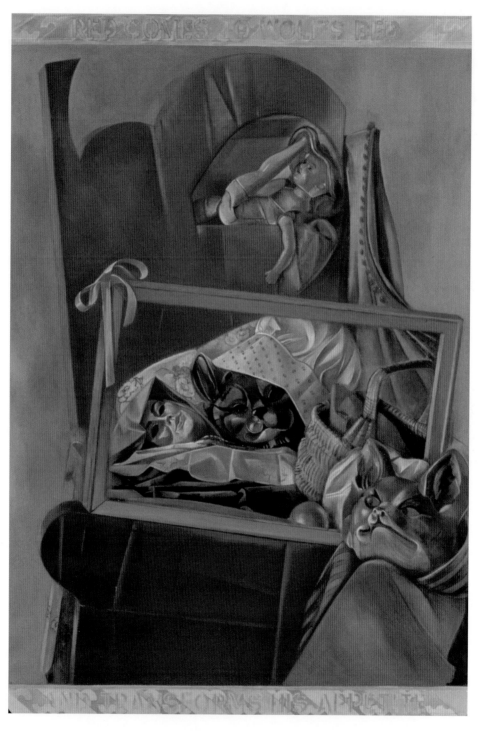

7. Ora Lerman, *Red Comes to Wolf's Bed and Transforms His Appetite*, oil on canvas

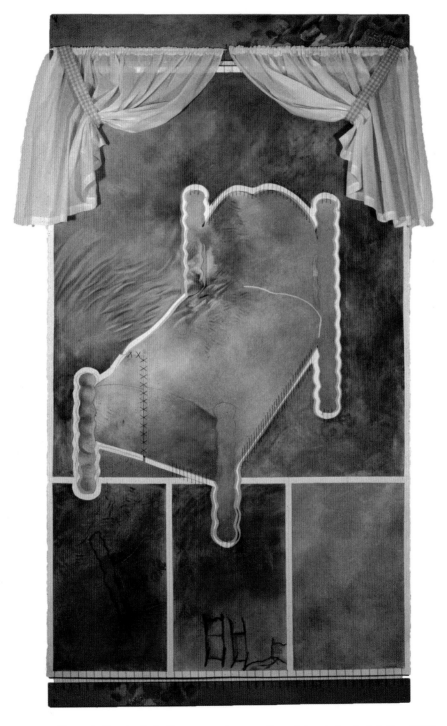

8. Sabra Moore, *Selling the Bed*, oil on gessoed paper with curtain, window installation, 1985

9. Bibi Lenĉek, *From an Interior*, 4 (Green), oil on canvas

10. Sabra Moore, *A Roomful of Mothers (Classified: Big Pages from the Heresies Collective)*

11. Sabra Moore, *A Roomful of Mothers*, Xerox quilt with family stories from *Heresies* Collective

12. Marilyn Lanfear, *Every Night She Latched All the Windows & Locked All the Doors & Put…*

13. Sabra Moore, *Opening Doors Work* (view with doors open to Sabra's story)

14. Emma Amos, Will You Forget Me?, acrylic on canvas with African weaving

15. Mimi Smith, *Knit Baby* from *Knit Baby Kit*, 1968, yarn, undershirt

16. Kazuko Miyamoto, *Woman on Stepladder,* laser transfer on silk

6

Fathers, Daughters, Mothers, Sisters, Friends, & Fellow Travelers from the Past

When I went to college, my father gave me this advice for the times when I might need help: "Carry a dime so you can call me." He was over two hundred miles away, but I still felt a kind of naive confidence in the idea of this thin silver dime. When we women at *Heresies* started working on the Mothers, Mags & Movie Stars issue, we decided to go around the room and describe our class backgrounds. Most of us started with our fathers, whose class was quite clear based on how he earned money. It was harder to figure out the class of our mothers and to work our ways through the issues of power and protection that clouded these relationships. Many of us had mothers who worked outside the home as teachers or nurses, but these jobs had usually been earned through a slow process of part-time education while raising children. Holly Zox described her mother's first job in a note: "Mom's jobs/teacher in an inner-city public school/was pregnant

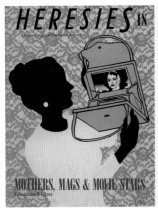

1. *Heresies* #18 cover 2. Carol Sun, *Herstory* 3. Patricia Jones, page art, *Mammies*, Mothers, Mags & Movie Stars #18.

with me the entire time she had the job/I was there!" Often, the mother's education had been paid for by the male spouse at a cost to the relationship, as I witnessed with my parents' repeated arguments about Mother's superior education.

Some women in our group were uncomfortable with the categories of class, feeling that their mothers transcended such labels. Patricia Spears Jones described her mother's struggles to earn her nursing certificate: "She was a black woman living in the still rural South. As far as I can make out, she belongs to none of the class-defined labels: 'working,' 'under,' 'lower middle,' and my absolute favorite, 'petit bourgeois.' My mother does not know French! I think she and many others are of a very unique aristocracy."

Others had mothers who had gone to college before marrying. Lucy's mother worked "as a secretary for a church, a professor, a Broadway producer, a very rich woman . . . while my father was away in the war." Sue Heinemann tried to figure out how her Jewish mother fit into an upper-class mold: "In my mind, true upper class looms as white Anglo-Saxon Protestant." Their mothers either gave up jobs as the fathers advanced or had jobs that kept them in a separate, and lower, class from their mates. In most of our stories, there were small painful details; we daughters were picking up the threads that unraveled from the unfinished work of our mothers or grandmothers. From another of Holly's notes: "Grandma should have been in business; instead she was a bitter mother." Or Patricia: "Mama had a beautiful voice and became a preacher singer (the singer that solos before the preacher delivers his sermon)." Her mother stopped singing when she finally got work as a nurse. Patricia thinks of her own poetry as singing.

I have already described the ways my Grandmother Caroline's death led me into making constructed sculptures. I was propelled by a sense of obligation and need. I was not alone in my reaction. Many artists in our circle started making works that addressed their female

4. Marilyn Lanfear (both), *Table with Ink Paintings* 5. *Sara Crew* 6. Diana Kurz, *Freedom Fighters* (*Portrait of Remembrance* series)

relatives. I cannot think of a male artist who felt a similar need. Male artists were already placed within the history of art. They were in a dialogue with the art movements that preceded them. We women were creating our own dialogues. Consider the visual conversations between Alice, May Stevens's institutionalized mother, and the revolutionary thinker Rosa Luxemburg. The two disparate women sit talking across class, circumstance, and time until one dissolves out of the painting series. For a time, Alice assumes center stage, sitting in her print dress and throwing rose petals at the viewer. Then, we see Rosa disappearing into the water, the site of her murder. These days, May has moved beyond her forebears and paints only the shimmering water replete with the ashes of her husband Rudolf. Faith Ringgold collaborated with her mother, Willie Posey, in sewing her early life-sized doll figures of people from Harlem, using an actual mother, not a symbolic one, to make her statement. Marilyn Lanfear has created sculptural tableaux about her family in Central Texas, using the symbolic language of furniture or clothing reconstructed in unexpected materials, such as lead or wood. Emma Amos made a series of wall hangings using laser transfer prints to tell her family's stories for an installation in Atlanta, Georgia. More recently, she posed with her daughter, India, to create photographic images wearing Ku Klux Klan costumes—a kind of political cross-dressing that demystified the terrorism of Emma's childhood. Lorraine O'Grady did a performance comparing the likeness of her dead sister with Cleopatra through photos and texts. Ora Lerman made a series of cryptic still life paintings bordered by a poetic text exploring her parents' diaspora from the Ukraine to Kentucky. Then, at one point, she was finished with her family and started making symbolic works about her own life. Diana Kurz, after painting loosely brushed nudes for a decade, suddenly made an intense series of oversized portraits and historic scenes based on the photos of family members from her native Vienna that perished in the Holocaust.

7. May Stevens, *Forming the Fifth International* 8. Lorraine O'Grady, *Sister IV, Miscegenated Family Album*

Other women sought to situate themselves within a community of artists by painting portraits of fellow women artists or by painting large tableau works showing groups of women artists and writers. I think these works are attempts to create a lineage. I remember seeing a photo of the suffragist Susan B. Anthony sitting at her desk in her lacy collar and satiny dress flanked by a wall full of photographs of her sister suffragists staring back at her. It was a satisfying image. I felt the same way when I would enter my great-grandmother Lillie's bedroom. The walls were crammed from floor to ceiling with photos of her kin, these relatives her seat of power. We children would whisper about a photo of our Aunt Ruby, her bare shoulders bordered with a diaphanous cloth, convinced that she was naked beyond the picture frame.

The works that feature large groups of women have usually been in the form of paintings or collages. Tomie Arai created a huge Cityarts mural in 1974 called *Wall of Respect for Women* showing the history of women on the Lower East Side in the form of a large tree. In ascending order, women are caring for children, washing clothes, cleaning, selling apples, working in the factories, and going on strike. The apex shows women of all colors in solidarity. Emma Amos made a series of small watercolor portraits of women friends and colleagues that she showed in a gridded installation at the Studio Museum in Harlem. At the opening, we all posed for a group photo. Faith Ringgold painted at least two quilts with various women shown grouped outdoors. There is a party atmosphere of the smiling participants framed inside an ornate pieced border. In my *Roomful of Mothers*, we women from *Heresies* form a community by proxy with our mothers as generational stand-ins. Mary Beth Edelson amended history by making a collaged *Some Living American Women Artists/Last Supper* in 1971. Georgia O'Keeffe stands in the place of Christ, and a rowdy group of women artists crowd the table around her and fill the picture's borders. Sylvia Sleigh kept adding to her series of women artists—some were painted as closely framed

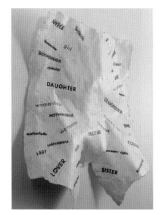 

9. Sharon Gilbert, *Etymography* 10. Emma Amos, *The Gift* (44 watercolor paintings of sister artists and friends)

faces while others stood next to their artworks or posed as goddesses. Sylvia also made two well-known large-scale paintings of the founding women of A.I.R. Gallery and SOHO20 Gallery. These works are often paired with May Stevens's symbolic 1978 painting, *Mysteries & Politics*. A very young Harmony, Lucy, and others are silhouetted in color against May's giant black-and-white painting of Rosa Luxemburg. But Joan Semmel broke the mold of this fledgling canon by painting a horizontal three-panel portrait of a faculty meeting, called *Faculty Frieze*. The viewer is across the table from a group of male professors intently listening to an unseen speaker, and the lone woman, Joan, is also unseen; her role as the invisible instructor is a wry commentary on her position at school.

Judy Chicago's *Dinner Party* was similar in intent to Mary Beth's *Last Supper*—to place women artists in an historical context of our choosing. Mary Beth's collage is modest in scale, but it has a kind of energized participation with the faces of the women artists obviously cut out and pasted over those of the disciples, interlopers to the party. Judy's party is the opposite of Mary Beth's: elaborate, grand, pristine, gorgeous, intricately crafted, empty, and serene. No one is invited to sit down. The winners of history have been selected, and we are there to pay them homage. Judy had worked with many women to create the *Dinner Party*, but not as collaborators. Her model was the Renaissance workshop with a master and pupils; and it had some of the political pitfalls I sensed in the *Artist and the Quilt* project. There was a lot of trepidation among other artists when the *Dinner Party* came to the Brooklyn Museum in 1980. I might even call it resentment. Here was the most famous installation by a woman artist and it had finally come to New York. We artists held back at first, and then trooped over in ones or twos. When my line finally snaked into the gallery, I surprised myself by the rush of pleasure I felt from the beauty of this installation.

11. Mary Beth Edelson, *Some Living American Women Artists/Last Supper* 12. Kathy Grove, *The Other Series: After Durer*

People used to remark on the packed look of the pages of *Heresies*. We would talk about leaving some white space on the page or creating a quieter, more refined sense of space. But we had so much to say and too many people to include. The same applies to these burgeoning family and social histories. We made artworks about our mothers and grandmothers, but rarely about our fathers. May used her father as an archetype in the *Big Daddy* series protesting the Vietnam War. Kazuko used a subtle photo of her elderly father in several artworks. He is seen only from the back, nude, passing through a doorway. Ora painted her father's artifacts from the Ukraine in an effort to understand the family's exile. Catalina occasionally utilized phrases found in the poems of her father, Nicanor Parra, in her artwork; *Let the Pope Pay the Ex(t)ernal Debt*, one collage read. Males are there aplenty in artworks from the seventies and eighties, but usually simply as penises or as provocative nudes. Sylvia is the exception. She painted over sixty portraits of her husband Lawrence, and her portraits of male nudes depict them as beloved individuals.

In 1990, Miriam Schapiro made a series in which she repainted Mexican artist Frida Kahlo's artworks. In one painting, Miriam and Kahlo are depicted sharing a studio, but I doubt that Kahlo would have been comfortable with their collaboration. This series was an extension of Miriam's physical appropriations of anonymous women's needlework to make her earlier large-scale collages and an indication of Kahlo's emergent status as an icon.

Kahlo and O'Keeffe still hold the monopoly on the Famous Women Artists title. Both women were married to powerful (philandering) artists who promoted their careers; some writers consider both artists bisexual; and neither had children. Kahlo painted herself as an icon of suffering within a Latin context of healing art. If you visit her house in Mexico City, her extensive collection of *recuerdos*, the small tin votive paintings meant to be placed in church as a prayer for recovery, greet you on her walls. O'Keeffe's flower paintings are also seen as portraits or

 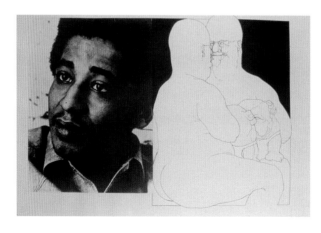 

13. Catalina Parra, *Let the Pope…* 14. May Stevens, *Big Daddy & George Jackson* 15. Kazuko, book page, *Body*

icons despite her vehement denial. Her second New York exhibit was preceded by her partner Stieglitz's exhibit of her nude photographs, and the flowers have become stand-ins for O'Keeffe's sexuality. Both women continue to fill the role of woman as symbol even though that was not their artistic intent.

After thousands of years as goddess, muse, mother, or drudge, it is daunting to break the mold and emerge as creators of images and ideas. Some women artists chose to embrace the symbols, and thus the proliferation of Great Goddesses. Others decided to play with history by taking the road of Mary Beth and inserting ourselves after the fact. Kathy Grove made a series of beautifully reproduced large-scale photographs of famous paintings in which she did the opposite: she removed the symbolic woman, leaving a blank. Cindy Sherman created a series of photo tableaux in the early eighties in which she tried on every possible female stereotype and deflated them with her witty reenactments. Sherman is one of the feminist artists who expressed her conviction only in her artwork, but not through acting in concert with other women artists.

Most of us read Linda Nochlin's *Art and Sexual Politics: Why Have There Been No Great Women Artists?*. Nochlin described how women artists from the past were usually associated with artist-husbands or artist-fathers and how few women artists there had been. Many of the women associated with our various groups had artist or writer partners: Nancy Spero and painter Leon Golub, Cecilia Vicuña and her then-partner Claudio Bertoni, Louise Bourgeois and curator Robert Goldwater, Sylvia Sleigh and critic/curator Lawrence Alloway, art critic Arlene Raven and sculptor Nancy Grossman, Joyce Kozloff and writer/photographer Max Kozloff, Lucy Lippard and ex-husband painter Robert Ryman, sculptors Ana Mendieta and Carl Andre, painters Edith Isaac-Rose and Bea Kreloff, Mary Beth Edelson and Robert Stackhouse, Miriam Schapiro and Paul Brach, performance artist Donna Henes and photographer Sarah Jenkins, painters May Stevens

16. Sylvia Sleigh, *Invitation...* (detail) 17. Miriam Schapiro, *Love's Labor* 18. Kathy Grove, *The Other Series: After Delacroix*

and Rudolf Baranik, Pat Passlof and Milton Resnick, and Willem and Elaine DeKooning. This is the short list. I followed the same pattern with Roger. Did we prove the persistence of Nochlin's thesis? Were these men or women in our lives more powerful than we were? I would call these partners confederates, but there was definitely a pattern. Bernice Steinbaum and Paul Brach curated a show about the same patterning for Steinbaum Gallery in 1984 with an overlapping list of artist-couples (*1 + 1 = 2*). Curator Melinda Wortz observed in the catalogue, "using the theme of couples as an exhibition organizing device opens up new avenues for looking at art. It suggests that we pay attention to connections and relatedness among art works, rather than uniqueness and originality."[1]

In 1981, California performance artist Suzanne Lacy had come to town and invited all of us feminist artists to a meeting. The flier read, "How long has it been since women artists have all met together in one room?" In fact, it hadn't been long at all, so we were surprised at her assumptions. But most of us admired Suzanne's work and came to meet her. Lacy was known for her choreographed performances that involved large groups of women. Her work evoked a stylized halftime at a football game or an elegant political demonstration with Suzanne in the role of cheerleader turned griot or singer of historical tales. Instead of celebrating male power or military victory, she honored the power of marginalized women. In her 1984 performance *Whisper, The Waves, The Wind*, 160 elderly women dressed in white marched onto the beach and sat down at 40 card tables draped with white cloths. Their prerecorded conversations were played from a neighboring cliff and the audience descended among the floating words to mingle on the beach with the narrators.

We sat on folding chairs in a circle for Suzanne's meeting and talked together. She quickly realized her mistake and joined us as simply another feminist artist or organizer, relinquishing

19. Faith Ringgold, *key to The French Collection* 20. Faith Ringgold, *Sunflower Quilting Bee at Arles*

her role as arbiter of disparate groups. She was from California, and the women's art movement there differed from our movement in New York City, partly because of physical conditions. We lived in a city where people walked on the street or crammed together on the subway or suffered the summer heat by escaping to the front stoop. You had to drive to meet anyone in California; things there seemed more purposeful and planned. New York lent itself to street actions, exhibits in vacant windows, fliers on a post, and words scribbled on a billboard. We ran into each other. It only took a few hours for a crowd to pour out to protest a catastrophe or for everyone to meet going from one opening to another. Most of us were also active in other movements as well and didn't confine ourselves to women's issues alone. The women's art movement in New York never remained tidily in one corner.

21. Clarissa Sligh, *Reframing the Past* show card 22. Grace Graupe-Pillard, *The Wonder Women Wall*

7

When Things Fall Apart, Other Things Come Together

Linda Peer and I were walking across the Brooklyn Bridge, heading back to our Brooklyn neighborhood after a *Heresies* meeting in Lower Manhattan. It was 1985. Brooklyn was still considered the other side of the intellectual tracks, and this magnificent bridge was quite a track to cross. Whenever I felt closed in by the crowds in the city streets, I would walk to the middle of the Brooklyn Bridge and feel a momentary sense of expansive space. You climb a wide footbridge that takes you above the traffic and ascend to the apex of the curve, standing between the tall arches inside a sort of squared gazebo where you can look up or down the East River. If you let your eye follow your mind past the tip of Manhattan, you sail straight into the Atlantic Ocean and then choose to cross all the way to Europe or veer back to Africa. I had actually done that on the Queen Mary as a student embarking on my Fulbright year in England. As we neared the Verrazano Bridge, it seemed impossible that the ship could find a passage under the curves of that bridge. But soon, we had sailed free of visible land.

1. *Heresies* issue #20 cover 2. Martha Wilson, *Nancy Reagan...* performance 3. Janet Pfunder and Janey Washburn, show card

We were talking about the meeting. "I feel like there are two groups: you and Ellen Lanyon versus Kay Kenny and Sandy De Sando. But I have the feeling that most people want *Heresies* to continue," Linda said. Lucy had remarked that she had been in *Heresies* when it had worked, and it clearly wasn't working now. "If we could somehow stop being under this weight of promises for future issues. I don't want us to be mortgaged to issues we can't produce." One collective was still working on the Mothers, Mags, & Movie Stars issue and soon another group, with Emma Amos at its core, was meeting about a Satire issue to pair with it. Emma described our issue as vapid. "What's vapid about class?"

Heresies had moved out of the Cable Building into more modest offices that we shared with another arts group. The magazine had a small paid staff. In 1985, the staff included Sandy, who did the day-to-day office work, Kay, the office manager, and Sue Heinemann, who was in charge of the production of the magazine. All were part time and no one supervised their work. We simply noticed when things got done or when they didn't. I think it was Ellen who started questioning what Sandy was actually doing. If *Heresies* couldn't control the staff, Ellen reasoned, we should simply fold. I agreed that we should confront Sandy, but it was awkward to have this discussion. The staff members were also on the collective and had a vote on any decisions we made. No one wanted to exercise authority within our horizontal structure. After the criticisms of Sandy's job performance, nothing was decided. Things were left the same, but with hurt feelings in the center. Ellen and I were seen as the bad guys for raising this issue.

I was riding home on the subway one afternoon, reading Tzvetan Todorov's *The Conquest of America*, and fell into an impassioned conversation with a stranger about mixed-race identity and the impact of the Spanish conquest on the Americas. As we parted, we introduced ourselves. She was the archaeologist Elizabeth Wetherford, a member of the first *Heresies* collective

4. Chris Costan, exhibit announcement 5. Avenue B Gallery group show 6. Linda Peer, *Untitled* sculpture

whom I had never met. Later, I told Lucy about this encounter: "I often meet people on the subway through reading books."

Some women from the collective were involved with the new galleries opening on the Lower East Side. Linda Peer was showing her ceramic sculptures at Gracie Mansion; Chris Costan had an exhibit scheduled for Avenue B Gallery. Chris brought the artist/dealer from that gallery to see my studio. He seemed to be flaunting his Texas accent and could barely detect my own. He didn't like my use of materials. He described one of his own works composed of stuffed rabbits and other artifacts and toys. "It's really a piece about dust," he solemnly told me.

Most of us were working on the *Choice Works* show for the *PAD/D State of Mind/State of the Arts* events. The openings were designed to coincide with Ronald Reagan's State of the Union address, just before my birthday. I was making a sculpture about my abortion in Guinea in the shape of a full-sized wardrobe with double doors. The form was based on the chifforobe in Mother Gladys's bedroom with one side opening into my story and the other into Aunt Opal's story about her baby Bobbie. Mother blamed Grandmother for the infant's death. "People let sick babies die." Roger built the wardrobe for me, and Kate came over to help me sew the tall paper panels into the doorframes. I started looking through my journals from Guinea and my annotated desk calendar in which I alluded to my abortion in code, never directly describing the hemorrhaging. A Danish entomologist friend in N'Zérékoré had obtained the leaves Guerzé women used as an abortifacient and sent them to me with a recipe. I found his letter. "You must boil the leaves a long time, then sift? the water? and drink a glass or two. Bonne appetite!" I felt like I was talking to my twenty-one-year-old self, boiling her/my experience into visual form, cutting out photos and handling my own images like paper dolls. I ended up with a numbered list of fourteen

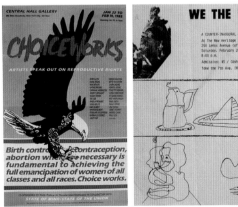

7. Kathie Brown, *Choice Works* poster 8. *Counter Inaugural Cabaret* poster 9. *State of the Mind/State of the Union*

phrases—to synthesize the fourteen weeks of searching for a resolution—and printed them on both sides of one door.

We had a *Heresies* meeting at my Warren Street place while I was working on the wardrobe. Josely liked it even in its stark, unfinished form.

One side had an open drawer at its base that I filled with an actual speculum saved from work at the clinic and three duplicates in various soft materials. I think I am the only person who has ever beaded this uncomfortable medical instrument tightly sewn shut with an ornate web of beaded and knotted strings. I started painting the piece only two weeks before the opening. I often feel an artwork is almost finished once I have created the form, only to work and rework the paintings for weeks after an exhibition. I completed the side about my abortion, but left the second door closed on the story about Opal's unwanted baby.

I dream that I am in a room with many women. The movie star Elizabeth Taylor is there; her body is covered with long white hair like a fur suit, with red spots on her stomach and pink nipples showing through the hair. I tell someone, "She got a chinchilla implant."

Roger and I delivered *Opening Doors Work* to the gallery with the oil paint still wet. Lucy passed on the street as we were unloading the sculpture and rushed to help bring it inside. She left us at the elevator just as a flower deliveryman appeared, laden with bouquets. We all three struggled to fit into the elevator—no one giving an inch between the flowers and the wet wardrobe. I got the giggles and couldn't stop laughing. During the opening, a visitor stuffed his coat into the corner between my sculpture and the wall. I noticed the look on his face when he discovered the pink paint streaking his jacket as he left.

Few artists have made artworks about abortion or contraception. The opening was subdued; viewers seemed uncomfortable. Susan Crowe had welded an armored torso that she

10. Sabra Moore, *Opening Doors Work* (all), beaded speculum 11. Hand 12. Closed doors 13. Opal's door open

placed inside a fence labeled "U.S. Government Property." Christy Rupp's oversized drawing of a woman with a coat hanger was painful to view. Paulette Nenner showed one of her crucified coyote figures. Mimi Smith made word clocks with time running out. Art critic Kim Levin mentioned Sue Coe's graphic poster about an abortion clinic bombing in a review. Sue's black, white, and red paintings are expressive examples of social realism; Candace Hill-Montgomery told me she had dreamed of Sue's print emblazoned with "$5,000" across its surface. Some of the editors I worked with at American Heritage Publishers came to the opening. "Are the artworks in the show for sale?" one asked. "Of course, but who's going to buy a seven-foot wardrobe about abortion?" "Someone with a lot of money could." The evening after the opening was my birthday. I returned to the gallery to finish the interior side of the sculpture, sitting on the floor in the empty room, hand painting a text of a dream: *I walk along a Venetian red beach with red water carrying a tiny multicolored casket. I meet an old man; his name is Ashanti. He says. "Give it to me. It's mine." I give him the casket.* Roger painted a birthday card with me stomping on worms—capitalist worms, ringworms, sexist worms; the worms are shouting, "Ouch!"

Josely and Kathie had organized events during the show. They used my title for *Speaking Pictures*, a poetry reading by some of us artists. I read poems addressed to Mother Gladys and to the fetus I aborted, projecting family slides against the window/curtain left over from the *Classified* exhibit. The window distorted the images as I read, silhouetted in shadow. But Candace's work stirred the most controversy with her interpretation of the theme. She did a performance piece, first showing a slide of herself not moving followed by an image of a full-bodied woman dancing to music. "I thought this was a show about creativity and reproduction," she said coolly, and then introduced a young man who laid out his painted T-shirts for us to buy.

  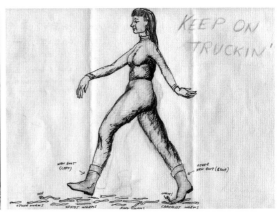

14. Sharon Niemeczyk, *Heresies* #14 15. Sabra at work on *Opening Doors Work* 16. Roger Mignon, *Keep On Trucking*

Later, she commented on my reading. "At first, when I saw your slides, I thought we were doing something similar."

I was working on a new magazine, *American Heritage of Invention & Technology*, and had almost completed the photo research for the first issue when an editor warned me that my work would not be credited on the masthead. Only the male staff editor and designer would be named. I went to see Byron Dobell, the managing editor and former editor for *Harper's Magazine*, and listened while he explained the rationale. "It's corporate policy; you're not on staff." "It's your prerogative, but I have choices too," I said. "I didn't know it was a stipulation of the job. You're one of the two or three best picture editors I've worked with; I'm not a fool." He relented. His wife was from Tennessee with a similar background to mine. "I forgot about the different value system of people like you." Maybe I was learning how to wear Betsy's visibility cloak.

Josely had suggested we organize a project together. We started meeting at her brownstone to develop ideas. Her house had that peculiar undertone of ease that comes from class security, though I was slow to recognize the signs until our trip together to Brazil to install our show some years later. The parlor floor was spare—a white crocheted Brazilian hammock hung in one corner of the room near a seating area with brown leather couches and a glass table. There were very few books and no clutter, unlike my place. Josely had a devoted maid, Maria Inez, who would serve us snacks and who also, I learned, helped make her artworks. She and her husband, Ernest Chanes, considered themselves socialists and were activists in Cuba support groups. They were physical opposites. Josely was short and intense with curly reddish hair. He was tall with a beard edging his chin like an Amish farmer; Catalina Parra told me her kids called him the Pilgrim.

17. Ilona Granet, metal sign, *Curb Your Animal Instinct* 18. Sabra reading, *Choice Works* performance

Reconstruction Project was still fresh for both of us; that exhibit incorporated a historical event into our contemporary experience. Now, we both wanted to organize an international show for artists to collaborate directly about current issues. Josely suggested pairing Brazilian and American artists, drawing on artists from her native country. We quickly decided on an obvious title, Connections Project, adding the Latin word Conexus because "in Portuguese, Connections Project sounds like plumbing." We thought about the idea of letter writing or sending out a kind of information net to see what issues mattered most to artists in these two places, and then we came up with a questionnaire. "Don't be intimidated," we wrote, "We have tried to include the entire world." We asked artists to rank their five favorite issues out of a list of fifteen. "What is your fantasy &/or reality about. . ." each question stated, followed by an issue. As the votes came in from the artists we had invited, some issues quickly evaporated. No one wanted to make art, for example, about the penal system, money, the media, or power, but many women were interested in the themes of death, race, environment, shelter, and three or four other ideas. Some suggested ways to refine the concepts: sex and beauty got absorbed into body; war became part of death. May Stevens selected the theme of religion with one caveat: "I can't stand the topic religion. Please call it spirit—so it has as much beauty and validity as body, birth, etc." Some artists balked. Liliana Porter refused at first because she thought she had to write an essay rather than create an artwork.

The New York City Women's Caucus for Art (NYC/WCA) was also organizing shows for another upcoming national conference in New York City, a series called Liberty. . . And the Pursuit of Liberty, based on the format of the 1982 Views by Women Artists project. Josely and I were looking for a space for Connections Project/Conexus as an independent exhibition during the same conference and found ourselves competing with the WCA for venues, always losing out to

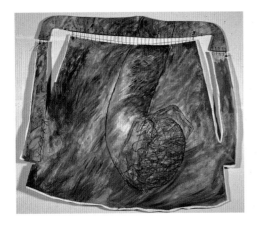 

19. Sabra Moore (both), Gladys Apron #2 with Nest (series of four) 20. Gladys Apron #1

the larger group's effort. I was still active with the local board, but not with the steering committee that was organizing *Liberty*. I was being attacked in writing for my work on the board; a friend of Annie accused us of being an "elite group" incapable of "moving forward." I defended myself. "Rather than 'holding on,' I chose to not be involved at all in the planning and development of this project. . . . I do mind that, having chosen to build on my concept, *Views* became a negative example, to outdo, rather than a positive example to make grow."

I had arranged to do another window installation at Windows on White shortly after the opening of *Choice Works*. I was still thinking about my visits with Mother Gladys and the pathos of her failing health. My nephew had photographed her lying in bed in her familiar room, her arm curled behind her head as she lay against the pillows and the covers crumpled around her. At first, this photo seemed sad, but then it assumed a classical form in my mind; her gesture looked like that of Michelangelo's *Pietà*. She kept asking, "Why are you photographing me in bed?" That became a mantra for paper text curtains in the triple store windows. Mother Gladys had given me an apron, and I made four painted paper apron replicas in various materials. I brought in straw, smooth logs of driftwood, the little beds from the SOHO20 Gallery windows, and the full-sized Xerox quilt made for the Atlantic Gallery show. At night, the pieced quilt and painted aprons glowed against the backlit straw and wood like stained glass. Between working on the installation and my day job, I often arrived late to our weekly *Heresies* meetings. Lucy said I was the "latest person she knows." I wrote in my journals. "Despite the conflicts, I feel *Heresies* meetings center me and give me context."

My landlord had sold the Warren Street building while we were working on *Choice Works*, and I was preparing to move into Roger's loft on Pearl Street. My sunny apartment had been rent

21. Sabra Moore, installation, Windows on White (all), *Gladys Apron* 22. Triple windows 23. *Xerox Book Pages with Gladys Apron*

controlled; thus, the harassment during *Views by Women Artists* to make me leave. I agreed to be bought out by the new owners, tucking money into the bank, hoping for land.

The east face of the Pearl Street building had indented spaces designed for a row of windows that had never been installed. Roger had once chipped out a small trial opening into one of these window blanks and then covered the hole with cardboard. A male starling found the hole and would practice his full-throated song each morning, facing the sun. This gave us an idea. Roger and I spent many weekends after I had signed the contract to move working on his loft, chipping bricks out of the closed window spaces, stacking the bricks into piles, and sorting between boxes of mortar and reusable bricks, bringing in a wall of light. We were still working when it was time for my move; the plastic we used to temporarily cover the window spaces kept billowing in the wind.

Everyone was encouraging me; I was leaving the sanctuary where I had fled C fifteen years earlier. Sue Heinemann said, "It's nice to try something different in a new space." Donna Henes wanted to come photograph what she called "shrines," the arrangements of objects and photos scattered around the apartment. In the midst of packing, Mother called to tell me that my grandparents had moved out of the nursing home and were back in their house. I called them. "We're living high off the hog," Daddy Chess said. "I wasn't happy; I kept thinking about rats gnawing my quilts," Mother Gladys added. "Are the quilts all right?" "I haven't looked." I told her about my move. "Are you going to live alone?" "No, I'll share a place with Roger." "I haven't met him." "Yes, you have. You've forgotten."

Alone in the apartment with all the boxes packed, I touched the empty walls and I touched the floor, trying to circle the energy and happiness I had felt living there back into my own body. Now, it looked no different from the many apartments I had painted. Roger and I went

 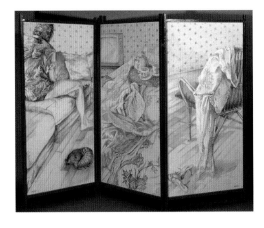 

24. Catalina Parra, *Welcome Home!* 25. Bibi Lenĉek, *Untitled*, screen 26. Catalina Parra, book page, *Race*

to Josely's opening a few days after I moved into the loft. Marithelma was at the gallery, freshly returned from giving a lecture in Kansas. She had never seen the Great Plains, and the flat horizontal vista had made her physically ill. We saw Catalina, and I talked about my move. "You put the magic there and you took it with you," she said.

Sharon Gilbert, Bibi Lenĉek, and I, cohorts from *Views by Women Artists*, were organizing a show called *Latitudes of Time*, which was scheduled for the fall in the former Huntington Hartford Museum, now City Gallery under the aegis of Organization of Independent Artists (OIA). Sharon gave birth during this project as well. Elena had been born during *Views by Women Artists*, and now, a boy, Elery, was about to arrive. We had asked Lawrence Alloway to write a catalogue statement, but when he got our exhibition description, he refused. We three had all contributed ideas to the concept and, in true democratic fashion, had listed every idea—*cosmic time, recorded time, recycled time, transformed time, big time, standard time, waste of time, golden time, time out, no time, on time, timeless, out of time, time bomb.* Lawrence disagreed with the concept of cosmic time. He felt that cosmic time did not exist. "I could write a review. A review can be an argument, but a catalogue statement is a representation of the show."

I was getting more comfortable in our Pearl Street place, though I was still adjusting to the noise and the dangerous passage home from the subway at night. It felt natural to share a place with Roger, and many friends had lofts nearby. Linda Peer lived around the corner, and Carol Sun, who had recently submitted page art for the Mothers, Mags, & Movie Stars issue, was down the street. One afternoon, I walked back over to my quiet haven on Warren Street to retrieve a bird feeder I had left in the garden and revisit my old studio. The new owners were architects, so they had been renovating. All the ornate moldings on the ceiling were gone, but my painting wall was still there with its fragments of gessoed lines and bits of paint colors. They had taken down

27. Sharon Gilbert, birth announcement for Elena Floris 28. *Latitudes of Time* curated by Gilbert, Lenĉek, and Moore

the plasterboard wall near where I had slept and had made a strange discovery. Hidden inside the wall was a canvas covered with blue calligraphic writing in Arabic, probably written by an Egyptian who had once owned this house. They had it translated. It was a plan based on various configurations of the number 7 and a grand scheme tying the house's address, 232 Warren Street, to the birth of Jesus. That cosmic view had been nestled near my head as I slept all those years.

Kate and Frankie both had artist residencies at the Helene Wurlitzer Foundation of New Mexico in Taos for the summer. I had applied for a residency for the following year, so Roger and I drove down to New Mexico to visit the foundation, finding our friends on the verge of breaking up their long relationship. I kept thinking about ideas for an artwork for *Latitudes* as we visited petroglyphs and made our own migration in reverse among archaeological sites, moving from Bandelier to Chaco Canyon to Mesa Verde and over to attend corn dances at the contemporary pueblos of Jemez and Santa Ana. Mother Gladys was about to celebrate her eighty-fifth birthday in a year filled with my grandparents' many migrations between their house and the nursing home. We got to Texas in time for the party. "We talk about you every day. We'll be in bed and Chess will say, 'I wonder if Sabra is in bed.' I'll say, 'I don't think so.'"

I had started a new project for American Heritage Publishers, doing the photo research for *Pride of Place*, a companion book to the television series on architecture by Robert Stern. I was at work one Monday morning when Josely called me. Ana Mendieta had jumped out a window the day before, she told me, falling thirty-four stories and killing herself. "Everywhere I would go lately [to see granting agencies], Ana had just been. You never know." By evening, we learned that her husband, Carl Andre, had been arrested. Every woman in our circle had an opinion about Ana's death, and many women had divided loyalties. Carl had been an important voice in the art left as a minimalist—the movement that radically broke with painterly expressionism—and a

29. Roger Mignon photograph, *Sabra at Chaco Canyon doorway* 30. Ana Mendieta. *Untitled* (*Silueta* series)

social activist. He had been a founder of the Art Workers' Coalition. Some people did not want to believe he could have killed Ana. Carl had been their friend, their lover, their cohort, and their chess partner.

I was never a close friend, but I liked Ana, and when she died, I identified with her. She had been unlucky; I had been lucky. Only one of C's friends had been willing to believe me when I called for help: the oldest friend who had known him at college. But he had comforted C, not me. The others acted like I was crazy and refused to believe that he was detaining me, trying to strangle me, drawing a tombstone on the wall with my name, stalking me, and threatening me with guns. Faith Ringgold called me. "This will be a test of the art world. Will they turn against someone who is famous? I know a black painter who stabbed his wife twenty-six times. He's out after one year in a mental institution. He's doing fine. In my opinion, Carl should be pushed out a window."

But Carl was not pushed out a window. He got bailed out of jail by Frank Stella, and he was there, in a corner, at Ana's memorial. I wore a red Chinese blouse to her memorial. I couldn't wear black—the everyday art world's uniform. My grandfather had died of a heart attack when I was seventeen, and I wore my favorite red sweater to his funeral as well. Red gives heart. Someone had prepared a wonderful slide show of Ana's work for her memorial. May Stevens came over, crying, to say that Ana had become one of her own *siluetas*; "[she] fell like a cat, fell and hid, alone on another roof." As I was leaving the memorial, Patricia Jones gave me two gladiolas—one red and one white—from the big bouquets flanking her photo. "But then you have to press them," I said. "No, enjoy them, let them fade, think of Ana—that's why I love flowers." Patricia understood the symbolism of flowers for a funeral better than I.

31., 32. Ana Mendieta (both), *Untitled* (Earth-Body works, Caumsett State Park, Long Island)

We were still working on *Heresies's* Mothers, Mags & Movie Stars; now, we had to add a memorial statement for Ana. I suggested that we write something about violence against women, but all the other collective members got upset. "We can't! He hasn't been indicted. We don't know," Lucy said. "Someone overheard two women at the memorial say, 'Let's lynch him.'" Others talked about "innocent until proven guilty." We ended up dedicating the issue to Ana, "who fell to her death in suspicious circumstances on September 8," and focusing on the importance of her artwork and her contributions to *Heresies*.

I called Josely to tell her about the collective's response. Some women had been invited to a meeting at Carrie Rickey's loft with Martha Bashford, the assistant district attorney, to gather information about Carl's patterns of behavior towards women. The prosecutor needed our help. "People often feel sympathy for someone accused of murder; his suffering is visible, the murder victim is dead." Ana's sister Raquel was there, the poet Jayne Cortez, Nancy Spero, Donna Henes, Ruby Rich, Ana's Cuban friends whom I had never met, and others; all of us trying earnestly to recall any bit of information that would help build a case towards indictment. After one exchange of stories, someone joked that they should just indict all the minimalists for their treatment of women. Martha Bashford had opposed letting Carl out on bail. "Where could this man go?" his lawyer argued, referring to the fame of his sculptures. "He could go two hundred miles upstate and no one would recognize him," she replied. She told us that most suicides that jump from buildings wear a lot of clothes, and Ana was only wearing underpants. "Only very psychotic people jump nude, and Ana doesn't fit that pattern." She also felt that if they were arguing, Ana would have grabbed a robe. There were so many small details that made us doubt that she had jumped—her small stature versus Carl's bear-like build, her fear of heights and nervousness about the windows in their thirty-fourth floor apartment, and her strong nature, her

33. Ana Mendieta, *Untitled* 34. *Heresies* issue #18 dedication page to Ana 35. Ana Mendieta, *Untitled* (incised leaf)

ambition, and her artistic success. In the recorded 911 call, Carl is heard saying, "My wife is an artist, and I'm an artist, and we had a quarrel about the fact that I was more, eh, exposed to the public than she was. And she went to the bedroom, and I went after her, and she went out the window,"[1] like Hannah's little bird in reverse. I don't know if our leads helped, but Carl was indicted. Later, he was acquitted in a non-jury trial. Carl is still famous. Ana is famous now too. She has probably won their argument about fame. For years, I carried a set of small cards I had made (the size of a name card) with, "We remember Ana Mendieta," in English and Spanish, framing one of her *siluetas*. The card was reversible. If one encountered a Carl Andre sculpture in a museum or gallery, you could simply drop the card on top of his horizontal work and an image of Ana's *silueta* would land facing up.

A few weeks after Ana's death, friends seemed to be walking around like they had swallowed canaries. A show was in the air. Guerilla Girls had surfaced as a new voice, the self-described "conscience of the art world," making midnight forays into the streets downtown to paste up their witty commentaries on sexism. Now, they were presenting a show at the Paladium nightclub, featuring *Some Great Women Artists*. I was not included. I went to the show with Lucy, softening my feelings a bit. "I think Mary Beth Edelson organized this," I said. Then, the canary grin, "No one is supposed to tell who is doing this, but it's not Mary Beth." And we walked into the exhibit facing a big Mary Beth painting on the wall. I ran into Nancy Spero. "Where's your piece?" "I'm not in the show." May came over (May was in the show, Sandy was in the show, and Vivian was in the show; nearly everyone I knew was in the show). "What do you think about the show?" "Partly, I can't separate my feelings about Sandy from the show; partly, I like it; partly, it's elitist, using the women's movement to get the media's attention. They never come to democratically

36. Guerrilla Girls postering, *What Do These Artists Have in Common?* 37. Mary Beth Edelson, *Coming Round*

organized events." But May was not deterred. Sandy directed the entire hanging, she told me. "She learned from hanging all those *Heresies* shows; she commands respect."

I used to buy glass for framing my drawings from an old man on Atlantic Avenue, Mr. Block. His father had been a glazier before him, and his little shop was filled with sixty years of smoky clutter. When I lived on Warren Street, I would walk to his place, and he would send me home with my oversized piece of glass nestled inside an oak carrier that resembled an elegant picture stand. Later, I would return his father's handmade tool. We learned that Mr. Block was closing his shop, so Roger and I went by to wish him well and present him with a bottle of Scotch, his favorite drink. After his retirement, I would stop occasionally and ask the storekeeper next door for news of the glazier. He was found dead one day in his tiny apartment. When the police investigated, they discovered that Mr. Block had been quite wealthy, with money concealed throughout his modest room, and a neat row of unopened bottles of Scotch lining one wall.

Roger and I had been working every weekend on the loft, and my studio was at last finished. I was making a clothesline sculpture for *Latitudes* using images of my childhood house left over from *House Book*.

We had visited that house in the summer, and Roger had photographed me talking with a former neighbor next to the backyard clothesline. I repeated frames of that photo on one side of a tiny photocopier accordion book I was making with a discrete text about using the washeteria. One side was about washing and the reverse was about ironing. I planned to give away copies of *Wash & Iron* at the show, mounting a box of books next to a mannequin hand holding a wire net bag. Visitors could take a book and leave a coin or a word in return (*Give & Take*). I gave away fifty-six books at the opening. Faith Ringgold was in the show and she introduced me to Marilyn Lanfear, newly arrived from Texas and the only other person in the room who had been

38. *Guerrilla Girls* Palladium exhibit card 39-40. Sabra Moore (both), *Give & Take* (left & right) 41. *Wash & Iron* book

to a washeteria, where the women washed their clothes in big tin tubs by hand, wrung them out on a wringer, and took them home to hang out on the clothesline to dry.

Mother Gladys's dementia waxed and waned, and with her poor health, she made more frequent stays in the nursing home. "She's lost her mind. She thinks we're living down in the country in one of those houses done burned down." I called them at home. "Gal, it's got so I can't make her mind." "I never promised him I'd mind. He is always telling me, when I won't do something, I promised him I'd mind. When we married, I wouldn't have done it if I'd had to mind. All I remember saying is 'I do.'" Mother visited us for Thanksgiving. She came alone; she had broken off her relationship with Larry. The landlord had let the boiler run out of oil, so we had no heat in the loft. Roger and I scurried around setting up electric heaters to keep her warm. Mother had only seen my family-based artwork in slides and now she was seeing the actual works. She had already reacted to an article Ora wrote for *Arts Magazine*, featuring four artists whose work deals with loss. Ora had included the window installation for *Gladys Dress/Gladys Story* and had made a few factual errors about my family. "It's an insult to a Southern person," Mother insisted. She looked in silence at the wardrobe sculpture about my abortion, but cried when she saw the gentle clothesline sculpture I had made for *Latitudes of Time* and objected to my mentioning the washeteria in *Wash & Iron*. "Your work moves me, but I see a lot of hurt. I want your work to be lovely."

We were finally pasting up the Mothers, Mags, & Movie Stars issue; I was meeting in the evenings after work at Kathie Brown's typography shop to help design the pages with others and work out the last details of the editorial statement. We were using a photocopier version of *Roomful of Mothers* for the editorial page. In our statement, Lucy wrote, "We were sad to discover that we were not influenced by art." But I countered this idea in my journal, listing the art I saw

42. Marilyn Lanfear, *Pink Organdy Blouse* 43. Ora Lerman, *Geese Lay Golden Egg*s 44. Marilyn Lanfear, *Diana's Huipil...*

growing up—"gourd dolls, reproductions in the Bible, quilts, fabric patterns, signs, movie mag-azines, the aesthetics of food, the arrangement of rooms, family photos." Roger was in Florida; his mother was in the hospital with a rapidly growing cancerous brain tumor. Our Mothers issue felt painfully pertinent.

It was almost Christmas when I flew to Florida to be with Roger as his mother lapsed into a coma. He had kept vigil at her bedside by photographing her. "At times, I feel I am her," he told me on the phone. This time, I couldn't draw as the plane flew over the fields of Virginia and headed down the coast. I sat writing out a grim list of murders and deaths in my journal, thinking about violence as a commonplace occurrence. Ana and Carl were first on my list, and then Grandmother's second husband Chester Bryant and Opal's baby Bobbie. Even Daddy had accidentally inflicted a violent death before he met one himself—a young man riding a motorcy-cle had been killed one night crossing in front of his train. Lucy's father, a doctor, had also had an odd brush with murder. He was sitting in a coffee shop and noticed a despondent man at the counter putting colored pills into his coffee. He recognized poison and jumped up, knocking over the coffee cup and interrupting a suicide. A year later, he saw a photo of this same man in the newspaper being arrested for killing another person.

Carol Sun invited us artists in Dumbo to celebrate the Year of the Tiger, 1986, at her loft near the bridge. We needed a celebration. We shot off fireworks in the snow to chase away the evil spirits—our efforts echoed by the noisy conflagrations in Chinatown just across the river. I ran into her neighbor, Rebecca Ballenger, who had helped with the publicity for *Views by Women Artists*, and we talked about the upcoming WCA conference in February. "You should have gone around lecturing about *Views* and about the MoMA demonstrations instead of Annie."

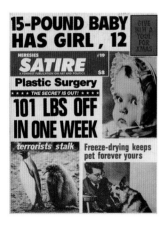  

45. *Heresies* issue #19 cover 46. Sabra Moore, *A Roomful of Mothers montage*, *Heresies* issue #18 47. Flier, *Heresies* issue #18

Although Susan Gill was the current NYC/WCA president, Betsy Damon was the conference chair and the issues of visibility were again present. The curators' names were on all the
exhibition cards, but none of the artists were listed. I was trying to negotiate among the competing camps; after all, Annie and I had been friends before all the crowing. But it was hard to attend
an event obviously patterned on *Views by Women Artists* that denigrated our contributions. I ran
into Faith in the hall. "This conference is a lot like the one you did." "It's exactly like the one I
did," I responded. "You set the standard," she said, "Everybody has to live up to that." I was appearing on a performance panel with Cecilia Vicuña, May Stevens, and Josely Carvalho—artists
whose work related to family or cultural issues. Cecilia had just returned from visiting her native
Chile after a long exile from the Pinochet regime. "The junta has been defeated culturally, but
not politically. That will take time. All our books were destroyed; our whole generation was killed
or dispersed in exile. Now, people are beginning to return. The young people receive us so gently." She stood in front of a darkened slide rattling a shell necklace, summoning the dead. She
had made a performance when she was in Chile, physically dissecting the word PARTICIPATION
(PARTICIPACIÓN) into parts on the ground, reconfiguring the letters to read YES TO PASSION
(PASIÓN), affirming life-giving Eros as a political act.

It took me many years to see that I also summon the dead with the work I have made
about my grandmothers. I think of myself as addressing these people, but Marina once pointed
out that most are dead. I showed slides with Mother Gladys, Daddy Chess, and Mother Gladys's quilts, reading poetry against the slides. In one photo, I am laughing on the porch with my
grandparents. It struck May Stevens as surprising that my grandmother was short and that my
grandfather had no hair on his bare chest. One poem was addressed to the fetus I had aborted.
"When I think of you, you would be twelve. . ." A mixed-blood woman from Virginia came up to me

48. Cecilia Vicuña, *Cementerio* 49. Carol Sun, *Maternity* 50.Cecilia Vicuña, *Precario/Precarious*, Exit Art

later that day as I was talking to Jaune Quick-To-See-Smith. She clasped my hand. "You were talking about a baby you lost or an abortion." "I was." "I had an abortion myself. I live in Virginia. I wanted to set up a consciousness-raising group to talk about this, but no one was willing." "You know," I said, "these are things we aren't supposed to say, and they are difficult to say, but when I've said them, people like you come up. I felt I did the right thing to have the abortion. But I still think about that person that didn't make it here." Now, we were both gripping hands. "A psychic helped me," she said, "These are spirits who aren't ready to be born yet."

Camille Billops hollered at me. "You were listed in an anthology of black women artists. I told them you're white." I felt embarrassed. "Don't worry. The Klan won't come after you." "It's not that. I don't want to claim a place that isn't mine." Vivian was standing with us. She knew what had happened with C. I found myself telling Camille about the Black Emergency Cultural Coalition and the shows organized by Henri Ghent. "It wasn't so common, in that period, for whites to show with blacks," she acknowledged. We all went into the conference dinner together, but I sensed that Vivian would have preferred sitting at the table with Betsy.

I dream that Ana Mendieta walks into a gallery where I am showing artwork. She is very playful and gay. "Sit down," she tells me, gesturing to a bench. She keeps bouncing up and down, making the floor sway. She starts arranging an assemblage with a huge sweater that hangs upside down. A baby boy is in the room and a man who promises to care for him. Ana and I walk outside down an exterior stairway into a dark snowy yard, talking intimately as if we share a secret. Armed men appear. They kill the boy. They kill Ana. I see her shadow fallen across the snow.

We had a WCA meeting after the conference and I went. Betsy started claiming, "This conference was the best conference we have had. It was the first time the WCA has reached out to black women." "You're talking about not being competitive Betsy, what does that mean?

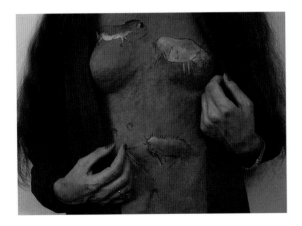 

51. Virginia Maksymowicz, *The History of Art*, body cast 52. Virginia Maksymowicz, *The History of Art*, body cast

It's not the first time. I started the practice four years ago. There had to be at least two minority women on every panel we did. That was our rule. It was the rule for curators too. It's offensive for you to say that this is the "first time." I haven't lived my life that way." "Sabra, I didn't mean it that way. I know you are a person who has dedicated her life to political change. I didn't know you had had that rule. Then, we are following your work." Now, Jackie Wray stepped in. "But Betsy, how can you say you didn't know?! I called you last fall and told you about our rule." "Jackie and I come from Texas, Betsy. This is not a light matter for us." "Well, I knew Sabra was like that. I knew there was a minority presence, but I didn't know it was a policy."

Jennifer Dunning reviewed the WCA series of shows on *Liberty* in the *New York Times*. I congratulated Annie and wrote Dunning a letter, sending the article Lawrence had written about *Views by Women Artists* four years earlier. "Your article made me feel that times have changed a bit." Annie had just been chosen as the national WCA president; she resigned from the local board with a two-page letter of advice and complaint to Susan Gill and others with a copy to the WCA National Archive. "Whatever may be the truth of this matter, this board has acquired an unfortunate reputation for being uninterested in outside opinion or new ideas." I was astonished at the tone. "Underneath the pompous tone must be hurt feelings," I wrote in a personal letter. "In terms of brushes tarring themselves, where do you think the Board got its 'unfortunate reputation'? From your continual characterizations of the Board, the majority of whom worked on the Conference with you. I have had hurt feelings myself, but I have never attacked you publicly . . . you have not practiced the same reticence." There had been a spate of letter writing. Sylvia had shown me a lecturing letter that felt like a breach of friendship. "I can remember the not-so-long-ago time you considered yourself a 'child' of Sylvia & Lawrence."

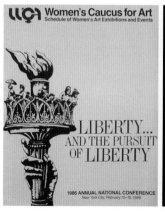

53. NYC/WCA conference poster 54. *The Clocktower* (three exhibits) 55. Annie Shaver-Crandell, tenure/birthday card

"About Sylvia," Annie replied, "your reaction to my note to Sylvia suggests that you see her as a wronged innocent. . . . A while back, Sylvia finally admitted to me that it was she who torpedoed Betsy Damon's nomination for chapter president, and then added, . . . 'Well, you know I consider Betsy a force for evil loose in the Caucus.'" Around this same time, Joan Watts resigned from the board "with some sadness and some relief." She was moving to Santa Fe. "It is regrettable that Annie . . . does not recognize or at least acknowledge the significant role she has played in the creation of this polarization." We were all invited to a meeting at Annie's loft, celebrating the *New York Times* review and the successful shows and events. Her letter to her steering committee had a different tone. "We know how good we are; now, others have a chance to see it all spelled out too." In September, Betsy was elected president of the NYC/WCA, running against Linda Selvin. Sylvia was defeated as vice president. Annie was among the former friends insisting that Sylvia's attention would be compromised by her care for Lawrence. Betsy had solicited endorsements from prominent artists, including May Stevens. This shattered May's long friendship with Sylvia.

Some weeks after the conference, Marithelma asked me to host a party at our loft for a visiting Canadian artist, Freda Guttmann. Freda was making an installation about the massacres in Guatemala for Powerhouse, a Montreal women's cooperative gallery. She had seen *Recon-struction Project* and wanted to meet me. She was using one of Marithelma's poems with an image of massacred Mayas tossing their decapitated heads like footballs underground like the Hero Twins of the *Popol Vuh*. Catalina Parra came to the party, and, soon, we three were planning shows for Montreal—one for *Reconstruction Project* paired with Freda's installation and one for Catalina. I showed Freda around the studio, pulling out the artworks about my grandmothers. She had also Xeroxed her mother's dresses when she died. It was Catalina's first visit to our

56. Sylvia Sleigh, *Arlene Raven & Nancy Grossman* 57. Photograph, Sylvia & Lawrence 58. Sylvia Sleigh, *Howardena Pindell*

Pearl Street loft. "I loved your other place," she said, "but this place is fantastic." The firecrackers had started to work.

The York Street subway station near the loft was notorious for muggings, but I had always been lucky in the city, partly because I am tall. You exit the train and go up a long flight of stairs, turn, ascend another flight, and then step out at night onto a completely deserted industrial street with the traffic roar from the bridge nearby muffling speech. I didn't usually ride this line at night, but I had grown used to our neighborhood. It was raining. As I rounded the top of the steps, I saw three teenaged boys, but I ignored them, opened my umbrella, and started walking down the block to our door. I heard them running after me. They knocked me down, hit me in the mouth, snatched my purse, and were gone. I didn't even cry out. The next day, I changed all the locks, bought new keys, and repaired my broken earring. A week later, Donna Henes called for help. She was organizing an event to save their loft building in downtown Brooklyn slated for demolition. She wanted to publicize a little-noticed park across the street and summoned her fellow artists for a park cleaning and decoration. Roger and I made a giant cloth leaf that we hoisted onto a tree, and then we started cleaning the filthy little park. I had forgotten to bring tools, so I was using two sticks to pick up trash. I reached over to pluck up a potato chip bag thrown behind a bench. It was heavy. Inside was the wallet of an Ecuadorian woman, minus money, of course, but stuffed with photos and cards from her entire life. I sent it back to her with a note, telling her that I also had been mugged, but finding her wallet had restored my balance about that event.

I went to another WCA panel on the ubiquitous topic of funding. The painter Joan Snyder had been the only woman on a National Endowment for the Arts panel that awarded grants to painters. Nancy Spero's slides were shown and passed over. "The men couldn't see the work," Joan told us. "So, I said, what if Spero's paintings were ten feet tall and done by a man?" Nancy

59. Donna Henes (both), *Dressing Our Wounds in Warm Clothes*. 60. Card with new address

got the grant. Josely and I had been applying for grants for *Connections Project/ Conexus*. We had found a venue at the Museum of Contemporary Hispanic Art for 1987 and had been meeting with Petra Barreras from New York State Council on the Arts (NYSCA). She had championed us with the selection panel, just like Joan Snyder. "The men thought the project was like *We Are the World*. Even though the exhibit was unorthodox, it was worthy of the money. We wanted you to have the book." NYSCA awarded us $5,000 for a collaborative artists' book/catalogue.

I had sent the clothesline work and the *Wash & Iron* book to a show in Seattle organized by Robert Costa, called *Feminist & Misogynists Together at Last*. The gallery gave away over one hundred books, recreating the *Give & Take* project, and I looked forward to receiving the paper responses. At the *Latitudes* show, it had felt like "opening 150 fortune cookies" to read the responses. But the Seattle show obviously had set a different tone from the one in New York; many of the papers contained violent or abusive comments.

I dream that I visit Grandmother's house and look across her swept dirt yard towards the woods. I see a tall pointed tower rising above the woods and realize that what I have come to find has been altered by the nearness of this structure.

At our photo meetings for *Pride of Place*, architect Robert Stern had exhibited an odd sense of humor, adopting a fake Chinese accent when the work of I. M. Pei was shown or jokingly offering to push me out a window when we disagreed. He knew that I had been acquainted with Ana Mendieta. The book was on press when Forbes bought American Heritage Publishers and abruptly closed down the book division. All the other book projects were cancelled. I was a free-lancer, temporarily out of work. But I was also about to leave for a three-month artist's residency at the Wurlitzer Foundation in Taos, so the timing was fine.

61. Sabra Moore, *Wash & Iron (...& rinse water. We washed by hand. I liked to put my hands inside the bluing water)*

Roger drove out to New Mexico with me. We planned to stop in Texas on the way and take my grandparents to their house for a short visit, and then he would fly back from Albuquerque. Roger needed a respite as well. His father had come back to Brooklyn for his eightieth birthday, bringing a photo of his wife's gravestone and a snapshot of Marie, his middle-aged housekeeper, wearing a bathing suit. He was already planning to remarry. As we went further south, towns gave way to open fields and the soft Appalachian Mountains. I felt a visceral relief soaked in green after months of pink brick and steel girders.

62. Sabra Moore, *Wash & Iron (...preferred the hand iron, I could do difficult clothes, like his railroad cap, sprinkle first...)*

8

A Room of One's Own

We each had our own small adobe house at the Wurlitzer Foundation in Taos, New Mexico. Mine was house number six. It was nestled into a compound with two other resident houses with big cottonwood trees giving us privacy from each other. The bare dirt was visible on the walkway paths, reminding me of Grandmother's place. There was a narrow backyard with a clothesline; a wire fence separated the house from a pasture thick with weeds. Chowpeña, the resident horse, systematically grazed the pasture all summer, consuming all of one favorite weed before moving onto the others. I arrived just as the magpies were fledging in their immense stick nests, creating a daily avian drama in the yard.

After all the talk and struggle, I embraced silence, taking walks before sunset and rushing out of the studio to watch the clouds as they shifted. My sense of smell expanded with the sweet earth. It was my first uninterrupted period of work in years and my longest time near the places of my childhood since leaving Texas in 1964. I started filling the studio with the

1. Roger Mignon photograph (both), *Sabra in yard with Chowpena* 2. *Looking for art inside caves at Tsankawi*

sun-bleached sticks and bits of rusted metal I found on my walks. At night, I would make a fire in the kiva fireplace and burn any discarded bits from the workday, and then work again until almost dawn. I started writing poetry fluidly again. I had almost given up poetry after C stole my poems and held them captive for weeks, finally returning them seeded throughout with his ominous notes.

The residents formed a little community. The poet Sam Allen was in a house nearby, and down the path, Owen Levy, a novelist from New York City. Sam had been in Africa with Langston Hughes and had visited Guinea. Sam, Owen, and I fell into heated discussions about African and African American literature. "How could you like Toni Morrison's character Sula?" they demanded, indignant at my opinion about this transgressive woman. Victor Bumbalo, a playwright, was also there, and a painter from California, Ellen Koment. When Victor stopped by my house a few days after my arrival, he said, "You've already made it your own." Occasionally, we would gather across the road at the Wurlitzer house and visit with the foundation's director, Henry Sauerwein. Henry was a linguist who had come out to Taos in the late forties and had befriended Helene Wurlitzer and the writers and artists surrounding Mabel Dodge Luhan. The Wurlitzer house had a fine collection of Pueblo pottery, *colcha* weavings, Navajo rugs, Taos school paintings, photographs by Paul Strand, and all kinds of unexpected artifacts. Henry would give us tours, allowing us to handle ancient pots or regaling us with stories from his many years in Taos. One pot had black tadpoles painted around the rims; I loved the layered quality of images painted on a sculptural form. Henry could be acerbic; one evening, he launched into a vitriolic attack on Owen's day job as a publicist for Ntozake Shange and Broadway productions, but Owen could hold his own. "Thank you for a lacerating experience," he said on parting. Henry retold the comment with relish the next day.

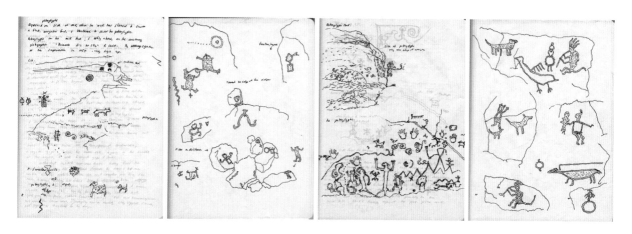

3. Journal pages, Books #40 and #42 (all), Chaco Canyon 4. Rock art, Lyden 5. Bandelier painted cave 6. Lyden

Ellen and I started taking small trips together, finding the huge petroglyph site along the river a few miles below Taos and going to ceremonial corn dances in the pueblos. We took watercolors and drawing books to record images from our jaunts. Ellen abstracted the landscape in her paintings as the Taos school painters of the twenties had done. "Ellen works with vastness, but I work with closeness," I wrote. I planned to make my piece for *Connections Project/Conexus*, but ideas for other artworks started forming in my mind inspired by the art in the adobe churches, the woven stripped blankets, and the detritus I kept collecting on my walks. I started a small work shaped like a washboard with painted horizontal strips of paper sewn inside a wooden frame, and then attached a twig "raft" at the base with a cutout of my childhood self, standing alone, and printed the word LAND on its frame. Years later, Linda Peer bought this work as a talisman to help her find land in Utah; it was the piece that got me grounded into my summer studio.

Other ideas were flowing. I went out to the hardware store and bought planks of wood to construct a form like a human-sized wooden doorway based on the kimono-shaped doors of the Chacoan great houses. The odd shape seemed designed to allow entry into a room with arms laden and elbows extended. I traced one of my short-sleeved blouses and cut out the shape as a hole into the doorway, saving the cutout blouse for a later work, and then tied gessoed sticks to fill the opening, creating a network of elaborate wooden ribs. I was thinking about the widening of the hole in the ozone over Antarctica as I worked. The assembled form looked evocative against the brown studio wall, chalky white with fresh gesso, awaiting painting. I ran into Harmony Hammond at a corn dance at Taos Pueblo, and she came over to visit. Somehow, I thought Harmony would be able to envision the work I already saw in my mind simply from looking at its white surface.

7. Sabra Moore (all), *Door* showing "ribs" (detail) 8. *Door* 9. More "rib" 10. *Land* with baby Sabra on raft

Ellen invited a Taos friend, Elyse Frank, whose husband was amassing a collection of Hispanic *santos* and *retablos*, to visit our houses. I expected her to understand my references to those traditional forms, but she thought I was a conceptual artist. So did Ellen. "Well, I do have concepts," I said. When I visited Harmony a few weeks later in her studio in Galisteo, I told her about this comment. "People need a label. They don't understand that you are combining two or three different disciplines. Just trust your feelings and go with what is happening here." She had just returned from a hike in Canyon de Chelly and described her encounter with strange hissing ants.

Roger had been invited with four other artists to paint a temporary mural along a wooden fence in front of the New York Aquarium in Brooklyn, and I was following his progress in our phone conversations. While he was standing on the sidewalk painting his composition of whales and sharks, passersby would make comments. A Japanese man complimented him on his drawing; another requested the addition of seahorses; and one man stopped often to watch. He hoped to be reincarnated as a sperm whale and enjoyed seeing the emerging painting.

I had been developing ideas for my piece for *Connections Project/Conexus* and had chosen shelter as my theme, but I was waiting on a packet from my Brazilian collaborator, Maria Do Carmo Secco. Two pairs of artists were both working on one theme for an exploration of eight issues among thirty-two participants. Each artist was supposed to share images with her partner. I had sent Maria an envelope with a series of words and cutouts related to my family. Josely and I were working together long distance as co-organizers for this project. She had chosen the theme of body and planned to make an artwork using feet, but her collaborator wanted to work with hands. Just before I left for Taos, we had assembled lists of names for the *150 Artists Book* from the recommendations of the core artists. I sent out sixty postcards inviting artists to create

11. Roger Mignon in front of temporary mural at the New York Aquarium 12. Mural in progress with paint buckets

book pages, and the replies were arriving in my post office box. When an artist accepted, I sent back a piece of heavy watercolor paper for her page art. I was happy that Louise Bourgeois wrote to accept, writing a note in her round script that echoed the bulges in her drawings. When Maria's packet of images arrived, she included a photo of a Brazilian house that closely resembled the adobe where I was working. She had translated a quote from Gaston Bachelor: "It is necessary for us to touch the primacy of shelter. Besides the life situation, we must discover the dreaming situation."

Frankie suddenly arrived from New York; her relationship with Kate had completely ruptured. She showed up at my door in a hailstorm, and I was glad to have a kindred artist in Taos. "Your work is changing; you're moving closer to myth." I objected. "I want to keep firmly rooted in social and family concerns." My studio was littered with bits of found objects, Indian pots, little twig and gessoed artifacts I had been making, bags of kapok collected from trees, and four elemental paper house shapes. My painting had changed from flat waves of color to reflect the dappled light and intricate ground I had been absorbing on my daily walks. "I feel a body change," I told her. "I'm getting used to walking outdoors whenever I need to look at clouds."

Mother also arrived for a weekend. I drove her from the airport in Albuquerque along the road winding through the Rio Grande Gorge as we ascended to Taos. Mother was excited and started remembering how we used to make mud figures with Red River clay and how Daddy would sing as he drove us down to the country to visit his parents. I introduced her to Henry. "Why didn't you teach your daughter anything?" Mother couldn't detect his affectionate teasing of me. She started explaining that I had been very quiet as a child.

I finally felt free to finish the painting for the Brazilian collaboration, starting with the materials I had been collecting. The words that I printed on the surface now seemed obvious—*Shelter*

  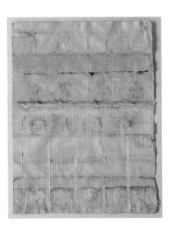

13. Frances Buschke, *Untitled* collage 14. Letter from Louise Bourgeois 15. Frances Buschke, *Untitled* collage

Is Material. I painted four sewn panels with images evoking mud, wood, rock, and straw, and then suspended little house forms with the actual materials from the top frame. I had collected a bit of discarded adobe while watching parishioners mud plaster the famous church at Rancho de Taos and sewed the thick adobe into a kimono-shaped plastic sleeve, and then spent an afternoon weaving a straw house embellished with porcupine quills, tying a twig house, and adding a rusted metal cutout from my walks. I was eager to finish this work before Roger came for a week's visit.

I dream that I am flying to New York, moving like a swimmer through the air, pulling a cloud behind me.

Roger and I went to corn dances at Jemez and Santo Domingo Pueblos, returning with the drumbeat echoing in our blood. I went to dances in twelve pueblos that summer. The dancers repeat the same dance eight times in one day, and each pueblo dances the same dance, just as the cycle of nature repeats. But each repeat is also a variation, and each variation deepens your understanding. I took him to the petroglyph site that Ellen and I had visited, and we spent days drawing and scrambling among the embellished boulders. Marithelma wrote me. "Don't get too used to that paradise because New York is worse than ever."

Kate sent Frankie boxes of her books and paintings, and as Frankie opened each box, she thought everything was damaged. I came over to help her unpack. Nothing looked damaged to me. It was Frankie who was damaged, like the bandaged and tortured papers she burned and distressed to make her artworks.

A new resident arrived, Jack Perla, a musician from New York. He did not need to select a category for the works I had been making; his music mixed metaphors as well. One day, he brought over the poet Mei-Mei Berssenbrugge, wanting to borrow my typewriter. She asked me if I

16. Christine Moore visiting Sabra at Wurlitzer Foundation studio 17. Drawing rock art at Lyden

knew of Richard Tuttle's work. "No, but I've heard his name." "I like your work," she said. "That's quite a compliment," Jack said. "Mei-Mei is a severe critic." She was heading to New York to collaborate with Tuttle on a book of poetry for the Whitney Museum. "The curator told me they had spent forty-two man hours selecting the poet." "You should put that in your book."

I had been wanting to visit Jaune Quick-To-See Smith, and my residency was coming to a close. Jaune was in *Reconstruction Project*, and now she was working on a piece for *Connections Project/Conexus*. Frankie and I went to a dance in Acoma in early September and then drove to nearby Corrales to visit Jaune. We got introduced to her "lap horse" and her chickens that roosted in the trees at night; her children were absorbed in homework as we three settled into talk. Miriam Schapiro had been a mentor to Jaune, but that relationship had frayed. "Artists like Miriam spend all their time in these huge warehouses and never go out. Miriam has five assistants." "Do you work with assistants?" "No, I wouldn't know what to do with them." "Neither do I. I like to do all the technical work myself. In my pieces, there's a lot of tying and sewing. While I'm doing that, other things happen with the painting." Miriam had criticized Jaune's use of color. "That affected me for a year." She had once stayed with Jaune for four days. "All she wanted to do was go to stores. She looked outside and saw nothing." Jaune brought out some starburst quilts that Sioux women make, and I told her about Granny's Texas Star quilt. "The morning star is sacred to the Native American church," she said. "Then, we got it [the star quilt pattern] from you." "No, I think we got it from you."

In the fall, I headed back to New York City with our pickup truck stuffed with my three months of artwork, holding the promise of a new residency for 1991 in my heart, passing again through Texas, watching for green turtles crossing the road, and trying to remember the rules. Things were becoming harder for my grandparents. Mother Gladys had recently mistaken Daddy

 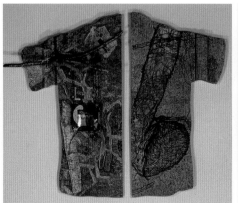 

18. Jaune Quick-to-See Smith, *Courthouse Steps* 19. Sabra Moore, *Left Over* 20. Smith, *Sunset on Escarpment*

Chess for an intruder and hit him over the head with a flashlight. Another time, he pushed her. She fell and broke her arm. They were put into separate rooms in the nursing home. I thought of the stories they had told me when I had stopped to visit on the way to New Mexico. They were talking about my grandfather's Aunt Belle. "She was the meanest woman; she only came around at hog-killing time. She treated Granny terribly." "She was brave if she treated Granny badly," Mother interrupted. "That was early on." He continued the story. "She always wore a pistol. They were going to hang her husband. She came with a knife and told them she would cut them open. She cut him down from the tree. Later, someone killed him. He was what you would call an outlaw."

Roger met me in Texas, and we stopped again in Clarksville on the way home. Daddy Chess handed me Aunt Belle's yellow pitcher. "Don't break it," he said. I wrapped it carefully and thought, "This pitcher belongs in the country, but maybe I belong in the country too." We went with him to visit Uncle Buddie. Uncle Buddie had recently married his childhood sweetheart, my Daddy's cousin, Emmadele. They were living on a farm right across the field from Grandmother's old place—the one I often visit in my dreams. We walked across the pasture to the house site, now bulldozed, and I struggled with my memories to unscramble the landmarks. I could only find the well and her catalpa tree; her road was overgrown with brambles. Arrowhead Ranch, the new owner of the land, had changed the road, pulled down the house, cut the woods, but left the pecan trees. Mother Gladys was sitting in her room at the nursing home when we got back. "Every time you come to see me, I'm sick."

After Texas and Tennessee, you turn north. The light changes when you cross the Mississippi, losing its dazzling clarity and softening as the air becomes moist and then grays with

21. Sabra Moore, *Woodsman* (artist's book, detail) 22. Emmadele Lewis and her mother Mitty in Grandmother's living room

pollution. I was heading back to New York City and the intricate jockeying for position after months of keeping my feet warm against the bare earth.

During my first year in college in 1960, I stayed at the Scottish Rite Dormitory, a building that looked like a set from *Gone with the Wind* with its white columns and a long sloping lawn. Our dorm mothers strictly enforced a curfew and lectured us about sex outside of marriage—"like tracking mud onto the carpet." We residents had a system of self-governance with student advisors on each wing. I can't remember the issues clearly now, but the dorm mothers tried to limit this student system, and we organized a demonstration. One evening, as we all sat at the big wooden dinner tables in the downstairs dining hall, we refused our desserts en masse by turning the empty dessert plates upside down. It seems quaint now, but I felt my first heady rush of empowerment at this dainty exercise of passive resistance. I wrote my father an indignant letter, expecting his praise and describing the dorm mothers' abuse of authority and our actions. He wrote back a long letter in his fine script. "I'm going to tell you how the cow ate the cabbage," he said, and proceeded to warn me that you can never win; it is better to not resist or fight; they will beat you down. That is how I learned as a young adult that my father had been defeated.

I always struggle with these mixed admonitions of class solidarity and danger learned from my family. We were encouraged to excel, but there were limits of getting too far ahead of the community. "Don't get a big head." Artists with a different class background simply seek more visibility without ambivalence.

There was a Women's Caucus for Art (WCA) demonstration scheduled against the Guggenheim Museum shortly after my return. Betsy Damon coordinated this action as president of the New York City/WCA; I still sensed the atmosphere of innuendo and whispers from her election campaign. The rally was called "Now You See Us." It was more formal than our demonstration

23. *Now You See Us* protest flier 24. Guerrilla Girls invitation to Guggenheim protest 25. NYC/WCA Art Gala benefit

two years earlier against the Museum of Modern Art (MoMA), and many of us were asked to speak. I decided to question why all that wonderful Native American art was housed in the Museum of Natural History alongside the stuffed animals and the dioramas rather than in an art museum. Howardena Pindell asked why curators like Lucy Lippard hadn't included more artists of color in a recent benefit exhibition for the Center for Constitutional Rights. Lucy spoke about the Guggenheim and its architecture, calling it a giant Dairy Queen. Harmony was there, visiting from New Mexico. Vivian Browne came over and patted my stomach, teasing me about my tummy fat. And then we all went downtown together to watch Faith Ringgold give a performance at the New York Feminist Art Institute, where she dragged a sack across the stage to symbolize her eighty-eight pounds of lost weight.

I was back. I unpacked my new work and started inviting friends from the neighborhood to come visit. Rebecca Ballenger came over and liked how I had combined materials. "I can see how you would get a lot of pleasure in putting things together; you like to organize and make things stronger." Harmony came over and saw the finished version of *Door*, which was no longer chalky white. I had printed the words about the ozone hole that echoed in my mind as I painted. She objected to the text, feeling that the words limited the artwork. Harmony paints abstractly and was working on a series related to the death carts in New Mexico.

Kate came, eager to see how my stay at the Wurlitzer had affected my artworks. She was starting a new life without Frankie and planned to visit every gallery in SoHo, determined to find a dealer. Josely had a party and many of the artists in *Connections Project/Conexus* were there. Liliana Porter described how her work was changing and becoming more painterly. "My work too," I said. "Everyone is moving in a different direction." I went over to American Heritage

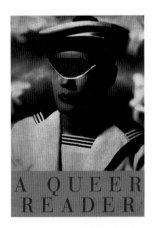  

26. Harmony Hammond, *A Queer Reader* 27. Catalina Parra, *The Human Touch* 28. Vivian E. Browne, *The Chief's Attendant*

Publishers to look for work. I thought, "If I lived in New Mexico, my life would fill up with activities there too, but at least I could go outside and look at the clouds."

I dream that I am bicycling with Roger, but our bicycle is actually a mule. "I save the New York Times *to feed it," he says. "Shouldn't it be eating hay?"*

Roger was working on a solo show for Atlantic Gallery. He was making a series of seven-foot pastel drawings based on slides he took while visiting me during my residency. He combined images of birds with the *descansos*—memorial crosses marking the places where people died—that dot the highways. I was still adjusting to my return, constantly comparing the golden afternoon light filtered into our loft beneath the massive bridge with my memories of the clear light in New Mexico. I had dinner with Ora, and we were talking about our mutual longings for the country. She was planning to buy a farmhouse in Pennsylvania. "I realize you might want to buy a place in New Mexico instead of here." She voiced my feelings. As I was leaving the red mesas past Taos on my way to Texas, I had pulled off the road, unable to see through my tears. The next day, I told Roger I preferred to buy land in New Mexico with the money I had saved. He agreed. "I love it there for different reasons than yours. It's fine with me."

I went to check on my artist's books at Printed Matter, trying to catch up with my book orders. I had just finished making ten copies of *Wash & Iron* and was working on *Artifact/Artifice*, a new book based on my childhood illustrated Bible, where I also kept the paper dolls I had made from cutting up a Sears catalogue. Printed Matter called my accordion-folded book *notes, notes* a best seller because I sold three or four books a year. Each one sold for $40, and I got 50 percent. It cost me $10 to print and took about three hours to produce, but I berated myself for my lack of enthusiasm for making more copies. "Don't freak! We love your books, but we hadn't heard from you in such a long time." They had taken my books out of the catalogue and

29. Roger Mignon, *Forces of Nature #2* 30. Halloween evening opening 31. Roger Mignon, *Forces of Nature #1*

told buyers that the books were out of print. "Do you have any back orders?" "We do now." I was eager to share my longing for New Mexico with the new staff person, Susan Wheeler, who had been at the Wurlitzer Foundation with Kate and Frankie. She had hated Taos, a place "with no sense of irony."

Mother and I talked on the phone. To my surprise, she told me that Mother Gladys had been gravely ill; they thought she was dying, but she had suddenly improved. "Honey, I want you to do something," Mother Gladys had asked. "Don't let me die. Chester wants me to live." "She's still doing what Daddy wants her to do," Mother complained.

I helped Roger hang his show and loved how the large pastels looked on the walls. The series of birds and *descanos* faced charcoal drawings of nude symbolic women in tai chi poses on the opposite wall. Carol Sun and I had posed for the drawings. At the opening, Linda Peer said, "the amazing thing was seeing you and Carol at the same height."

After the opening, I called Mother again. It had been about two weeks since our last conversation. We had been back and forth from the vet during this time. Our orange cat, Saskia, named after the golden-haired woman in a Rembrandt painting, was very sick. "Mother Gladys is dying." I was shocked; I thought she had recovered. "Why didn't you call me?" "I told you, you knew; everyone has been down to see her. I'll call you when she dies, or Nancy will call." The next morning, Nancy called. Mother Gladys had died during the night with my aunt Mary Jane by her side. I went back to Texas for the funeral, riding in the truck seat behind my grandfather to the cemetery. "Didn't she look pretty, gal?" he said, patting the armchair in grief for his wife of sixty-seven years. "I know they put paper in her mouth to make her mouth so pretty, but didn't she look pretty!" He called her "my little heifer" and "my little corn shuck," an erotic term if you consider the form of the growing corn plant. We stayed the night after all the kin had left, eating

32. Roger Mignon (both), Daddy Chess closing window reflected in mirror 33. Guest bedroom with mirror and spindle bed

the food that people had brought and looking through Mother Gladys's memory boxes of cards and photos. "I'm sitting here studying the times I stormed at her. It's hurting me. Nothing has hurt me like this." "I know, Daddy," Mother said pointedly, referring to her own loss twenty years earlier. "But you were young; you could work it off. I'm an old man." Two days after the funeral, we went with Daddy Chess to the bank. He withdrew all his savings—$1,657 that my aunt and I counted twice for him. Then, we drove to the funeral home and he made the first payment on her funeral.

Our cat, Saskia, died shortly after my return. Roger printed out the photos he had taken the year we visited the old cemetery in the woods with my family. Gladys is strong and pretty against the sky. We sent them to my grandfather. I told Josely about the box of memories that Mother Gladys had called her Sad Box. "You should go there immediately and document everything; Xerox what you want. They will think you are crazy, but you should do it." Instead, I made a list from memory of the items in that box, noting also what she kept in the two chifforobes that were their only closets. The list was modest—the Sad Box, her Bible, boxes of the greeting cards people had sent, empty matchboxes filled with receipts, and their clothes. In the hall, she kept her quilts carefully stacked. "What interests me is the way she organized her memories," I wrote.

I dream that I go to Gladys's house. Someone has thrown out her metal bed; it is lying broken outside. I pick it up and put it in our truck, along with some parts from a rocker. I go inside. Mother has removed all the oval photos of the children from the bedroom wall and replaced them with photos of herself, looking very well dressed and young. I go into the guest room and find the Sad Box. I take it and put it in my bag.

Connections Project/Conexus was scheduled to open at Museum of Contemporary Hispanic Art (MoCHA) in January, and Josely and I were collecting the artists' book pages, most

34. Roger Mignon (both), Mother Gladys & Daddy Chess at Briggins Cemetery 35. Gladys storytelling about tombstones

arriving by mail. Each of the 32 artists had selected 4 other artists to make pages, so we anticipated around 150 art pages. We planned on making nine booklets, one for each theme plus a *Documentation* booklet; all reproduced by Xeroxing six hundred copies of the original pages. We used the photocopier machine at the typography shop of our fellow *Heresies* member, Kathie Brown. We loved the way the stamped envelopes from both the United States and Brazil looked, so we divided envelopes to use in our designs for the thematic booklet covers, each of us designing half. Now, our shared belief that "the project itself is an artwork" was taking tangible shape. Josely arranged to print the silk-screened packets that would house the nine booklets at the *Silkscreen Project*. Each packet had to be trimmed, folded, glued, and tied with a maroon ribbon. Somehow, we imagined this could be produced in one or two weekends, but it took about three months. I tallied 79,450 photocopies for printing the book pages and covers on Kathie's machines. We had to recruit helpers for modest stipends; the poet Sapphire made copies with us one weekend.

We went over to visit Lucy, sitting together on a couch under a dusty mounted buffalo head and facing the walls of her loft densely layered with artworks, posters, and ephemera by artists in our circles. We wanted to show her the design format for *150 Artists Book* and spread some of the book pages across her table. She agreed to write an introduction for the *Documentation* booklet, calling our project "vast and fearless." "Carvalho and Moore printed each booklet themselves—a combination of whimsy and ideology that is a metaphor for the stereotypically labor-intensive tasks that women both love and hate."

Josely and I were working on *Making It Happen*, an essay on our collaboration, for the same booklet. We taped a conversation that I laboriously transcribed, winnowing sixty handwritten pages into three. "Both of us are products of hybrid cultures," Josely observed. I added,

36-39: Covers, *150 Artists Book (Connections Project/Conexus)* designed alternately by Josely Carvalho and Sabra Moore

"I think we both feel a kind of dissociation from the cultures we come from, but still feel their pull. . . . We're both inside and outside."

Louise Bourgeois was making a book page. One Sunday, I went by her house with Roger to pick up the page. Louise lived in a nineteenth-century brownstone across the street from Sylvia. The interior hadn't been painted for years, so the whole house had an antique feeling. There were stacks of papers, books, and magazines on every surface; Louise couldn't find her small page. We walked through the rooms, looking on tables, lifting books and papers without success. She offered us a glass of brandy; we sat down and drank, and then left. Roger wanted to drive out to his childhood neighborhood in Astoria, Queens, near another imposing nineteenth-century iron bridge. We poked around under the bridgeworks and walked over to stare into the abandoned public swimming pool, with its conical cement islands beached in the center, where he had played. Back home, Louise had left a message. The drawing was found. I collected it the next day—a double-sided drawing of women with quirky hairdos; one in red lines with the face cropped abruptly below the nose and her hair twined upward like a broom. Louise drew the woman's head on the reverse side in black with her hair twirled in a spinning plait leading off the top of the page. She called this side, *la belle pendue*. I thought this hairdo was a product of Louise's zany imagination, but I later saw an Aztec statue with the same vertically twisting style.

Things were working again in *Heresies*. We held a dinner meeting at Lucy's loft to welcome back Betsy Hess, a founding member who had been living in Washington, DC. Betsy had been a painter, but now she was writing art criticism for the *Village Voice*. Faith Wilding, a collaborator with Miriam Schapiro on *Woman House* in California, had also moved to New York City and joined the collective. We cooked together and crowded around the little table, talking and laughing. "For a while, I thought we would fold," Lucy said as we cleaned up. "There was a nice

 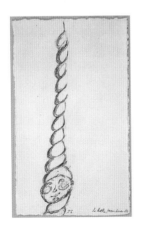  

40. Cover, *150 Artists Book (Birth)* 41-42. Louise Bourgeois, *La Belle Pendue (verso & recto)* 43. Cover, *150 Artists Book (Death)*

energy tonight. I don't know what we accomplished, but it was fun." "I think it's working now because we've broken ties with the old collective."

I dream that I am standing in my childhood backyard, about to embark on a trip. An odd woman is in the yard with me; she seems special; she might not be human. She is handing me flowers, one at a time, which I eat.

Catalina Parra nominated me for a Guggenheim Fellowship. She liked the work I was doing about my grandmothers. "You are preserving their stories; so many other people are involved in materialism." Her grandmother had eleven children before she was twenty-six. One was Catalina's father, the poet Nicanor; another was the legendary singer and artist Violeta. "My grandmother was very poor and sewed these fantastic clothes for her children using every scrap, and when she was old, she made amazing curtains that looked like stained glass." Catalina had finished her artwork for *Connections Project/Conexus*: leaves and feathers stuffed into pockets of a translucent shower curtain, following in the tradition of her grandmother, but using her own materials, like I did in my artworks. I left feeling ebullient and set about asking for letters of support—Lawrence, Ann Harris, and Lucy all agreed. "I liked your project," Lucy later told me at a party, "and I wrote you a good letter, but you don't stand a chance." She was right.

Josely and Ernesto went to Brazil for the holidays, and I was left to finish the edition of *150 Artists Book* on my own. When she returned, she hired helpers to finish her share of the packets. Roger's fiftieth birthday was three days after Christmas, and we decided to throw a huge New Year's Day party to celebrate. I cooked for two days—salty ham, black-eyed peas for good luck, meat pies, cornbread, chess pies, and eggnog; the house filling with familiar smells and with friends bringing kids' presents for Roger's new decade. Sylvia walked over to look at my freshly completed painting *Door* at this party—the one based on the Chacoan doorway. A few of

44. Cover, *150 Artists Book (Food)* 45. Silkscreen packet with ties, *150 Artists Book* 46. Cover, *150 Artists Book (Spirit)*

us were standing around with her. I asked Lucy what she thought about the words describing the hole in the ozone layer; unlike Harmony, she liked them. Some friends from my house-painting days were there, including Bolivian historian Brooke Larson and her husband, Carter Bancroft, whom I first met as I was wallpapering their kitchen and Brooke entered with a T-shirt emblazoned with the words "Radical Historian." Our neighbors in Dumbo came; the artists whose works we would soon hang were all there; and sister Heretics and the WCA friends who had survived our rifts—all of us eating together for good luck.

The following week, Josely and I started hanging *Connections Project/Conexus*. It was a difficult process and took three days. In addition to the 32 works on the wall, we had to arrange 150 book pages into thematic groups along stands that resembled narrow peaked houses and place the pages on both sides of the peaks. Josely had brought her maid, Maria Inez, and she and I stretched canvas tightly across each stand. Josely couldn't climb on ladders, so I hung the show with her directing. "I thought you knew," Kathie Browne said later, referring to her experience hanging *Choice Works* the previous year. I finally had to call Roger to come and help me as Josely focused solely on arranging and rearranging the phalanx of dried turtles lining the floor under her diaphanous silk-screened artwork. I had to remind myself that we had brought different skills to this project; my writing and exhibition design skills complimented her connections to the artists in Brazil. The director of MoCHA, Susana Torruella, came over as the show started to take shape. "I know Josely's work, but which is your artwork?" I showed her. "I couldn't have planned it better! It's my favorite in the show." The gallery's carpenter was standing nearby. "That's Sabra's work? At least it makes sense." At the opening, I met an artist named Gladys Triana. "I was watching what you went through hanging the show. Who are you? Do you have a painting in the show? Do you work for Josely?" "I'm the co-curator."

47. Installation with book pages 48. Kazuko and Iole de Freitas, *Body* 49. Sabra Moore and Maria do Carmo Secco, *Shelter*

The opening was packed. Susana wrote us later about "the tremendous center of interest, energy, and good feeling" that the exhibit generated for MoCHA. That night, the energy was
palpable. The painter Juan Sanchez came to see Marina Gutierrez's work and saw mine as well.
"You should see this woman's work!" he told her, "she's a clone of you!" Petra Barrera came to
wish us success, gratified to see the fat stacks of photocopier book packets for sale that NYSCA
had funded. I introduced Vivian Browne to the anthropologist Johnetta Cole, and we stood there
looking at Vivian's artwork. "Does it make a difference that it's women? It makes a difference!"
Harmony walked into the gallery. "I thought you were in Galisteo!" "You can walk up to me at an
Indian dance, but I can't walk up to you in New York!" Most of the New York artists were at the
opening; some had come during the installation, eager to see how their work looked with their
Brazilian partners. Two paired sets of artists had worked independently on each theme—birth,
shelter, race, environment, body, food, spirit, and war/death—without seeing the other's work.
Only some of the collaborations were obvious. Marina, for example, had incorporated a drawing
sent by Maria Lidia Magliani into her artwork on race with paper flaps over women's stomachs
that could be lifted to reveal dark secrets of forced sterilization. Maria Lidia had simply painted
an elegant knotted cloth. This show was our ideal artists' community: women from various cultures, classes, ethnicities, and levels of reputation showing their works together in a dialogue
with each other even if the dialogue was imperfect. It was art in context; for some, there was
too much context, but not for me. Josely had organized a series of films by women filmmakers
that we showed on various evenings, so the show kept attracting new audiences. One night, a
woman attended who was working on a bibliography project; she only wanted to see the works
by minority women. "But the point of the show is collaboration across ethnicity," I reminded her.

50. Sabra, Sharon Gilbert, and Kathie Brown at opening 51. Installation, Sophie Tassinari and Jaune Quick-To-See Smith, *Race*

The day after the opening, I went by to read the guest book and enjoy a more peaceful look at the show. Betsy Hess and Kim Levin had signed the book for the *Village Voice*, so it looked like there would be a review. There was a phone message from Ann Mancuso at the *New York Times*. She was planning to write an article for the culture section and wanted to set up an interview. We all started jumping around and hugging. We called Josely. The next day, there was no phone call, so I gratefully stayed in bed, exhausted from the installation. That evening, Josely called to tell me that she had met with the reviewer on her own. They had talked for an hour and a half. "Why didn't you call me?" She acted surprised at my dismay, but I felt like our project was suddenly breaking apart along class lines. So, I called Ann and arranged to bring her the installation photos she had requested—a selection of works by ten pairs of artists. It felt emotionally like a photo research meeting and blunted my feelings at missing the interview. The article appeared in the Sunday *New York Times* on my birthday. I opened the paper to see that they had reproduced my own work, *Shelter is Material*, paired with Maria do Carmo Secco's piece, restoring a temporary balance to the events. Willie saw the review that morning. "Hey, Marina, here's an article about that show you're in, but it doesn't mention your work. Do you want to see it?" "It was right," Marina told me, "that they mentioned you and Josely. You did all the work. I was happy your piece got reproduced. After all, we're clones."

Betsy Hess was reviewing the show for the *Village Voice*. I ran into her at a party at Lucy's just after she had finished writing her article. Women can be hard on each other. "I loved the show when I first saw it. I loved your piece; it's like a jewel in the show," she told me, "but when I started to write about it, it fell apart for me." She disliked all the draped cloth. Most artists had made new works based on the themes, but some of the more established artists hadn't taken the show very seriously and many brought existing works. May Stevens brought a wonderful text

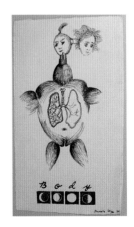

52. *150 Artists Book* (all), Mirtes Zwierzynzki, *Birth* 53. Mimi Smith, *Shelter* 54. Emma Amos, *Race* 55. Pamela Wye, *Body*

piece made for *Artists Call* with a Pablo Neruda poem hand-lettered in Spanish and English—*The blood of the children in the street is like/the blood of the children in the street*—onto a white canvas, ignoring that people spoke Portuguese, not Spanish, in Brazil. Faith Ringgold's solo show had just opened at Bernice Steinbaum Gallery, and she was criticized for sewing the show announcement into her artwork. The connection to her theme of food was tenuous, but she called excitedly when she picked up her "gorgeous set of booklets." Ida Applebroog brought a drawing for a larger work that Betsy later saw in her studio; she hadn't had time to make a separate piece. Everyone, including Betsy, loved the book pages and the photocopier version of the book. Visitors could walk among the little roof-shaped stands, viewing a plethora of visual commentary on the themes. "We could move the book pages around within the theme so weaker pages didn't stand out, but we couldn't move the paired artists on the wall." "Why did you lock yourself into that format?" Betsy queried. *The Village Voice* again selected my painting as the illustration. Our ideal community was not entirely egalitarian in action.

Weeks later, after a *Heresies* meeting, Betsy and I took up the threads of this discussion. "We're going to spend our lives under capitalism," she said. "Maybe," I said. "Maybe!" We argued about the importance of quilts. She thought that women artists had done a good job bringing an awareness of quilts as art into the mainstream. I felt that these objects hung on a wall like paintings had been denuded of their cultural roots. "The dominant culture has adopted the form, but not the content. Quilts serve a function; the context of women working together could serve as a model to change the art world," I said. "That's ambitious," she said coolly. "What is feminist art?" "Art that changes the context and content of art," I insisted. "The context?" Betsy would agree with Susan Wheeler about irony.

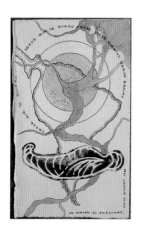   

56. Faith Wilding, *Environment* 57. Laurabeatriz, *War/Death* 58. Maria Lidia Magliani, *Race* 59. Ida Applebroog, *Death*

Freda called to confirm that *Reconstruction Project* was scheduled to be shown in two artists-run venues in Canada. The first was for Powerhouse Gallery in Montreal in a month; the second at Eye Level Gallery in Halifax in the fall. I was making a new artwork. Henry Sauerwein called to offer both Roger and me residencies at the Wurlitzer for 1988; I would still keep my residency for 1991. Josely and I took a break from our tattered collaboration even though we still had to arrange for taking *Connections Project/Conexus* to Brazil. And Marina asked me if I made prints. "If you consider photocopier books printmaking, then yes." The prints and drawings curators at MoMA had contacted her about a show and asked for recommendations of other artists. "I'll find out."

Vivian Browne had a show at SOHO20 Gallery right after *Connections Project/Conexus* closed. Many people at the opening had just come back from the latest WCA conference in Boston. I hadn't gone. I ran into Camille Billops. "Are you sending your artwork with me to Canada?" I asked. "No, don't you do your own work anymore?" Camille was still upset that I had hung her small, framed artwork above the doorway during the installation of *Reconstruction Project* at Artists Space. She had ignored the size requirements and her small artwork didn't fit with the other seven-foot-tall monochrome works on the wall. But the other artists were excited about the new venue; some were making new works. Holly Zox had a new job, working as a carpenter for the US Department of Veteran Affairs (VA). "Though I'm the first woman in engineering at the VA, I'm getting to be one of the boys. Last week, I won at spades four out of five days. I'm also doing artwork." She found her piece "a little dusty, but otherwise in good shape." When I opened all the boxes in Montreal, there were many surprises.

Kazuko sent a disturbing work with a photograph printed in black-on-red knit cloth, showing herself with a gun to her head. Catalina's piece was also made of cloth, but it was black and

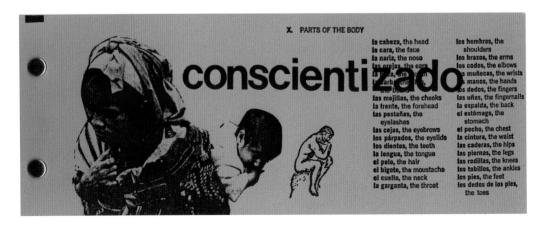

60. *Conscientizado*, a three-part book: 1. Freda Guttman 2. Sabra Moore 3. Barbara Lounder/Guatemala Solidarity Projects

shiny with round vinyl records sewn in rows, a contemporary concept of writing in glyphs. *Recon-struction Project* had been reviewed by several magazines when it was at Artists Space. Most of the articles were positive, but the reviewer for *Women Artists News* had less empathy, calling *Reconstructed Codex* "a cacophony of political art slung across a low green platform."[1] She sin-gled out the artworks by Jaune and Colleen, evidently stung by their temerity to "inanely" criticize European culture. Jaune had made a strong collage with a text that listed the unacknowledged contributions by Native American people to mass culture. She never discussed this review with me, but I felt that her new piece for Canada reflected self-censorship: a simple drawing of a Maya figure made with paint on cloth. I made a new artwork also; I wanted to conflate personal and societal loss. Using Grandmother's thrown out chair back as a mold, I made four papier-mâché curved forms and joined them like oversized yellow backbones suspended from the wooden chair back. It looked like a dress. A tiny yellow chair perched beneath the artwork. The dress was par-tially framed inside a stepped wooden mantle with a text from Diego de Landa: *Quite a distance away was a pyramid, so large and beautiful that even after it had been used to build a large part of the city they founded around it, I cannot say that it shows any signs of coming to an end.* Marina couldn't send her yellow panel decorated with cornhusks; it had won a purchase price at the Cuban Biennial and stayed in Havana.

Roger and I drove the show to Montreal and installed it as a companion to Freda Gut-tman's show, *Guatemala! The Road to War!*. Freda had suspended a camouflage net over her entire installation of papier-mâché curved walls and paper *huipils* in the style of Guatemalan fabrics. Each low wall represented a village; abundant wall texts described the bloody repres-sion. You felt as if you were entering an encampment as you passed between the two exhibits. Catalina was in Montreal as well, installing *A Winter of Anxiety*, her solo show at a sister gallery,

61. Canadian Installations, *Reconstruction Project* (all), (red wall), Correa, Grove, Peer, Kazuko 62. (yellow wall), Jaramillo, Moore

Articule, alongside Barbara Lounder's exhibit *Trouble Dolls*. Our four shows were part of a Guatemalan solidarity project. Barbara, Freda, and I found time to make a skinny collaborative artists' book together, each contributing ten photocopier pages to *Conscientizado*, which we sat around assembling and sewing at odd moments.

The Canadian galleries were a revelation. Powerhouse was a feminist gallery, an artists-run space with government funding. The gallery had paid staff, fax machines, and artists' stipends—luxuries our New York City galleries couldn't afford. Roger returned to New York City while I stayed at Freda's house and participated in panels and talks. I was invited to speak one evening at the Canadian equivalent of the BBC on a program called *Brave New Waves* and spent two hours seated with an interviewer in the big stuffed leather chairs of the station, talking about wanting us artists to reorient ourselves towards the native history of this continent. "This is not political art; it's art placed back into the serious context where art belongs. In previous centuries, art always had a context." During the break, the interviewer told me that he was glad I had said that. A few days later, I rode the train back to New York City, sleepy with fever and exhaustion, waking to glimpse icy lakes and fields of snow as the train twisted toward home.

The next week, MoMA curators Deborah Wye and Wendy Whitman called. Marina had recommended me, and they had sent me a letter asking to see some of my artists' books for a show they were organizing on "printed matter with social or political content." "You sent us some great stuff." They wanted to see *Reconstructed Codex* and the book for *Protective Devices*. "We already have the *Connections Project/Conexus* book in the library." I wrapped several little books in wax paper and was ushered into a pristine white room. I started to unwrap the books. "Don't put them down there," Deborah told me, indicating a tiny amount of dust. The books had come from my fuzzy studio, but it was pleasant for my works to be treated with respect. I had been

63. Freda Guttman, *Guatemala: The Road to War* 64. *Reconstruction Project* (black wall), Costan, Buschke, Carvalho

working and reworking the little folding book *Wash & Iron*, which was based on two clotheslines from my childhood, and also brought along *Making* and a few other books. They were surprised as I unfolded *Reconstructed Codex* and revealed its full size, and we talked excitedly about ways it could be displayed. They glanced at the other books; *Protective Devices* now looked like an ugly duckling. The curators were mostly interested in the books from the two recent collaborative projects. "That's nice enough, isn't it?" I wrote in my journal, and answered myself, "Yes."

Faith Ringgold had organized a show called *HOME* for the Goddard Riverside Community Center that included artists from the black art, women's art, and political art circles. I was making a large paper house, called *Elemental House*, with paintings of one of the four elements on each side. Roger and I went around Lower Manhattan looking for abandoned crate wood, and he constructed a little wooden cart for the house. It moved like a child's wagon or like the death carts of Northern New Mexico. As usual, I was still painting the night before the delivery date for installation. Everything was going very well until I got to the side for the element of air. I had planned to paint oversized feathers and worked intensely, finishing near dawn. The house was constructed with a framework of small branches piercing the sides. Suddenly, my painting looked grotesque, like a bizarre smiling face with the sticks as eyes. Once I saw this, I couldn't stop seeing it. As the sun lightened my windows, I rubbed the painting out and started over.

Perhaps, my panic painting the air side was a result of selling *Air House* that spring to a woman collector from Los Angeles, a stranger to me. I felt a sense of loss. It was one of the small houses I had made at the Wurlitzer, which I had painted in response to an abandoned magpie. The magpie mother would feed her babies on the ground near my studio window, but she stopped feeding this one. It just sat there all afternoon, calling, so I tried to feed it by digging

65. *Guatemala Solidaridad* card 66. *No Aid to Guatemala*, Toronto 67. *Reconstruction Project*, Eye Level Gallery, Halifax

worms and bugs. Around dusk, it died. Many magpies suddenly appeared as I buried the bird, filling the branches of a nearby tree and emitting a cacophonous chorus.

At the opening, Faith came over with two men I had not seen since leaving C seventeen years earlier: painter Cliff Joseph and printmaker Bob Blackburn. "Do you know these guys?" Faith asked. A pause. "Yes. I know them." "I love the way you said that." We all laughed. "Do you remember me?" "Yes, we wondered what had happened to you," Cliff said. "These kinds of shows bring people together again." Marina and Willie came up. Willie had seen my artwork, *Gladys Story*, at the WCA show in Clocktower Gallery. "I went back and analyzed it. You have to do that to be sure it was really good." We went around looking at all the artworks; I loved the fine twig house by Noah Jemison. Then, Marilyn Lanfear did a performance: *True Stories and Some That Really Happened*. Bernice Steinbaum came over. "A tour de force," she said, referring to *Elemental House*. But, later, I thought, "talk is cheap," since Bernice never included me in any of the shows at her gallery.

One day while walking to work, I ran into Betsy Damon. Betsy started talking about her ideas for the NYC/WCA even though I had mostly stopped attending meetings or events. She wanted to establish two new boards. One would be an advisory board that would meet twice a year and be composed of two art critics, a lawyer, and a publicist. "Betsy, I think you're seeking validation from experts," I said. The other board would be composed of "really important people" so that the WCA could go after big funding. "Funding for what?" "So we could initiate, not just respond," she replied. She wasn't good at paperwork, she explained, so she was just "laying out ideas." Young women who weren't ready for membership on the board would do most of the real work. As for herself, she said, "my career has really taken off. I could have a gallery now if I want it. As I get more successful, people will want to work with me."

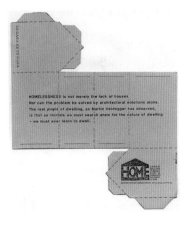

68. *HOME*, curated by Faith Ringgold 69. Sabra Moore, *Elemental House* cart with *Earth/Air/Fire/Water* sides

When I first moved into our loft, there was a derelict car dumped on the small triangle of dirt between a stone fence and our building. Eighty-one Pearl Street had been built to fit the Brooklyn Bridge, and the brick wall had been sliced diagonally on the bridge side, leaving this lot. I convinced our landlord to let me make a garden there. Somehow, the car got removed. One morning, Roger and I started to dig up the ground, unearthing metal, bricks, glass, and what I hope was not asbestos. The neighbors stopped to look. Obadiah Fisher, the jeweler on the third floor, and Barry Johnson, a painter, came by. Barry said, "This is really a ritual act of someone who loves a garden so much she'll do anything." "I know that it's quixotic," I said, "but I got tired of coming into this building and not being able to look around." Soon, Barry came back out with seeds and planted some pumpkins. He worked as the head of maintenance for the Cooper Hewitt Museum, so he promised to bring peat moss. He found a stone in the basement embossed with the word Thames, and we installed it on an abandoned sculpture stand too heavy to move. As the garden took shape, offers to contribute plants and materials mushroomed. Another neighbor, Scott Miller, who worked on commercial fishing boats, offered to supply fish heads as fertilizer. Kate came over from Cobble Hill with a bucket of worms. Frankie had been calling from Taos, threatening to kill Kate or to kill herself; it was a relief to talk about gardens. Soon, ladybugs found the site. I planted only hardy things—moonflowers, morning glories, honeysuckle, impatiens, clematis, and alyssum. Ora brought some wild rose cuttings from Pennsylvania. Mother mailed me an althea cutting; Sylvia gave me some of her wisteria. Tending a garden centered me. I kept adding notes and drawings in my journals as the seeds sprouted and matured.

The other artists in the building kept adding to a collection of street artifacts that we placed around the borders of the flower beds—bits of metal, railroad spikes, stones, and broken glass. I would often remove trash that had blown in, but no one vandalized this site. One day, a

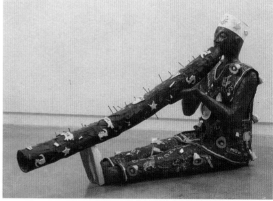

70. Sabra Moore, *Air House*, oil on gessoed paper 71. Willie Birch, *Song for Mother Earth*, papier-mâché sculpture

Jamaican deliveryman stopped to ask about the morning glories. "Now, if you lived in the country, you'd be fine. I can see you know what you are doing."

Daddy Chess turned ninety in June. I went to Texas so that he could come home from the nursing home for four days. I needed to stay in that familiar house as well. There were twenty-six kinfolk at his party—children, grandchildren, great-grandchildren, and cousins of various degrees. He cried. Mother got angry that he cried. Then, he and I went back to their house. It felt forlorn without the presence of Mother Gladys, so I threw myself into cooking. I fried catfish and potatoes, and then I learned he didn't like potatoes. "I guess you and Roger eat a lot of potatoes," he commented. He sat and read his cowboy novels, and I cleaned the yard, pruning and weeding Mother Gladys's day lilies and her flowering bushes. We watched the mocking birds and the red birds. I looked at Mother Gladys's quilts, which were neatly stacked in the hall chifforobe. I particularly wanted the plain white one, intricately quilted in white thread with no pattern. This was the only quilt she had from her mother, who had died when she twelve. When the quilt started to wear out, she had stitched a white cloth over it, preserving the old quilt. When you hung it on the line, you could see her mother's red zigzag pattern inside, revealing its secret heart like a palimpsest.

Daddy Chess kept telling stories—stories about a pig-fetching dog named Sam Riley that could bring in the wild sow and her piglets, and dark stories about murders in the family. His Uncle George ran a gristmill and heard that you could make a lot of money in Kansas City, so he went there with his grist stones. He had to ask for help to get back home. "I finally saved enough for him to come back with his stones, but he could never bring back the motor." Daddy Chess was very particular about his corn plants, Mother had told me. One summer she and Mother Gladys planted two rows of peanuts. "We loved peanuts. We pulled up a few of his corn plants

72. Pearl Street garden showing Manhattan Bridge arches 73. Pearl Street garden near Front Street corner with day lilies

to give the peanuts more light. We enjoyed delicious peanuts that year, but we never got to plant peanuts again." He talked about a childhood friend who was Choctaw. "His mother had a grease hole," meaning an oil well. "We're part Indian too," I said. "Honey, I don't know. Maybe Grandpa Greer; I think he was Indian."

Emmadele and Buddie came to visit. They sat around telling stories too. Emmadele used to love going over to "Aunt Caroline's place" to play with my father's toy trucks. "Frank made the best trucks. I had to be very careful with them. He made them with old skate wheels and the tin from Prince Albert cans. He would flatten out the tin and turn it wrong-side out, and then shape it like a bullet." Daddy Chess and I drove over to the nursing home to pick up the box of photos Roger had printed for him. "I thank you for the pictures. They mean a lot to me." Seeing her pictures was still very emotional for him, so he kept them in the box we had sent and took them out sparingly. I met his ninety-six-year-old roommate, Mr. Will, who had been a farmer like Chester. "Do you live in Dallas?" "No, I live in New York City." "New York City! What do you do for a living?" "I'm an artist." "I went up there once. I couldn't figure out how people made a living."

I went to spend a few days with Mother before returning to New York. We weeded her garden as well. She talked about Daddy's family. "I think you will have the Lewis white hair," she told me, referring to my long auburn hair. She talked about Caroline's sister, Aunt Jane, "my favorite. Her hair was black with a just a little gray. She showed the Indian blood."

When I came home, I went over to the Brooklyn Museum to meet Deirdre Lawrence, the principal librarian. She wanted to look at my artist's books and buy the *Reconstructed Codex* for the museum. To my surprise, she brought out books that she had already bought at Printed Matter, my "best-selling" *notes, notes* for one. Then, we looked together at the wonderful nineteenth-century photographs of Mayan ruins taken by Alfred Maudeslay. She mentioned that the

74. Daddy Chess in Briggins cemetery 75. Chess going into kitchen 76. Picture of Mother Gladys from box

curator, Charlotta Kotik, was reviewing slides by women artists for possible exhibitions. The next week, I sent a sheet of slides with a proposal for an installation called *Words/ Woods*. I think this was a little like showing Harmony the gessoed panels for *Door*, imagining that she could see what I envisioned. I wanted to make a series of artworks about the cemetery in the woods near Acworth, where many members of my family were buried. I saw this as a way of looking at history and nature. A few weeks later, I received a polite note "doubting" that my artwork would fit into their program.

There were several issue collectives at work for *Heresies*. We had members of the Mother Collective on each issue—Robin Michals was working on the Art in Unestablished Channels issue and Avis Lang was part of the issue on Aging. I proposed submitting page art related to my grandparents' aging. Somehow, Avis and I fell into a discussion about my work at the abortion clinic. It was still a difficult subject for me, but Avis wanted to interview me. She had had an illegal abortion. "As soon as I left the building, I couldn't remember anything that had happened there." The page art morphed into Avis's interview. I called Hannah Wilke to ask if she would send something for the Aging issue. I liked the work she had made when her mother was dying of cancer. Hannah told me that she had just been diagnosed with lymphoma, the same disease that had killed her mother. "I am trying to be nice now. I saw some paintings of yours this spring—they were nice." When Hannah died in 1993, she had a posthumous exhibition at Ronald Feldman Gallery. The opening was a bit like a wake with her pink vagina bubblegum sculptures rendered this time in black and photos of herself saucily nude, revealing the huge lump that had grown on her neck. She had made a series of artworks using her hair. Rows of her shorn lockets were framed like calligraphy, creating a text that we could not decipher except for its bravery. When Roger and I were in Montreal, we spent an evening with Lani Maestro, a Filipino artist.

77. Robin Michals, *Just Kidding*, paintings with open books of racial stereotypes blocking women's faces

She had also made work with her hair, cutting her long hair and gluing it onto the gallery walls in homage to friends who had been tortured because of their political resistance while she had escaped to safety in Canada.

I had started working part time again at American Heritage Publishers, researching an article on the logjams that used to form on Red River, the river that had watered my grandparents' farms. The editor, Fred Allen, mentioned the photocopier book *Wash & Iron* that he had received at the *Latitudes of Time* show. The side with photos of my childhood clothesline read: *We would go to the washeteria, Mother & I/Inside, the steaming tubs with bluing & rinse water/We washed by hand/I liked to put my hands inside the bluing water.* "Because I think about it, it's my own memory now," Fred said.

Members of the Mother Collective were working on an anniversary issue to celebrate ten years of publication. By the time we completed the issue, it became Heresies: 12 Years; we worked two years beyond our anniversary decade. But we were able to organize a benefit exhibit for the magazine's first decade on time. Emma Amos, Kay Kenny, and I negotiated with the directors of the Lower East Side gallery, PPOW, for the use of the space, and I was chosen to coordinate the show despite Kay's objections. She had become increasingly critical of me, citing my frequent lateness to meetings. We met one evening at Sue Heinemann's loft to develop ideas for the show. Faith, Linda, Josely, Lucy, Emma, Kay, Betsy, and I sat around talking, trying to figure out a title; "What's Up? Heresies Is Ten Years Old! Issues that Won't Go Away? Issues" finally won. No one could decide on an answer to the core question of what is feminist art, so we agreed to sponsor a visual poll in the form of a call for postcards and create a wall of responses at the show. Emma wanted to heighten attention to the exhibit by asking famous people, such as Paloma Picasso or Gloria Vanderbilt, to participate. But would any of these women actually

 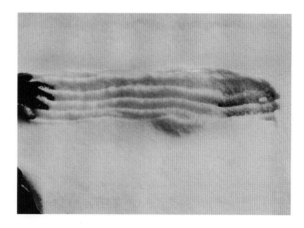

78. Hannah Wilke, *Brushstrokes No.6*, artist's hair on paper 79. Lani Maestro, *Incision to Heal* exhibition card

agree to come? I thought we should copy Martha Wilson and just impersonate famous people. We pictured dressing up like notorious stars such as Tammie Faye Bakker, Nancy Reagan, Fawn Hall, Phyllis Schlafly, and Imelda Marcos and arriving in fancy cars to infiltrate the opening. Then, we settled down and decided instead to simply invite all of us—our community of artists and activists who had participated in the magazine during the past decade, ten times ten—one hundred artists to show our artworks in a giant birthday party event (we ended up including 130). I went home and started working on my artwork for the show, aptly called *Running Out of Time*. The Contragate hearings kept me company on the radio as I painted.

Roger and I went over one evening to visit Sylvia and Lawrence. I told Sylvia about my spate of rejections from dealers and curators. Josely had tried to interest her dealer, John Terne, in my work. "I think he doesn't like your use of twigs, which I love," Josely said. Sylvia had experienced similar rejections. She told me that the artist and dealer Betty Parsons hadn't liked her work all those years they knew each other. Lawrence was in a wheelchair with his degenerating spinal condition, but this didn't affect his ability to regale his guests with caustic remarks. "Philosophy is for artists what ornithology is for birds," he commented, quoting his friend Barnett Newman.

Reconstruction Project traveled to Eye Level Gallery in Halifax early in the fall. I received a $700 stipend ("every artist receives a similar stipend," the Canadians explained) that paid for the trucking of the artworks from Montreal and for my airline ticket and the new poster I designed. Freda and Lani came to hang their companion show, and we had an intense weekend of work and conversation. I stayed one night with Barbara Lounder and Bob Bean; Barbara and I were already veteran collaborators from our shows in Montreal. They lived in a pristine farmhouse near Halifax; their artworks were also pristine. He was assembling a series of jars—one

80-81. Double page from *Heresies* issue #24, *What Is Feminist Art?* 82. Anita Steckel, *New Mona on New York*

consisted of wheat berries in a clean canning jar with a photo of a grain elevator inside. We talked about the corruption of local politicians. "They're hillbillies out here," he said, and I hoped he wouldn't notice the traces of my own accent.

Nancy Spero didn't frame her work. Its fragility was part of its ethos; a long panel of white paper with irregular edges with cutout figures depicting synthesized historical violence pasted along the panel and interspersed among printed words. Nancy's work was particularly meaningful for the artists in our circle both for formal reasons and for its depiction of violence against women—as well as its restrained eroticism. I simply pinned her seven-foot paper panel to the wall with pushpins. When I returned to Canada to install the Halifax show, I was informed that a small corner of her paper panel had been ripped. I wouldn't have noticed it, but there it was: a tiny triangle about two inches wide missing from the upper corner. They had saved the corner and I made a temporary repair. Powerhouse Gallery had insurance and offered to have it restored. When I returned to New York City, I called Nancy, expecting her not to care, but she was upset. "Will I have to sue you, Sabra?" she joked. "No," I said. I personally delivered the restored work to her loft after the Halifax show closed. We unrolled the piece together and inspected the repaired corner. It was fine. "I really appreciate your including me in these shows," she said. Nancy pulled out two of her folding metal chairs and invited me to sit down in the spare loft. Leon was working nearby, painting a large canvas, stopping briefly to criticize Nancy for leaving a light bulb burning. She made tea and then produced one Petit Beurre cookie, my favorite, from her kitchen cabinet, carefully replacing the box. We had seconds.

The sculptor Gertrude Barnstone used to stay in our loft when we would travel to New Mexico, driving up from Houston in her pickup truck. I knew Gertrude from various WCA events. She had studied welding as a young woman after separating from her husband, the architect who

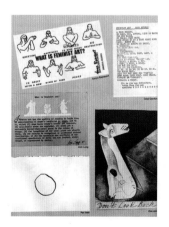
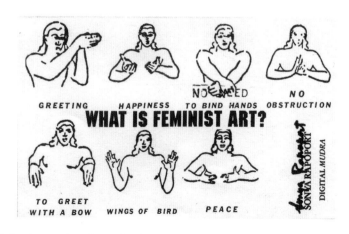

83. *What is Feminist Art?, Heresies* issue #24 visual spread continues 84. Sonya Rappaport, postcard response

had designed the Rothko Chapel at the Menil Collection. She supported herself and her children by working as an industrial welder, and that craft branched into commissions for brightly colored gates and assembled sculptures. A few weeks after I returned from Halifax, Roger and I went to New Mexico for a short visit. Gertrude stayed in our place, making drawings of our many cats that then appeared as cut out figures on her welded gates. Our plan was to camp at several archaic sites—Chaco Canyon, Keet Seel, Betatakin, and Mesa Verde—and visit friends. "You came a year too early," Henry Sauerwein said when we showed up at the Wurlitzer Foundation in Taos. Frankie was still living in town, but planned to leave for a residency at The Studio, a retreat for lesbian artists in New Hampshire. She had never removed her artworks and furniture from Kate's apartment in Brooklyn, so we agreed to move her things into a storage facility when we returned. My seventeen-year-old tortoiseshell cat, Sené, was sick when I left, and I feared she might die while I was drawing and hiking among the Anasazi sites. I kept dreaming about her; she was alive when I returned and my corner garden was still in bloom.

　　We decided to honor Lucy for the *Heresies* benefit at PPOW Gallery. It was our twelfth anniversary, and Lucy was the only member of the collective who had been a member consistently since its inception. The honor, of course, upset Lucy, whose métier was based on talking about other people and not about herself, but she agreed. I was still inviting artists to participate. I called Louise Bourgeois. "Did you like the book I sent you?" I asked, referring to *150 Artists Book*. "Not at all." "Why not?" "Because it only reproduced one artist. I don't think it was democratic." "But we reproduced everyone's work." "I've got to go." I called Joan Snyder. "I like *Heresies*." Michelle Stuart felt pressed. "I'm feeling like not organizing anything for a while," I complained. "I bet you are," she conceded. I designed an exhibition card with a drawing of a birthday cake bursting with candles and every participant's name listed. Emma and Josely liked

85. *Reconstruction Project*, (white wall), Zox, Gilbert, Smith, Spero 86. Spero and Savilli, book page 87. Spero, *Artaud*

the card, and May complimented its small size; others complained, in keeping with criticism/ self-criticism. In between, I was slowly making the paper sculptures for *Running Out of Time*—a series of thirteen small houses, each a symbol of nature and based on one of the four Aztec thirteen-year calendars. Roger constructed a base shaped like a little table, using my snaky pattern for the tabletop.

For two weeks, I had been keeping a listing by my telephone. Daddy Chess had suffered a stroke, and the list was my daily notation of the report by the hospital's nurse as his condition slowly improved. He had played dominos with Mr. Will the day before he fell. He had gone to his house and visited Mother Gladys's niece, Jewel, that same day. "I walked over to the house looking for her," he told Jewell. "I realized then I wasn't going to find her. I'm not satisfied anywhere without her." I arranged to fly to Texas to visit him in the hospital. Mother wanted to see me as well. "My nerves are running like a sugar tree." The day before my trip, Daddy Chess had a heart attack and died. Once again, I flew above the East Coast, watching a forest fire and drawing the shapes of the rivers as the plane neared Tennessee and the mountains flattened. Mother met me, and we drove down to my grandparent's house. At the viewing that evening, I struggled to recognize Chester without his felt hat. Everyone was remembering his gravel truck. The local florist had made a wreath with orange chrysanthemums and leaves. "I couldn't imagine ribbons for Mr. Parks; he was too masculine for that." We buried him the following afternoon next to Mother Gladys. After the funeral, everyone came back to their old place and sat around in the living room telling stories between eating and crying. I saw Mother Gladys's first cousin Mildred. "Sabra, you're supposed to still be a baby!" That night, Mother and I took the woman's way out of our grief and cleaned the kitchen, washing all the dishes from the donated food. She told more stories. Chester used to haul logs. He was a big man and could lift them off the freight cars

88-89. *Heresies: Issues That Won't Go Away*, PPOW Gallery show card 90. Susan Bee, *What is Feminist Art?* postcard

by hand. Sometimes, he would bid on cutting logs in the woods; he would hire my Daddy's father, Harry, to help figure the number of board feet a tree could yield. Harry was illiterate because he had quit school when he was nine to work in the logging camps to support his widowed mother. But he had the ability to figure linear feet or the weight of an animal simply by looking. If Chester got the job, he paid Harry.

I slept that night in Mother Gladys's back room. It was her workroom and bedroom and housed two big metal-framed beds and her sewing machine. "She was always working on a quilt when I was a child," Mother said. "At night, she would roll the quilt like a scroll and hang it above the bed, and then resume working the next day." She was still quilting as her health failed. One time, Mother went to visit her in the hospital. Mother Gladys said, "Christine, I've been trying to finish you a quilt, but I realize now you'll have to finish your own quilt." Mother and I kept looking for that unfinished quilt and finally found a box of neatly folded and cut cloth squares. She gave it to me. The next day, Buddie and Mary Jane, Mother's siblings, returned and each adult child removed their own baby picture from the bedroom walls where the children had kept watch for over forty years. They divided the quilts and the dresser scarves. Each child took five quilts; I asked for the white quilt and the morning star quilt that my great-grandmother Lillie had pieced. I carried the quilts back with me on the plane. I also asked for Daddy Chess's loose denim jacket, the one he often wore. I discovered that he had been carrying around her last grocery list in his jacket pocket.

Shortly after I got back home, my cat, Sené, died. I had now lost a cat with the death of each grandparent. Africans give people nicknames. Sené was one of my names when I lived in Guinea; it meant, "you are the color of gold." I named the tortoiseshell cat for her golden-striped

91. Roger Mignon (both), Doorway into Mother Gladys's empty kitchen 92. Dining room with *Last Supper* reproduction

arm. Just before I left N'Zérékoré, Niankoye, the Guerzé man who helped us keep house, named me Gah-may, meaning, "wherever you go, you will be respected."

       We had visitors. The traditional Nigerian carver Lamidi Fakeye was in town staying with us before traveling to give workshops in Missouri. We had met in Ibadan over twenty years before; he often stayed with us en route to his various teaching projects. We would go on arduous shopping expeditions to buy gifts and supplies for the crowd of family and friends who awaited his return—pointy-toed shoes for women who had supplied sheets of paper with their penciled foot outlines for size; carving tools; watches; calculators; film; cameras; hair dye; children's books; and wrestling videos. We would go the length of Canal Street, and then try our luck along the discount stores on Fourteenth Street. Roger and I gave a party and invited our neighbor, Obadiah, and my old Peace Corps friend, Maggie Rodgers. Obadiah, or Obie as we called him, had grown up in the projects in Cleveland and had become an orphan at eighteen when the woman he called his grandmother had suddenly died. He had learned his craft as a jeweler at Kenkeleba House, a cultural center we Peace Corps trainees had visited from nearby Oberlin. When Martin Luther King, Jr. was assassinated and Cleveland had erupted in flames, Obie simply got on a bus for New York City and never returned. Marina and Willie Birch also came to the party. Willie brought along photos of his own artwork to show Lamidi, but scarcely looked at his carved sculptures. Lamidi noticed the disparity. Lamidi was impressed, however, by Obie's modesty and his work as a silversmith. The Metropolitan Museum of Art had commissioned Obie to make all the lost wax casting reproductions sold in the gift shop during the Tutankhamun exhibit. Shortly after Lamidi's departure, Freda arrived from Canada, coming to help hang the *Heresies* benefit at PPOW Gallery and to honor Lucy.

93. Photographs of three babies on Gladys's bedroom wall 94. Lamidi Fakeye and Roger in front of *Oh Grandma...*

Freda and I installed the show for three days with a changing array of helpers—Faith Wilding, Merle Temkin, Robin Michals, Emma, Linda, and Josely. Robin had painted political murals on the building next to PPOW, so she knew the neighborhood and the gallery well. Josely and I had reconciled, "closer for the distance." Perhaps, we would write about our experiences organizing the show. She arrived late one evening when our energies were flagging, bringing wine and cookies. The works kept being delivered throughout the installation, and each had its own set of delicate instructions. Nancy Azara's wooden mask was made with a complex arrangement of sticks. She had drilled a single little hole in the back so the mask could be hung on a nail, but it leapt off the wall when we hammered another nail across the room. The sticks scattered. Robin and I gathered them up and called Nancy, who rushed over to the gallery, very upset by the accident, and restored her piece. We hung the wall of postcards. Ora sent one of a dog facing backwards—*Don't Look Back*. Mine had two words ornately painted, *Subject Matters*. Not surprisingly, I had run out of time for completing all thirteen houses, but I arranged eight across the snake-shaped table set into the corner.

Since the show was also a birthday party for *Heresies*, Carrie Cooperider had baked a beautiful cake. I had drawn a big birthday cake replete with candles on the invitation. I went to the upscale restaurant where Carrie worked to pick it up, entering a room filled with mirrors punctuated by portraits of ballerinas. All the cooks were excited by the extravagance of the cake, which was decorated with a thicket of sugary blue cornflowers and a phalanx of dime-store rings.

The opening was packed with women artists from all the various groups; many had worked on an issue collective or the Mother Collective. When we brought out the cake, I asked every woman who had worked in any way with *Heresies* to come up and get a ring. We gave out all the rings. "It's been a long time since I've seen this kind of bonding event," Betsy later told

95. Fakeye's photograph of Owen, Fabio, Obie, Maggie, Sabra, Roger, and Marithelma
96. Carol Sun and Linda Peer at *Heresies* event

me. Then, we had a ceremony for Lucy. Each collective member had made an artist's book page, which we presented one at a time for her to place in a box. When May's turn came, she said, "it has to be said," and handed her a page: "I Love Lucy." Avis Lang gave a performance as the *Representative of Ladies Against Women*, referring to *HER-sies* and *MRS. Lippard*. We even managed to sell a lot of artwork, albeit mostly to each other. Michelle Stuart bought Louise Bourgeois's small marble house, Emma bought a piece by Donna Henes, Joan Snyder bought a collage by Nancy Spero, I bought a little wooden wolf piece (*Catch Me If You Can*) by Holly Zox, and Nina Yankowitz bought a drawing by Ida Applebroog. We had allowed the artists the usual gallery commission, so people contributed good artworks.

Ana Mendieta was having a posthumous retrospective at the New Museum. Roger, Freda, and I went to see the dense show. I knew Ana's work well, but had not seen the full-size tree bark works she had been making in Rome shortly before her death. They leaned against the museum walls like giant husks with her *siluetas* carved inside. Ana must have been trying to figure out how to make permanent works based on the ideas for her earthen *siluetas* that continued to exist purely as photos. She had also engraved big tropical leaves framed behind glass. Lucy had loaned the amazing little branding iron that Ana had commissioned in the form of her handprint. There was a video in which Ana danced again and again in a pink satiny dress at a party celebrating her Prix de Rome and I found myself crying in the darkened room.

We had not healed the rifts in the women's community caused by Ana's death; most of us called it her murder. It was simpler for me; I had not been a friend of Carl's. I had lunch with May. She wanted to discuss her conflicted loyalties with the two. "They were both drunk; no one will ever know what happened." I disagreed. "They were both drunk, but only Ana is dead."

 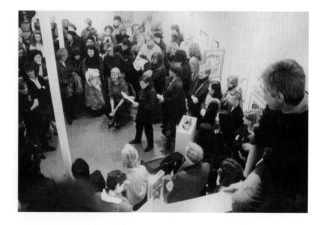

97. Roger Mignon (all), *Heresies* party honoring Lucy Lippard: Eating cake and taking rings 98. Reading dedications to Lucy

Mary Beth Edelson had written May a letter with a quote from Carl Jung: "You mustn't forget the dark side."

Lucy and I went to a panel at the New Museum. She was considering becoming inactive with *Heresies*, moving over into our catch-all category of associate. After all, we had given her a gold watch at the benefit. The panel was a discussion between essentialists and deconstructivists or structuralists, depending on the country of choice for the feminist theoretician. The audience was packed with women artists from the various camps—feminists, anti-feminists, lesbian activists, Great Goddess worshippers, political activists, and agnostics, like myself, in regards to theory. The debate made a wry contrast between academicians for whom these ideas were an intellectual exercise and those of us practitioners who felt a call to action for our beliefs.

 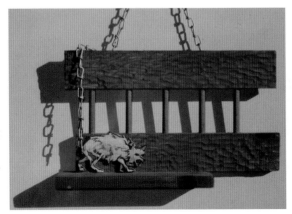 

99. Readers Lang, Carvalho, Heinemann, and Lanfear 100. Holly Zox, *Catch Me If You Can* 101. BIOTA fashion performers

1. Frances Buschke, *Towards Me the Darkness Comes Rattling/Reconstruction Project*, 1984

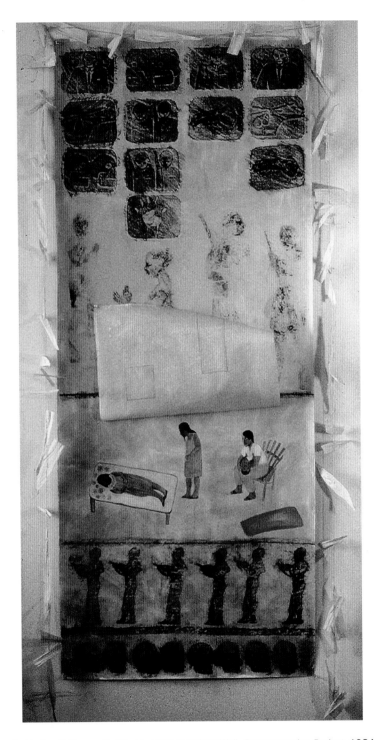

2. Marina Gutierrez, *Untitled* (unveiled), Yellow Wall, *Reconstruction Project*, 1984

3. Helen Oji, *Untitled (Volcano Series #48)*, Black Wall 4. Sabra Moore, *Renew*, Yellow Wall

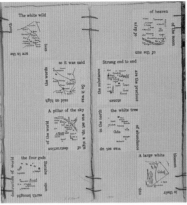

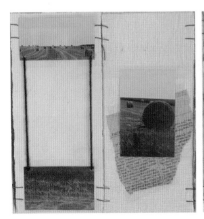

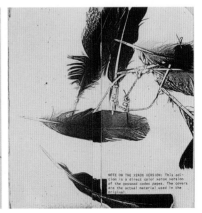

5. Double Pages, *Reconstructed Codex* (top to bottom): Colleen Cutschall, Sharon Gilbert, Chris Costan, Kate Correa, Holly Zox, Jaune Quick-to-See Smith, Catalina Parra, and Sabra Moore

6. Liliana Porter, *Reconstruction, Yellow Wall, Reconstruction Project*, 1984

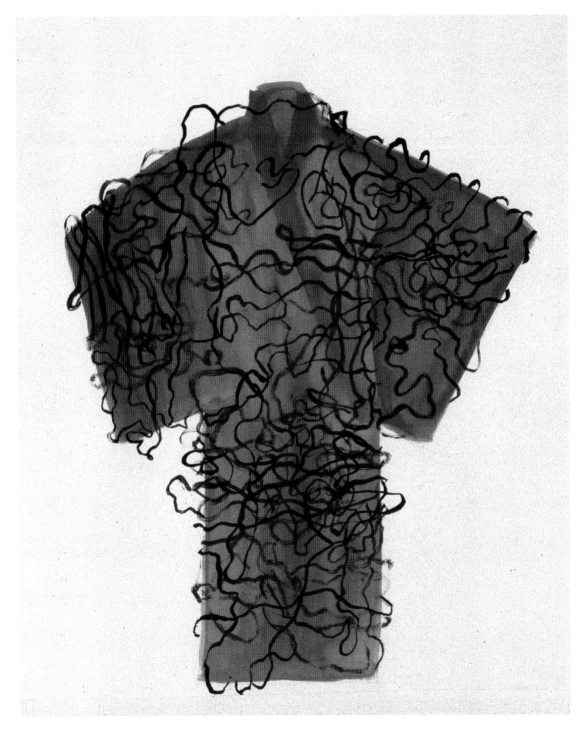

7. Kazuko Miyamoto, *Untitled*, watercolor drawing of a kimono on paper

8. Sabra Moore, *Door*, oil on gessoed wood, found branches, painted and tied

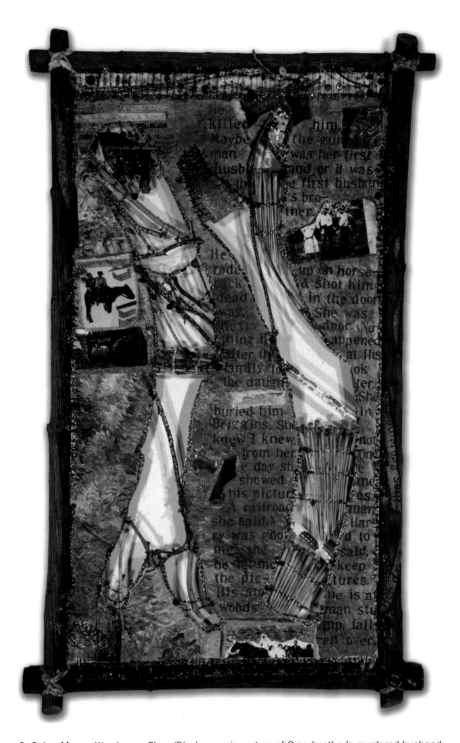

9. Sabra Moore, *Woodsman, Place/Displace* series, story of Grandmother's murdered husband

10. Sabra Moore, *Lillie's Peaks* with *Gypsy Baby Cart* emerging, *Place/Displace* series

11. Sabra Moore, *Not a Civilian*, Place/Displace series, rubbing from tombstone of Dane Lewis

12. Book pages, *150 Artists Book, Connections Project/Conexus:* Vivian E. Browne, Michelle Stuart, Carolee Schneemann, Nancy Chunn, Sabra Moore, Charleen Touchette, Marina Moers, Vida Hackman, Grace Graupe-Pillard, Pat Mercado, Katie van Scherpenberg, Howardena Pindell

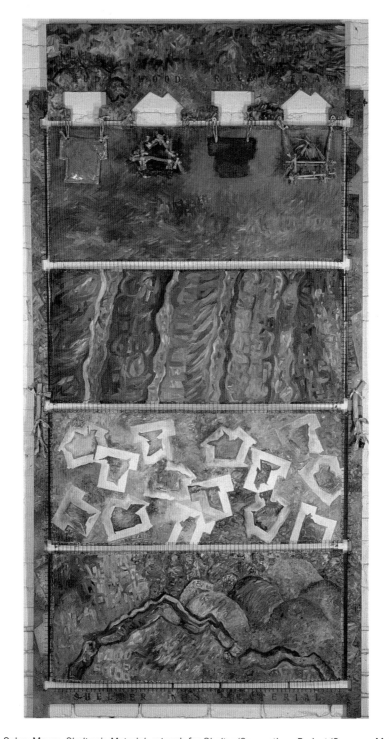

13. Sabra Moore, *Shelter is Material*, artwork for *Shelter/Connections Project/Conexus*, MoCHA

14. Marina Gutierrez, *Race, Connections Project/Conexus*, MoCHA, 1987

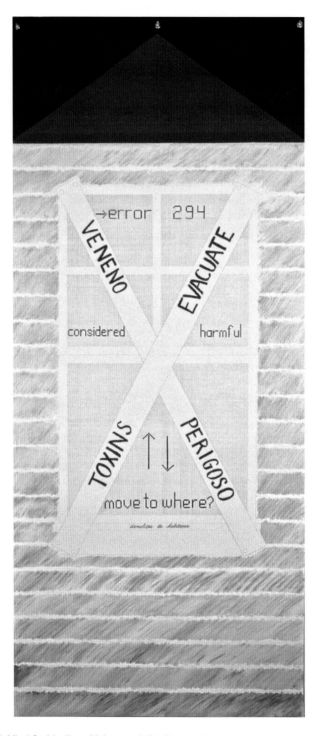

15. Mimi Smith, *Error 294*, artwork for *Shelter/Connections Project/Conexus*

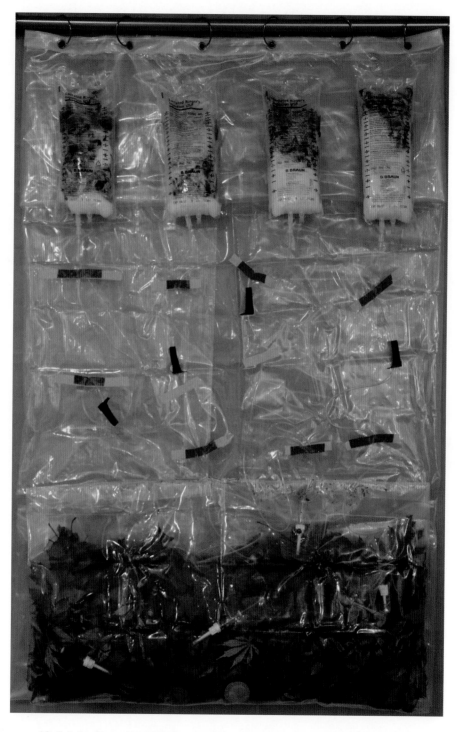

16. Catalina Parra, *Mortal Body*, artwork for *War/Death, Connections Project/Conexus*

17. Sabra Moore, *Preservation Work*, artwork for the Canadian venues of *Reconstruction Project*, yellow wall, 1987

We Move Into the World & Take Our Issues with Us

"We're in the citadel," Day Gleeson exclaimed. All of us, accustomed to our opposition from outside an institution like the Museum of Modern Art (MoMA), were now celebrating an opening with our works and actions honored. *Committed to Print: Social and Political Themes in Recent American Art* was the 1988 show that alarmed art critic John Russell, who wrote an exasperated review in the *New York Times*, offended that he recognized so few names of the selected artists. Of course, we all knew each.

The show was divided into various rooms by theme. *Reconstructed Codex* resided in the room on War/Revolution near an etching by Marina Gutierrez, called *Soldiers and Civilians*, in which lines of silhouetted figures from the two groups are repeated until they gradually and violently intersect. Marina brought her mother to the opening. "Imagine! My daughter's work is on these walls!" The installation was immaculate. The *Reconstructed Codex* was stretched out elegantly like an accordion inside a climate-controlled box inset into one of the walls. "Do you

1-2. Arlene Raven and others look at unfurled *Reconstructed Codex* during opening of MoMA's *Committed to Print* show

like it?" Curator Deborah Wye rushed over and hugged me, "Of course, I like it! It's beautiful!" Most of the artists who made pages for the book were at the opening. Kate came over with her new partner, Lisa, and handed me a rose. "It's so wonderful to see this work treated with respect," Robin Michals said. "This is like a Latin American show; it's so political," Liliana Porter exclaimed. Sylvia came to show support. "Your work looks good," she told me. "It's a good show if you like this kind of work."

We wandered around looking at all the artworks, most of which were by artists in our circles. *Connections Project/Conexus* (*150 Artists Book*) was in the Gender room near the iconic *Some Living American Women Artists/Last Supper* by Mary Beth Edelson and May Stevens's *Rosa Luxemburg* print. Nancy Spero's *Hanging Totem II*, replete with tortured witches, was in the same room; though Nancy had work displayed in almost every room. Emma Amos's beautiful and disturbing print, *Take One*, made for the *Art Against Apartheid* show, was in the Race/Culture room. This print justly received a lot of critical attention. Emma had intersected repeated drawings of the same bound and blindfolded nude woman with arbitrary bands of color labeled "black, white, colored." Over 120 artists and collectives were in the show, including the *Heresies* collective represented by the issue most of us had criticized: the oversized Women's Pages.

"All the outsiders are inside," I wrote in my journal the next day as I sat savoring the thick catalogue. The timeline at the back listed most of the exhibits we had created over the past decade, giving official credence to our interlocking movements. The museum had bought extra copies of each artist's book so that viewers could thumb through the pages at the exhibit. The curators had also arranged for artists' books from the exhibit to be sold at the museum shop. I delivered ten copies of *150 Artists Book* to the bookstore before the opening. "They're nice," the store manager said, "you should see some of the others."

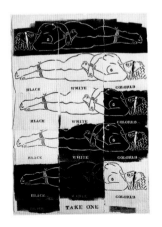  

3. Emma Amos, *Take One* (stencils) 4. Cover, *Committed To Print* 5. Cover, *Heresies* issue #14, Women's Pages

I dream that I am trying to escape an enemy, running across roofs and down stairways, bumbling into a room with Mayan frescoes and rushing out past a dance hall. Suddenly, I am on a dirt road. It is cold and snowy. Two big white birds looking improbably like pelicans are skimming the air. One is trailing blue ribbons from its outstretched wings. The sun comes out and the sky fills with people parachuting and I am flying among them.

I was still trying to juggle my day jobs. "Maybe I'm working too much," I thought, "though there doesn't seem to be too much money." Just before the opening at MoMA, I was called to do the photo permissions for *Power of Myth*, a book based on the public television series of conversations between Bill Moyers and Joseph Campbell, and I was invited to a meeting at Doubleday with their editor, Jackie Onassis, and others. Here was a conjunction of events with powerful people or institutions and all I could think about was how I had nothing to wear. Roger wisely suggested I wear something I already had. "You can't compete with Jackie O." I went, determined to arrive on time for once. The meeting room was full. Jackie O. was dressed plainly in black, eager to serve everyone coffee. She had brought her own sack lunch. I was introduced to the Campbell book editor from the University of Texas, Betty Sue Flowers. "You look familiar," I said. "You look familiar," she said. "I'm from Texas too; my family comes from Clarksville, well, Acworth actually." "I know Acworth." "I was just there for my grandfather's funeral." "I was just at my grandfather's funeral too; he's from Clarksville." I remembered what the preacher had said at Daddy Chess's funeral: "What is missing is Mr. Parks's gravel truck. Mr. Mirabelle is in the next room. He used to sell gasoline to Mr. Parks." We had seen each other at our grandfathers' wakes. Now, everyone was looking at us.

Each of us was given an impressive bound notebook with photos and lists of all the book illustrations—though, later, this illusion of preparedness was simply that. A third of the

6. Sharon Gilbert talks to Liliana Porter at MoMA opening 7. Lanfear (hat) and Amos in *Economics/Class Struggle* Room

pictures had never been selected and there was a two-week print deadline for publication. Jackie O. sat next to me and noticed that I was hurriedly writing notes on each blank page. Doubleday's art director, Alex Gotfryd, was showing us the design for the cover; the title, *Power of Myth*, was emblazoned above a pre-Renaissance painting of Adam and Eve in the garden. Bill Moyers was on the phone from Texas, telling Alex that he had to find a different image for the cover despite the tight publication deadlines. Adam and Eve are not a myth in East Texas, he insisted. No one there would buy a book called *Power of Myth* with a painting of Adam and Eve on the cover. So, the designer switched to a dragon, leaving believers from a more geographically distant cultural tradition to safely protest.

I rushed around finding the missing images and arranged a week later to meet again with Jackie O. and Alex Gotfryd. The accepted method is for a photo researcher to bring in many alternatives and allow the designer and editor to make the illustration choices. I began that meeting by presenting a selection of photocopies. Jackie O. turned quietly to me: "You and I think alike. You should take more responsibility and just pick what you like." Then, she left for a luncheon with the writer Joyce Carol Oates. "It's terrible," she whispered, "I don't usually have lunch. Your pal, Marshall, wants to see you." She was referring to Marshall De Bruhl, the managing editor of Bantam Books. "Jackie was quite taken with you," Marshall told me. I had freelance work for many years from Doubleday and Bantam after this encounter. I would use Jackie O.'s elegant empty office at 666 Fifth Avenue during the afternoons when she didn't come into work. Marithelma and others used to tease me about my "friend," whom I never saw again.

Carl Andre's murder trial was taking place during the first weeks of the *Committed to Print* show. Ruby Rich called to urge me to attend, but I couldn't make myself face the trial. Josely, Howardena, Juan Sanchez, and many other artists and friends were going daily to offer support

8. *War/Revolution* Room with *Reconstructed Codex* next to W. Wiley guitar 9. Marithelma Costa and Sabra at opening

to Ana's sister and mother. Carl had been able to waive his right to a jury trial, so the verdict was solely in the hands of the judge. His lawyers used photos of Ana's bloody *siluetas* to argue that she was unstable—an "unconscious suicide" whose artworks prefigured a death wish—and to raise doubt about the sequence of events the night she died. The deli worker who testified that he heard her screaming had a history of hearing voices. Marina described the scene in the courtroom when Carl was acquitted. He was sitting by himself, reading the newspaper, and showed no emotion. The judge told Ana's supporters, "Be quiet and leave now."

I dream that I am walking up the yellow gravel driveway to Mother Gladys's house. Daddy Chess is bareheaded and standing in the yard, talking to Mother. I go over and hug him. I know somehow that he is dead and briefly visiting us. "I've seen Lillie," he says, referring to his mother. "You've seen Lillie!" I reply.

It was a bitterly cold winter, but we bundled up and went out to see the shows of friends. Nancy Spero had a solo exhibit at the Cash Gallery, and May was installing two huge photo murals related to the murder of Rosa Luxemburg at the New Museum. Roger and I met Ora after Nancy's opening to watch a performance of a Korean woman shaman, Hiah Park, at Asia Society. We were all comfortably seated in the big auditorium as she danced with her drums and shawls. She began "fishing" the audience, and I felt literally pulled out of my seat when she gestured directly to me. She had already pulled others to join her on the stage. The drum was pounding, and I pranced towards her, mimicking her motions. She gave me a red banner and draped a red robe over my shoulders, and I followed her drum beat, feeling momentarily energized by her amazing plucking of me. We touched flattened palms. The drum stopped. She retrieved the red banner, and I returned to my ordinary seat between Roger and Ora.

10. Sabra Moore, *Flowers* (series with grandparents walking into cemetery) 11. Sabra Moore, *Leaves (double)*

May had taught a class on women artists at School for Visual Arts (SVA) for many years; she was retiring and asked me to apply. SVA had already hired the artist Barrie Karp, who taught at several schools, but Barrie invited me to come speak. I decided to focus on my own work rather than the collective shows or *Heresies*, bringing up issues of class and difference. Afterwards, a young student came over; he was from a little town in the Ozarks, "where everyone knows everyone." Now, he felt different in both places. "What did you mean about not leaving your class?" he wanted to know. "Remember that the people in the city won't be able to understand the culture in the Ozarks, but you know both." "Are you saying the two are equal?" "Yes. It's something you'll have to struggle with before you find your way." After the discussion, Barrie came over. "Your work has a kind of playfulness. I used to work like that when I was a child. Then, I got involved in serious painting. I don't have that kind of feeling anymore."

On the spring equinox, Roger and I experimented at home with standing eggs on end as Donna Henes did in her outdoor performances. Three erect eggs stood on the gray painted floor of our loft until our orange cat Beowulf came over, sniffed, and knocked them back into their proper horizontal positions. I had talked on three panels in one week and needed a respite—a *Heresies* panel with Faith and Emma at MoCHA a panel on cross-cultural issues at the Schomburg Center for Research in Black Culture in Harlem that Betsy Damon moderated (the panelists were diverse, but the audience was white), and a panel on ethics and aesthetics at SOHO20 Gallery with Miriam Schapiro, Gino Rodriguez, and Terry Fugate Wilcox. Miriam refused to introduce herself or describe her art, proclaiming that her work was well known. I was left to fight alone with the men against the concept of universal values in art.

A few weeks later, Josely and I drove the artworks for *Connections Project/Conexus* to New Bedford, Massachusetts for a venue at the university gallery. I had been apprehensive after

12. Josely and Sabra hanging art in New Bedford 13. Installation, Pacheco e Chaves, Applebroog, and Bueno, *War/Death*

our conflicts during the installation at MoCHA, but we ended up working well together. We were united in anger against the absent gallery director and stoked our resentment over a meal at a Portuguese restaurant in town. Later, we told May about our travails. "Rather than criticizing him, you should ask him for a one-person show," she advised. We had gone to May's studio to select a different artwork to take to Brazil. Josely did not want to be embarrassed by exhibiting a Spanish language piece in São Paulo. May was twenty years older than me, and I admired her youthful spirit, but her openness often contained a barb. Each time she saw me, she had to mention my height.

I was back at work in my studio, making a series of small memorial pieces about my grandparents. I thought of them as bulbs in the ground and called the series *Leaves & Flowers*, using repeated laser transfer prints of the two walking into the cemetery in Acworth. I was also including fragments of that photo in *Flowers*, a small photocopier book edition for the International Society of Copier Artists' (ISCA) summer 1988 *Annual Bookworks Edition*. Roger was organizing materials to pack for his upcoming residency at the Wurlitzer Foundation in Taos. I would join him there in the fall. Ann Harris had asked for slides for a talk she was presenting at the Asia Society in June, shortly before Roger's departure. A dealer had told her recently, "If I can't get it in nine seconds, it's not art." This had set her thinking about us artists who made contemplative work versus the mammoth-scale paintings she called "importance art." She had selected some slides of my painted house sculptures to show alongside Harmony's series on *descansos*, the roadside memorials in New Mexico, and Ora's finely crafted narrative still lifes. She described our artworks as "beautifully resolved and morally considered." We went with Sylvia to hear her talk.

Our editorial collective had been meeting all spring for the anniversary issue of *Heresies*, replete with disagreements about the cover design and the selection of articles. The magazine

150 Artists Book pages, *War/Death* (both): 14.Cilia Colli, 15. Maria Lucia Carneiro, 16. *Connections Project* installation

was starting to get attention from outside writers with the concept of "importance" always in the fore. Ruth Bass had interviewed many of us for an article in *ARTnews*, but then mentioned only the three or four participants who were well known in the art world. Moira Roth, an art history professor at Mills College, was also writing an article; we considered her an ally since she had known Faith Wilding in California. We suggested she select twenty things to discuss from the twenty-three published issues. I was feeling the lack of class diversity in the magazine and wanted to introduce a Dear Heretics page. I wrote a series of letters from imaginary people from various regions and backgrounds, hoping to spark a fabricated dialogue, but I couldn't interest anyone else in developing the idea. Some of us had proposed a cover design with a grid of snapshots of all the women from the various collectives, similar to a high school yearbook. I liked this idea; Betsy called it "silly and trite." I had to agree with her, however, that printing a collective photo implied that the magazine was at a finish point. "It shocked me when Lucy felt like she would leave after we gave her an award," Betsy said. "You have a point," I added in exasperation. "I may be feeling like leaving." So, we started thinking of alternate ideas for the cover; mutants or Wonder Women were favorites. "The mutant definitely should have fur," Kathie suggested. "But that's like nature versus culture," Betsy countered. "Only if you set it up that way," I insisted. "Woman is identified with nature, not culture; the problem is that man is not identified with nature." Betsy and I argued. "But technology hasn't failed." "There are two holes in the sky." We returned to the idea of werewolves.

The summer of 1988 was fantastically hot. I was researching photos for *American Heritage of Invention & Technology* again and still finishing a project for Marshal at Bantam. "It looks like we're winning the war against the planet," the editor Fred Allen observed. The newspaper described the weather in the city as "tropical," but tropical without the monkeys or the oversized

17. Christy Rupp, *Humanitarian Aid* 18. Vanalyne Green, *Trick or Drink* performance 19. Nancy Burson, *Cat Woman*

flowers of N'Zérékoré. The city was digging up the sewer line in our street, so the gas in our building got turned off. The gas company refused to restore service until we residents corrected the violations they discovered with the installations of our hot water heaters. Our landlord refused to help.

It was hot; we took cold showers. Roger had left for Taos, calling me each night from the various towns where we often stayed together. When he reached Taos, Henry greeted him. "When is Mother Moore arriving?"

Clive Philpot called; he was the curator for MoMA's artists' books collection and wanted to buy a copy of *Reconstructed Codex* for the museum. "I was just showing your book to someone this morning; it's wonderful. I'll pay whatever you choose." He made an appointment for me to show him my other artist's books that fit their parameters of "multiplicity and availability." I got another request for the *Reconstructed Codex* from the Social Science Research Council. They wanted a copy for their lobby, assuming I would donate the book for free.

Clive sat in a light-filled office with a big window opening to the street. I liked how he dressed in a blue shirt and red tie. We sat down as I opened my box of books and he checked for the titles that the museum already owned. He had cofounded the PAD/D archive with Lucy. She was teaching this year in Colorado; we both missed her. "She had to leave," Clive said. "She was getting too fragmented here." I had brought *notes, notes*, *Making*, *Artifact/Artifice*, *Wash & Iron*, and the newly completed *Flowers*. I described *Gladys Sad Box*, part of the *AKIN* series I was developing with family stories, each book "one step removed" from the way my kinfolk might see the same story. "I think we should have all of them," he said. *Committed to Print* was about to close. "We are already talking about what comes next." My prices were modest. I sold the *Reconstructed Codex* for $125 and the small books for around $15 each, but I felt rich as I left his office.

 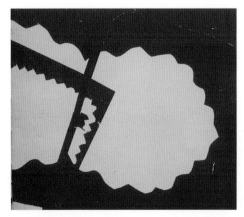 

20. Sabra Moore (all, limited edition photocopier books), *Artifact/Artifice* 21. *4/TELLS* (Opal) 22. *4/TELLS* (Caroline)

I was building my painting racks in the evenings, taking advantage of Roger's absence to get a lot of work done. I built the racks laying on their sides while listening to Jesse Jackson's speech at the Democratic National Convention, and then called our neighbor Barry to help me stand the first one up. He came upstairs with a new girlfriend from California. She recognized my name. She subscribed to *Heresies* and was active in the California WCA. Our animated conversation made Barry nervous, and he rushed out with his friend as soon as the rack was standing upright. I waited until Robin Michals visited to lift the second painting rack. Robin had just left an Artmakers mural project because of the personalities of some of the artists; we talked about conflicts in *Heresies*. Issue twenty-three, Coming of Age (formerly called Aging), was in production, and the production itself had become an issue. Kay Kenny had hired a man/woman design team, headed by Gail Bradney, without consulting the collective. Kathie Browne had been working on the design and felt like she had been fired. Many members were uncomfortable with having a man participate in the design, but Gail promptly resolved all these issues by resigning, finding the entire process cumbersome. "I am happily un-committing myself from *Heresies* (rather than have myself committed)," she wrote. Our multitiered structure could be difficult for editors of the Issue Collectives; they often heard our opinions indirectly from reading the minutes. The women working on Aging requested a meeting after we described them in writing as rigid. Editors Penny Goodfriend and Wopo Holup sat down with Kathie and me to rework the design. That seemed to temporarily resolve the problems.

Sylvia and Bibi came to visit. I wanted them to see the *Leaves & Flowers* series I was making about my grandparents and to discuss problems I was having with another painting, *Animal/Vegetable/Mineral*. Bibi had once made paintings about the destruction of nature. "I can't bear to look at those works anymore." We went downstairs to look at the garden; all the

23. *Heresies* issue #23, Coming of Age 24. Robin Michals, *Armed to the Teeth* 25. 81 Pearl Street garden near loading bay

flowers were blooming. Sylvia told me about a plant called Fire in the Mist. "When it loses its blossoms, it's called Devil in the Bush because it looks spiky." I had read about a temple in Thailand that was trying to reclaim a stolen lintel sold to the Art Institute of Chicago. The missing lintel depicted creation while the remaining lintel depicted destruction. "It isn't right to have destruction without creation."

A few days later, I hosted May and Josely. We three stood in the garden looking at the flowers, the roar of the traffic all around, big trucks braking as they turned under the bridge. A rough-looking man stopped near the fence, a stick in his hand, missing teeth. "I passed by the other day," he said, "the flowers were all lying down, but now they look nice!" "They got knocked down in the rain," I said. He smiled. Then, our building's maintenance man passed by, wearing his ill-fitting blond wig. "Everyone around here carries sticks," May observed as we rode the elevator to the sixth floor. I showed them Roger's studio before we went to mine. He had hung the painting *Grunk!* on his wall with its repeated images of himself as a caveman brandishing sticks. "The sticks again!" We walked through the loft to my studio, which faced the windows opposite the bridge, and then sat down to enjoy supper together. Later, May telephoned me. "I hadn't realized your work was so manifest and manifold."

Marithelma and I went to see Richard Samuelson, a former member of Atlantic Gallery, perform in a play. I was catching up with visits to women friends before leaving for New Mexico. Marithelma had just returned from ten days staying on the beach in Puerto Rico. "I saw these black men just standing on the beach, not swimming. No one was talking to them. I went over and asked them what they were doing. They said they were looking for money. Because of the current, money washes up from all the beaches onto this particular beach and gets caught in

26. Sabra in loft near Roger Mignon painting, *Oh Grandma...* 27. Golden light coming into the loft under the bridge arches

the algae. One man showed me $29 that he had made that day. It's terrible in Puerto Rico now; there are only the rich or the poor."

Artelia Court invited me to come see the clay sculptures she had been making. We met while we were both working at Tree Communications and when I was doing my first photo research project on Japanese art. I had thought of her as a writer; she had written *Puck of the Drom*, a book on Irish gypsies. She was involved in a decade-long bitter struggle with her former husband, a photographer, over child support. Her daughter, India, made her first film in college about this pitched battle between her parents and called it *The Inheritance*. Artelia was intense, but she was also witty; I loved talking to her. We went around her apartment trying to figure out how she could empty her bedroom and create a studio for the sculptures she was starting to make—inventive three-dimensional portraits in clay of friends and kin painted in vivid colors. We exchanged stories about our stubborn moments of shyness. I would often avoid places where I had enjoyed success, not returning to visit people at Printed Matter or Artists Space, for example, after having well-received shows at these venues and easy relationships during the projects.

Gertrude Barnstone was driving up from Texas to stay in our loft during my residency in Taos. I had put off telling Fred that I would be missing an issue of *Invention & Technology*. "I don't want to endanger my position on the magazine." "You don't have to worry about that." I had lined up a fellow photo editor as a replacement. I told Alex Gotfryd about the pending residency as well. He often asked me to research covers for Doubleday. Alex was a survivor of Auschwitz; he and his mother had been imprisoned there. He was thirteen when the camp was liberated; his mother died the same day. Alex had just finished a book he had designed about her.

I shipped off some of the *Leaves & Flowers* series to complete in Taos along with another box filled with pages for *Gladys Sad Box*. Gertrude had arrived, the moonflowers had finally

 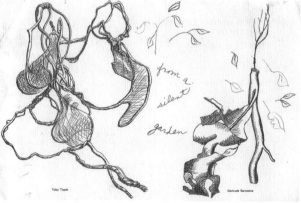

28. Sylvia's wisteria at Pearl Street garden 29. Gertrude Barnstone, *From a Silent Garden* show card

bloomed, and the weather had cooled. I fell asleep on the plane, waking to rows of clouds like the ones Georgia O'Keeffe had painted.

I had barely settled into my house at the Wurlitzer when Roger's brother called with the news of their father's death. This time, we flew together to Florida to bury Michael, Roger's father. "Stay as long as you need," Henry told us, "and come back." We sat in his parents' Florida apartment and called Michael's relatives in Italy. None of us spoke Italian, so I tried speaking in French and then Roger simply spoke in English, telling them that "Mike Mignon, née Michelangelo Mignone" had died. That challenging conversation made his death real for me; the boy who had immigrated alone from a mountain village at fifteen had died in Florida at eighty. He had shortened his name to suit his union organizing activities, eliminating the poetry. "My father had always lived in the real world," Roger said at the spare memorial. "He was a difficult and opinionated person, but he stood for what he believed. He had hoped to live long enough to vote for Dukakis." "Maybe, we could get an absentee ballot," someone quipped. A few days later, we flew back to New Mexico.

The land was there to comfort us. Taos is nestled between the Sangre de Cristo Mountains and a daunting rift formed by the Rio Grande River, leaving a vast plain opposite the gorge that glows violet and golden at sunset and is rimmed by another mountain range to the west. The sheer daily beauty is bracing. We started taking hikes together to gather my materials, finding nests of water-polished wood among the shiny basalt boulders that lined the river. Laden like burros, we would carry the collected wood back up the canyon in backpacks. My little house soon began to fill with found rusted metal and sticks of appealing shapes as I prepared to work. Alan Wells, Henry's assistant, asked me, "it's very exciting to see all of this. I think about you and Roger. He sits and paints. How does he stand this?" "We have separate studios."

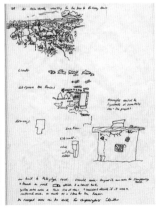

30. Roger at Tsankawi 31. Book #40, Sabra's journal drawings at Aztec Ruins 32. Book #40, drawings at Mesa Verde

This time, most of the residents were writers. Only Roger and I were visual artists. A poet and translator of Sufi poetry, Coleman Barks, arrived from his home in Georgia while we were in Florida. Ed Woods, a writer from Denver, was in the house across the field from mine. We residents met one evening to eat and talk. I used the word Eurocentric. "What's Eurocentric?" Coleman asked. "Is your work Eurocentric?" "No. As a woman artist, I have been left out of the dominant culture." I explained the ways I was trying to translate quilt making and women's experiences into my artworks. Coleman insisted that he was entirely involved with the feminine, with rivers, the Tennessee River, in particular, and its swelling and flux. "I find a certain kind of ambition today in women that is not feminine." "It's not ambition," I said, "it's anger." "I know about Kali," he replied.

The editors for the anniversary issue of *Heresies* were making final selections while I was in Taos. Faith Wilding sent me a packet of poems for my vote. "I know you are having a wonderful work-filled time, but your collective never sleeps and its long arm can reach you even in Taos." She had included minutes from the most recent meeting along with proposals for new issues and a description of ongoing conflicts. "Kay expressed—and I think it has been evident to most of us for a long time—that she has a lot of anger and frustration with *Heresies* and that, in fact, she has come to an impasse with our organization and also personally with the members." I felt a kind of anxiety about the discussions on art. "Why not assume that my work speaks for itself and simply look at other artists' work without comparison?" I called Obie to see how things were progressing with the gas service in our building. The gas was still off and someone had set the mound of discarded tires on fire in the lot under the bridge. A few days later, another miscreant came during the night and dumped a boiler in the same lot with the

33. Sunset near the Rio Grande Gorge above Taos, New Mexico 34. Storm clouds from Pearl Street loft windows

smoldering tires. The US Environmental Protection Agency sent out men in white hazard suits to clean up leaking asbestos.

Roger only had a couple of weeks left in his residency; we had planned to look for land. We drove out to Abiquiu to visit Kate and Lisa. They had settled in New Mexico and were building a house near the Chama River.

My journals are filled with the drawings from our hikes to the river, the shapes of the rocks and clouds, the outlines of petroglyphs we found, and notes about the colors of the sunsets and the changing hues of yellow flowers as the nights grew chilly. I drew detailed plans for the artworks I was making, but wrote almost nothing about the two places we went to look for land until Roger left and we had made our decision. I had only indirectly alluded to our land search even though in my mind I had "fantasized, pictured, plotted, hoped, made actual (still in process) this land search." My reticence made me remember the date book I had kept in N'Zérékoré with its pithy notations about my search for an abortion, the "opposite emotion" to my joy in finding land, when I had "plotted, hoped and unraveled my unwanted pregnancy. Those actions led to my decision to leave N'Zérékoré, my emotional expulsion from a rural place, and these actions lead to the reversal of that long-ago decision and my reclamation of a place of beauty." I wrote this in my journal the evening I returned from taking Roger to Albuquerque to catch the plane back to Pearl Street. I stopped ritually several times on the way back to Taos, gathering red earth near Jemez Pueblo, yellow dried grasses from Valle Grande, and fire-singed wood from the road near Bandelier. We had made a bid on ten hilly acres in Plaza Blanca near Abiquiu on top of a mesa spotted with piñon and juniper trees, with both red and white dirt, bisected by a hanging white canyon, and framed by the same two mountain ranges visible in Taos. Roger was back in the loft

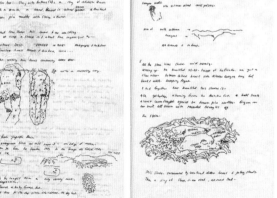

35. Walking around Stone Lions shrine, Bandelier 36-37. Journal Book #40, Sabra's notes and drawings at Stone Lions

by the time I returned from my meanderings. He called me; he liked the new painting racks and the "art show" I had hung in our long, skinny hallway.

I dream that we are looking for land inside a huge cafeteria with long rows of white tables. A collection of bulky stripped rocks line one table. Roger tells me, "A mesa is a table."

I invited Henry and Alan to come with me to see the land that we were buying. Henry had known Georgia O'Keeffe; he had found her affected. "Why did she have to dress only in black?" One time, a mutual friend, Bud Johnson, was thirty minutes late to visit her in Abiquiu. "The door was locked and that was it. He never visited her again." Henry had vertigo, and I was nervous that the drive to our place along the steep mesa road would be difficult. As usual, I addressed this problem by cooking an elaborate picnic with fried chicken and pie. I do not consider fried chicken to be fast food; it was our Sunday meal growing up. Later in my stay, when two New Mexican writers, Pat D'Andrea and Karen McKinnon, came as residents, I cooked for them. "I knew you were serious about frying chicken," Pat later told me.

I met the realtor to check on the survey and spent hours hiking along the site lines, tying tiny strips of cloth to the trees and setting cairns in the rocky places so that Roger would be able to see the boundaries when we returned the following summer. I drew a little map with tree and rock formations marked in place. Kate and Lisa came for a tour and invited me to dinner to meet other artist friends from the area, all women. On the drive back to Taos along the dark canyon that follows the river, I flushed an owl, its great wings swooping away from the windshield. Joan Watts, an ally from the New York City WCA struggles, had settled in Galisteo near Harmony's studio; she drove over another day to visit. "You've found something wonderful for about a tenth of what we paid in Galisteo." I felt blissfully saturated with land.

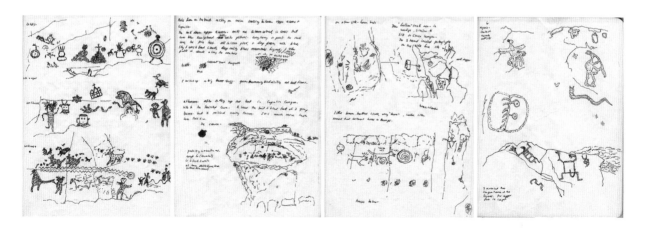

38-41. Sabra Moore, journal drawings, Book #40, including painted cave at Bandelier National Monument

Henry had been puzzled by how green the trees were on this dry mesa. "There must be a spring somewhere." He also had an "overwhelming sensation of hanging gardens," but his vertigo prevented him from joining Alan and me as we hiked across the white canyon to explore the red earth on the opposite flank. When Pat D'Andrea came with me another afternoon, we followed the interior canyon into the wide arroyo below and discovered a seeping spring at its entry marked by petroglyphs of horned water snakes. Years later, I realized that the whole mesa was dotted with ancient rock mulch gardens; their rock-lined grids subtly visible in the red earth. Henry knew how to read the landscape.

Roger was meeting me in Texas for the drive back to New York City. I had stopped at a diner in Tucumcari with the pickup truck stuffed with my collected wood and artworks in progress, and learned that Bush had won the election, defeating Dukakis. I had cast an absentee ballot. By buying land, I had finally done something that my kinfolks could appreciate. "I always knew Sabra was smart," Mother's first cousin, Daphne, had told her. I suddenly felt an urgency to find a venue for a solo show and exhibit the series of family-related artworks I had been making. None of my efforts at interesting a New York dealer had succeeded, but a dealer in Rancho de Taos had offered me an exhibition space for an unspecified date. He liked my use of found materials. "There are more artists here than you think working like this." Ann Harris had introduced me to Josephine Gear, the director of the Whitney Museum at Philip Morris. I had sent slides. "Ann was right to ask you to send these," Josephine had said, but no studio visit had materialized. Josely's dealer had said he liked my work, but felt it didn't "fit" his gallery; Fabio's dealer had told me the same thing. I didn't do the obvious and apply to one of the women's cooperatives. My hesitancy puzzles me now. Perhaps, I had enough collaboration in my everyday life.

42. Sabra stands with Kate Correa in front of Kate and Lisa's adobe construction 43. White canyon on Plaza Blanca land

Faith Ringgold was having a show at Bernice Steinbaum Gallery, and we went to the opening, running into many women from the WCA that I had hoped to avoid. Marilyn Lanfear was back in New York working as an assistant to Bernice. She invited me to visit her studio. We went down the street to see Leon Golub's show and ran into Lucy, who was back from Boulder. "Did you feel the earthquake?" "No." "I've spent a lot of time in South America; I recognized it. Call me; we should talk about the Southwest."

Ora was back from her residency at Giverney. She had made a beautiful series of paintings with flowers; some were simply studies, but others were composed as narrative still lifes based on the story of Adam and Eve. We ate together at Sylvia's house for Thanksgiving; she brought slides to show Lawrence. "Ora doesn't want to waste a minute with Lawrence," Sylvia told me.

I had unpacked my new artwork and reassembled the human-sized sculpture I was making. It was called *Lillie's Peaks* and looked like a double-roofed house; the painted paper peaks were enclosed in a wood fence made from tying found wood with cloth strips. When I showed these works years later in New Mexico, people thought of them as shrines. I was still painting the four panels that formed the peaks and had stretched the papers on my studio wall. One side represented the river while the other side represented the woods; a dark story was printed on the inside panels. It was, after all, part of a series about the people buried in Briggins Cemetery. I had finished two more small houses, *Earth House* and *Water House*, and also made a curtain work showing Gladys lying on her bed and a text printed across a painted frame. You could lift the curtain and see her clothesline out the window.

Roger and I went for a walk in our neighborhood, heading towards the East River. We knew the two old men who lived in a rough camp near the parking lot with their dogs. A police car

44. Sabra Moore, painted paper panels on both sides of right "peak" and the facing ends, *Lillie's Peaks*

was parked near their camp. We stopped to talk. "A man was driving in here, going thirty miles an hour. He went right into the river. He got out, but his car's down there under the water." He was stroking one of the puppies. "You know, Paul and I have lived here many years. One time, we were sitting here. Paul said, 'Look!' I looked. A man went right over. It took them days to find him. Another time, we saw a big bag come floating up. It was two bodies, all cut up." We left and walked over to the nearby storefront where artists from the neighborhood made window installations, and then circled back to Pearl Street. I collected some seeds from the moonflowers before we walked upstairs.

Marilyn had sublet a studio on Grand Street, spending time in New York before her house in San Antonio was sold. The quilt work she had made for the *Artists & the Quilt* had told a true story about the dissolution of her marriage. Her room was filled with the lead blouses and soft cloth chairs she was making—the clothes like armor and the chairs insubstantial and malleable. She was working on a barber chair for an artwork about her grandfather, an oilman who was shot dead while waiting to get his haircut. "He had been messing with a local girl and her family had him shot. The murderer, a man named Teal, was never prosecuted." I had a similar story about Grandmother's second husband. Marilyn collects death stories; she asked to collect the story I was printing on *Lillie's Peaks*. My great-grandmother had had long hair that she wore in a bun. Her daughters had wanted her to be more modern and wear her hair short. After she died, they cut her hair and gave her a permanent. We were all startled when we saw her in the open casket. Marilyn told me about visiting a cemetery where the magnolias were so big that the leaves looked like animals when they fell on the ground. Her artworks were like the quilts with stories embedded or like the Inca's string *quipu* that acted as a spark for memory. But these

45. Sabra Moore (both), *Lillie's Peaks*, side view with panels in place, open door 46. *Gypsy Baby* (cart detail)

stories depend on a reader who knows how to unravel the content in the knots. In New York City, only a few of us were readers.

I called Lucy and we arranged to have dinner together before a *Heresies* meeting. I brought her photos from the land we were buying, and we joked about an "old age home for artists" in New Mexico; she was thinking about buying land there as well. Both of us had been bitten by the beauty and quirkiness of petroglyphs and had been tromping around to improbable sites looking at rock art. She asked about my artwork. "You haven't had a show in a while." We walked over to Emma's studio for the meeting. We were figuring out how to reorganize the magazine; the new structure was still in flux. Four issues were in various stages of completion, starting with the Anniversary, Women on Men, Education, and Latina issues. Lucy and Josely had volunteered to be editors for the incipient Latina. Should the office and the collective be separate? Kay was currently office manager and a member of the collective. Everyone felt that she needed to choose where she wanted to concentrate her energies. Betsy had proposed a structure to allow *Heresies* to respond to current issues and publish on a more regular basis. We would keep the core half of each issue thematic and open to outside participation, but institute regular sections or columns that members of the core collective would write or edit. This reduced page size would make the theme section more manageable and accountable since it would be held within the firm-developed arms of the sections. We all proposed our favorite concerns. Kathie wanted an ecology section; Avis, cartoons; Betsy, a feminist art section; I wanted oral history or regionalism; Lucy, activist art; Josely, an international column with writers from other countries; someone wanted gynecology or romance; and Emma, an advice-to-young-artists column and a simian section on men. No one could later remember who had suggested sections on divorce, Satanism, or animal-of-the-month. "What if someone takes a hate to a particular column? It's

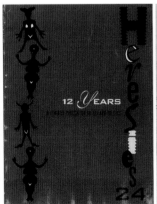  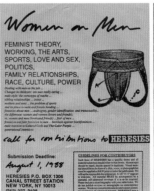 

47. *Heresies* covers (all), 12 Years, issue #24 48. The Art of Education, issue #25
49. Women on Men flier (unpublished) 50. Latina, issue #27

happened before, and that person just goes off and licks her wounds." Emma observed. "There should be an understanding that this person is in charge of her section," I replied. Lucy called for guidelines and deadlines.

Everyone stood around after our discussions looking at Emma's work, loosely rendered energized figures framed like wall hangings with strips of African cloth. Emma used to be a weaver, and her love of cloth and texture was apparent. Lucy was planning to include her work in *Mixed Blessings*, the book she was writing on artists of color. "I like Emma's work. Many artists invite me to their studios without bothering to read what I am writing about." I told her how *Connections Project/Conexus* was often seen as a Latina show rather than as a collaborative project between diverse artists. "It's because so few people do that." I felt that I was holding a string that no one knew how to read.

The Anniversary issue was about to be pasted up, and many of the ideas and articles I had advocated were dropped during my stay in Taos. I sent a letter to the members of the editorial collective, but no one wanted to discuss it in a meeting—our usual method for handling conflict. Only Kathie Brown commented. "It's a good letter—not bitter the way it could seem." Faith Wilding wrote me, "we got burned out, and then Linda left and you were gone and so things did fall apart." I was particularly upset about deleting a double-page visual with Sylvia's male nudes and was fighting to restore and round out with additional artworks a section we were calling "the penises." Nancy Spero called. I told her I had been in New Mexico and excitedly described the land we were buying. She though this would be disruptive for my artwork. "Did you get a grant?" "Yes." "Did you organize out there?" "No, I painted." "You didn't organize the Indians?" "No. I did my own work."

51. Ora Lerman in her studio with maquettes for painting 52. Bea Kreloff and Edith Isaac Rose send greetings from Italy

Ora had a party to show slides from her residency in Giverney. She invited Patty Hagen, who wrote a garden column for the *Wall Street Journal*. I knew her sister, Shelly, and we fell into a passionate discussion of urban gardens. I told her about the vegetable garden that my Warren Street landlord had tried to destroy. When the neighbor next door died, the new owner immediately cut all the apple trees in his backyard and installed sod. On Sunday mornings, he would mow the tiny lawn wearing pajamas. She wanted to visit our Pearl Street garden. We quieted as Ora showed slides, but Patty kept up a running commentary. The gardens at Giverney were not a restoration at all; Monet had grouped the flowers in waves of color and never planted the bright patches that now line parts of the garden. The current gardens are sprayed, so there are no birds or butterflies. A slide of the pond fed by the Epts River flashed against the wall. "The Epts is the inept," Patty murmured.

Marilyn returned my studio visit and came over to see my new work. "You don't make it easy to read your stories." "People have to want to read them," I said. She looked through my collection of wood from New Mexico. "It's so wonderful to talk with people who don't laugh at you. I've been teased a lot about my collecting."

It was almost Christmas, and Roger and I brought home a sweet-smelling pine tree. I pulled out the box where I kept my colored lights, suddenly looking at it closely. It was the wooden champagne box that C had given me as welcoming present when I abruptly returned from England, abandoning my Fulbright scholarship. All these years, it had felt like opening a casket when I pulled out the lights. Why had I kept this painful reminder? I emptied the box and put it in the bag of discards I was taking to the Salvation Army. Roger and I had bought Hopi rings at the annual Pole Climb in Taos Pueblo, browsing among the jewelers' tables set up along the edges of the dirt plaza. The sacred clown had just finished lowering the bags of food suspended from

Sexual relations permeate our whole life, and the correct analysis of the place of sex in the life of an individual is an important step in the evaluation of his character and psychological disposition. Sex can be either an integrated part of an individual's life — though with modern educational methods this is rare — or it can cause disharmony in that individual's life. It can be either an immense force or creation or an equally strong force for disintegration. Disharmony in sex accounts for the majority of modern problems, and it is almost certain that sex, or more exactly repressed sexual energy, is the basis for many nervous and mental diseases. An overemphasis of sexual functions can be as destructive as under-emphasis; they are both misuses of fine energy. When the little finger is quite obviously isolated from the other fingers, difficulty in relationships must be immediately suspected [115], a difficulty in relationships having been diagnosed it is necessary to give a more exact analysis by means of other parts of the

DAVIDSON

53. Marilyn Lanfear, *Genie's Headpiece*... 54. Nancy Davidson, *card* (detail) 55. Marilyn Lanfear, *Aunt Opal's Hat*

atop a silky thirty foot ponderosa pole, and we could all breathe again after he had balanced himself perfectly on the pinnacle, his arms extended in a wide embrace of the sky, and made a resonating series of whoops before nimbly sliding to earth. We had decided to go to city hall in Brooklyn and get married. I called Marithelma to ask if she and Fabio would be our witnesses. "I'll get out my velvet suit."

I dream that Roger and I are driving along a white dirt road on our way to visit Pat D'Andrea. Everything is suffused in light. People on horseback are riding towards us, but the horses get their hooves caught in deep cylindrical holes and can't advance.

Lucy was returning to Boulder in January, so Josely gave her a send-off party. Everyone was together that evening, enemies and friends. I ran into Noah Jemison, Lucy's partner at that time, a fellow Southerner and friend of Willie Birch, who had gone to school with Ana. We started talking about growing up in the South, and fantasized organizing a show called *South Up North*. Betsy Damon was there, and Betsy Hess, along with our fellow Heretics on the Anniversary issue. Josely had work in a show on landscape and the body that had just opened at the Bronx Museum of the Arts. "I mentioned you to the curator; she knew who you were." I felt left out. I thought, "The undercurrent here is plaint; everyone feels left out of something. Edith Isaac Rose and Eva Cockcroft complained to me about being left out of *Reconstruction Project*. I just complained to the editors of the Anniversary issue about the changes they made while I was in Taos." The music was playing; the complaining didn't really matter. We all started dancing.

Josely and I had been trying to get funding for taking *Connections Project/Conexus* to Brazil. The Museum of Contemporary Art, University of São Paulo (*Museu de Arte Contemporânea da Universidade de São Paulo*) had invited us, and we finally had a date for February 22, 1989, but we had no money. Only Varig Airlines was willing to help; they were donating one roundtrip

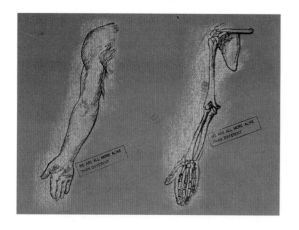 

56. Edith Isaac Rose, *We Are More Alike than Different* 57. Show card, Museu de Arte Contemporañea, São Paulo

ticket, which Josely and I would split, and free transport for the artworks as luggage on the same plane, but offered no insurance. We decided to ask the artists to divide the costs of insurance and explained our reasoning by describing our two-year efforts in a letter. "The community-based organizations felt that we should be able to get corporate funding—the show was going to be in a museum; the corporate sources felt it 'didn't fit into their campaigns'; the government sources felt we had 'too many non-American names'; and the Brazilian museums felt they 'couldn't afford' to fund the transportation with hard currency even though they could fund the show within Brazil. Once again, we have to turn to *ourselves*—women artists—to support our shows." The insurance cost was steep—$135 per artist. Ida Applebroog called, outraged that no one would give us funding. "I know what the Brazilian museums are funding. Why are we so far down the pecking order?" Mary Beth Edelson declined to purchase insurance on principle. All the other artists agreed. I started to draw up detailed plans and patterns for ways to pack the artworks into a minimum number of boxes. *Shelter Is Material* didn't fit the airline's space requirements for luggage, so I also started making a new artwork. I designed the new version in horizontal paper strips that could be sewn together and folded to fit into a narrow box with a low stick fence hinged along the center.

I dream that I look out the window of our loft. The view is fantastic; a deep canyon is suffused with light. I think, "How have I never noticed what a beautiful view this is?" I wonder, "Do I have the same view from my studio?" I go to the window, but see only the low buildings that line the street.

Sally, my former housemate in N'Zérékoré, came to visit with her mother shortly after my forty-sixth birthday. Her mother had grown up in Texas, and I showed her *Lillie's Peaks* and some of the other artworks I had been making about my family. She seemed ambivalent that I

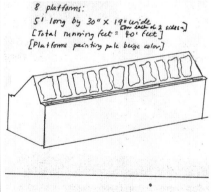

58. Sabra Moore (all), *Shelter Is Material #2* (detail) 59. *Shelter is Material #2* 60. Sketches for book page stands

was celebrating the culture she had rejected. She left Texas as a young woman "to go where the action was." "Levittown in 1949," Sally interjected. I thought of my mother and the emotional distance she had traveled by moving away from the country; the same distance I have "tried to travel back" to in making theses artworks. I had been printing laser transfer images for *Shelter Is Material #2*—my grandfather in the wooded cemetery, my hands, and direct copies from a straw nest I had made in Taos. I used clothespins to attach the series of sewn paper panels to a wire stretched along a wooden plank, paying homage to the clothesline.

I dream that Roger and I are walking around our land. I spot a horned toad and feel happy. Then we spy a badger, sunning itself, and a big tawny bear, asleep like a dog. We back away quietly, but the bear follows us. We climb into the pickup truck and she sticks her front paws into the wing glass. I try to be friendly, but I am nervous. She is a bear. I stroke her big tan paws. "Don't worry," I tell her, "we won't bother anything here." Suddenly, we are standing in a cafeteria. The bear is with us, but she looks like a woman. She orders blueberry cake.

Josely and Ernest were planning to stay for two months at their beach house at Guaratiba, a fishing village near Rio de Janeiro; I was going to be in Brazil for two weeks. "It will be a vacation for you," Josely said. "You can stay with my family in São Paulo while we install the show, and then come for a holiday in Guaratiba with us." I needed a holiday. I was trying to finish my freelance projects, make the boxes and collect the artworks, and complete my new piece; we were still working on the Anniversary issue of *Heresies*. Time was running out. Barbara Strauch, the editor for the birthday calendar I was researching, was getting exasperated, expecting me to finish the photo selections before my trip. I went over to gallery onetwentyeight to meet Kazuko and pick up her piece, and then went down to Chinatown to enjoy dim sum with Catalina. Their works would go together inside one of the boxes I was making along with Liliana's piece. Catalina

150 Artists Book pages: 61. Vira and Hortensia Colorado 62. Liora Mondlak 63. Marilyn Minter 64. Karen Shaw

was upset with Josely. She had agreed for Josely to photograph her dancing bare breasted, but then felt exploited when she saw her silk-screened images repeated on the artwork Josely had shown at the Bronx Museum of the Arts. "When you come back from Brazil, we have to start seeing each other and doing things together."

I was making everyone frantic. Roger had to help me finish the boxes as I kept sewing the panels for the new *Shelter Is Material* artwork. "And how do I feel about all of this?" I wrote, describing the crazy last minute rush, "Glad to have made my new piece. I really like it." When we got to the airport laden with the three boxes of artworks, Ernest and Josely were waiting nervously at the desk. Officials from Varig Airlines had met Josely when she arrived with the Brazilian artworks—we had saved the packages used for the shipment to New York City. Now, we watched as the rest of the works got checked onto the airplane and we prepared to board the flight. "I was afraid you wouldn't come in time." Josely said. "Keep trying," Ernest added, "maybe someday you'll get it right." "I did get it right, Ernest. I'm here." Standing in line to board, I felt like I had just run a race. I spied Tak Inagaki en route to São Paulo as well. It was a relief to encounter a friend who wasn't mad at me. One in ten residents of São Paulo are Japanese, Tak told me; he was filming a program for Japanese television. The Varig complimentary ticket had been issued in Josely's name, and she and I had split the cost for the second fare, my ticket. As I settled into my seat, ready to nap after my marathon of work, I realized that Josely was sitting in first class and I was sitting in second class. "She got half for first class and I got half for my class." I hadn't even thought of buying a phrase book in Portuguese.

The airplane descended to São Paulo, the city enclosed within green mountains, a mammoth church visible on a hill. Peering from the taxi windows, I spotted familiar trees—baobab and umbrella—and felt again the heavy moist air of the tropics. We arrived at a guarded apartment

150 Artists Book pages: 65. Betye Saar, *Body* 66. Kathie Brown, Food 67. Michiko Itatani, *Spirit* 68. Mary Beth Edelson, *Spirit*

house, and I went upstairs to leave my bags with Josely's mother, Janjyndra, and meet her live-in maid, Maria, a black woman from Bahia. Lamidi had visited Bahia on several occasions. "They are more traditionally Yoruba than we are now in Nigeria," he had told me. Josely and Ernest were staying with her nephew in another gated house nearby. We drove to the museum to check on the boxes and meet Rejané Citron, the curator. I was relieved to discover that many of the curators spoke either English or French. Lawrence Alloway had curated a biennial here some years earlier and had accurately described the museum to me—a modern building with a wall of glass, slightly shabby. I had unpacked my bags in my room at Janjyndra's and left my boots sitting on the floor. When I returned, each boot had been placed neatly inside a plastic bag.

I dream that Josely and I go into Mother Gladys's house. She precedes me and leaves me to hook the screen and lock the door. It is dark inside. I wonder where Daddy Chess is, and then I discover that someone is driving a tractor; he is riding in back.

Janjyndra and I pretended we could understand each other by talking in a combination of English, French, and Portuguese; I gathered that her father had been a general. "I used to have a big house with four servants." Her apartment was immaculate with delicate furniture. I joined Josely that first evening to eat at her nephew's house. He and his wife had twin boys and two live-in servants, a couple with a three-year-old girl who lived somewhere south of the city with her grandparents. "Couldn't she live with her parents at your house?" I asked the nephew's wife. "I wouldn't want her to."

Many of the Brazilian artists came by the museum as we were installing the show. I met my partner, Maria do Carmo Secco. "I thought you would be small and blond," she said. Like me, she had made a new version of the artwork she had shown in New York. Photos and words (*An Empty House Is a House without a Dream*) bristled prominently from the accordion-shaped

150 Artists Book pages: 69. Judy Blum, *War/Death* 70. Eva Cockcroft, *Race* 71. Leticia Parente, *Race* 72. Marilyn Lanfear, *Food*

portfolio in the center. "I wanted to show the most fundamental aspect of a woman—the house, the bed, and the presence of a man, the hat." I mentioned Diego Rivera's hat hanging in Frida Kahlo's bedroom. We both laughed.

I was beginning to feel like I was in an aquarium, moving through the continuous rain from one type of enclosed space—the guarded residencies—to another—the museum. I had no sense of the city and had not walked outside since our arrival. We were all eating dinner at a restaurant in a hotel near Janjyndra's apartment, and as we finished, I said, "I'll walk back alone to the apartment." I had been watching out the taxi windows and thought I could find my way. Josely seemed startled. "At least go into the hotel and get a map." I wandered along the streets and discovered a beautiful park and a hint of a lush forest like the one in N'Zérékoré, which I entered like finding a lost friend. The next day, I told Rejané about my walk, and she made out a list of places I could visit on daily walking tours, showing me how to find the town center. She gave me a map and explained how to use the very efficient subway system.

The museum galleries had heavy moveable partitions that an older man named Joã had arranged for us. He only spoke Portuguese, but my French helped me get the gist of what people were saying. I was hanging Faith Ringgold's piece when I noticed Josely and Ernest talking with Rejané and another curator named Marcos. I walked over. The previous day, Josely had been fretting about the way her artwork was hung, upset that it was separated by a small space between partitions from her partner, destroying "the ritualistic aspect" of their collaboration. We were now halfway through hanging the show; moving her work would mean rearranging everything else. I was upset that we would have to ask Joã to move the partitions again, but the others insisted. When Joã returned from lunch, I wanted to apologize. I asked Ernest to translate for me; he refused. Maria came in. "What is happening? Why are you taking everything down?"

  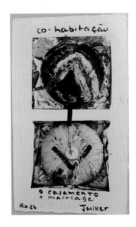 

150 Artists Book pages: 73. Lygia Pape, *Environment* 74. Sharon Gilbert, *Environment*
75. Judith Miller, *Shelter* 76. Erika Rothenberg, *War/Death*

Maria asked. "I am very angry!" I said. She understood. "You are very tired." I told Josely: "I feel embarrassed to ask Joã to do the same work twice simply because you didn't like how your piece was installed." "You don't understand. This is Brazil," Josely replied. "No, I do understand. This is about class." "It was Marcos who felt the show looked bad." "You should have come and talked to me first," I insisted. "I'm not a translator," Josely said.

Now, it was our turn for lunch to bid Maria do Carmo Secco goodbye. She was returning to her home in Minas Gerais province. I was sorry to see her leave. "I feel very easy with you," I told her. Anna Mae, the museum director, joined Rejané, Josely, Ernest, and me. She had lived in Austin ("the only place where I experienced discrimination"), and also in Birmingham, England, where I had had my thwarted Fulbright, and Nigeria ("in Nigeria, I am white"). "We live in the same places."

Joã had finished moving the partitions by the time we returned. Actually, the show did look better. Newspaper people came, and a crew from the television station arrived. I snapped their picture as two men stooped low alongside Marina's veiled painting and blew heartily to make the cloth move and reveal the painting underneath. Another man quickly filmed. The wall works were completely installed, and now we had to arrange the book pages. I had sent the museum the patterns for the house-like pedestals we had used at the Museum of Contemporary Hispanic Art (MoCHA). Josely and I started arranging the cases around the room, but Ernest kept intervening with new ideas for their placement. Finally, I said, "Ernest, there can't be three people deciding." He got furious and cursed me, storming out of the gallery. "Now, you've really hurt Ernest," Josely said. "I don't think he should be involved in designing the show." "Why not? He's been helping us; he has a right." "No, he doesn't; he's not a curator. Roger would never do this." "Well, you should tell him that." I went over to Ernest and said, "I'm sorry I hurt your

  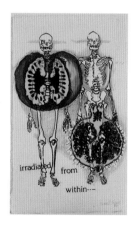 

150 Artists Book pages: 77. Josie Talamantez, *Race* 78. Tomie Arai, *Race* 79. Susan Crowe, *Food* 80. Alice Brill, *Environment*

feelings. I really appreciate the help you've given, but Josely and I have hung this show twice; I designed the cases myself. We've worked three years on this project; our names are on the show; we should decide the design." "I don't give a damn about your three years or your ideas for the cases. I don't like your method of operation. I've watched you all day and I don't like the way you behave." "What don't you like?" "I don't have to tell you now." He stomped out again. I invited Josely into the bathroom for a private conversation, furious now. "I've gone to a lot of trouble to come here; I've probably lost a quarter of my freelance income. I know you feel that this is Brazil, but my name is on this project too. You and I are responsible for this project, not Ernest." "Look, I know Ernest. He was wrong to speak to you like that. Give him time. He's like this; he'll calm down." "He's not my husband, Josely, and now he's made me mad. I'm not going to be beholden to someone who dislikes me." "He doesn't dislike you." Now, she was trying to kiss me on both cheeks. We were both crying. "I don't have to go to Guaratiba. I have enough money." "But Guaratiba is my place too. I want you to come." We ate together that night at Janjyndra's, Ernest and I avoiding each other.

The next day, Josely met me at the museum without Ernest; I had figured out how to walk by myself from Janjyndra's apartment. We finished arranging the cases and book pages easily. A photo had appeared that morning in the newspaper *Jornal da Tarde* showing us hanging the show. Ours was not the only exhibit; many people were coming in and out as we were working. I met a broad-faced woman named Erdina from the Workers' Party who was mayor of her town and two other women involved in education. They were excited about an exhibit focusing on women. Anna Mae told us, "Out of fifty-three ministries, only three are headed by women—psychology, nursing, and here." That evening, Josely's niece described attending a meeting where Erdina

  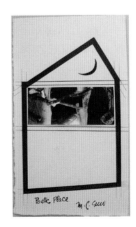 

150 Artists Book pages: 81. Sophia Tassinari 82. Jaune Quick-To-See Smith, *Race* 83. Maria do Carmo Secco 84. Louise Neaderland, *Shelter*

spoke. "I had never been in a room with so many people with poor clothes and bad teeth." When Erdina entered, she was stunned by the intensity of the people's response.

One of the artists, Alice Brill, had studied in Albuquerque. She invited me to spend the weekend after the show opened at her country place in Itu. I decided to accept and then travel alone to Rio de Janeiro for a few days before going to Guaratiba and returning to New York. Everyone seemed comfortable with this plan despite Janjyndra's opinion of Itu. "There's nothing there, only little buildings." I had been following Rejané's walking tours. I found a leafy park full of craft vendors and browsed among the objects. There was a bluntness and massiveness in the jewelry; the earrings I fingered weren't heavy, but oversized. I bought a pair. It felt like an African market with tie-dyed cloth and leatherwork purses and belts on display. I bought a flimsy layered blue dress that looked like nothing I would ever wear. I had discovered the stand-up street luncheonettes serving big plates of black beans and rice with tiny cups of black coffee. A Japanese woman was standing nearby; I greeted her in French. "Do you like Brazil?" she asked me. "Very much," I replied. "I don't like Brazil," she beamed and giggled. I wandered under an overpass and found people selling buckets of bright green turtles and tiny orange fish. The light poles along the street glowed with beaux art designs among the vestiges of the forest creatures swimming in these buckets. A crowd gathered to listen to three country musicians playing guitar, drum, and tambourine. I stopped to look at a man playing a hurdy-gurdy with a bright green parrot perched atop. A blind man was selling needles in cutout packets printed as baskets of flowers, and another man had slim alphabet booklets in Portuguese. I bought both, and then noticed an old woman and girl sitting against the stone railings of the overpass. They had laid out cards and cowrie shells. I hadn't had the cowries cast for me since I lived in Guinea and longed for a reading.

150 Artists Book pages: 85. Angela Leite 86. Sumiko Arimori, *Environment* 87. Kathy Grove, *Race* 88. May Stevens, *Spirit*

After the drama of the installation, the opening was placid. I met more of the Brazilian artists. Ana Barros seemed disappointed to learn that I didn't have a dealer and that we had had to raise money for the show. Her artwork sounded interesting, however. She described a video she had made while living in Los Angeles. A young woman repeatedly offers her breast for nursing; the viewer has to kneel on an altar rail to watch the film. "In Brazil, they don't like craft-based work; they like the newest technology."

I was running out of money and needed to cash my traveler's checks before going to Itu. I had gone to the bank, a hotel, a travel agency, and the American Express office without success. The currency was in flux and no one would cash the checks. Josely sent me to see a man named "Leslie," a friend of her niece, but failed to warn me that this would be a black market transaction. I went to the right floor, but couldn't find his office and no one would direct me to his door. Finally, I managed to call her niece for clearer directions. Josely and Ernest were leaving for Guaratiba that evening; Rejané and I were going out for dinner. Alice and her husband, Julian, were picking me up the next afternoon to go to Itu. I overheard Janjyndra complaining to her maid Maria, "Why didn't she go to Guaratiba with the others?" Saturday was the maid's day off; she was worried about preparing lunch. I was relieved when Rejané arrived to explain clearly in Portuguese that I was leaving the next afternoon and that no one would have to prepare any meals for me. "She's very traditional," Rejané explained as we sat drinking "little county girls," a sugarcane whisky served in bars with fried strips of manioc. "She's one of those we call the four-hundred-year families."

Rejané mapped out my last walking tour—the Japanese neighborhood, the open market, the railroad station, and the main cathedral. São Paulo is cosmopolitan; I didn't stand out. A black woman stopped me on the street to ask for directions in Portuguese and laughed when

89. Josely Carvalho, *Rebirth* (left), Liliana Porter, *Birth of the Face...* (right) 90. Brazilian TV filming Marina Gutierrez art

I replied in English. The buildings seemed to go right to the sidewalk, presenting a closed front of scrubbed cerulean blue walls topped by ochre colored roofs. The market was shaped round like a stadium; art nouveau stained glass domes depicting bucolic farmers gave the meats and vegetables a holy glow. I stepped among cages of tiny birds and rabbits and bought a sack of speckled quail eggs, and then made my way past the red brick railroad station to the cathedral. People were selling amulets along the road. I tried to understand the instructions for the most efficacious use of the ones I purchased. As I neared the church, there were beggars grouped among the palm trees. The bases of the trees had been white washed, giving them a bulbous appearance as if someone had tied a belt tightly around their trunks. Small crowds were gathered around performers—a man who ate cigarettes and another with a clinking instrument in his mouth. I circled the big plaza as it started to rain and entered the cathedral. The light was somber. When I exited from a different door, the forest again announced itself in the form of many cloth bags arranged along the ground. There seemed to be one hundred open sacks, each containing a different bark, leaf, or powder. It was almost time to meet Alice and Julian. I took a cab to the museum to look once more at our show and say goodbye to Rejané and Marcos. My work was finished; we hugged.

It was dark when we arrived at Itu; the sounds of cicadas and tree frogs greeted us. "The earth smell alone is enough for me," I wrote in my journal later that evening. There was a fine meal of rice and beans prepared for us by Alice's cook and her daughter that was laid out on a long colonial-style table. The house had a big veranda and the furniture was simple, but massive. We served ourselves to my relief. Alice had migrated to Brazil in 1933 with her mother; both were German Jewish refugees. Her father, a "Bohemian painter," went back to Germany, refusing to believe in the imminent danger; he was soon imprisoned and killed. "I didn't know I

150 Artists Book pages: 91. Beatrice Leite, *Spirit* 92. Faith Ringgold 93. Jerri Allyn & The Waitresses, *Food* 94. Sarah Swenson, *Spirit*

was Jewish until I was ten," Alice said. She described her struggles as an artist, making clothes, working in batik, and painting. We talked about the show; she seemed disappointed that I did not make money with my art. "The show was better than I had expected. Please tell Vivian Browne how much I liked her work." I tried to describe the women's art movement and the feminist and cooperative movements. "Latin American women don't like feminism; that's for Nordics. . . . I never had time for groups; I had to work and raise my children." Her daughters arrived. "We have to stop talking. I feel tired; I am not used to talking so much. Usually, they [Julian and her daughters] are the ones who speak."

I took a shower before going to bed in the redolent darkness. As I turned on the water, a tiny tree frog startled me by jumping against the shower wall, revealing its translucent pink feet in the bathroom light.

The next day, we walked around, looking at the cluster of family houses. Alice's daughters, the caretaker, and Julian's sister all had houses within an open compound. We talked more about the show. Alice had been disappointed with *150 Artists Book* because the art wasn't reproduced in glossy color. "We made the entire edition by hand," I explained. "The museums wouldn't have bought this book if it had been mass-produced." "I thought it was the best you could do." She assumed we had been paid as curators. "I'll explain this to the other artists. I think they didn't understand that you did this for idealism."

Itu was a small colonial town with a pretty park and outdoor market with baskets, embroidery, crochet, and lace work for sale. Julian took me to see a plain ochre church. I was unprepared for the splendor of Brazilian baroque style art and architecture. Inside, everything was carved and patterned in blue and white. The oversized saints reminded me of Ora's dolls with metal crowns adorning the heads of Mary and Baby Jesus. There was still time to swim in

150 Artists Book pages: 95. Margot Lovejoy, *Birth* 96. Back cover, *Documentation* 97. Linda Herrit, *Death* 98. Rose Viggiano, *Environment*

a pond before leaving for my plane to Rio de Janeiro. I floated in the warm water as butterflies drank from my wet towel.

My journals are filled with the drawings I made in Rio de Janeiro while I stayed alone at an inn near Ipanema beach, sitting outside and sketching the fantastic loaf-shaped mountains. I went to the botanical gardens and stood inside the folds of a fromager tree similar to the ones I had known in Guinea, its smooth roots undulating like skin from the ground, and then I walked into the bamboo grove and lingered among the palm trees—the forest near N'Zérékoré a physical memory rising like steam into my body.

I had agreed to spend two days with Josely and Ernest in Guaratiba, a fishing village built up along hills that rise steeply from the sandy beach. The town was small; most of the beach belonged to the military, and there was a newer section where wealthy Brazilians and foreigners had built houses. I liked their house; it was open and plain, and you could walk easily onto the beach. "There had been a big kitchen, but that was ridiculous for us," Josely explained, showing me the small kitchen that was closed off from the rest of the house by a door; the place where the maid worked. I had been visiting churches in Rio de Janeiro after my introduction to Brazilian baroque style in Itu, and was curious about the church in Guaratiba. Neither Josely nor Ernest knew where it might be. The next morning, Josely and I took a walk, strolling up the steep road into the village; blue bell-shaped vines lined the path. Many houses had been painted with depictions of Saint George; the yards were hard-packed yellow dirt like Grandmother's place, with children playing and chickens pecking at ease along the ground. In some places, banana trees were growing. We found the church, which had a big cross in the shape of a prickly pear. I went to sit in the luxuriant grass of the churchyard, wanting to watch the dark ocean waves along the beach from this high vantage. Josely stayed on the path, afraid of snakes. She was talking about

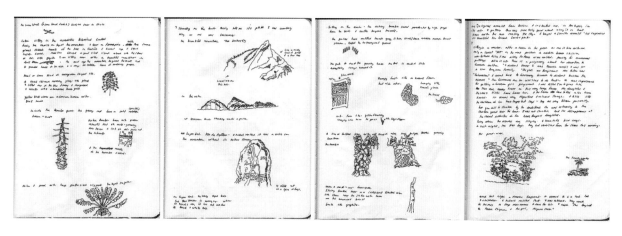

99-102. Sabra Moore, journal drawings, Book #49, including trees and mountains near Rio de Janeiro

us doing another collaborative project as if nothing had happened at the museum. At sunset, I went out alone to swim, the waning moon reflecting itself in the water as I rocked in the waves. I noticed a homemade altar to Saint Peter along the beach and followed a path, quickly finding a second church.

My plane left the following evening, and I needed to be at the airport in Rio de Janeiro by nine, three hours before departure. Simone Michelin had offered to take me to the airport. Simone was one of the core artists in *Connections Project/Conexus*, having been paired with Mary Beth Edelson on the theme of spirit. She had photographed the show at MoCHA, and we had visited each other in New York; I had been hoping to see her. I spent the afternoon uncertain about how to get to Simone's apartment in Rio de Janeiro. Josely and Ernest "didn't feel like driving." I could take the bus or get a ride with Josely's friends, Teté and Alfred, who had come to Guaratiba for an afternoon visit. We got into the city around the time I was supposed to be at the airport, but no one seemed concerned. Teté stopped to check on her film playing at a local theater before looking for Simone's apartment. Simone was waiting for me. "Why didn't you call me? Josely told me you were staying in a hotel in Rio de Janeiro. I told her that you could stay at my place." I loved her apartment; there was no maid. "I assumed we would all meet together; I depended too much on Josely." We had a cup of tea, and she showed me her artwork of figures enclosed in various kinds of boxes. Then, we left for the airport, stopping on the way to pick up a journalist friend who was collaborating with Simone on a project about endangered trees in the Amazon. This was getting late even by my relaxed standards for time. We got to the airport twenty minutes before flight departure, and Simone and her friend left me at the door to rush inside with my bulging luggage. "The flight is closed." I almost wept as I stood before the stern Varig worker, but I was not the only one. Many worried people were grouped nearby. I was mentally evoking the

150 Artists Book pages: 103. Josely Carvalho, *Birth* 104. Maurie Kerrigan, *Spirit* 105. Aviva Rahmani, *Birth* 106. Glenna Park, *Shelter*

Mayan goddess who repairs bee wings, having adopted her in spirit to calm me during airplane takeoff and landing. The electricity went off. Then, lights came back on; we were all allowed to board. A woman did a quick manual check of my luggage, mildly disgusted as she fingered my packet of rolled eucalyptus bark and the bag of hollow quail eggs nestled among the amulets and booklets I had collected.

Lamidi had called while I was in Brazil. He was doing a workshop in Amherst and had forgotten to bring his address book from Nigeria, but he finally located our phone number. I told him about finding African food and seeing all the familiar tropical trees in São Paulo.

"You really got to know Africa; you lived in a very remote area," Lamidi said. I described my difficulties with Josely in Brazil; they had met. "You have been going your own way and doing the same thing for a long time, like I have." The flowers had started to sprout in our Pearl Street garden during my absence, and my freelance work with Barbara had also survived.

I dream that I find a big bowl filled with ash, with bits of porous, broken pottery inside. I take the pieces out and start trying to put them back in order.

I went over to the *Heresies* office to see what needed to be done for the Anniversary issue. Sue and Kathie had started designing pages even though we were still editing articles and making changes with selections. By default, I had agreed to edit Harmony's article on women tinsmiths in New Mexico. Betsy and Sue had both refused after receiving Harmony's note in the fall: "Needless to say, I know how the editorial and production process seems to work. . . . I assume the piece needs editing, but I care very much *how* it is edited. Some sense of context and history is important so that the three interviews don't come off as *quaint*." I called Harmony to discuss her article before mailing my edited version. She knew about our land and had once looked at a parcel near ours, but had found it too hilly. "I have to think about getting moving vans

150 Artists Book pages: 107.Anésia Pacheco e Chaves, *War/Death* 108. Caroline Stone, *War/Death* 109. Frances Buschke, *Spirit* 110. Cecilia Vicuña, *War/Death*

in and out to transport my artwork." Harmony was working on a new series of large-scale paintings in combination with rusted tin roofing she had collected from abandoned dumps in canyons
and arroyos. Her article on traditional tinsmiths was connected to this new series, making editing
more delicate.

Harmony wrote *Heresies* another letter after receiving my edited version, complaining
about "too many choppy paragraphs that read like a report," but she had managed to condense
her article. We were still bargaining with each other about some of the selections. Sylvia's "penis
page" was back in; I had redesigned the page, and the other editors felt more comfortable with
its format and the new additions of artworks. No one, however, wanted to use my faux definitions
in the introduction: "pe-nis (p⊠'nis) n., pl. –neses or –nes (-n⊠z'). [Latin, a tail] 1. The male organ
of sexual intercourse. Mammalian. Formed in embryology by an inversion of the female organ of
sexual intercourse [vagina]. 2. Cultural & religious organ [see editor's note]."

In passing, Sue mentioned that she and Kathie had dropped my apron-shaped artwork
from *Cunts/Quilts/Consciousness*, a survey article on feminist art that Faith Wilding and Miriam
Schapiro had written, "because you have the other page." "I might prefer my artwork included in
the article instead of the page art I was making," I responded. No one had eliminated Faith or
Miriam's artworks because they were writing the article. It seemed unfair. My sister editors had
rejected the Dear Heretics letters when I was in Taos. Only Faith had liked what she called "your
stories"—my efforts to introduce other voices by writing and answering six fake letters ("Bring
your problems to Heretic. She solves matters relating to love, sex, politics, social relations, art.
. . . Meteorological enquiries not accepted"). Sue could understand my anger. "I realize it feels
like you went away to Brazil and we dropped your work again."

111. *Heresies* anniversary issue #24, double page, *Historias* by Harmony Hammond 112. Sabra Moore, *Gladys Apron*

I was back at work on a series of artist's books called *4/Tells*, wanting to complete the four booklets in time for a Women's Studio Workshop grant application. Each booklet had a different shape and told a dark family story. One was the story of my aunt Opal's unwanted baby; I was using valentines she had made by cutting out deckled hearts from magazine pages. I inserted a photo of Opal petting her horse Diamond into the valentine's window. Another booklet simply repeated a photograph five times of a smiling Gladys in the cemetery with one word of the text under each photo—*She Thinks She's Not Pretty*. It unfolded in color like a skinny accordion. These four booklets were related to *Lillie's Peaks* and the other sculptures I was planning about kinfolk buried in the Acworth cemetery. My usual method was to assemble family photos and ephemera and make multiple photocopies in various proportions, and then make cutouts and keep recopying until I got the grainy images I preferred. One evening, working late at American Heritage, I was using the photocopy machine with my stacks of cutouts clearly visible as the editor walked by. Luckily, she didn't seem to care.

Kazuko and I started planning a show that I would curate at gallery onetwentyeight to mark the imminent end of the decade called *Running Out of Time.* "You know so many people," Kazuko said, "I feel I could learn from you." I later wrote in my journal, describing ideas for the new show: "The opposite from working in *Heresies*, where I feel at a dead end." I was gradually contacting all the core artists to tell them about the Brazilian show. We had gotten positive critical attention in the newspaper and on television; *Istoé Senhor*, a glossy weekly magazine similar to *Time Magazine*, had published a review by critic Radha Abramo, focusing primarily on the Brazilian artists, but also mentioning Vivian and Ida. Despite Anna Barros' opinion about craft, Abramo had liked my homage to the clothesline. Sylvia and Lawrence invited Roger and me

113. Sabra Moore, *Photocopier limited edition book 4/TELLS (Caroline), "…her son were alive, it would be different…"*

to dinner to hear about the trip. I had been right about the blue dress; I brought it as a gift for Sylvia. The layered drapes looked wonderful on her, not on me.

I dream that I am in the country. I pass a fence and notice a sandy ditch filled with frag-ments of glazed and colored pottery. I start gathering the pottery shards. The colors are dazzling in the vivid light. Then I find all kinds of dolls, Indian dolls and a doll couple hidden behind a big female figure. I pick up the couple. I am not sure if I want to keep the big woman doll.

Ernest called me. He had just come back alone from Brazil and had brought our art-works as luggage in the four cardboard boxes Roger and I had constructed. One box was miss-ing: the biggest box containing the pieces by Liliana, Catalina, and Kazuko. "I feel like I've been molting," I wrote after receiving this news, "now, I've got to come out again." There had been a commotion at the airport. The clerk at the check-in counter knew nothing about Varig's agree-ment for free transport of the artworks, and Josely had to loudly insist that a supervisor come to the counter. Both Josely and Ernest had seen all four boxes checked in as luggage on the plane. Her theory was that an airport worker had probably stolen the biggest box, thinking it was valuable. It was, but perhaps not saleable by a thief. Catalina's artwork was a shower curtain stuffed with leaves; Kazuko's was draped silk printed with images; and Liliana's was the one most obviously "art"—silk-screened images printed on paper. I spent a month exchanging letters with Steven Pincus, who had arranged the insurance with Lloyds of London ("It is a large box, and I feel it could still be found"), with Varig Airlines ("Due to the commercial nature of these items and the gratuitous handling provided, responsibility for this unfortunate disappearance cannot be accepted") and with an adjustor named Vinnie Apesa, who never held out any hope that the artworks could be located. They simply vanished. A couple of months later, Catalina, Kazuko,

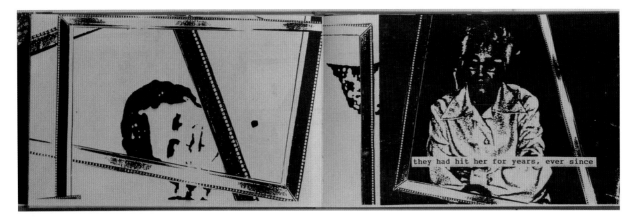

114. Sabra Moore, *Photocopier limited edition book 4/TELLS (Caroline)*, *"...they had hit her for years ever since..."*

and Liliana all received checks from Lloyds of London. Kazuko told me she tried to think of this as a sale rather than a loss.

Josely was back in New York; we were seeing each other frequently at *Heresies* to flesh out the plans for the reorganization. She acted like nothing had happened in Brazil. Michael Oren, an art historian, had presented a paper at the WCA National Conference, "Is the *Heresies* Collective an Avant-Garde?" Josely and Emma had represented us as respondents, armed with a sheaf of suggested questions from the collective. "Is it usual for a male to be given a forum by the WCA to critique women's organizations?" "How do the workings of women's collectives compare to those of men's?" We Heretics had supplied a response to that query. "Q: Men's what? A: Men's collectives. Q: Are there any?" In May, we learned that Oren was donating his archive of research on *Heresies* to the Archives of American Art, but including only Harmony's interview. She called Betsy for advice. Other issues were more pressing, however; restructuring the office was on top of our list. We met later that month with Emma, Avis, Faith, Betsy, Kathie, and me in attendance. Josely and Kay were both sick, but Kay, to our surprise, had invited the entire editorial collective from the Women on Men issue to attend. One of the editors, Kate Gleason, revealed that we had been denied our National Endowment for the Arts (NEA) funding, and then we learned that our subscriptions were down. When the editors left, we voted on the plans we had discussed since winter. The newly revealed financial crisis added to our sense of urgency. We decided that the staff should be pared down to a managing editor, a production manager, and a part-time office assistant. We selected Avis Lang as the new managing editor and voted to fire Kay, who would remain on the core collective. We gave Kay a month's notice and a month's severance for her one-day-a-week job and asked Emma to call her with our decisions. A couple of weeks later, after Avis came into the office to start her new job, Emma wrote a long, polite letter

 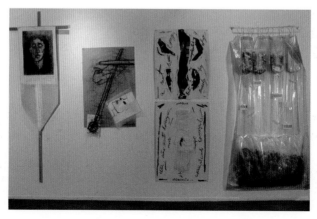 

115. *150 Artists Book* page, Liliana Porter, *Birth* 116. Installation wall, *War/Death* 117. Page, Ellen Lanyon, *Environment*

to Kay. "We desperately need the check book, check stubs, up to date check register, deposit slips. . . . I went to Merchants [Bank] today and discovered that though I am listed as the President of *Heresies*, I can't sign checks. A bit of a bind, since I don't know who Palmer Fuller, the other possible check signer, is. . . . The bank gave me a record of checks written this month, so I noted the $12,000 check to the Fidelity Cash Reserves. What is this for?" She also asked for the postal box key, the key to the storage shed in New Jersey, the corporate stamp, tax forms, and the missing design boards for the Women on Men issue.

Lucy had just returned from teaching in Boulder and immediately asked to come back onto the core collective to help us fight what the district attorney later called Kay's "larceny" and her "childish response to an organizational dispute." We met at Lucy's loft as more details emerged with Josely, Robin, and Penny in attendance as well. Kay had been threatening to resign for over a year, but her response to Emma's phone call had been a venomous surprise. "Does this mean that Avis will work for me?" "No." Her husband, Larry, a lawyer in whose joint bank account our $12,000 now rested, accused *Heresies* of firing Kay "when she was under the knife." We hadn't realized that she had been hospitalized for an entopic pregnancy. Despite her medical emergency, Kay had acted quickly before Avis came in to start work. Phone records showed that someone—we suspected Sandy De Sando—had called Kay's house daily from our office as our subscription mailing lists, back-up computer tapes, and all the materials relating to the Women on Men issue vanished. We discovered from bank statements that Kay had written another $3,000 in checks right after Emma's phone call. She paid herself in advance for her projected last month's work and the severance we had promised, wrote out checks for severance and vacation pay to her assistant, Jo Tavernor, and made payments to Sandy De Sando, Kate Gleason, and the designer Nancy Rosing for unspecified work on Women on Men. We later found Kay's

118. Josely Carvalho, *Turtle News*, spectacolor lightboard, One Times Square 119. Erika Rothenberg, *Is God...?*

typeset article for that issue, calling herself a "woman's group junkie" and criticizing collective action. When our lawyers, Arlene Boop and Dannie Alterman, called Larry, he insisted that Kay was using the $12,000 "for purposes related to *Heresies*."

The position of president had always been a nominal one, purely for legal purposes, but Emma had now been thrust into an active role that she didn't seek. We needed a new president. Avis suggested Josely as president, and Betsy nominated me. It was awkward. Betsy turned towards me and said, "You make the nomination." I could see that she had written down Josely's name, so I nominated Josely. We didn't need more complexity. I wrote about the meeting in my journal that night. "The President has mostly to do legal things like help Avis open a new bank account. Josely can do that with ease."

Sandy had been calling each of the *Heresies* associates. She told Ida Applebroog that we had been trying to subvert the publication of Women on Men, so Kay took the money to "publish her issue." Avis found a letter that Kay had written to the NEA, claiming that the editors for the Anniversary issue "embarrassed" her and insisting that the Women on Men issue be published first. Robin told us that Kay had tried to convince her that I was incompetent and shouldn't be organizing the benefit at PPOW Gallery. We had to start getting our side of this debacle out. Avis agreed to write the associates. Robin and I agreed to draft a letter for us to send to the editors and contributors of the Women on Men issue, informing them that Kay was no longer authorized to speak for *Heresies* and that *Heresies* was temporarily suspending production on that issue. After all, Kay had the money for publication; we did not. We asked our lawyers to get an injunction against Kay.

I dream that I hear noises on the other side of the loft and see men and women coming up through the floor. I "catch" them, but then realize that I am trapped with them inside our place.

120. Theodora Skipitares, *Micropolis (Six Portraits & a Landscape)* 121. Bibi Lenček, *Endangered*

The men push me towards the wall and threaten to rape me. I am prepared to fight. I call out to the women, "Why don't you stop them?" The women say, "We can't stop them, but we'll read to you."

Lucy had just been in New Mexico visiting Harmony, and we found a moment during the meeting to talk about something other than Kay. Harmony had finally settled on a place in the village of Galisteo near Santa Fe; she was buying a historic stone building, a former wool warehouse, perched near the Galisteo Creek. "I know Harmony; she will make it wonderful. She always lives with a certain style . . . we have to get together and talk about the Southwest."

Powerhouse Gallery was making a video documentation of women artists who had exhibited in the gallery and wanted to include many of us living in New York. I had agreed to host an afternoon at our loft. Sarah Drury, a video artist whom Emma had recruited for the Education issue, lived nearby and would come over to film the fifteen-second spots. Not everyone from *Reconstruction Project* was available. I got a letter from Holly Zox:

> I ran off to Seattle to become a jockey. Honest! I live on and care for a forty-acre thoroughbred ranch outside of town and gallop horses at a nearby training center. . . . I wouldn't have known how to finish that sentence about Powerhouse Gallery, but I would have enjoyed sitting in your loft with everyone. I think *Reconstruction Project* was the nicest "art thing" I was part of in New York, and you always did serve the best food in town.

Catalina, Sharon, and Donna came over and a couple of other artists we didn't know were also there. It felt like a party after the daunting series of meetings for *Heresies*. I showed them the new work I had made in Taos, and then each of us did a fifteen-second video sitting

122. Janet Culbertson, *Faces of the Peconic* 123. Harmony Hammond, *Fan Ladies on the Edge*

near our windows. Mine was very plain. "Less is more," Donna said. She had prepared a chant, holding her dog. Sharon read a poem; a German artist held up a fish across her eyes; and Catalina read a statement. "This is not like other people's houses," Sarah said as she packed up her equipment.

I dream that I go to see Catalina. She lives in a huge apartment, with many rooms and a grassy lawn inside. My second cousin Daphne comes to visit, wanting to see our land. "It's across the street," I say. We cross the road; it is wooded, like the forests in Maine. We see an odd house set in a fantastic landscape. Icebergs are floating in a lake ringed with craggy mountains. Everything is cloaked in a silvery mist. Suddenly, we realize that the land is sinking under us. We rush back into the little house, which is actually a boat.

My proposal for Multiply: Artists Organize Artists Organize Art, a panel on collaboration, was accepted for the February 1990 WCA National Conference with the stipulation that Josely could not be included because she had been a panelist the previous year. I had been planning to write her about our conflicts in Brazil, and now I needed to tell her about the panel as well. She had been calling, wanting to visit. "This is your friend from the jungles of Brazil." She responded a few weeks later, in the midst of the crises with *Heresies*.

Frankly, I could not imagine you had so many grievances . . . . I would rather meet with you, sit down and discuss with you how I perceived these different situations. . . . I and my family received you in Brazil with open arms. . . . If my family have invited you to so many dinners, it was because they wanted to include you as an insider. . . . Have you thought that some of these misunderstandings could have been cultural?

124. Artelia Court, *Aquifer* (front) 125. Ida Applebroog, *Two Women II (after de Kooning)* 126. Artelia Court, *Aquifer* (back)

I replied, "I am not encouraged by your letter. You make it sound like I am simply object-ing to having eaten *too many* wonderful meals with your family."

Our letters had now gone out to the associates and the contributors of the Women on Men issue, and not everyone was supportive of the collective. Kay had evidently also sent out let-ters, stating that she was fired without warning. She continued to refuse to return the money and had hired a lawyer. Performance artist Jerri Allyn was at first reluctant to sign the amended per-mission form giving *Heresies* sole right to publish her artwork for Women on Men. "I do know that if it's true that Kay was fired, never given a warning, and no one still part of the 'legal' collective will talk with her; this seems particularly harsh." She suggested mediation. I replied with copies of bank statements and our minutes regarding the notice and compensation we had offered Kay.

> I, for one, am incensed that she felt she *could take* these monies—these mon-ies were raised by our mutual twelve years of *unpaid work*, time, love, artwork, begging work from others like ourselves, conversations, words, hauling stuff, etc., which had built *Heresies* into *Heresies*. It made me ashamed and mad that Kay could just *take* the money, no matter what she felt.

Jerri sent us her permission form.

Joyce Kozloff responded to Avis's letter. "This is going to be unpopular with you, but I think you should just publish Issues #24 and #25 [Anniversary and Women on Men issues] and then *fold*. I really feel that *Heresies* no longer makes sense—it comes out once a year, many people believe it ceased to exist years ago, the issues are uneven, but mostly, it just feels very

127. Jerri Allyn, *4 Story House* 128. Joyce Kozloff, *Pornament Is Crime* series 129. Jerri Allyn, *The Waitresses*

seventies and tired to me now. (This is blunt—I'm sorry.)" I seemed to be the official respondent for disgruntled mail. I wrote:

> I understand your dismay at this drama. What disturbs me is your feeling that *Heresies* should fold. Do women really control so *many* institutions that we can simply toss *Heresies* out because you no longer like it? I don't subscribe to the idea of decades of art—that concept seems more related to consumer packaging. But I am curious what factors you see as "seventies"—the desire to act collectively?

I was trying to finish up *Lillie's Peaks* and the other two photocopier books for *4/Tells*, complete my freelance jobs, and get ready to go to Abiquiu in late August. We were planning to camp on our land and build a shed. Friends were coming by the studio to visit; Linda Peer, who had resigned from the Anniversary issue, liked what I was doing with *Lillie's Peaks*. I had started sewing the paintings as twin-peaked ridges rising above the rectangular-tied fences. Linda helped me figure out how to make a mate for the juniper wood I planned to use in a sculpture called *Woodsman*. The installation series about my family that I had long envisioned was gradually taking shape. I took the train up to Boston to visit May at her artist-in-residence studio at the Bunting Institute, bringing some of my recent photocopier books. May was working on paintings based on photos of her institutionalized mother pulling petals off a flower. I showed her the book I had just completed for ISCA, *Place/Displace/Replace*; the images were dreamlike silhouettes derived from photos I took inside Mother Gladys's house during my final visit. I loved the indistinct outline of Daddy Chess closing a window with the curtain billowing, his back stooped

130. Sabra Moore, (all), *Photocopier book 4/TELLS (Opal)* "...they had to cut away the tape..." 131. "...the trial all right..."

with age. May found it too abstract; she disliked the tiny photos of Opal repeated inside the valentines, wanting a bold, clear picture of my aunt. But I saw Opal as captive to her difficult life circumstance framed inside the heart-shaped window.

I dream that I visit Marina in her house. It is labyrinthine and huge, like a school. There is a steam bath in a side room, where Willie is soaking. Marina tells me her cancer treatment is completed and we dance with joy like schoolgirls, twirling around and around.

Elyse Taylor, who was part of the *Pieced Work* show I curated for *Views by Women Artists*, was organizing a project called *On the Move*. Thirty-two artists were contributing narrow horizontal panels that would be assembled into five quilt-like artworks, 4´ x 8´ each, for the *Arts in Transit* installation in the subway station on Forty-Second Street and Sixth Avenue. The installation would be up for six months near the main library where I often went for research, so I would see it when we returned from Abiquiu. I delivered my paper panel to Elyse and found her reaction odd. "I hope you didn't work too hard on it—it's wonderful."

Roger and I went over to city hall to get our marriage license. Fabio had asked me when we planned to marry; we would be ready when we returned. We had to raise our right hands and swear that we were who we said we were while standing there in line among couples of every size and shape, and then we filled out forms listing the names and birthplaces of our parents. I loved the sense of genealogy. When we got back to the loft, we discovered that one of the newts Artelia had given us was shedding its skin like removing a set of pajamas. We watched as two tiny cellophane feet disappeared down its throat.

I dream that I am in New Mexico on a hilly dirt road. I have been painting a large oblong bumpy rock. I want to open it, so I climb the rise and drop the rock down. It splits open cleanly,

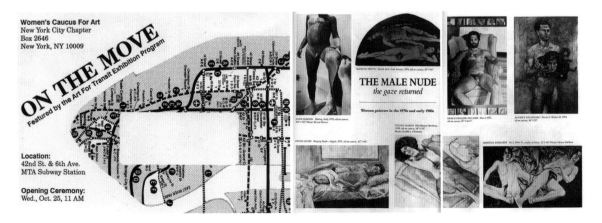

132. *On the Move* subway installation card 133. *Heresies* issue #24, double page, Sylvia Sleigh, *The Male Nude...*

like a fossil rock. Inside are beautiful black and white paintings on two concave sections like the paintings on pots.

I was still working with Sue and Kathie to finish the mechanicals for the Anniversary issue before leaving for New Mexico, and took the layout that I had designed for the "penis page" to show Sylvia. Her reaction was visceral—"I can't wreck my career." She sent me a letter just as we were leaving. "I love you, but I hate the layout; I hate the title and have no choice but to withdraw the whole thing. . . . I took a great deal of trouble to have everything as near as possible in size to ensure equality and I think that my layout was elegant and equable." I called Sue from Roanoke. Sylvia was my friend, and I had straddled the chasm between her sensibility and that of the collective, getting caught in the morass myself. Standing there talking to Sue on the pay phone, we decided to restore Sylvia's original double-page layout and title (*The Male Nude/ the gaze returned*) and move the artworks by Nancy Grossman and Judith Bernstein that we had added to the following page. I sent Sylvia a postcard as we headed south towards Tennessee.

134. Sabra Moore, *What Is Feminist Art?* card, *Subject Matters* 135. *Vital signs: Artists Respond to the Environment*

10

How to Be in Two Places at Once

Road signs advertising "Tucumcari Tonight" start in Amarillo with garish billboards displaying the names of the town's many motels. We were back in New Mexico, rising early to turn onto a narrow blacktop winding through red cliffs and past humped rocks shaped like giant turtles, taking the scenic back road into Abiquiu as a ceremonial entry to the month's work building a shed on our land. We startled vultures congregated beside a ranch fence, feasting on the carcasses of three dead cows, and then we passed pronghorn antelope grazing at a distance in a pasture with the ubiquitous ravens overhead. Otherwise, we were alone on the road after three days of negotiating interstate highway traffic. We stopped at a homemade Virgin Mary shrine set into massive boulders at the base of the steep road that climbs up to the village of Trujillo, and then we continued past pastures thick with grass. In another hour, we were in Abiquiu, rounding the two sharp curves onto the white mesa where we planned to camp. We parked above our place and started hauling our tent, tools, sleeping bags, lanterns, sacks of food, bottles of water, and

1. Cerro Negro frames the newly built shed and tent site on our land 2. Sabra unpacks the camping gear to set up tent

four straight-backed wooden kitchen chairs freshly found abandoned on a New York street. Were we home? It felt startling and abruptly silent as we walked around trying to select a level site to place the tent. We were surrounded by two distant mountain ranges; a white canyon opened a few yards beyond our stacks of gear, descending into a wide arroyo three hundred feet below. Cerro Negro was just beyond the mesa, her two gentle peaks like comforting breasts framing the sky. We sat down on the ground.

Kate Correa had settled along the river just beyond Bodes, Abiquiu's general store located on the main two-lane highway across from the village. Kate had offered us showers and a bed when needed during our stay. I planned to repay by cooking pies and cornbread. She and her new partner, Lisa Schwartzberg, had almost finished their house. Both were artists, but without the intense collaboration Kate had shared with Frankie.

My time wasn't completely free. I had brought the final stages of photo research work to finish for another Joseph Campbell book, this time for Harper Collins. We also had Jaune Quick-To-See's painting from *Reconstruction Project* to deliver, and I planned to refine the proposal for *Running Out of Time*, the show I was organizing at Kazuko's gallery for December. But first, we needed to decide on a house site before placing the shed.

Georgia O'Keeffe had lived in Abiquiu; her house was visible on a bluff above the highway just as you neared Bodes. In legend, she is seen as a lone figure in a vast landscape, but she could stroll a short distance from her gate to the church plaza. Her studio window looked out over the highway facing Cerro Negro and the veiled white formations called Plaza Blanca, where we were starting to build. I loved the way she had created emblematic forms from looking at the land—the dark raven flying above twin snowy hills; Pedernal, the flat-topped butte to the west, which she painted repeatedly; rock crevices opening to the sky; and the dark crosses

3. Looking into Madera Canyon as the water flows after a rain 4. Roger works to erect the first frame wall for the shed

against the hills. But I could not stop looking down at the intricacy and intimacy of the ground; the distant view was not as compelling to me as the dirt itself. The ground was covered with subtle variations of color and texture—quartz pebbles in pink or white, smooth river rocks, black lava rock, orange lichen, milky agate tool fragments or obsidian chips, and the glistening black volcanic glass mined at Pedernal by earlier inhabitants. I would happen upon a source rock made of silky umber jasper carried by someone to this site centuries earlier. What at first looked to us as completely undeveloped land was in fact a place that had already been inhabited. We found fourteen thick shards near our tent—the remnants of a pot someone had dropped in the twelfth century where we were now camping. It was hard to get started on the shed amidst these constant discoveries. The clouds kept changing; the light would soften or turn golden against the cliffs. A red-tailed hawk would catch our eye. The nights were dazzling as we sat around our little campfire, watching the dense Milky Way or identifying constellations. We weren't alone. We kept seeing lizards—some with turquoise tails and others brown with bright blue patches under each leg. There were horned toads, my childhood friends, and collared lizards that ran like little dinosaurs on two legs. One night, we spied a badger lumbering along the road and another time, we surprised a fox. We kept count of jackrabbits and cottontails that popped up each evening as we returned from showering. Finally, we picked a site. It was obvious; we were already camping in the house.

We drove to Taos and saw Henry. "You should hurry up and move here." Joan Watts drove over in her little camper with Salynn, her partner at the time. We spent the next morning hiking in the arroyo, looking at the petroglyphs and pictographs I had been drawing. A spring was seeping up right where four horned serpents had been pecked into the lower cliff face by Pueblo ancestors. Pat D'Andrea came later to camp with Cecile Dawkins, a writer from Taos, bringing

5. Sabra sits astraddle the shed roof nailing down the roofing tin 6. Atop the finished shed roof with one shutter hanging

corn to roast. Pat had just returned from the headwaters of the Rio Grande in Colorado, still gathering stories and information for her book on the river.

Finally, we got to work. I sketched the layout of the L-shaped house and the placement of the shed nearby in line with the path we had worn, walking each day from the road to our tent. We had no electricity, so we designed a shed 8´ x 12´ based on the size of a sheet of plywood. It was a simple structure: a peaked-roof building with four small square windows and shutters that could be raised to cover each window. The door faced the canyon with its back to the road. We dug a test hole for pouring cement footers. There were no earthworms or roly-poly bugs; only a seventeen-year-old locust roused from its sleep.

We had been going over to Kate and Lisa's house each night to shower, but they were also having other visitors—new friends who had just returned from the Lakota Sun Dance and wanted to build a medicine wheel in the pasture near Kate and Lisa's house. Since none were Native American, it felt uncomfortable. I needed to soak in a bath and to finish sending off letters inviting artists to participate in *Running Out of Time*. We went for a weekend to visit Acoma Pueblo, stayed overnight in a motel at Jemez Springs, and returned with fresh energy to our thoroughly dry cement footers, ready to put up the framing for the shed. Roger and I nailed together wooden studs at the standard sixteen-inch centers for each of the four walls—like making large stretchers for a canvas. Each wall had a small square window opening already framed in place. We had completed the plywood base and raised the first wall, securing it with three-inch nails, and then we lifted the eight-foot-wide corner wall. Roger was standing on a ladder ready to join the two walls. I was standing below the skeletal shed, looking with dismay at the visual effect of the rectangular structure against the rounded hills. A breeze came up and Roger shouted,

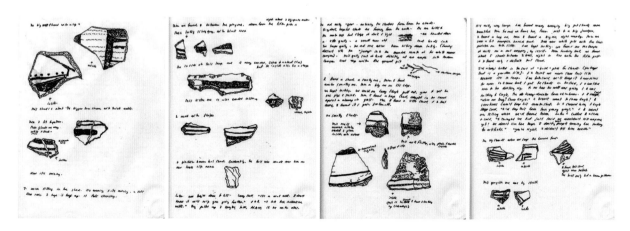

7., 8., 9., 10. Sabra Moore, drawings from Journal Book #52: Abiquiu black and white shards found at various sites on the land

"Hold it!" I saw the wall falling towards me and found myself standing inside the small square window space; only my heel got roughly scraped.

We got to spend our last night before leaving for Brooklyn sleeping in the shed and savoring the silence. The slightest breeze had made our tent flap and billow. The falling wall had taught us our second lesson about wind: the gently rounded twin hills at the top of our road had been smoothed into shape by ferocious winds. The imposing skeletal shed settled down into the modest structure it actually was once we faced it with plywood and nailed corrugated tin on the roof, containing the space. We packed away things: the four chairs, the juniper roots I had saved from digging the footers, a few special rocks I had found, and some of our camping gear. We locked the shed and left.

Roger had been taking photos, so I showed them to my aunt and uncle when we stopped in Avery on the way back. "Do you want to come over and build my barn?" Duel asked. It worried him that there was so little grass—nothing for feeding cows.

There were stacks of mail to sort on our return. Many friends were having shows: Howardena Pindell was exhibiting at Cyrus Gallery, Linda Peer was making a window installation, and Kathy Grove was doing something entirely new for a show in Boston. Kathy did photo retouching as her day job, and now she was using this skill for a series of large-scale photos altering famous paintings. Many women have added female figures to historical paintings, but Kathy responded to the proliferation of allegorical women by removing them. The bare breasted revolutionary in Delacroix's *Liberty* was etherized into space.

I had dreamed twice that Sylvia had died; in each dream, I was crying, so I called her. We had not talked since her letter about the *Heresies* double page of male nudes; the issue was

11. Howardena Pindell, *Autobiography: The Search: Chrysalis...* 12. Vernita Nemec, *Surface Tensions* performance

on press with Sylvia's original design included. Lawrence answered; he seemed a bit startled to hear my voice, but then our conversation became normal again.

Artists were responding to my invitation for *Running Out of Time*, most agreeing to participate. I decided to make a card by composing an image in the photocopier machine, direct-printing my hands, the square snapshot of the rain forest road in N'Zérékoré, a tiny childhood ceramic doll, and a wooden toy cow—all scattered across the glass bed of the copy machine. The decade was ending; I had invited nine artists and was also planning an evening of readings, *Nine Times for the Nineties*. My artwork with the same title as the show had been sitting unfinished in my studio since the PPOW Gallery benefit two years earlier. Now, I was completing all thirteen houses. "Do you make a show in order to finish pieces?" Faith Wilding asked me. She had a point.

We called Marithelma and Fabio to meet us in the Manhattan Municipal Building as our witnesses; Roger and I got married on October 6. We sat with other couples waiting to be called in for Justice of the Peace Mrs. Vines to perform the ceremony. Signs admonished us to "Have Your $5 Ready" and "No Soliciting Witnesses." Soliciting wasn't necessary; our friends arrived on time. We exchanged Hopi rings and kissed, and then we walked down Atlantic Avenue for a meal together. We didn't want a party; it was too late for wedding gifts of skillets and sets of dishes; we each kept our names. Roger was at work on a card—our way to share the news with friends and kin. We had taken a timed photo of the two of us posed inside the skeletal shed in our work clothes, looking out the opening of the window that had fallen around me. "Sabra & Roger Got Married" was printed in plain type beneath the photo. Later, Kathy Grove and I compared notes about people's reactions; she and Larry had made the same trip to city hall. "Does everyone ask you, 'is it different'?" When people had insisted on changing her last name on

13. Sabra and Roger waiting with witness Marithelma Costa at Brooklyn City Hall to get married 14. Photo for our wedding card

letters addressed to them, she had responding by reversing the names, Larry Grove and Kathy List. "That stopped it."

I dream that I am traveling around the world by swimming across the ocean. The water is dark and cold, but I can see through it. I am able in places to walk on big rocks. Then I reach a narrow place, like an alley. The rocks there are translucent ultramarine blue, round and smooth and pierced with holes. I gather them up. Then I am in a museum rearranging the paintings.

Kazuko's gallery onetwentyeight was a storefront on Rivington Street in what was then a Dominican neighborhood on the Lower East Side. The heating was erratic, but the space intriguing; it still had a mosaic floor from an earlier use and a display window suitable for art installations. Kazuko took me next door to see the basement wine cellar for the kosher winery; she wanted us to use both spaces for the opening. The cellar was damp and had bright yellow walls and a long U-shaped stand-up bar. A Japanese friend named Mako was living in back of her gallery. We three sat together looking at the photos I had brought from our land. Many friends were buying land away from the city. Vivian Browne had just bought a place in Bakersville, California with her partner Vida Hackman, and Linda Peer was looking for land in Upstate New York. The next week, Joan Watts showed up at our loft, visiting friends in New York. I pulled out the photos of the shed. "It's not quite finished," I said. "What does it need, curtains?"

I ran into Sue Heinemann at Roundtable Press, Inc.; we both had freelance work from them. "Everything that could go wrong did go wrong on the *Heresies* issue," she told me, but at least it was finally on press. A few days later, we had a meeting. Things were still unresolved with Kay Kenny; various people had tried to mediate, but we were not even able to retrieve the boards for the Women on Men issue (not, as Faith wrote regarding Lucy's comment, Women against Men). The injunction against Kay was still in place. Emma had been working with the

RUNNING OUT OF TIME

9 Women Artists Take a Planetary Turn To The 90s
VIVIAN BROWNE • MARINA GUTIÉRREZ •
EDITH ISAAC-ROSE • KAZUKO •
SABRA MOORE • CATALINA PARRA •
MIMI SMITH • MAY STEVENS •
FAITH WILDING

NOVEMBER 11 – DECEMBER 2, 1989
Opening Reception, Saturday, November 11, 7–9 pm
After-Opening Party next door at Shapiro Wine Co., 9 pm on
Closing Event, **9X for the 90s**, Sat, Dec 2, 7:30–9 pm

one twenty eight
128 Rivington St (betw. Essex & Norfolk), NYC 10002
Gallery Hours 1–7 pm, Thurs–Sun • (212) 254-6608

15. Kazuko, show card 16. *Running Out of Time* exhibit card with photo of road in N'Zérékoré 17. List of participants

Myth/Education issue; it would move into the slot reserved for Women on Men. Our logjam of publication was finally easing. Penny and I were asked to organize the party for the Anniversary issue in early December—we were inviting Jerri Allyn and Robbie McCauley to perform, and everyone promised to cook.

Our Peace Corps training group was having a reunion in New York, the first since 1964. Maggie was the only Peace Corps friend I saw regularly. One of the reunion organizers, Gina, told me, "You're the person everyone has been asking about." That made me nervous—living in Guinea had been a keystone experience for both positive and negative reasons. Roger went with me. Carol Munday, the only black volunteer from our group, came over. "You were so colorful in training," she said, "but what has happened to your accent? I was expecting to hear that accent." Carol was from Tuskegee; she had also lost her Southern accent. I saw Carol Zeitz; we had been close friends before she moved to California. "What happened to your hair? You've turned gray. I was expecting your beautiful auburn hair." "When I was a child, it was this color." "You should color it like I do." She had stopped dancing and was now a therapist.

At the time I was trying to leave C, Carol Zeitz was living nearby in Park Slope with a boyfriend. I ran to their apartment one afternoon, weeping and dragging the few possessions I had grabbed on the way out the door. C had come to their building that night, threatening to bomb the apartment. I could see that they were afraid; I went back to the loft. "You were there during the violence," I said. "But I haven't experienced violence," she said.

May called when she received my packet of cards for *Running Out of Time*. "Usually, I don't send cards to a group show, but I love your card so much. Those hands look like wizened black hands." "They're my hands." It took three days to install the show. I became immersed in Kazuko's Japanese-in-New-York art community, a cultural discovery for me. Roger felt we

18. Installation, gallery onetwentyeight 19. Sabra Moore, *Running out of Time: 13 House Count*, based on Aztec calendrical images

shouldn't hang any artworks in the damp wine cellar, but it seemed safe for such a short period of time. I only hung my own artworks there—three of the *Flowers* paintings I had made for my grandparents based on repeated photo transfers of them walking stooped through the gateway to Briggins Cemetery. Kazuko was enthusiastic about the winery, and she hung tiny kimonos along the yellow walls and a target with black cloth feet. I draped a pink striped cloth to frame my small paintings like a curtain. "For the Chinese, red is the color for anything new; they use it with babies." I told her about the shape of the doorways in Chaco Canyon, and she told me how it felt to give birth to her son Eizan: "like a train coming out." The next day, she made a kimono doorway in response to my Chaco story, visualizing the transit of Eizan from her vagina.

I ran back to the gallery next door to receive artworks. Mimi Smith, bundled against the cold, brought some of her clock series. She kept on her coat as we stood in the gallery and talked. Her mother had the same sort of tumor on her spine that was slowly killing Lawrence. Catalina appeared with her father Nicanor, carrying her artworks made with X-rays. Marina brought a mixed media print with ominous houses; May delivered a painting about her mother; Vivian brought a series of small artworks with her veiled trees; and Faith Wilding delivered a painting of a strange mermaid. I went home to finish the last house, the one for *fire*, and returned the next morning to complete the installation. Bea Kreloff and Edith Isaac-Rose met me to help hang the show and install Edith's drawings of bones. I felt happy to have finished all thirteen houses, each a symbol of nature, crowded together along the snaky tabletop. I had made an accordion folded paper text about the Aztec concept of a decade, albeit a thirteen-year decade, and attached it to the wall. There were four time periods, each configured by a symbol. *House* was one, and I planned to make works for *rabbit* and *knife*. Mako thought it looked Japanese.

20. Marina Gutierrez, *No Shelter* 21. Sabra working at gallery 22. Faith Wilding, *Godot's Tree, a dream...*

We didn't have to worry about the heating in the building at the opening—the narrow space was packed. "Sabra pulls these things out of a hat," Vivian said. The Anniversary issue was out, and people were excitedly passing around copies. Barrie Karp invited all of us to come the next day to St. Patrick's Cathedral for a "No More Nice Girls" action. I ran into Elyse Taylor; I hadn't seen her since delivering my panel for the composite quilt installation in the Forty-Second Street subway station. I had recently gone into the subway to see how it looked. Mold was already growing between the panels and the Plexiglas. "Don't mention it to me!" Elyse said. "One of the artists told me she knew her piece would be destroyed during the [subway] show." "It wouldn't be all right with me if my work were destroyed," I countered. I volunteered to help her temporarily remove the framed panels and try to kill the fungus. The woman who had mounted the artworks had used wheat paste instead of archival glue, and then had promptly sealed them inside the Plexiglas frames without allowing adequate drying time. We all drifted over from the gallery to the winery; the kosher wine was old and terrible. Outside, the moon was full.

I dream that I am traveling with Kazuko. We are standing in the rain under a catalpa tree in a place like Grandmother's front yard. A man says, "Don't stand under that tree; it might thunder." We move to a doorway. The man says, "It looks like a tornado is coming." I run out to look, hopping deftly over embankments slick with ice and snow. Then everything vanishes, leaving only air.

Three weeks later, we closed the show with visitors again crowded into the gallery for a performance night. Mostly, we artists did the readings, but Lucy and Marithelma also came to read. Kazuko had been practicing an eerie piece with sounds and a scream. I read from Diego de Landa against slides of Mother Gladys and Grandmother's doorstop doll. Catalina and May read their own poetry, and Marina talked about her disrupted Taíno heritage. "It's like the early days at A.I.R. Gallery," May said. "I love it." Lucy thought the show was "great, but lost in that space."

23. Mimi Smith, *Racing Against the Muck*, installed at *Running Out of Time*, gallery onetwentyeight

The benefit party for the Anniversary issue was a few days later, followed quickly by a *Heresies* meeting in the office. Linda Peer had written us a letter complaining that her name was not listed as a member of the editorial collective even though she had worked for over a year on the issue. It was true that she had quit before publication, but she found the omission "hurtful and . . . ungenerous." Emma complained that her name and artwork were not listed in the table of contents; I was in the same "category of nameless art." Other artists in that category included everyone whose postcards were reproduced for the "What is Feminist Art?" section. We had misprinted Kate Millet's artwork, but Kate had not yet complained. The new issue was already selling well; Myth/Education had a very good designer at work, Mary Sillman, a woman I knew from Doubleday Publishers. We had one clear fundraising idea: printing T-shirts from the cover of the Anniversary issue with Miriam Schapiro's red and black graphic cutouts spelling out heresies. We still hoped to implement our ideas for columns once the current issues were all in production, but we were already $8,000 in debt to the lawyers with no hint of resolution with Kay. What was a reasonable schedule for production given our finances and the drain of the embezzlement? "We need interim goals." Kathie Brown suggested two issues per year as a feasible goal.

I had been completing some of my photocopier book editions, amassing a fine stack of sewn books for the Saturday Book Fair sponsored by the Center for Book Arts. I felt I should start participating in more book art venues. I laid out copies of *Place/Displace*, *4/Tells*, *Wash & Iron*, and other small books with dark family stories, and then I noticed that all the other tables were filled with beautiful calligraphy books, marbled papers, finely bound blank notebooks, and other immaculate examples of traditional book art. People would approach my display, pick up a book, leaf through it, and quickly put it down and head over to the next table for more delightful

24. Installation view, Mimi Smith, *Running Against the Muck*, foreground 25. May Stevens, *Fore River*

objects. A young woman stopped to look. "Do you work with *Heresies*?" she asked. She had just completed her senior thesis at Yale on *Heresies* and had recognized my Xerox work.

I dream that I am going to get married, but first I have to perform. Other people are getting married dressed in formals with frilly ruffles. I decide to tell a story. People come to listen; my sister Nancy is there. I tell about Mother and I sewing Nancy's wedding dress, but this story upsets my sister.

Roger and I decided impulsively to fly to New Mexico for the week of Christmas; we were eager to visit our place. "It's like being in love," Jackie Wray had said. In three months, the rough-cut wood had shrunk in the dry climate and a mouse had found its way inside, but otherwise, nothing had changed. On Christmas, we drove over to Taos Pueblo for the Deer Dance, standing with others in the cold to watch the solemn line of men dressed as deer, elk, or buffalo enter the plaza. The animals hesitated as they neared the circle of dancers until two Deer Mothers approached and a white-suited hunter invited them to enter. The drum and chanters filled the space with sound. A child dressed as a mountain lion would subtly point towards a deer or elk and a sacred clown would ritually shoot it with his tiny arrow and then haul it out of the circle. At a certain undefined point, someone approached the Deer Mothers and removed their cloaks, and then the dance simply stopped. The next day, we drove back to Abiquiu with a friend from the Wurlitzer, Sidney Hamburger. We walked up to enjoy the view from the ledge above the shed and promptly found a tiny bird point arrowhead in our path. Then we noticed three people walking across the ridge as if this was a familiar path. A little girl ran forward, then stopped in surprise at seeing us, and we, for the first time, met our neighbors on the mesa.

We returned to New York before New Year's Day in 1990. I had made a date to have lunch with May, but arrived twenty minutes late. She was furious. "No one does this to me!

26-29. Sabra Moore, details (all), *Running Out of Time, 13 House Count: Fire, Forest, Deer, Forest*

You did this to me once before in 1982. The only people who are late are Hispanics." "But, May, I am a Southerner. I tried to call you." "You live here, you're busy, and someone told me you're always late. How can you do this to people?!"

A couple of days later, Sylvia called and left a message on my phone machine. Lawrence had died early the previous morning. She was alone with him in their bedroom when he had a heart attack. I got dressed and took the subway to her house, agreeing to accompany her to the bank to make sure she would have access to their account while his affairs were being settled. Sylvia was much older than Lawrence. They had met at an art history class when he was seventeen; she was unhappily married to a painter, taking a class at his behest. We had gone to many of Sylvia's birthday parties, singing "Happy Birthday" around a cake that never revealed her age. I thought it was Sylvia who concealed her age. At the bank, I tried to avert my eyes as she filled out the forms listing her address and age, but it wasn't necessary. Lawrence was the one who had wanted her to appear younger.

"I'm really glad you're here," she told me as we sat in her kitchen, writing up a list of friends and colleagues to invite to his memorial. Lawrence had once been a curator at the Guggenheim and a critic for *Artforum*, but during the past ten years of his illness, he had been enveloped primarily in Sylvia's circle of women artists. Many of the more established male artists and colleagues had simply stopped visiting. Sylvia asked me to call Roy Lichtenstein and a few others. She talked about how hard it had been during his progressive paralysis to forgo the intense eroticism that they had both enjoyed.

Lawrence looked like a baby in his casket as we crowded into the packed room for his memorial; Sylvia had hand-sewn the plain shroud, leaving only his face visible. Roger and I stood in the back next to Ce Roser, Maureen Connor, and Ellen Lubell. Maureen and I were crying

30. Sylvia Sleigh (all), *The Bride (Lawrence Alloway)* 31. *Lawrence Alloway* (tondo) 32. *Lawrence Alloway with Bowtie*

quietly, but everyone else exhibited composure. Stephanie Rauschenbusch turned and asked me if I was all right. Various artists stood and spoke about Lawrence, most describing how he had written about their artwork. He had recently completed a catalogue essay for May while also working on an article about Matisse. He had told May that he was writing "Matisse in the morning, and May in the afternoon." Roberta Flack praised him for being one of the first critics to notice her paintings, and Catharine Stimpson lamented the loss of his uncompleted survey book on women artists.

There was a reception at Sylvia's house after going to the gravesite; it would be a couple of hours before everyone returned to Twentieth Street. Sharon Gilbert, Roger, and I decided to walk over to see the Velasquez show at the Met. We three were standing with Bibi in front of the funeral home, waiting to see Lawrence's coffin exit. "He's already gone," Sharon said, "the limousine follows the hearse." We had turned the corner to walk to the museum and almost stepped on our flowers resting on the sidewalk. The hearse was parked nearby, and we stood there as Lawrence's coffin was briskly wheeled out the door and loaded into the hearse. Only we three friends were accidental witnesses to his departure.

The reception was like an art opening, as befitted Lawrence. Sylvia seemed gratified that Alex Katz and other artists who had neglected them came. Lawrence was self-taught and didn't finish university, but he was able to straddle both the art world of money and power and the cooperative art world that we inhabited. I remembered his discomfort, however, when I met Sylvia one evening to go with her to the opening of the Andy Warhol show at MoMA. "Are you going to change clothes?" he asked, disapproving of the informality of my dress. "No." Many friends from our women's circle were there—Ann Sutherland Harris, Ora, Bibi, Sharon, Joan Semmel, Nancy Spero, and others. Roberta Flack came over to suggest I might pose for one of her oversized

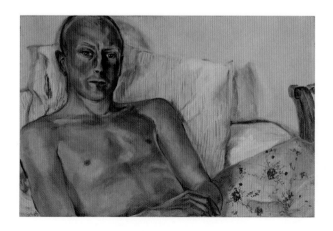

33. Sylvia Sleigh, *Lawrence in Bed (Ditching)*. 34. Joan Semmel, *Self Portrait on the Couch*, 1983

sculptures. "You have such a beautiful face." Would I try grimacing like Medusa so she could see my expression? I couldn't.

Lawrence's death brought some old friends from the WCA closer again. Ora and I visited. She had been experiencing discrimination in the academic world. At a recent panel, the two male panelists were paid honoraria, but not the women. They convinced the men to donate their stipends to a homeless shelter. I told her about the cemetery-related sculptures I had been making and how I wanted to have a solo show again; it felt like my time was constantly swallowed up by freelance jobs. Ora encouraged me. "No one else is working like you; your work is highly original."

We met again for *Heresies*. I wrote the minutes. "In penance for not sending out the December 3rd minutes, I have been assigned to write *double* minutes." The first topic was fundraising. Ida, Joyce, and Miriam had suggested an idea for a curated benefit exhibit, and Bea Kreloff offered to help by contacting the progressive funding resource, Black Star. I felt weary and welcomed the help "only if it meant *actual work*, not simply suggestions for others to execute." People had been criticizing the effectiveness of the PPOW Gallery benefit: we had raised $10,000, but netted only $5,000 after paying 50 percent to the artists. Betsy wanted to discuss our plans for the number of issues produced yearly. "An issue needs an adequate shelf life," Avis said. "We only sell our issues when they've gotten moldy," Betsy countered. She was astonished that we had agreed to two issues yearly as an attainable goal. "You don't work up to being a quarterly. . . . You set a goal and make it happen." So, we returned to the problem of money. Betsy envisioned a big public event and a "public person" to help us. Lucy suggested partnering with another group and mentioned the recent highly successful NEST benefit. Of course, we were not El Salvador or AIDS, the beneficiaries of that effort. Everyone liked the idea of partnering with MADRE. Someone mentioned corporate money. No one liked that idea. We returned to our

35. Ora Lerman, *As the Sun Sets in Sidilkov, Eggs become Golden Suns* 36. Edith Isaac-Rose, *Milagros*

T-shirt enterprise, thinking about printing two different shirts, the red Anniversary issue cover with Miriam's cutouts and the black Activists issue cover with its transgressive list of names that women were called. Josely would do the printing. We begged Betsy to beg Ida Applebroog to draw a heretic at the stake for a third T-shirt. "Every Heretic Needs a Stake," Lucy quipped, offering a slogan. We had no trouble agreeing on colors. Avis offered to beg cartoonist Nicole Hollander to draw her character Sylvia reading *Heresies* in the bathtub. We agreed with four votes "yes" and one vote "no."

Marina was having a solo show at SOHO20 Gallery. Roger and I picked up her artwork; she insisted on paying us for the transport. That same day, I took my two small houses and Sharon Gilbert's artist's book over to Cooper Union for the *Primal Forces* show that was part of the upcoming WCA Conference. When I went a few days later to see the installation, I noticed that a cloth tie for *Water House* needed adjusting. I asked permission from the guard. "Another artist was here earlier and re-hung her piece." It was Josely, unhappy with same artwork that she had hung and re-hung at both venues for *Connections Project/Conexus*. I found myself missing our friendship.

Lucy had just organized a big show looking back on the Vietnam War. It got me thinking about women, war, and the artworks I was making for the *Place/Displace* series. Each of the thirteen sculptures I was planning told a specific story about someone buried in that country cemetery in East Texas—one man had been murdered; another had his Union infantry regiment on his tombstone; Opal's dead baby was buried there. War and violence stood in the shadows. I had read about a Mayan goddess whose bravery in giving birth was seen as equivalent to a warrior's bravery in war and thought about how I had survived my incomplete abortion and C's violence.

37. *Heresies* event flier for issues #18 and #19 38. Nicole Hollander cartoon 39. Miriam Schapiro's T-shirt design

Barbara Moore was interested in looking at my artist's books, and I went over to visit her at Bound & Unbound, her bookstore and house in Chelsea. Her husband had been affiliated with the Fluxus movement, and word-based and found object art filled the house. I felt immediately at home. Sari Dienes, one of the founders of A.I.R. Gallery, had made a small bottle glass window that illuminated the front door. Barbara was packing up a book by Joseph Beuys as I arrived; we had recently seen his show at PPOW Gallery. I sat down and unwrapped my box of books; most were from the *AKIN* series of family stories, but I had also brought collaborative books such as *150 Artists Book* and *Making*. Barbara was worried about the archival quality of color Xerox, but loved the black and red photocopies in *4/TELLS*. "You have a real gift for handling simple materials." I was happy when she bought six books, but I later wrote in my journal that I wished "I had gotten more than the $55 check I stuck in my pocket."

It was again time for another WCA Conference in New York, and I was preparing a statement for the panel I was moderating, "Multiple: Artists Organize Artists/Organize Art," with Jerri Allyn, Freda Guttman, and Donna Henes. I traced two threads of experience that had led me to work collaboratively—the idea of artists as fellow workers, which was based on Daddy's union organizing, and the concept of a common language, which was based on my grandmothers' quilts. Diana Kurtz later remarked on the denim shirt I had worn. "At first, I thought you had underdressed, but when the slides went on, the sequins on your shirt sparkled like stars." The panel was a bit like *Heresies*; everyone said too much. Only Donna was prepared with a succinct statement and carefully honed visuals. I offered to forego showing my slides to make room for the next panel, but the audience insisted on seeing a rapid display of artworks from *Connections Project/Conexus* and *Reconstruction Project*.

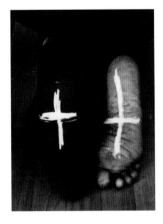

40. Back cover, *Heresies* issue #24 41. Marina Gutierrez, *Biography 42*. Maria Magdalena Campos, *A Woman at the Border*

I went out into the corridor and ran into Roger. "Avis is crying," he said. She was sitting along the wall with Emma. Her partner, Ron Wolin, had been struggling for years with cancer and now, he had gotten much sicker. Emma tried to calm her. "He's weak, but is he eating?" "Yes." Then Faith Ringgold appeared with Harmony and Bea. "Congratulations." I looked blank. "It must be going all right if you can't remember." Sharon Gilbert appeared, and we went together to the *Transgression* panel. We parted afterwards—she to hear the Guerrilla Girls and I to attend Harmony's panel. I loved seeing Kazuko's string sculptures in outdoor locations and Joyce Kozloff's playful "pornaments," and was surprised to see that Harmony had included my artwork *Door* in a quick overview of works by many others. Harmony and Joyce were complaining about the technical support for the WCA panels, calling the women yentas (busybodies).

I ran into Diana Kurtz again in the corridor. She had read my interview with Avis in the *Heresies's* Coming of Age issue. She had had an abortion at Women's Services in the early seventies and thought I had been her counselor. "This woman with long blond hair who was an artist; I'm pretty sure it was you. . . . It was my first experience of feminism. We were in a group session; there was a black teenager, a woman in her forties, and a couple of other women. I was pretty male-identified at that point. It was the first time I realized we all had this *body* in common."

May Stevens was being given an honor award, and I rushed after work to catch the chartered school bus to Newark. Helene Aylon and I squeezed into the last vacant seats. "I'm going for May," I said, catching my breath. Bea was seated behind us with Nancy Azara and Marilyn Lanfear, visiting from San Antonio. I moved over to talk with Marilyn about the artworks she was making that were also based on a family cemetery. When we got to Newark, we wanted to see Emma's show, but it was closed. She was there, looking glamorous in a white leopard skirt, and asked the guard to let us sneak into the gallery. He loved her show filled with paintings of

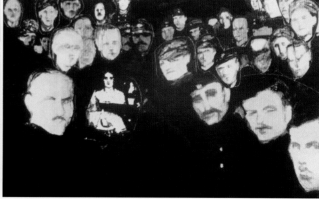

43. May Stevens, *One Plus or Minus One*, installation at New Museum (both), *The Second International* 44. *Eden Hotel*

people falling "into the hell of Western civilization"; she had autographed a program for him. Vivian Browne was already inside the auditorium. "I saw you earlier, walking through the corridor. You looked so serious and sort of sad; I wasn't sure it was you." Betsy Hess joined us; she had just been to see *Bad Girls*, a show "built around the premise of Hannah Wilke with gum stuck all over her body." The awards ceremony had started; several women were being honored. Santa Clara Pueblo painter Pablita Velarde said, "I think we all deserve it," and the audience cheered. I stayed behind to congratulate May. "Sabra! I'm glad you came! When I saw Josely and didn't see you, I thought you wouldn't come because you were still mad." She turned to Betsy and told her how I had kept her waiting for lunch. "Sabra! Late! May, Sabra is always late." Now, Vivian and I were giggling. Thalia Gouma Peterson insisted I come hear her paper on Miriam Schapiro's studio, and Eleanor Tufts, an art historian from Dallas, was trying to remember which year I "had arranged the programs." That night, I wrote, "Friends, enemies, comrades, artists, writers; quite a few of us now have a *real* history between us that has settled into a kind of ease."

I was working on a new photo research project for Doubleday editor Nan Talese, *O'Keeffe & Stieglitz: An American Romance* by Benita Eisler. Benita was a friend of Susana Torruella and had seen *Connections Project/Conexus*; her husband, Colin, was an art historian. For the first time, my day job had merged with my art life, making me feel, as I wrote later in my journal, "a little tender and vulnerable." Benita had gone to Abiquiu to do research at O'Keeffe's house and had found the area "desolate." Stieglitz was "a genius" and O'Keeffe was a painter who had "betrayed her gift for commercial success." "We may disagree," Benita said, "but I'd love to know what you think."

I dream that I am receiving an award. "It won't be a dress," someone says, "it's just called that." A large audience is seated as a woman reads the award, handing me three books and a

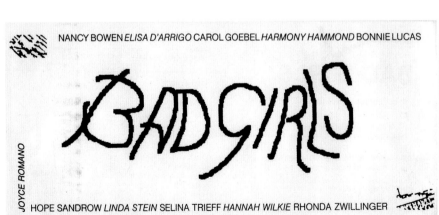
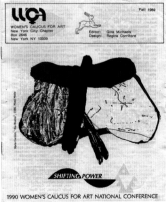

45. *Bad Girls* show card 46. NYC/WCA newsletter illustration, *Shifting Power*, 1990 WCA National Conference theme

three-cornered hat. I start to make an acceptance speech, but everyone gets up and heads to a food table. "Go ahead; enjoy yourselves," I say. I walk into a large room wearing my hat and carrying my books. Betsy Hess and Faith Wilding are there. "You should have gotten the award. You've been honest and direct. You say what you think." "Yes, I've made enemies; about half of the women in this room are enemies."

Avis's partner, Ron, died shortly after the WCA Conference and all of us Heretics attended his memorial. Roger remembered him from Vietnam Veterans Against the War. Ron had been executive director of the Cartoonists Guild for fourteen years, thus Avis's connection to cartoonist Nicole Hollander. The same week, I passed by the subway station at Forty-Second Street and saw that the mold had found my panel—spores of every variety were spotted across the painting. I called Sharon Vatsky to ask again to remove my artwork. "This has made Elyse physically ill; everyone has blamed her and no one has praised her." Oddly, no one seemed to notice the irony of the caption next to the molded artworks, "The NYC/Women's Caucus for Art supports women artists."

We Pearl Street tenants had been on rent strike for three years. Like many loft dwellers, we had joined the Brooklyn Loft Tenants Association and registered our building with the New York City Loft Board as part of a slow process to bring our buildings up to code and give us legal rights to live in the spaces we had renovated at our own expense. Our rents were frozen until the building violations were corrected, ending the cycle of renovation followed by eviction that had bedeviled artists in the past. We had been meeting regularly with the Loft Board to try to force our landlord, Jerry Rachman, to make some basic repairs. We wanted a secure locked front door and locked mailboxes to replace the heterogeneous collection of open wooden mailboxes we had each constructed. We also wanted the hallway painted. Paul Watson, the die cutter on the fifth

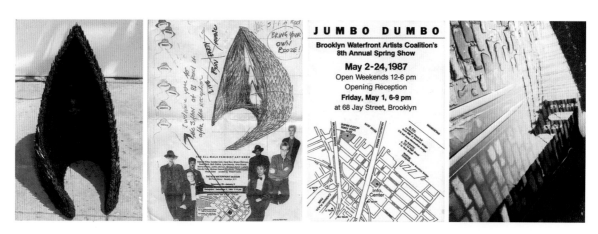

47. Brynhildur Thorgeirsdottir, *Hervör* 48. *All-Male Feminist Art Show* 49-50. Card, *Jumbo Dumbo*

floor, estimated that it had last been painted around 1973. The landlord wanted the rent we had been squirreling away in an escrow savings account, so he finally agreed to these three initial repairs. Barry Johnson, our neighbor on the third floor, was in charge of maintenance at Cooper Hewitt and noticed that each floor had asbestos sleeves around the heating pipes and advised Rachman to simply leave the sleeves undisturbed. Roger and I were home the day the two painters started working in the hallway. One was Albanian, one Yugoslavian; neither spoke English. We glanced out the window and saw the stacks of asbestos sleeves thrown out on the sidewalk. I called up the New York City Department of Environmental Protection, and a short time later, men arrived in white hazmat suits and stretched yellow safety tape across the sidewalk. The landlord was shouting at them as they stood impassively, letting him rant. At the Loft Board meeting the following week, Rachman insisted that asbestos was harmless. "It won't hurt you!" He had used asbestos for years in the burlap sacks made by Rachman Bag Company, the factory formerly housed in our building. The chairman, David Klarsfield, listened calmly and then added, "You know it's illegal." The street had been cleaned at our landlord's expense, but our halls were still contaminated. We now had permission to spend some of our escrow account to hire asbestos abatement workers to clean the hallways. As I left the Loft Board and headed uptown for work, I passed a group of Andean musicians playing their flutes on the street. Later, returning home, I saw the same musicians performing in the Forty-Second Street subway next to my molded panel. It softened my sense of injury, hearing the mountain music permeate our damaged artworks.

I took the train to New Haven to look through what was called the Wastebasket Collection, a series of photographs and papers that Stieglitz had discarded and O'Keeffe had later donated to the Beinecke Collection at Yale. Even though Stieglitz took over five hundred photos of O'Keeffe, only fifteen were outside the purview of the Georgia O'Keeffe Foundation. The

51. View of Manhattan Bridge from sixth-floor loft fire escape 52. Front Street building with rental signs in background

foundation didn't like Benita's book, so I was scrambling to find images that they did not control. As I walked into the research room, I passed two little chairs lined up primly between two small paintings in the hallway. They had belonged to Gertrude Stein and Alice B. Toklas. The painting of Alice was by Dora Maar and the one of Gertrude by Picabia; Alice had sewn the cushions of each delicate Louis IV chair with a needlepoint design by Picasso. I could imagine only Alice sitting on either improbable chair. Picasso was also on my mind. I was now researching a second book, *Matisse and Picasso*, by Françoise Gilot, the only one of Picasso's wives who had left him; these two research projects double blurring the boundaries between my art life and my day jobs.

The Brooklyn Waterfront Artists Coalition had a yearly show during the month of May often located in one of the vacant loft buildings and coupled with outdoor installations in various locations. The painter Jackie Lima was the coordinator; she was planning to paint the Manhattan Bridge inside a circle drawn on the street. I proposed doing an outdoor piece as well. The river attracted me. Its shore had been altered—the bays lined with wood and squared off for ships to dock, its strips of sand now cluttered with trash, but I wanted to see it as a natural waterway between two islands. There was a suitable bay just down the street shaped like a U and flanked by an abandoned building and the Con Edison plant. I would be able to climb down at low tide and walk alongside both buildings to reach the water. I planned to construct a series of grass rafts—like small floating islands or oversized lily pads—that I would tie into a web stretched inside the bay. At the end of the month, I would cut the strings and let the raft islands float out into the river. The materials were all natural and biodegradable: sod, planks, branches, and sisal string. I called the installation *This Is a Place Where the River Joins the Islands*, and started making the rafts, testing them in the bathtub. They seemed to float.

53. *This Is the Place Where the River Joins the Islands* (all), Roger holds web of *Grass Rafts* 54. Roger tosses a *Grass Raft*

We ran into Jackie Lima drawing out her circle on the street below our windows as we rolled a dolly with the first ten rafts tied together and ready to install in the river. I carried a ladder; Roger brought his camera. We laid the grouping out on the cobblestones, and then I bundled them into my arms and descended the ladder into the water while Roger held onto the end strings. This was my first time launching the grass rafts, so I simply hurled them into the water. They splashed in a snarl as I started pulling on the various strings; a few floated, but most turned upside down as soon as the water soaked the sod. We were attracting passersby. The police came three times. "Officers, we're installing an artwork." "Where?" "Here," indicating the forlorn snarl of sod bundles. A Japanese man stopped his bicycle. I explained that the rafts would become flotsam in the sea. "Like a blessing," he said. Later, I thought, "if I were Zuni, I would feel that the river had rejected my offering." In a couple of hours, I had gotten some control by continuing to tie and stretch the web, but then the tide suddenly swelled, the river rose, and all the rafts flopped upside down again. This would definitely be a process piece. I came each day for three days, working at night in the loft improving the construction, making new rafts, and hauling others out of the water to add rudders and wood. The two cops stopped by. "We came again last night to look," the woman said. "It's looking better." "I still don't get it," the man said. "This is an island and here is the river. I'm making a piece about that." I was kneeling along the water on the third day, leaning over to nail into the wood and add more strings, when I noticed a man and a woman approaching, wearing hard hats emblazoned with the Con Edison logo. "Who gave you permission to do this project?" "No one." I corrected myself: "Or rather, the Brooklyn Waterfront Artists Coalition." Had I "gotten permission from the Coast Guard?" "No." When I returned two days later, they had cut all the strings from the Con Edison fence and installed con-certina wire alongside both buildings, making it impossible for me to enter. The web of rafts was

55. Sabra working on web of *Grass Rafts* near trash at low tide 56. Close-up of *Grass Raft* lying on the cobblestone street

still attached on the street side, so I could climb down onto the trashy beach at low tide and get access to the river. This is what I kept doing throughout the month of the show. I would retrieve the strings and retie the rafts and Con Edison would cut them down again.

Sylvia came to dinner with Catherine Stimpson and her partner, Liz Wood, while I was in the middle of the struggles with the sod rafts. We looked around the studio as I described my ideas for the *Place/Displace* installation; I had finally finished sewing the twin roofs of *Lillie's Peaks* and had started the *Gypsy Baby* cart that would fit inside. "You know, you are being blocked by corporations," Catherine said. "Here, you can't get to your family's cemetery because the lumber company owns the woods, and Con Edison seals off your strings for the grass islands. You are really a dangerous woman." They followed me into the kitchen so I could finish frying chicken. I pulled out some of my artist's books, and they sat looking together through the four booklets in *4/Tells*. "You've produced a minimalist novel," Catherine said after reading the pithy texts describing the birth of Opal's baby and the abuse of Grandmother by her children. "I could teach a whole semester of my women's studies course with this statement." Liz was a musicologist; she thought my books were musical. "I hear the stories as I select the progression of images."

Heresies seemed stalled—it was impossible to brainstorm for new issues or to implement our ideas for columns when we were mired in the legal dispute with Kay. Our lawyers' fees were mounting. Avis had finished the report to New York State Council on the Arts, putting the best face on the fact that over $12,000 of their funding was still missing. Her energy was fractured after Ron's death, spiraling out into the obsessive club hopping she described to me one evening. Josely was rarely at meetings, but Avis conveyed her opinions. I was feeling like leaving the collective. As I walked into the meeting, everyone was talking about *The Decade Show*.

57. Sabra tying ropes for *Grass Raft Web* near Con Edison plant 58. Stringing *Rafts* from facing side near derelict building

Emma and Josely were in the show, as well as many artists who been in my projects such as Catalina, Jaune, Nancy, and Cecilia. Betsy was writing a review. Its subtitle was "Frameworks & Identity in the '80s," a topic close to my heart—identity aptly described the artworks and installations I had been making about my family. One of the curators was Susana Torruella Leval; I couldn't tell myself she didn't know about my work. The show was in three venues, and I had already gone to see the section at the New Museum and enjoyed it despite my envy. I told Emma I liked her prints. "I didn't see you at the opening." "We went the next day." "Good."

Josely had an installation at the Museum of Contemporary Hispanic Art that included repeated silkscreen prints of Catalina's face. I ran into Linda Cunningham at the show. "The white artists all have international reputations," she said, wistfully trying to figure out why she had not been invited, "like Cindy Sherman or Nancy Spero." We walked outside; it had started to pour. I hurried into the uptown subway to meet Marithelma for our shared readings at the East Harlem Music School. A few days later, May and I discussed *The Decade Show*. "I really believe in this multicultural idea," May said. "Of course, that's the way things should be," I agreed, "but I would like to have been included." "What can you expect? In order to make way for new voices, they have to limit the number of white people. They picked the very best political artists." "Well, May, I can still mind. My work fits more with the so-called minority artists. In what way is Leon Golub's work about identity? It's like having two categories."

I had gotten used to the garbage in the river—a rusted motorcycle, a bed frame, old tires, bits of plywood and planks, rubber tubing, metal and wood fragments. One afternoon, as I was wading in the water retying rafts, something white swirled and caught my eye. My neck tingled; I had grown up with cottonmouths and water moccasins. I got out of the water and put down my string and scissors. A dog skull was floating, and near the chalky skull, a very large

59. Sabra tying *Rope Bridge* near trash 60. *Rope Bridge* mirroring Manhattan Bridge
61. Unfurling *Rope Bridge* across from Con Edison

dead snake. I fished out the skull and went to get Roger. We returned with the camera. The snake looked foreign and poisonous with a pattern of orange and brown on its back and a creamy white underbelly. Roger pulled it out with a stick and photographed it, and then returned it to the water. All the artists seemed to be on the street: Jackie Lima and our neighbors, Brynhildur Thorgeirsdottir and Barry Johnson. Brynhildur had just gotten a Pollock-Krasner Foundation grant. "I'm getting good at whining," she said. In the loft, I had started working on a narrow rope bridge to suspend across the sixty-foot girth of the bay during the last weekend of the show. I invited them to come.

I dream that the bay is like a swimming pool filled with people cavorting among my sod rafts. Roger and I are riding in a motorboat. I wonder if the boat will manage to move around the grass islands without getting caught in the strings, but we maneuver nicely. The water is clear and silvery. It feels very satisfying to think that now I can easily repair and right the rafts while sitting in a boat. Then, I too am in the water swimming.

When I lived in Guinea, I had once crossed the Diané River on a *pont de liane* (a vine bridge). These amazing suspension bridges were woven out of raphia and looked like elongated hammocks with circular pads at intervals along the base. The bridge swayed as you walked; there were crocodiles in the water below. I was holding tightly to the sides when I had to make room for a man crossing deftly from the other side with a bicycle balanced on his head. My miniature bridge was far less serviceable, but it made a visual echo of the Manhattan Bridge nearby as we celebrated the closing weekend. Roger and I went the next day to release the last of the rafts and retrieve the rope bridge. We were just in time; an incipient thief had not been skillful enough to finish untying my knots.

62. *Rope Bridge* floating across water 63. *Documentation Blueprint* (detail) 64. *Grass Raft* (detail) in water

Catalina invited me to meet her at the Studio Museum for third venue of *The Decade Show*. "I am squeezing my jobs into tighter and tighter spaces," I told her, but I went. We walked into the gallery facing Joe Lewis's intense piece about AIDS, using neon, photos, and numbers to commemorate its impact. We moved over to look at Alison Saar's carved woman with a heart of nails. "And you should have been in this show," Catalina said. "I think there's a kind of racism," I said, "The white artists are picked for their names and the minority artists for their work." "Though it's the white artists who are mentioned in all the reviews," she added. We wandered over to the outdoor African market, and I bought a beautiful cloth doll. I had never told Catalina about C; she had had a similar brush with violence in Spain.

Nelson Mandela had been freed from prison in South Africa after twenty-seven years; he and Winnie were in New York City for a parade to celebrate his release. I tried to walk over the Brooklyn Bridge, but the bridge was blocked off and helicopters were hovering overhead, so I jumped into the subway for Lower Manhattan. The street was jammed with expectant people, mostly black; I crowded in for a view. The Irish bagpipers from the New York City Transit Authority were marching down the street. "You have to give them credit for coming," a man dressed in a suit said. "They're paid," his friend replied. Then, the high school bands came strutting past. The Palestinians appeared in formation followed by a golden Chinese dragon, then more dragons, the sanitation workers marching together, more police, finally, an odd-looking glass house mounted on a flatbed truck came into view. Winnie and Nelson were standing inside like saints, waving, and Mayor David Dinkins was beaming beside them. Jubilation mounted inside the crowd like a huge wave of relief. Free! Free! "I've been waiting for this all my life," the woman near me said, both of us grinning. I had been looking for Roger. Then, I heard my name. Obie came pushing towards me, resplendent in an African dashiki and soft Yoruba hat. We hugged. Now, everyone was

65. Catalina Parra, *It's Incontestable Again*, 1992 66. Howardena Pindell, *Autobiography: (Africa) Buddha*

dancing. The police kept shouting that Broadway was closed to pedestrians, but we all spilled onto the street, propelled by the rhythms in our hearts.

Lucy was back from Boulder, and the full collective met at the *Heresies* office. Kay's lawyers had written us with an offer to return $8,440 in segments in order to publish the Women on Men issue. Despite the injunction, she had spent over $2,000 for typesetting and had paid herself $1,300 for design and editing. Our lawyers conveyed our consensus in their reply.

> First, the problem with the proposal as framed is that it focuses on a question
> of the publication of the Women on Men issue, which my clients believe is sim-
> ply a red herring since the publication never was and has never been an issue.
> On the contrary, the real issue in this matter is your client's liability for funds
> taken and thereby, the consequent damage to the corporation in counsel's fees
> and other additional costs as a consequence of the taking as well as monies
> spent by her and paid to her without corporate permission.

I went out for a beer with Faith and Betsy. All of us were disheartened. We sat around trying to figure out how we could make Kay uncomfortable. Obviously, lawyers did not faze her.

I had printed fifty blueprint posters for my river installation and gave one to Benita Eisler at our photo research meeting. She described how she had felt flying over New Mexico. "The country is too big; there are all those empty uninhabited spaces." "I find those spaces reassuring." She had found several Stieglitz photos at the National Gallery that had never been published. Some showed a nude O'Keeffe toying with her abstracted fiddlehead fern sculpture with her knees flexed and the sculpture grasped between her toes. Another showed the same

67. Pages, *Making* (all), Lucy Lippard, text written over Sue Maberry graphic 68. Moore 69. Nicky Lindeman

sculpture placed provocatively in front of the veiled opening of *Music-Pink and Blue II*, the 1919 painting whose erotic content O'Keeffe had always denied. The National Gallery would allow Doubleday to publish five of these photos, so Benita wanted me to go to Washington, DC to make the selections. She handed me her research sketches. As I descended into the Forty-Second Street subway for home, I discovered that our artworks had been taken down. No one had called me, but I felt relieved.

When I picked up my artwork from Elyse, it looked moldy but intact. I had already purchased archival chemicals to kill the mold and started carefully removing the backing attached by wheat paste and then cleaning the painted surface. The curator for *Arts in Transit*, Sandra Bloodworth, had assured me that the mold would simply "dust off." It did, but it had also eaten the rabbit skin glue in my gesso, so about half of the painting dusted off into powder as well, leaving only splotched paper.

Emma called to ask me to pose for a watercolor portrait. She was painting a series of women artists "whose work and mien I like," and had already drawn Joyce Kozloff, Martha Wilson, Carol Sun, Camille Billops, Howardena Pindell, and herself. She worked quickly, and then let me see the rather calligraphic portrait with touches of lavender. I liked it. Emma had been a weaver before she focused on painting. We talked about the importance of cloth and about our own aging as we ate lunch, avoiding the subject of *Heresies*.

In a few weeks, Roger and I were going to Abiquiu to have our well dug. Mother called to talk about finding water. "They bring up a bore and check it periodically. . . . You can hear it coming." Her voice got excited as she remembered; it was nice to hear her speaking with pleasure. "I was sitting on the cultivator. I was about eight and I felt the ground. I said, 'Here comes the water.' They didn't believe me. Then, the well man shouted. That was it." Uncle George, her

70. Emma Amos, *The Gift* (all), Joyce Kozloff 71. Camille Billops 72. Carol Sun 73. Sabra Moore

favorite uncle, was a water witch. "He believed it. He would get a peach tree limb, forked, and he would find water. We used to believe a lot of things people don't believe now. . . . Are you going to put a pump down in the well?" "I don't know." "If you don't put a pump down, they have to line the well and bring the water up in a bucket. Do you remember Granddaddy's well? He had a long bucket like a sorghum syrup can, which he would lower." Roger interrupted, "They lay a metal casing." Her voice changed. "I'm sure it's different now."

We had another meeting with the Loft Board. The asbestos had been removed, so now we needed to discuss the many remaining code violations and when we would release rent money for these repairs. Our landlord had managed to force several tenants out, referring to us in one meeting as the "surviving tenants," a name we had adopted among ourselves. I wrote the letters for our building, creating a record by simply describing the things that had happened. Recently, the super had started camping inside one of the vacant lofts. We could hear various women hollering outside for Fox to come open the door; we had always called him Louie. He banged on all our doors one evening, sounding drunk and demanding the rent. I wrote that down. When we came into the meeting, everyone looked up and then continued reading my most recent letter. Obie complained that the landlord was demanding a key to his door; he was refusing until the building was more secure. "Oh, you don't want Fox to have your key?" David Klarsfield asked.

Freda was coming to camp with us while we were Abiquiu. She had already booked her flight from Montreal, so we had a deadline for arrival stamped onto our road trip. Sylvia was also coming to visit; Joan Watts and I had pitched in together to buy her airline ticket. She wouldn't be camping. I had finished the copyright permissions for Gilot's book; she thought I had been "crafty finding the pictures." I had finally understood that some of the people I was writing to in France held grudges and were reluctant to grant her permission; that was the crafty part. I was bringing

74. Manhattan Bridge from Pearl Street fire escape 75. Looking down Front Street from loft 76. Buildings along Jay Street

work with me to finish in the shed—writing the photo credits and caption notes for *Invention &*
Technology, testing the patience of the editor, Fred Allen. This time he was angry. Marina had
given my name to Greg Sholette, one of the founders of a new collective, REPOHistory. He called
just as we were leaving, asking me to participate in a project in the fall making street signs at
various sites in Lower Manhattan. Marina and Willie were also making signs; we would all be
working together.

　　Mother sent us five hundred dollars to acknowledge our marriage, so we had extra money just when we needed it. She wanted to treat her daughters equally she told me, and so she
sent me the same dollar amount she had given Nancy for her wedding in 1958 without regard to
the thirty-two years passage of time. It was pouring when we drove onto the mesa, but our shed
was dry, and we quickly unpacked and headed back out to pick up Freda at the Albuquerque airport. I had met Freda's deadline, but missed the one for my photo-editing job. We had brought a
guest tent and set it up behind the shed for visitors. One morning, Freda spied an animal trotting
up the slope towards our outdoor kitchen. She had been reading Tony Hillerman mysteries and
thought it was a coyote. "What's that?" "It's a dog," Roger replied. A spare and spotted adoles-
cent blue heeler had found us. We gave her some chicken and set down to breakfast. Suddenly,
the bulging clouds gave way and a torrent of hail descended, making the nearby arroyo roar
with churning rocks and water. We scattered for shelter. I thought the dog had run away, but she
crawled out from under the shed when the rain stopped. We named her Sunday for the day she
appeared and for her easy holiday spirit.

　　We needed a driveway before the well could be dug. Kate had recommended Larry Parnell, a well driller who lived nearby, and he recommended Mike Sandoval and Jerry Dutchover to
plow a road. As we were walking around looking for possible routes, Jerry hollered and I jumped

77. Returning to camp in the shed 78. Roger and Sabra eating breakfast outside shed with Sunday Dog nearby

back to avoid stepping on a rattlesnake poking out from the ledges near the canyon. Jerry headed to his truck for a shovel, but we didn't want to kill animals, even snakes, branding us as city dwellers. That evening, I got out my snake book and read about rattlesnake habits; they hunt at night. Mother would already have hoed it to bits. We met Henry Sauerwein a few days later at the Santa Clara corn dance. He was happy about the dog, but worried about the snake. I recognized the painter Pablita Velarde from the WCA awards ceremony in Newark as she went over to one of the dancers and took an ear of corn, kissing it in blessing.

We now had a post office box, and I enjoyed the trips to the village, picking up our mail and running into neighbors. I had sent off the photo credits and caption information for *American Heritage of Invention & Technology* magazine to Fred while Freda was still visiting. One afternoon, I found his terse acknowledgement, which was then followed a few days later with a letter firing me. He criticized my "inability to function within the mundane time sense of the office," something that had taken him five years to notice. He added that he hoped to keep my friendship. Another day, a note arrived from Barbara Moore, thanking me for the "moving documentation of your sod island piece. What a wonderful use of blueprint! Will it fade away?"

Jerry Dutchover had worked for the US Forest Service and gave me advice about how to plant native grasses to restore the scarred land where they had plowed the road. We could now drive down and park near the shed, making everything easier. A second rattlesnake had also appeared. We took Sunday to the vet. She described a way to catch a snake with a stick and a string, deposit it in a camping freezer, and take it up to the mountains. "Catch them one at a time. Make sure you jump away when you release them." We weren't convinced of our dexterity. Doris, a clerk at Bodes General Store, alarmed at our dilemma, brought me a paper bag filled

79. Sabra talking with her mother (standing in red) inside the white canyon 80. Sitting with Sunday Dog facing canyon

with Osha, the resinous root used to repel snakes or cure sore throats. I threw it liberally along the ledges. A few days later, Sunday surprised another coiled snake.

Sylvia arrived. She stayed with Joan Watts at her new house in Galisteo before coming to Abiquiu; I had found her a room at a motel near the village. The land reminded her of the south of France, "though the scale is bigger." "Joan told me your place was austere, but I don't agree. It's so varied and intricate." She was eager to paint, so we set up chairs overlooking the big arroyo and started making watercolors. Sylvia cut out the tips from cotton gloves so her hands wouldn't burn while she painted. Later, she told me, "You looked quite right in that landscape."

I started planting grass seeds and mulching with hay along the banks of the new road before Larry tried to drive down with his huge well rig. The long derrick got stuck at the curve in the road and it took hours as he hopped the inflexible rig, but it finally got set up where we had decided to drill for water. Larry and his well-drilling partner, Gayle, collected soil samples every ten feet and then, as the well bore descended deeper, every twenty-five feet, checking the dirt's color and texture for moisture. They would dump delicate scoops of earth from the well bucket and lay them in regular lines. It looked like a minimalist art installation. Later, I collected the samples and numbered them by depth, placing a little strip of paper in each bag. Gayle was from Oklahoma. He had worked in uranium mines. "That went down." Then, he moved to Texas to work on oil rigs. "That went bust." Finally, he decided to drill water wells. "I love finding water for people. New Mexico grows on you."

We didn't hear the water coming out of the ground like Mother had as a child. Larry's wife, Ann, came over one evening after a week of drilling, bringing her two children and their dog. We had bought beer in anticipation, and Pat D'Andrea had brought us a clay turtle from Santa Clara Pueblo for luck—it was sitting in the window of the shed facing the drill site. The half-moon

81. A chair and table set up for Sylvia Sleigh to paint a watercolor of Madera Canyon 82. Sabra and Sylvia above fields in Abiquiu

was up, and the steady *thump, crunch* of the well rig had become a familiar and worrisome sound. Floodlights illuminated the rig. They had drilled beyond 625 feet without finding any water. Red gravel started coming up. The dogs were barking. "Water's coming," Gayle said. "It's not a gusher," Larry said. Water poured out the top of the pipe.

Carla, the senior editor at *American Heritage* magazine, sent me a note. "I just wanted you to know that I am really very sorry about what has happened regarding your job at *Invention & Technology*. . . . I think it's very likely that your contributions here will come into sharper focus as time passes and everyone calms down." Byron Dobell wrote to invite me to his retirement party. "Whatever the specifics, I always appreciated your wonderful eye." In the meantime, I had just lost half my income and our savings would barely pay for the water well. It was weak, only pumping up about two gallons per minute, but I was still basking in the memory of the bale pipe releasing its sweet flood of reddish-brown water. We had been making discoveries: we found rectangular rock lines dotting the mesa across the canyon from our shed and thick black-and-white patterned shards near the grids. I drew the broken pottery and made detailed notes about their locations. "I feel connected to the land," I wrote, "after planting grass seeds."

83. Enjoying the flow of well water near the new well house 84. Leaving the house site en route back to Pearl Street

11

There Is No Peace

There had been a ferocious hailstorm, and lightning had struck the parking lot next to our build-ing on Pearl Street. Police had found a dismembered body stuffed into garbage bags near Vito Acconci's loft. Obie filled us in on the news. Our dog, Sunday, had been good in the truck, visiting easily with people in Texas, and staying quietly in motels en route to New York, but the bridge sounds when we pulled into the loading bay terrified her. She balked at the elevator, so I carried her up the six flights of stairs to our loft.

A few days after we had unpacked, Kazuko called to invite me into a drawing show at gallery onetwentyeight. I still had photo research work; I would continue to do the calendars for American Heritage Publishers with Barbara. Fred had written again describing why he had fired me, noting the "magnificent job" I had done at *American Heritage of Invention & Technology*. "Fred is upset at losing your friendship," Barbara told me, "you should forgive him. To forgive is divine." "I'm not divine." I went by Doubleday to check on Benita's book and ran into Alex Gotfryd, the

 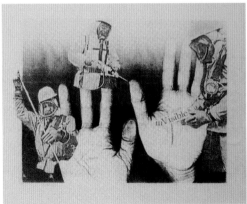 

1. Marina Gutierrez, *What Goes Around Comes Around* 2. Sharon Gilbert, *Hands/On* 3. Shirley Smith, *Tornado Watch*

executive art director. I liked working with him researching book covers. He would say, "Come talk to me, do you have a minute?" "You've spoiled me," he told me after I returned from my first residency at the Wurlitzer Foundation in Taos. He had been liberated from the Vaihingen an der Enz concentration camp in Poland on his thirteenth birthday; his mother was freed the same day at Auschwitz, but she died shortly afterward. Alex had something to tell me: he had AIDS. He planned to keep working and "maximize and savor" the time he had left to live.

REPOhistory was organizing the Lower Manhattan Sign Project; artists would select a street and make a sign about something that had happened in that location, repossessing a forgotten history (thus, the name of the collective). I went to my first REPOhistory meeting at their crowded upstairs office near Broadway and Lafayette. They shared the space with the War Resisters League, an organization whose mission sadly never went out of fashion. "The dynamics of these meetings," I wrote later in my journal, "are really altered by the male energy." I was used to the complex intimacy of *Heresies*. Lucy was at the meeting; I hadn't seen her since we got back from Abiquiu. We went out for a drink with Leela Ramotar and Hattie Gossett. I had to tell them about finding the matrix of rock lines on our land. "Are you going to report it to an archaeologist?" Lucy asked. "Not until we build our house." "Or return it to the Indians?" Hattie Gosset suggested. "Actually, archaeology is a Western idea. I'd rather leave it alone as is and live with it."

A few days later, we had a *Heresies* meeting. "I've never seen you so brown; you're pink," Avis said. "But I get very dark; I have Indian blood." "How can that be?" Avis retorted. "I get brown and I don't have Indian blood," Lucy said. "Emma is a black red man," someone added, illogically ending the banter. We got down to business. The National Endowment for the Arts (NEA) had overturned the recommendations of their own peer panel and denied funding to performance artists Holly Hughes, Karen Finley, Tim Miller, and John Fleck. Many artists and art institutions

4., 5., and 6. Cindy Carr, *Adventures in Art & Politics*, cartoon strip for *Heresies* flier

were taking stands against what was being called blacklisting based on the "homophobic, misog-ynistic and racist agenda" of a far right-wing minority gaining authority within the NEA. *Heresies* had been awarded an NEA grant, and we had to either accept it or refuse it. "How can we accept this grant and still call ourselves *Heresies*?" someone said. No one wanted to be complicit with blacklisting. But what about Viva Latina, the only issue collective currently meeting? Would our refusal kill this issue in the same way Kay had killed Women on Men by her theft? We voted to refuse the money. I agreed to write a press release. Emma was moderating a *Heresies* panel on art education (If You Don't Go to Art School, Can You Still Be a Famous Artist?) at Cooper Union in a few weeks; I would announce our decision during this event. Then, we brainstormed about other ways to raise money. Perhaps, we could auction a portfolio with works by every artist who had been part of the collective. We adjourned our meeting, having come full circle with a new version of the same ideas. "Everyone loves your drawing," Emma said as we left, referring to the watercolor she had painted of me in the spring. She had almost completed forty portraits for her series, *The Gift*.

Roger and I had been taking turns walking Sunday, usually going up to the park in Brook-lyn Heights and letting her run with neighbor dogs. One morning, we had gone over together to buy the Sunday *Times*. Roger was carrying the paper, and I was a bit ahead with the dog straining on the leash, eager to get to the park. We turned off a side street and cut across a little court-yard. Three men were standing near the subway entrance a short distance away—one was near a flower planter, two had their backs to me. What I noticed first was their stillness; they were frozen in a tableau. It made me pause. Then, I saw the gun pressed against one man's neck. The flow-er planter man saw us and ran off towards the park, the scene fell apart; I found my voice and screamed. Then, we all clustered together around the robbed man. People started coming out of

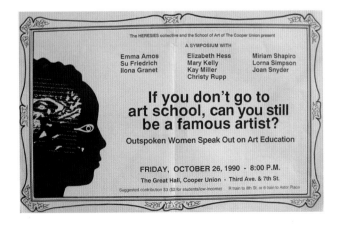

7. Cindy Carr, *Adventures in Art & Politics* (detail) 8. Flier for *Heresies* panel on Art Education for upcoming issue

the subway, including our neighbor Alex. "Forget it. It's all right." "No, call the police." Plainclothes men appeared and went off with the victim in search of the gunman. Roger and I started walking back to Pearl Street with Alex and our dog.

I was making a new artwork for Kazuko's drawing show, pulling apart the word *d-raw-ing/dra-wing* and ironing laser transfers from the cutout photo of Mother Gladys lying in bed. I had started another artwork incorporating a spoon from her house, called *Art-I-Fact*. Kate was in town and came by to visit. She thought *Lillie's Peaks* looked like a "medieval reliquary." I was making progress on the series of artworks for *Place/Displace*, copying the letter Caroline had penciled onto the back of the photo of her murdered husband. "I think that idea of her using the photo to communicate with the absent loved one is similar to my feelings about making these works," I wrote in my journal, affirming Kate's intuition. Roger had started painting as well; he had arranged a still life in his studio with some of the Acoma Pueblo pots we had bought at the dances. Sylvia called; she had succeeded in auctioning Lawrence's collection of pop art at Christies. Her finances had vastly improved, and she wanted to start collecting works she admired by her women artist friends.

Mako was at the gallery, touching up the walls, when I arrived to help Kazuko hang the drawing show. "It's wet!" I told him as I laid my painting on a stand. "Again!" Kazuko had to rush out to pick up her son, Eizan, but others were there, and we started unpacking artworks and laying them around on the floor, leaving spaces. Several pieces were missing, including a drawing by Sol Lewitt. The painter Amy Kalina returned with Kazuko and Eizan. "I was excited to see that you were going to be in the show." "How?" I thought to myself. "It's my mental state that no one knows my work." Then, the missing pieces arrived. I had met Linda Shapiro when we had the opening party for *Running Out of Time* at her kosher winery next door, and she came into the

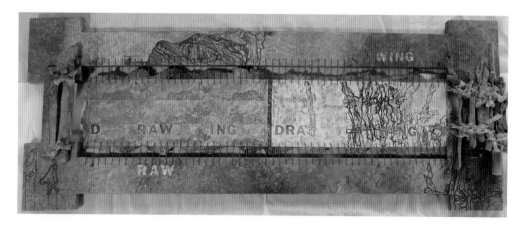

9. Sabra Moore, *Dra- Raw- Wing* for *Drawing Show* at gallery onetwentyeight

gallery to see the show. "Sabra, I love your work. I can't afford art, but if you ever start to throw something out, don't throw it, give it to me."

Avis called me; there had been a round-robin of phone calls after the *Heresies* meeting. Lucy had called Betsy with some ideas about how we could honorably accept the grant; Betsy agreed that the timing was off and we needed to reconsider our decision to refuse the NEA funding. They called Avis. I was in the middle of writing our press release, but now we would rehash the issue at the next *Heresies* meeting, so I went to Emma's panel without the pressure of making an announcement.

Barbara and I took the train to Providence to research Brown University's nineteenth-century collection of Civil War lithographs. "Scott wanted me to fire you," Barbara told me, referring to the Forbes financial manager. "I thought we weren't working with Sabra anymore. Fred and Richard told me you had had trouble with her as well," Scott had said. Richard Snow had replaced Byron when he retired; Fred had moved into Richard's position. "We had one problem, two years ago, and solved it," Barbara had replied, referring to the spring I went to Brazil with Josely. The train was rumbling along the coast, giving us glimpses of oversized osprey stick nests perched atop the electrical poles. "I told him, I love working with you. It was Richard who fired you. Fred really had no choice."

My studio faced a row of nineteenth-century brick buildings, including a former elementary school and a vacant brick factory; I could look into the interior courtyard of the factory from our sixth floor windows and enjoyed seeing the softened yellow and reds of the old walls. The Watchtower, headquarters of the Jehovah's Witness, had bought that row of buildings, and they started to raze the entire block. Each day, booms would shake our building, adding an aura of uncertainty as the walls collapsed into rubble. On the other side of our building, two men had

10-11. Roger Mignon, photos of demolition of Jay Street buildings purchased by the Watchtower

dug a deep trench under the bridge that looked like an archaeological dig, and then refilled the hole. Roger and I walked over to look at the broken crockery they had unearthed and found a translucent bottle opalescent with age. The radio and newspapers were filled with talk of an impending war with Iraq. I was working on two artist's books for a show at a library in Oregon, *The Book as Vessel*, curling papers like dried leaves and incorporating laser transfers from my river piece in the spring. I pulled out one of the mannequin hands I had stored for years and painted it like the river, suspending a net bag of paper leaves from its outstretched fingers. The hand would be mounted onto a board surrounded by the words, "It Won't Hold Water." It grounded me to be working.

Our *Heresies* meetings kept getting bogged down. We couldn't reach consensus about the NEA grant despite having voted twice to reject it or about how to reorganize the magazine. Betsy was convinced that we needed a fully funded and staffed office similar to the offices at the publishing houses for my day jobs. I was walking to the subway with Kathie Browne after one of these discussions. "Betsy is like a girl who won't date a boy if he doesn't have a college degree," she observed.

We went to a book party for Lucy's *Mixed Blessings* at Exit Art; many friends from my collaborative projects were in that book. May came over as I was talking to Noah Jemison. "Noah, do you think multiculturalism is here to stay or is it a fad?" May asked. "Well, it's been around for a long time; it's not new. . . . I don't actually think in those terms." "Obviously, the world is multicultural," I added. Noah walked down the stairs with Roger and me. "She's a nice woman, but that comment builds a barrier. I wanted to talk about the repudiation of socialism, what she thinks of that." We still had the idea of collaborating on a show we would call *South Up North*.

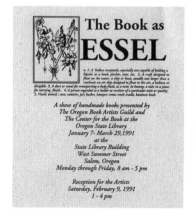

12. *The Book as Vessel* exhibit card 13. Sabra Moore, *It Won't Hold Water* for *Book as Vessel* show

Jerry Kearns stopped Roger to ask if he was making more of those large-scale drawings of nude women in tai chi poses. He had liked his last show.

I dream that I have to give a performance as part of someone else's art piece. I am in a big room like a gallery and the audience is already seated. I haven't prepared, but I go out and start to dance. I am unraveling a string, twirling it around. I have to speak and I do, even though it is all made up.

Lamidi was coming to stay with us for a few days before returning to Nigeria; we had a party for him in the loft. "I know two things: I know how to carve and I know how to eat. For the rest, I am foolish." Mei-Mei, whom I hadn't seen since Taos, brought a friend interested in Yoruba religion to meet Lamidi, not understanding that he had converted to Islam. "Do you talk to spirits?" her friend asked me. "No." "I ask because you have spirits hovering around you." "Oh, well, my grandmother and my mother believed in their dreams." "She has long hair and she's on your left side on your shoulder." This made Lamidi uncomfortable; we joked about it afterwards. Marina was out of town, but Willie and Noah came. I showed them *Lillie's Peaks*, and then Willie started telling stories similar to my cemetery stories about his family in Louisiana. His grandmother had Indian blood. "Mine too," I said. This time, no one challenged my identity.

We were all Southerners and knew how to place each other in a family context. Noah had gone to school with Ana Mendieta in Iowa. We got to talking about ambition and murder—"someone tried to kill me once." I was trying to describe how some country people were "complete": comfortable in their bodies and able to live at ease in the present; they had known people like that. "But you're talking like you're not complete; you are too," Willie said.

It was almost the end of the year, and the REPOhistory proposals were due. I had chosen Pearl Street on the Manhattan side of the river, which was named for the mother-of-pearl

  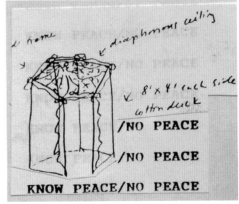

14. Lower Manhattan Sign Project (all), Tess Timoney/Mark O'Brien 15.Greg Sholette 16. Sabra Moore, tent, *Know/No Peace*

shell mounds left over from the Eastern Algonquian fisheries. These shells had been broken up to pave the streets. Eleanor Moretta, director of exhibits at Pratt Institute, had seen my slides at Artists Space and called me. They were planning a series of installations for the Pratt Manhattan Gallery; she liked my ideas for *Place/Displace*. I was surprised and pleased; I didn't think anyone ever looked at that slide registry. New Year's Eve heralded 1991 a palindrome year with a full moon rising. We went with Sylvia to Bibi's loft to celebrate together, and then drove her home and sat in the kitchen, talking. The celestial signs were auspicious, but the earthly ones were moving in the opposite direction. A few days later, Roger and I were demonstrating in front of the United Nations in vigil against the impending Gulf War. I was buying tomatoes and avocados at a grocery store when I heard the news that Bush had started bombing Iraq. The woman next to me turned and saw my face. "It's horrible," she said, "people are dying right now."

We all felt helpless as the bombing continued. Kazuko's gallery was going to be closed all spring for renovations, so she hadn't scheduled any shows. She and I decided to organize a peace project in the empty space. I thought we could make curtains, but Kazuko suggested tents. I liked her idea; it made sense for the Middle East. She would create a walk-in shelter by weaving branches and ropes, and I would design a nine-foot hexagonal cotton duck tent with a grid of ten-inch squares ironed into the canvas on all sides. Artists could participate by bringing squares to sew onto the canvas tent and objects to be placed inside the shelter. We planned to invite sixty or seventy artists to come to the gallery and add to our structures during a three-week period, culminating in an opening/closing event at the beginning of March and followed by a one-week show ending on the gallery's March 9 deadline for closure.

We called the project *Know Peace/No Peace*. Kazuko invited Todd Ayoung, Amy Kalina, and Kaoru Sato to work with us. I wrote the statement that we used to recruit artists, inviting

17. *Know/No Peace* installation (all), Kazuko building branch and rope shelter 18. Artists' names taped on ironed tent squares.

people to bring their squares or objects to the gallery on "Wednesday, Friday, or Saturday from 12–2 p.m. or Thursday nights from 8–10." Some of us would be there to help install.

> There is *no peace*. There is *no domestic peace*. Women, children & men are living throughout the city in *no shelter* or in makeshift shelters on heating grates, subway tunnels, parks, doorways, abandoned cars. . . . Women are getting battered and killed by lovers, husbands, friends, strangers, for their gender. Others are killed for their difference or race. There is *no international peace*. We are bombing Iraqis with bombs paid by our money that could have provided shelters here. We are making refugees of people we don't even know.

There was also no heat in the gallery, so the project presented us with physical challenges.

I was turning forty-eight, the age of Daddy when he died. "Now, I feel I am in uncharted territory," I wrote in my journal, "going beyond Daddy's life span." Mother called and asked if we were going to demonstrations. "Protests accomplish nothing." "Mother, our protests probably prevented Nixon from bombing Haiphong harbor with nuclear weapons." "I've had a difficult week. This thing in Iraq brought up memories."

Everyone was having a difficult time. At least I was busy ironing squares onto the sides of the tent with narrow borders between each square. The work was tedious but beautiful; it looked like a minimalist installation. I had had a lot of practice as a child, starching and creasing Daddy's railroad cap and overalls. Jackie Wray called; she had been glued to the television, unable to stop watching the mayhem in Iraq. Now, the oil wells were burning, spilling their waste into the Persian Gulf. She was glad to make a square. I went by Doubleday. Alex had been in the

19. Sydney Hamburger's hand steadies her square from inside tent 20. Artelia Court sews square as Tak Inagaki films

hospital, but was back in the office with his tiny dog, a pecan-colored teacup poodle, sitting on his desk. He was designing *Passion Fruit*, a square-shaped book of recipes and photographs, each print an elegant arrangement of fruit and flowers. The photos were his; I was researching the botanical illustrations. "It's more than a flower book," I said, "more felt." "You understand what I mean."

Barbara Moore had suggested I show the art dealer, Ted Cronin, my artists' books, so I made an appointment. "Don't show me anything that's not for sale," he said, adding that he doesn't handle Xerox books, my principal medium for multiple editions. He knew I sold books at Printed Matter, Inc. "I think Printed Matter exploits the artists, they shouldn't take 50 percent and they make you sell the books for so cheap. Dealers protect artists." "Really!" I thought, "usually everyone complains about dealers." He wondered what Clive had paid for *Reconstructed Codex*. "I asked because the Modern [Museum of Modern Art] is so cheap. . . . I can see that they would love your work; you should keep in touch." He ordered a copy of my newest book packet, *4/Tells*, disregarding his own opinions about photocopier books.

Roger met me one evening at the subway to help me carry my heavy book bags full of photo research work and Xeroxes for the copy of *4/Tells* that Ted wanted to sell. Our shiny red Toyota pickup was parked along the street under the bridge, but we didn't feel like stopping to move it into the loading bay of the loft. We were both tired. A neighbor called while I was cooking supper, his voice upset. "Pick up the phone. I have to tell you about your truck." His companion Caroline was unlocking the front door when she glimpsed a sand bag falling off the bridge. She turned in time to see the second bag land with a perfect bull's eye, hitting the center of our windshield, crushing the hood and shattering the glass. We called the police and all the neighbors came out of their lofts to stand cautiously and look up along the bridge structure as the officer

21. Amy Kalina installs *Know/No Peace* artwork 22. Unidentified artist holds his double square and sews from outside in

shined his floodlight. "It's an act of God," Kazuko said later. Or it was an act of forgetfulness by the workers repairing the tracks on the D train.

I had finished ironing all the square spaces onto the canvas sides. Kazuko was already at work on her branch and rope shelter, and now we were ready to install the tent. Roger and Artelia came with me. First, we suspended the wooden hexagonal structure from the gallery ceiling. Then, we hung the five canvas sides by looping green rabbit-headed Chinese baby pins across the tops of the screw heads protruding at regular intervals from the wooden frame. The whole construction worked. You could enter it and sit inside on a small bench. I draped a diaphanous black net over the top. A steady parade started as artists arrived off and on during our four open gallery days to install their works. Bibi Lenĉek, Sandy Gellis, and Mimi Smith were among the first. Kazuko's shelter was like a tunnel filling the back half of the gallery. "I am tired, but I feel good spiritually because I am doing my work." Her friend Harua Hiyama, a video artist, kept filming our process. One afternoon, he asked me to make an antiwar statement, but he spoke very little English and couldn't tell when I had finished. I spoke no Japanese. Marithelma came one day to see what we were doing and decided to assemble a collection of maledictions in Spanish and English. Someone else was arranging for texts in Arabic and Hebrew. I had found translations of Mesopotamian poetry about devastation and war to print along the top of the tent. Mimi Smith brought tiny brightly colored paper peace symbols strung into chains. She was no stranger to obsessive artwork; she had once knotted the outline of an entire room with button thread. Ayisha Abraham, whom I knew from REPOhistory meetings, brought a square. My ironing skills impressed her; she hadn't expected the tent to be so well crafted. She was in contact with relatives in India. "All the workers are returning from the Gulf; it's an economic catastrophe. Each worker can support ten people with their earnings." Bibi's husband, Tak, visited the gallery

23. Video stream of installation for Japanese television 24. Participants Kazuko, Penny Josephides, Roger, and Sabra.

when the tent squares were about half filled. He wanted to film our project for Tokyo television and returned the next morning with his crew. Many artists came to install their squares. Roger brought his camera to photograph the filming; Harua was videoing at the same time. I had to leave for a calendar meeting with Barbara right after Tak finished. I was inside the elevator in the Forbes building when it stopped at the American Heritage floor and there stood Fred, waiting to enter. He hesitated. "How are you?" "Cold. I've been standing in a freezing gallery being filmed for Japanese television."

I dream that Roger and I are traveling in our red truck with Sunday dog. We pass big bushy zebras and one comes over and sticks its head into the open window. I manage to ease its head out of the glass and roll up the window. We continue driving through a clear and open space.

Lisa Maya Knauer from REPOhistory stopped by the gallery to see how the shelters were progressing. She had been going to the Thursday night meetings of another group of antiwar artists at Washington Square Methodist Church; she wanted to come film our project as well. I noticed Betsy Hess and Faith Wilding walking along Rivington Street. "We both came to see how you were doing." Faith agreed to make a square. "I love how the tent looks with safety pins," she said. "It's my most heroic ironing job." I was attaching one of my own squares; a square with a curled text from the Sumerian city of Ur and falling figures and beds. Sydney Hamburger was standing on the ladder, sewing her whiskery square, while wearing earmuffs against the cold. The gallery was so cold, the glue shrank as Artelia and I smoothed out the translucent paper of Roger's dog skull soldier pencil drawing, crinkling the surface. Mimi, Roger, Artelia, and I had been doing paired sewing, attaching squares on both sides of the tent simultaneously. Then, May and Rudolf stopped by, bringing posters for *Outages*, a series of art actions planned for March 21. "Did Betsy come by?" May asked. "Yes. We tried to get Faith to do a square." "Betsy called

25. Detail of many squares installed inside tent. 26. Robin Michals & Sabra talk at opening inside partially completed tent.

us to find out what artists are doing about the war. I told her about the Thursday night meetings and this project. She had gotten your letter, but thought it was vague, about homelessness."

It snowed. We planned poetry readings and performances for the all-day opening on March 2. I recorded the sounds of water running in our bathtub to play for a performance I was calling *Oil Over Water*. Marithelma, Vyt Bakaitis, and other poets were coming to read. On the morning of the opening, the gallery was filled with artists finishing their squares. Jerri Allyn created her cutouts in the gallery. Sylvia brought Arlene Raven to see the shelters and add her two canvas squares: delicate pencil drawings about women's reproductive rights and the rights of animals. Ora got upset when Angela Frement spray-painted stencils directly onto the canvas and retreated onto the snowy sidewalk, but then returned to sew her lithograph. Michelle Godwin came with six squares; Sue Heinmann and Robin Michals with two each; Nancy Azara brought a big cutout heart. Underneath the bustle, we talked about the war and the levels of propaganda. Kazuko's shelter was getting filled up as well. Someone brought clouds; another artist brought peace cranes; and I brought a small green plastic Statue of Liberty wearing a map of the Middle East as a cloak. Mimi and I had become a team who could quickly sew two-sided. She was help-ing me install a square with a fiery glove. "Whose is this? It's beautiful." "It's mine." "I've seen you sew so many squares, it could have been anyone's." Suddenly, it was time to sweep up the threads, throw out all the cut paper bits, clean the floor, and put out wine for the opening. The poets stood inside Kazuko's branch tunnel and read poems against war. I sat down at a table with a white paper tablecloth and fluted wine glass, the water sound running, and calmly opened up a quart of motor oil and poured it into the glass until the oil spilled over the white tablecloth and seeped onto the floor. Kazuko went inside the tent, closed the flaps, and screamed and cried. Then, we stood around talking and drinking. Janet Goldner, Jerry Kearns, Linda Peer, and

27. Vyt Bakatis reads poetry near Kazuko's branch shelter 28. Sabra performing *Oil Over Water* at opening evening

others made dates to come install new squares during gallery hours the following week. There were still empty spaces on the tent. I hadn't seen Zarina Hashmi; she told me she had been feeling vulnerable as an Indian woman, unwilling to come outside onto the street, but now she would add a square.

Marshall DeBrul called me to work with him on a book project for HarperCollins Publishers, a new edition of *Bulfinch's Mythology*. Could I find an illustrator to make fifty drawings and also do the photo research for the illustrations? "But maybe you could do the drawings yourself?" I was tempted to try. A few days after the opening, I stayed up all night, making an ink drawing of Hercules with the two-headed dog Cerberus, having to figure out a style for book illustration as I was drawing. I was meeting the designer, Deb Brody, the next morning to present a selection of various illustrators for the project. "Go look at my drawing," I asked Roger when he woke up. He had studied painting with Philip Pearlstein at Pratt; I heard him chuckling. "There's something wrong with the way you drew the hand; the arm is like a tree. I could help by teaching you." "I don't learn that way." I just packed my drawing along with the photocopies from other illustrators, ignoring his judgment, and headed out to meet Deb. I decided to be forthright as I showed her all six samples, including my own. "I wanted to try my hand." She liked it. We faxed the illustrations to Marshall in Austin. "I like the first one." "It's mine." "Well, that's what I said at first. Why don't you do it yourself? It's simpler." I was excited. I needed to make money for my summer's residency at the Wurlitzer and the time Roger and I would spend working in Abiquiu. Roger had criticized the way I had drawn Hercules's hand, but I had simply copied the way the Greek artist had seen him: a hero with oversized thighs and a big stylized hand. I would learn from looking at art of the past in this concentrated manner; it would strengthen my drawing

29. Sabra Moore, *Bulfinch Mythology* (all), Cadmus slaying a dragon 30. Thomas Bulfinch 31. Hercules bringing the dog Cerberus

skills. I wrote in my journal, "It's an odd, closing the circle, from those vanished Guerzé drawings that Thanos kept." Roger had his doubts. "It's not your art. It's illustration."

My package of artworks from *The Book as Vessel* was at the post office, and I went by to pick it up. I quickly opened the box and found a folded handwritten note from the librarian in Salem, Oregon. Someone had stolen the mannequin hand painted like a river, managing to remove the four nails that fastened the base to the wall, deposit the wire bag with curled leaves on the floor, and then walk out of the library with the artwork during gallery hours with no one noticing. The director hadn't even bothered to notify me when this happened. Did they imagine I would meekly accept this loss without filing an insurance claim? The title of my artwork was *It Won't Hold Water*. It didn't.

Lani Maestro was in town for her show at Grey Art Gallery, an installation featuring over-sized drawings of ears. She came to the gallery the day we were taking the show down. Roger and Mako helped Kazuko and me disassemble the tent sides and pack them carefully into boxes. We were thinking of traveling the shelters as the war continued and asking artists at various venues to add squares. Lani and Kazuko were talking. "We Japanese look very young, but Mako told me, all of a sudden, we become old women." We laughed. "Old women!" We laughed again.

Fabio was having a party at his studio right after I negotiated my contract for the *Bulfinch* book. The drawings had to be finished by the end of May; I would be paid a total of $9,000 in three increments as I delivered the artworks. "Fifty drawings?" Fabio said, "You can do that in a day or two." Catalina Parra had just gotten a job teaching art at the State University of New York at Purchase (SUNY Purchase); she had "grown up" from her days working as a nanny, she told me. She understood how psychologically important it was for me to be paid for drawing. Roger

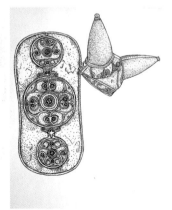

32. Sabra Moore, drawings for *Bulfinch Mythology* (all), Cupid with dolphin 33. Ceres 34. Celtic armor

had changed his mind as well. A few days later, Ora had a birthday and we toasted my new contract with Sylvia and Selina.

"Are you getting the REPOhistory mailings?" Ed Eisenberg cornered me at the opening for *AWOL*, an antiwar show of artists from the Thursday night meetings at Art in General. "Yes, I was having trouble making a sketch for my sign. I couldn't make a comp, so I just had to make the piece. I finally finished it last night." I was in time for the June exhibit of all the sketches for the Lower Manhattan Sign Project. Then, I ran into Yong Soon Min, who had organized the show. "I hadn't realized it was an open show. I would have sent a piece, but I had to work for money right after Kazuko and I finished our project." I had been drawing the Greek myths, noticing the "deeply eroticized male figures" that I described in my journal. I had been confused by the folds of one of the togas, and then realized that the artist had delineated the penis beneath the drapery. The Greeks weren't the only purveyors of eroticism. Twin cones protruded from Celtic helmets like breasts as if to arm the warriors with the power of the mother. Ear shapes varied wildly among the Greeks, Egyptians, and Celts. "I don't think it's because of genetics," I wrote. Linda Peer came over to my studio to look at the drawings. She thought they were "anthropological." I had drawn a frontispiece with the scowling face of Thomas Bulfinch framed inside a bronze mirror from Thebes. The mirror rested on the head of a standing woman. "Even if this drawing were anonymous, you'd know it was by a woman artist," Linda said.

I dream that I go into Fred's office and tell him about my job drawing for Bulfinch's Mythology. *He listens impassively. Then I go upstairs to a party, leaving a package of building materials in the hall. I go back and retrieve the materials.*

Diane Ruden, one of Nancy Davidson's students, invited me to give a lecture about my artwork to her class at SUNY Purchase. We had just seen Nancy's show at Marilyn Perl Gallery:

35. Sabra Moore, drawings for *Bulfinch Mythology* (all), an ensemble of divinities and mortals 36. Virgil holding *The Aeneid*

artworks on silk created by burning marks with a hot iron or rubbing pigments onto the smooth cloth surfaces. I talked about the women's art movement and the ways my artwork translated family history and intersected class. Afterwards, many students came over to look at my artist's books. "I had a feeling that the regular program was only inviting certain kinds of artists," Diane said. "Who?" I asked. "Artists from Yale."

Alex died before *Passion Fruit* was completed; the time he had left to "savor" had been very brief. Benita and I went together to his memorial at Doubleday. "He took off his oxygen mask and tried to speak, but we couldn't hear him," a friend told us. They handed him a pencil, but his writing was a scribble. "Write in block letters." So, he wrote again, "Thank you."

Betsy called. She had decided to "associate" from *Heresies*, our term for leaving the Mother Collective and becoming an inactive, or "associate," member. "What can I say?" she wrote. "When one can no longer do the work or win the arguments, it's time to move on." We talked about how Josely and Avis seemed to disregard our votes on the NEA grant. Faith Wilding was leaving as well; her tone was friendlier. "In no sense should any of you construe this as an abandonment or a loss of belief in *Heresies* and you—and all we've done together." "I'm probably quitting too," I told Betsy, but I went to another meeting at Emma's loft. Two women from Moscow had proposed collaborating with *Heresies* in publishing the first issue of their post-Soviet feminist journal, *IdiomA*, a ready-made issue for our moribund production schedule and a boost to our finances. I was curious to meet them, but came home dispirited. Lamidi called from Atlanta where he had been installing a carving. He listened to my complaints and then recited a Yoruba proverb: "When I can see my enemy, he can no longer hurt me."

"Hi Sabra, will you be here?" Avis penciled a note in red along the border of her agenda letter for the June *Heresies* meeting. I had delivered all fifty drawings for the *Bulfinch* book and

37. Cindy Carr, *Adventures in Art & Politics* (detail) 38. Cover, *Idioma Heresies* issue #26 39. Card for release of *Idioma* issue #26

earned the money I needed for my two months residency at the Wurlitzer; Roger would join me in late August for us to continue building in Abiquiu. I wouldn't be at the meeting. Avis struck a cheerful tone; the "acceptance" of "several current members' requests to become associates" was first on the agenda. In addition to Faith and Betsy, Lucy was leaving for the second time. She had been waiting until the "Kay business" was finished, but two years had passed and she couldn't keep waiting. Robin Michals wrote, confirming that she had been inactive for the past two years and had already left. I promised to send a letter from Taos, cutting ties after twelve years. Emma, Avis, Josely, Kathie, and Sara Pasti were staying. Second on the agenda was the "final vote on acceptance or rejection of the $10,000 NEA grant earmarked for Viva Latina." Avis was "preparing a fact sheet of our voting/revolting history on this question." Faith had already sent a letter voting "yes," citing "changes in NEA policy and legislation pursuant to lawsuits challenging the obscenity restrictions." I planned to abstain.

I sat up writing in my journal at the Lakeside Inn in Tennessee. We had driven six hundred miles, and Roger had immediately fallen asleep. He was sharing the driving to New Mexico and would then fly back to New York while I settled into the Wurlitzer to work on my installation scheduled for December. I had packed boxes of unfinished artworks and materials and was trying to mentally sort through what I had brought. Had I forgotten anything important? I had brought railroad spikes found under the bridge, the unfinished *Art-I-Fact*, and the mock-up for *Gladys Sad Box* to get me started. Eleanor Moretta had selected *Place/Displace* to be installed at the Pratt Manhattan Gallery for the series of four installations called *Charting the Inner Terrain*. Maureen Connor was making an installation as well; I admired her work. Eleanor had liked my ideas for echoing the massive curved windows in the Puck Building with an arched branch and stick gateway into my series of cemetery-based sculptures. I planned to iron images onto

40. Sabra Moore, *Bulfinch Mythology* (all), Odysseus tied to mast against harpies 41. Bacchus playing lyre with satyrs

curtains for the big windows and had gone to Todd's Copy Shop to print a stack of laser transfers. They were safely stowed in the truck. I was also planning to finish prints for a show on "electro-graphic art" at the Vasarely Museum in Budapest; Sharon Gilbert was sending work there too. "I hope this show will give your piece the attention it deserves," Eleanor told me. It was raining outside. Sunday dog was asleep on the motel rug; she had perked up earlier in the afternoon when we passed cows grazing in the fields. I thought of our dinner with Ayisha, her husband Jitu, and Zarina. The rain pounded outside their apartment as we sat eating. In India, they told us, they have a perfume for the smell that is released after rain.

The next evening, we were in Arkansas; I signed the motel registry and the woman noticed my name. "I knew a girl named Sabra Carver. Her brother was named Blade. Their mother said, 'I want my children to be sharp.'"

Lucy met us for breakfast at the Abiquiu Inn. Our truck was still packed; we hadn't driven up yet to see our place, so we all went together. "I notice we haven't mentioned the "H" word, as Betsy calls *Heresies*." I told her I was writing my resignation letter from Taos. "Well, I wanted to stay to finish it, but not if it's continuing." We were standing in the arroyo, looking at petroglyphs. She thought the "triangle" of rock art was unusual because of the pictures on both sides of the white cliff walls. "Usually, they just make drawings on the southeast wall." We sat along the ridge talking. "I can visualize you here now," she said. She was heading back to Boulder and would be in New York for the *Heresies* meeting. We caught up on news. Harmony had been awarded a Guggenheim; it was well timed. "Harmony felt like she had lost everything in the art world by coming here." I thought, "Lucy sees me as a lot more self-assured than I am; she doesn't realize the anguish I feel at not having more recognition for my artwork."

42. Sitting near petroglyphs in Madera Canyon
43. Sabra and Pat d'Andrea walking in Madera Canyon below the mesa with house site.

It took me time to settle into my studio, but I was back in the same adobe: House #6. I had errands to do: going over to our place to arrange with Jemez Electric Cooperative for the electricity to be brought up from the canyon floor, drawing a house plan, and figuring out how to build a foundation along the sloping ground. Roger and I collaborated long distance. One day, I soaked in the hot baths at Ojo Caliente on the way back to Taos, and then stopped to eat at El Taquita. "The ceiling has bloomed with yellow ribbons," I wrote. "Can there really be so many people from this valley who went to the Gulf War? It must be true." Each time, I would return to the Wurlitzer with found wood from the canyon. I was collecting materials in Taos as well, as Sunday and I took walks along Animal Shelter Road at dusk. The materials led me back to the three *Woodsman* pieces I was finishing.

Avis mailed me the minutes from the June 18 *Heresies* meeting at Josely's place; my resignation letter had crossed in the mail. I wrote it on the solstice in my studio rather than going to Abiquiu as Lucy suggested to see where the sun hit the rock art at dawn. There were some glimmers from the end of the tunnel with Kay. Her lawyers had unexpectedly come to court with a $12,000 check plus 9 percent interest and a box of the stolen materials, including the very out-of-date Women on Men mechanicals. No one was sure what this might mean; our lawyers had already filed a motion for summary judgment. *Heresies* owed many times that amount in legal fees. Emma, Josely, Avis, Lucy, Sara, and Kathie were at the meeting, and all but Lucy voted to accept the NEA; third time's a charm. "If we don't accept the money," Josely said, "we do what they want us to do: fall silent." She was working on the Viva Latina issue with Marina Gutierrez and Susana Leval. Emma said, "I keep thinking of what Janet Henry said, 'Take their goddam money; if you don't, it's immaterial to them.' I want to back out [of *Heresies*], but I don't want it to die." I rehashed the NEA vote in my parting letter:

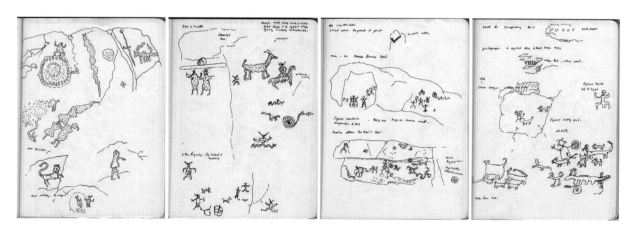

44. Sabra Moore, Journals #40 and #43 (all), rock art, Lyden 45-47. Chaco Canyon sites en route to Chetro Ketl

The dynamics of ignoring our group decisions aren't new. They are the same dynamics that led us to want to re-form when we fired Kay. The [Mother] Collective makes a decision. Because it is an open discussion, people often vote their ideals—what we think *Heresies* is (heretical)—but back home, other power interests come into play. . . . I've worked with *Heresies* without interruption since 1979. So, it feels a little odd to be stepping out. And I part with this observation: I think either *Heresies* finds a way to get *really* funded and develops the kind of paid structure Betsy envisions or it goes back to develop a mass base of volunteer labor and resumes its old structure. I don't think it can straddle the lines like it's doing now. . . . I've loved *Heresies* in many moments. But this phase will be minus my tender labor.

Mary Maughelli, one of the Wurlitzer residents, drove over to Abiquiu with me to see our land. Roger and I had already laid out the outline of the house with strings. I had been moving rocks from the site and tucking them under trees for restoration after the foundation was dug. During one visit, I had found twelve pottery shards right where our bedroom would be, so I drew them in place among the rocks before collecting the broken pieces. The floor plans were gradually taking shape; I would move through the site and picture the window spaces and imagine the doorways, and then I would measure and draw. Mary and I stopped to pick up mail. Greg Sholette had written, asking if REPOhistory could use a small version of my Pearl Street sign for a grant proposal. "It's one of the better pieces that was sent." I found a letter from Nancy Spero, inviting me to create an artist's book for *Burning in Hell*, a show she was organizing at Franklin Furnace. I thought of submitting *4/Tells* with its dark stories of Opal's baby and Caroline's abuse.

48. Emma Amos, *The Gift* (all), Josely Carvalo 49. Marina Gutierrez 50. Back cover, *Heresies* Latina issue 51. Lucy Lippard

Mary was a painter who taught at California State University, Fresno and knew Faith Wilding and Miriam Schapiro. Her father had emigrated from Italy and worked as a coal miner in Pennsylvania before moving to California. Like Roger, Mary didn't meet her Italian grandmother until she was grown. "My grandmother used the formal pronoun with my mother; she seemed distant to her." We were waiting for Flavio Montoya from Jemez Electric Cooperative to discuss how they would bring electricity up from the canyon. "Can you climb down the cliff?" he asked. "There are petroglyphs on the cliff, so you'll have to be careful. But you can climb down; I have." We planned a route with two poles leading to the house site. The workers would have to haul the cable up the cliffs by hand and set the holes for the sturdy poles seven feet into the ground. "Are you from Santa Fe?" "No, I live in New York now, but I'm from Texas. . . . It feels like coming back home to me." His wife was a *santera*; she made carvings of saints. We three joked about how hard it was to sell artwork.

My studio neighbor was Melvyn Ettrick, a Jamaica-born artist who knew Mel Edwards and Jayne Cortez. For the first time, another painter at the Wurlitzer was working with autobiographical issues and not simply me. I walked over to see his paintings. Two lovers—a stylized and child-like black man and a bigger, realistically painted white woman—were floating entwined in a sea of disapproving black faces flanked by the Klan. I was startled to feel tears rising behind my eyes. His painting reminded me of Frida Kahlo cradling Diego Rivera as a fat baby. We fell into an intense discussion of racism, class, and race mixing.

I had already started ironing laser transfer images on vertical strips of muslin to suspend across the oval windows at the Puck Building. Eleanor had called me with the sizes; each window was about fourteen feet wide and eleven feet high. Fragmented photos of Daddy Chess, Mother Gladys, trees, and tombstones were scattered across the curtains interspersed with

 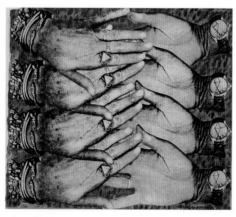 

52. Sabra Moore, Book #40, Lyden 53. Sabra Moore, *Peace by Piece #2* 54. Sylvia Sleigh, *Ravishing*, artist book

drawings of sticks. I had also started three versions of *Woodsman*, each telling parts of the story of Grandmother's murdered husband. My lovers were more abstract than Melvyn's. I had joined two pieces of found wood to create a low-standing arch, which looked to me like two people lashed together against an inescapable fate. My grandparents floating across the curtains frightened Melvyn; they reminded him of the newspaper photos of poor white Southerners from the civil rights era. "You know, this wood piece reminds me of a grave." "That's what it is." The murdered man's tombstone was shaped like a tree stump; he had belonged to the fraternal order of Woodmen of the World. I had traced the same embracing forms onto a wall work about the murder, cutting them out of thick paper to leave their negative images and sewing a translucent plastic toy gun into one of the openings. Melvyn felt that artworks about a murder should look more violent, but I wasn't interested in the violence. I was interested in Grandmother's survival; the hidden gun sewn into the opening felt like a scar that had healed around a harsh wound.

Sue Heinmann, another core Heretic who had left the collective, had moved to California and was in Santa Fe for a photography workshop. We drove out to Abiquiu and hiked into the arroyo to look at the rock art. Jemez Electric Cooperative had marked a nearby electrical pole with orange tape; it looked like electricity might be coming up to our house site soon. Sue thought we had selected the best location for building. We talked about the spate of resignations. Lucy had sent me a postcard. "Your letter caused quite a stir." She agreed with my criticism about how we had handled the NEA vote.

I dream that I am following women through corridors. One woman is about to give birth. She and a man go alone into a room and close a glass door, leaving us outside watching. I can see her huge vagina and then a baby girl emerges. The baby smiles at me with a big grin.

 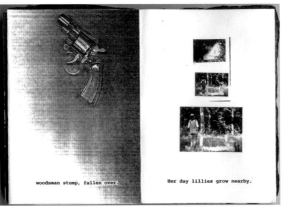 

55-56. Sabra Moore, *Woodsman* (both) cover, double page spread 57. Curtains hanging, Puck building

Every afternoon in Taos, it rained, giving us spectacular rainbows and sodden sunsets, belying the idea of living in a high desert. Mud and boulders the size of small cars rolled off the pink mountain onto the main highway that winds through the Rio Grande Gorge and into Taos, closing the road. It was the day of the corn dance at Santa Ana Pueblo, so I drove the long way across the highroad through Chimayo. I had just mailed off my prints for the electrographic show in Budapest, and promised myself that I would go to the dance and eat the noonday meal spread out on cloth across the same dirt plaza where the dancers and chanters had pranced and sang. Squatting with others to sample the chili stews and slices of watermelon felt like a true sacrament of the summer. As I got into the pickup truck to return to Taos, a wall of water descended from the sky, and I sat in the cab until the deluge passed—everyone running and laughing at the good rain that had followed the dancing. That night, it felt like I was the only person driving along the newly opened highway—with the rocks and freshly raked mud ghostly in the starlight.

Henry hosted a lecture for the residents at the Wurlitzer house and afterwards we got into a discussion about the Gulf War. One of the writers declared his support for the war, and I lost my temper, "screaming like a banshee," Henry insisted, reminding him of the one hundred thousand Iraqis incinerated in their tanks when panicked soldiers got caught in a traffic jam retreating from the Kuwaiti border. The war had ended without any real peace having been achieved; Kazuko and I would no longer try to travel our shelters. I ran into Melvyn at the grocery store the next day. "You were magnificent," he said. "It's the black world versus the white world with the brown world in between." Melvyn had gone with me to paint in Abiquiu a few days earlier. "It's such a pleasure, watching your love of this land. It tells me a lot about you—that you are comfortable here."

58. Sabra Moore, *Place/Displace* series (all), *Directions* (detail) 59. Tent for *Woodsman* (detail) (floor)

I had mailed the finished house plans to Roger, who would shortly be flying back to New Mexico. He liked them. We were baffled about how to build the foundation on an eight-foot grade and decided to hire an architect to redraw my plans with technical specifications. Henry was letting me store my artworks and materials at the foundation during the two months we would work on the house before returning to New York. My sister, nephew, and brother-in-law were also arriving, driving from Texas with discount-price supplies for our well, a water pump, heavy electrical wire, and a control box.

"When do we get to Harry's?" Julius, my brother-in-law, teased me as we drove up the bumpy curves onto the mesa. Everyone kept talking excitedly about Grandmother's farm, remembering the long drive on a dirt road. For once, my family seemed happy with my choices. The day after their arrival, we all went over to Taos to visit my studio. I had a few more days to work there and pack. Roger had been surprised at how much art I had completed. Julius read slowly, "Acworth, Texas. . ." He paused. "I like it. I like it." Nancy was silent. "Does Mother know?" "Not yet, but she's coming to the show. I'll tell her before the show." "Maybe you shouldn't," Nancy warned. Steven, my nephew, spoke up, "she thinks you don't know the correct version." "Well, she doesn't like anything negative," Julius added, "but that's reality." He started to talk about the violence in his own family. "I'm not pretending that I know the whole story. I'm telling what I do know; how I see it. We would each see the same story differently."

A few days later, I invited Henry to see the works I been making all summer; he never visited the artists' studios without an invitation. "You should be pleased with what you've done." He especially responded to all the sewing.

When we returned after storing my artworks, the poles were up. "Yes, it transforms the landscape," I wrote, "making the place less 'far-away' because with the electric poles will come

60. Sabra Moore, *Place/Displace* series (both), *Arrowhead* (detail) 61. *Not a Civilian* (detail)

a house. But the poles are tree trunks, so they don't look so odd." The ravens quickly found them. The next day, the linemen were there all day, rappelling up the cliff face on heavy cables, and then deftly stringing the wires, creating lines in the air across the mountain. We were back to camping in the shed, studying the architectural plans that John Midyette had made. It was nice to see the elevations prettily drawn. John had wanted to group the windows to create a big expanse of glass, but I insisted on keeping the same-sized sequential windows I had pictured from within the string outline. We can always walk out the door for a bigger view. He had solved the problem of the eight-foot grade; the house would step down as the land slopes, a few feet at two different levels, to conform to the L-shape configuration of traditional farm houses, nestling quietly into the land.

Lucy was writing regularly for *Z Magazine*; she had told me that she would mention *Know Peace/No Peace* in her article on artists' responses to the Gulf War. The magazine arrived. According to her article, I noted in my journal, our show had been organized by "a group of Asian-Americans." Kazuko had become anonymous, and my work creating the tent in the freezing gallery had become nonexistent.

Robin Michals, another former Heretic, sent a postcard. She and her boyfriend, Chino, were coming to visit. That night, we heard the great horned owl hooting softly as we settled into sleep.

Larry Parnell came to look at the equipment that my brother-in-law had brought from Texas. "That control box is worth a thousand dollars," he said, examining the box Julius had intricately assembled. He was an electrical engineer who was used to making industrial controls for cotton gins and other heavy machinery. "You could start your own store. . . . Now, if we could find a scientist…" Roger and I had started to lay out the well house and pick away at the hard

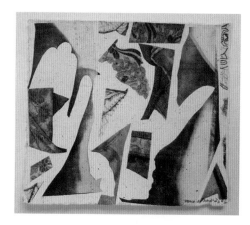

62. Sabra Moore (both), *Peace by Piece #1* 63. *Peace by Piece #2*, series of prints for Budapest exhibit

mounds of soapy dirt left at the mouth of the well, getting things ready for the pump to be in-stalled. We had to have water before we could start work on the foundation. Larry couldn't give us a firm date. We were still looking for someone to do backhoe work and others to lay the cinder blocks for the stem wall.

Rose Gutierrez was the manager at the Abiquiu Inn; we often stopped to chat with her after getting showers at their RV Park. She and her filmmaker husband had moved from Los Angeles to nearby Mesa Poleo twenty years ago at the height of the La Raza struggles. They had built their own house just like we were starting to do. He had unexpectedly died, but Rose had stayed and raised their daughters, Isis and Una. "This is sort of hard for Roger, isn't it?" she asked me. "Yes, he feels frustrated. He doesn't want to plan until things are definite, and, of course, you have to make plans." "You're from the country, you're used to it. You have to just go with it." She recommended Reyes Trujillo to help us with adobes. I hoped we could get that far; Roger had his doubts.

There was one juniper tree in the house site, so Roger cut it down. "Trees create space," I wrote, adjusting to its absence, "they make the landscape bigger and more complex." It rained, filling the holes we had dug for the well house footers. One morning, we found a spade foot toad, almost the color of the white earth, happily soaking in the tiny pond.

I dream that I visit May and Rudolf. "We are getting the foundation dug," I tell them, "but we may not be able to start the adobes." We talk about art. "I've worked twenty years, but have no recognition for my artwork."

I woke up and walked outside. Cerro Negro, the eight-thousand-foot mountain that we faced, was in a cloud. We had found someone for the backhoe work; Rudy Trujillo would start as soon as Larry installed the well pump. The night before, driving home from a dance at San

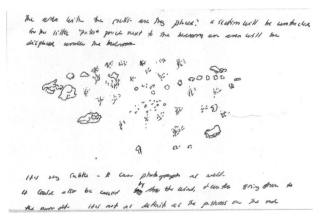 

64. Journal drawings of rock place where shards were found 65. Sabra Moore, *Grounded* (detail) showing feet on land

Ildefonso Pueblo, Roger and I were arguing. The sky filled with streaks of light—pure blue rays alternating with pink, then shifting into orange and gold. "The sunset is beyond argument," I thought, breaking through our discord. A coyote suddenly raced across the road before I had time to react, bounding safely to the other side.

The water pipes lay in trenches three feet below the surface with the electrical cable slightly above. I marked the lines with rocks so we could remember their location. Larry had to bypass Julius's complex system to make our modest pump work, but now we had an outdoor faucet with a blue handle. He held a mirror to the mouth of the well; the water had risen about six hundred feet; you could see its reflection. Roger completed framing the well house. That night at the inn, Rose commented, "Now, things will start to work."

We drove over to the village to meet Robert Garcia and get a permit to use the dump near the cemetery. We were starting to accumulate trash. "You must have good views," Robert said when I told him where we lived. "I have a good view too." We walked over to look across at Cerrito de Abiquiu, the bumpy pink mountain that faces Abiquiu Mesa with the Chama River curving along its flanks. "It looks like a ship." "Or like an alligator," I added. We were standing near a low wall made of pitted dark volcanic rock. He had helped his father build that wall. "I was bringing stones and he was setting them faster than I could bring them." He asked if we had found any rattlesnakes. "My grandfather used to give me the rattles," I told him, "I saved them in a little box." "We keep them too; we put then inside our fiddles." He gave us apples from his orchard and cota tea; we got the dump permit as well.

I went to the post office to send *4/Tells* to Franklin Furnace for Nancy's show. There was a letter from *Heresies* in our mailbox. Emma, Kathie, Josely, Penny, Avis, and Sara responded collectively to my resignation letter, defending their decision to accept the NEA grant. We women

66. *Heresies* flier for Viva Latina! 67. *Heresies* subscription flier, *Or Else*

who voted to refuse the funding, they wrote, "were quite cynical, at moments, about using the opportunity to look good while making a bold gesture of refusal to knuckle under to government intervention in the arts." They bristled at many of my comments. "No one was happy to receive your letter, Sabra, and certainly, no one was 'cheery,' to use your word, about having to accept people's resignations from the main collective. . . . Accepting people's resignations/associations graciously seemed appropriate to us rather than, for example, accusing them of abandoning ship." They hoped I was leaving with "more good feelings than negative ones. . . . Certainly, everyone feels that your participation has been invaluable, extensive, part of the very identity of *Heresies*—how can anyone think otherwise?"

Avis included minutes from two "open-by-invitation" meetings at the studios of Josely and Emma in July and August to recruit new members, breaking with the practice of inviting a woman to join only after she had worked as an editor on one of the Issue Collectives and learned how to create a magazine. *Heresies* would no longer be composed of people with a shared work experience. When *IdiomA* was printed in 1992 as a bilingual Russian/English special edition, there were twenty-three collective members listed on the masthead, but only three worked on that issue as editors. "On the way out of the meeting," Avis continued with her minutes, "Susan Crowe, displaying the right spirit to ensure a fine future for our quasi-venerable feminist collective, suggested we produce some *Heresies* shower curtains."

Roger woke early the morning of the autumnal equinox and noticed that Venus had risen right above its pictograph next to a red sun drawing on the canyon wall facing our place. We had finished building the well house. At night, the moon reflected off the tin roofs of the two little buildings, making them glow in the darkness like floating silver rafts. Rudy was coming in a few days to start digging the foundation. Mother arrived for the weekend. We were eager to show her

68. Invitation to meeting to recruit new *Heresies* members at Josely's house 69. *Heresies* meeting at Emma's house

the rock art in the canyon, but she didn't need much prompting to see the drawings. "I can see that my visual sense comes in part from her," I wrote in my journal. She helped me finish moving rocks from the building sites, not finding my behavior odd. It was she who taught me respect for the land; we always had a garden. To my surprise, she handed me a check as she was leaving. "This is partly a loan and partly a gift. You weren't there all those years for the dinners and gifts I gave to Nancy and the boys."

I was unprepared for the destruction of the excavation. The sandstone came up in great sheets, exposing raw white rock and marring the delicate lichens and plants on the surface. "We can't be innocent about the degree to which we have altered this land," I wrote sadly. Kate came over with champagne. "I feel wrenched. I don't think I could have anyone else come by today but you." "The excavation is the hardest part," Kate assured me.

Roger and I went to Taos for a reading by Ed Wood; he had been working on a novel during Roger's residency at the Wurlitzer. We ran into Henry. "When are you coming by?" I was still feeling obsessed about the damage to the land; it felt like I shouldn't be "out in public" until the site had been restored.

Mike Sandoval, who had plowed our road the previous summer, recommended Joe Gonzales to build the foundation. Joe brought Alvaro and Mike as his crew. The worst part of the digging was over. Now, there were big stacks of cement blocks placed at intervals within the site; the trenches would soon be filled to create a low stem wall. Adobes would rise from that perimeter. Roger was right; we would not lay any adobes before the time came to return to New York. We settled into a routine of work. One day, Joe brought antelope steaks to grill for lunch, and we all sat around our outdoor table to eat. We often traded snake stories; Alvaro told us a somber one. He had been crossing through the desert with other undocumented immigrants when a friend

70. Staking strings of house outline before digging stem wall 71. Roger and Sabra inside start of concrete stem wall

was bitten by a rattlesnake. They rushed for help to a nearby ranch, but when they got back, the man was dead. "Don't tell my family how I died," his friend had begged when they left him to seek help. The rancher reported them to the authorities, "but we had to go back with the body anyway."

Rudy was still working down the slope from the foundation, digging an eight-foot-deep hole for our septic tank; it looked like a tiger trap with its stony interior. A mass of rock and dirt was mounding up next to the hole. One of Rudy's neighbors needed this kind of soil rich in ash, so Rudy filled the bed of his dump truck with a brimming load and started up our drive. Roger and I were nailing slabs of barky wood over the plywood walls of our well house, and we watched as he passed. His truck stalled at the steep curve, and Rudy quickly backed down. Roger went over. "I stalled," Rudy said, and immediately started up, this time faster. Now, all of us were watching. The truck stalled again, and then started rolling back, picking up speed. Suddenly, it lurched to one side and flipped over, coming to a sickening stop upside down on its load of dirt. Rudy was still inside. We were all running uphill and reached the truck just as Rudy struggled out, unhurt, wiping dirt and grease from his face. The massive load of dirt had cushioned the cab. I ran back for water and a towel, my knees shaking. Rudy had purposely rolled his truck to avert a crash down the side of the hill. He washed his face, walked to his backhoe, and proceeded to spread the tons of dirt that had spilled out of the truck bed. Then, he hooked a chain onto the upside down truck, pushed it with the bucket of the backhoe, and watched as the truck flipped once again onto its wheels. That evening, I told Rose what had happened. "These guys from here are amazing; it's like getting back onto a horse after you've been thrown. You don't let it make you afraid."

The nights were starting to get cold. There was snow on Truchas Peaks. I called Barbara Strauch to see if I had work; Workman Publishing had renewed the contract for the Civil War

72. Joe Gonzales and crew lay concrete block for stem wall 73. Pouring concrete into stem wall near telephone poles

calendars. Roger also had jobs lined up to do mechanicals for an advertising agency. Rudy was almost finished laying the perforated drainage pipes for our septic tank. Kate and Lisa came over for a last hike with us, climbing Cerro Negro. As we ascended the slope, we could still hear the moans of Rudy's backhoe scraping the land; the small outline of our foundation was barely visible in the vast landscape that unfolded as we climbed higher. I found that comforting; it restored my sense of proportion about our impact on the mesa. Now, I understood why they called this "breaking ground."

Reyes Trujillo helped me restore the places where Rudy had dug. He was the dishwasher at the inn whom Rose had recommended. We worked well together, pulling out the broken chunks of sandstone and adding them to our rock pile and raking the ground to recreate the swells and slopes. I retrieved the surface rocks Mother and I had stashed under the trees, and we tossed them on top of a layer of straw and grass seeds. I hoped for snow to soak the seeds. "You work like a squirrel," Reyes teased me when I scooped along the dirt with my hands. He was a big cheerful man, somewhat childlike. He brought us his drawings of weeping unicorns with big eyelashes. His father had kicked his mother in her stomach when she was pregnant, he told me, and he was born with a big red lump on his forehead. He was still a boy when his father was killed in a backhoe accident.

We ate at the inn on the evening we were leaving, planning to spend the night and rest before driving to Taos to pack up my artworks for our return to Brooklyn. Our truck now had New Mexico license plates. We picked up our mail; my Daddy's cousin, Emmadele, had sent me a postcard. "You have a lot of Harry and Caroline in you." Rose and Reyes sat down to chat as we ate, and then we went to our room, looking forward to a warm bed. We were startled to find a stranger sitting in our motel room, watching television in his under shorts. "I knew there was

74. Sabra raking and cleaning site of completed stem wall foundation 75. A rainbow in front of Cerro Negro

something I had forgotten!" Rose said; she had double-booked our room. We climbed back in the pickup with our tired dog and drove to Taos, finding a motel late in the night. Henry was waiting for us at the Wurlitzer the next morning. "Why didn't you call me? I would have found room for you."

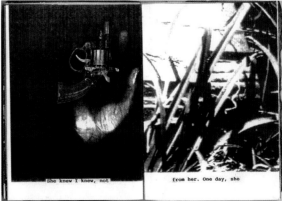

76-77. Sabra Moore, *Woodsman* (details), artist's book relating story of the murder of Grandmother's second husband

12

A Bird in the Hand

The big potted coffee tree and the bitter lemon tree in our loft had died from lack of water; plants we had nurtured from seeds. Someone had dug up the lantana and one of the altheas from the outside garden. One of the newts had survived; the cats were fine. The woman who had sublet our loft had left some of her art materials in my studio. I was anxious for her to pick up her belongings so I could get back to work; my installation was in three weeks. Pat D'Andrea wrote. It had snowed seven inches in Santa Fe; perhaps, the seeds Reyes and I had scattered were already settling into the earth. Roger kept describing our place as "out there," but I was feeling like "out there" was here in Brooklyn.

I went by to see Sylvia; she had gone to Europe with a new traveling companion from Chicago, a handsome young man named Robert. They were planning a trip to Egypt in January. I commented on all the new art she had bought. "But I still want an artwork by you!" She gave me a copy of the newly printed in memoriam book for Lawrence; several of us had contributed

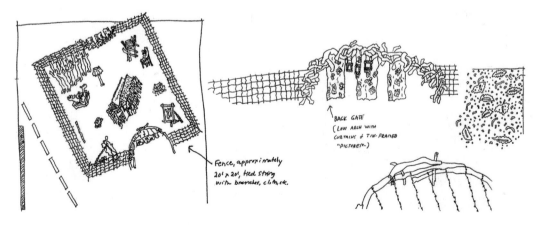

1. Sabra Moore (both), drawing for *Place/Displace* installation at the Puck Building 2. Drawings, gate and curtains

our recollections of him. Linda Peer had moved next door to our loft and came by to see my new sculptures, reminding me that I had agreed to trade my little artwork, *Land*, with her. She liked the way I had started using strips of metal to join or attach sticks and other objects to my artworks. "I may borrow that idea."

Bulfinch's Mythology was out, but the designer had cut apart some of my composite drawings, reduced sizes, and made other alterations without consulting me. As a photo editor, I always had authority to check for mistakes and approve the final design, but as an artist, my work had been "for hire." I went by to pick up my copies and retrieve the originals. The managing editor, Carol Cohen, was there. "This is the first time I have heard that you were upset. I agree that these are silly alterations." Five thousand books had already sold from the first printing of fifteen thousand copies. She promised to make changes in the reprint. "You're very professional," she told me, "of course, I wouldn't have allowed this if I had known." I wasn't entirely convinced.

I still had to finish *Arrowhead*, the artwork about Grandmother losing her farm to the owners of Arrowhead ranch, and *Not a Civilian*. I had made a photo transfer of my rubbing from Dane Lewis's tombstone with his Ohio Infantry Regiment engraved in stone, keeping in defiant touch with the Civil War. I mirrored the same shape in wood, framing the diaphanous cloth like a funeral wreath. It sat on a caned chair bound in place with cloth ties. There were other details to complete, including painting the text for the curtain above the gate. It would read, "The lumber company now owns the woods."

Kazuko had a solo show at Brecht Forum with multiple versions of kimonos in various materials—some with prints or drawings, some made out of rope. I found them "beautiful and uncompromising." Then, I managed to go see Nancy's show, *Burning in Hell*, at Franklin Furnace.

3. Sabra Moore, *Place/Displace* installation (all), *Not a Civilian* 4. *Woodsman* (tent cloth) 5. *Arrowhead*

All of us book artists were listed by name on the wall. For some reason, *4/Tells* was inside a glass case; the booklets didn't make much sense without being able to turn the pages.

The Pratt Institute sent a truck to pick up the artworks for my installation; I was still working at home as well, but I had ten days to install, although this would be interrupted by Thanksgiving. I started with the arched gateway and blue string fence, dividing the installation from the lobby of the third floor where students and teachers passed going to computer classes. At first, people were walking around the ladder as I suspended the curved sections of wood assembled in the studio. The text curtain hung across the top. By the end of the day, it had become architecture and people were walking through the arch as I continued tying a string fence stretching to the outer walls. A guard named Tim was seated at a desk near the elevators, watching my slow progress. "You've made me an arch!" he said, "I couldn't tell what it was going to be like. I have to thank you." A woman stopped to ask me about how I had printed the curtain images. "It's probably a secret," she said. I told her. Then, she told me how she melts crayons to make drawings. Another woman asked if *Woodsman* was my artwork. "Yes." "Is it for sale?" "Maybe." As I left that first day, Tim gave me his assessment. "You've made a good start. I am looking forward to the rest." He was from the South and asked me if I made quilts.

Roger came the next day to help me assemble *Lillie's Peaks*. I was feeling like a teacher with all the students stopping to watch. One man said, "It has a spiritual quality; it looks like a church." I told him about the cemetery. A student from Columbia came over. "This is fantastic work." He asked if he could show me some of his paintings. He had helped another of the artists install an outdoor piece with tree trunks at the Pratt Brooklyn campus. "We had to place them just so; he taught me that trees are greener on one side. I learned to look at trees differently."

 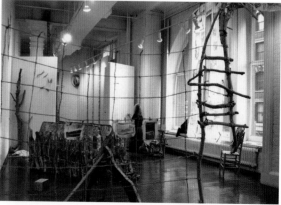

6-7. Roger Mignon, photographs of *Place/Displace* installation. Sabra making drawings of sticks on wall

Wendy Waxman was installing wire sculptures in a gallery beyond *Place/Displace*, making the wall bristle like an animal.

We all took a break for Thanksgiving; Sylvia, Ora, Artelia, and India came to eat at our place. Freda arrived the next day to spend the night. We went together to see a show at the Alternative Museum, *Artists of Conscience*. I had wanted to see Robin Michals's artwork. She had painted three women—yellow, white, and black—in immaculate realism like the three classical Graces; their faces were open books filled with racist and sexist comments. It was shocking and effective. Freda showed me slides of her recent work. I thought, "Freda's work is directed outward to the viewer in an effort to educate and 'profess,' but my work is about my own identity; it goes both ways—it permits the viewer to see, but it also expresses my own feelings. I am trying to figure this out as I make the work; I don't have my mind made up."

I had almost finished the installation—the artworks were grouped randomly within the fenced area like one might encounter them in a cemetery, each with a story if the viewer chose to read. The curtains were up, but I still had to paint drawings of sticks and roots onto the walls. Another student walked by; he looked Middle Eastern. "What culture is this? American Indian, Asian, African?" "All," I thought. "I'm the artist," I said. Thomas Broadbent stopped to look. "I have a friend who works like this, sort of primitive. You'll get a lot of attention." I had to go the next day for a dental procedure. I wasn't worried about the gum surgery, thinking it would only leave me with some soreness in my mouth. The opening was in two days.

Melvyn sent us a letter; I had to read it twice to understand. He had returned to California after the residency in Taos, and packed his Oakland studio, storing all his artworks at a friend's house in the nearby hills. He was planning a motorcycle trip throughout East Africa. They

8. Visitors stand near *Gate* with laser transfer *Curtain* 9. Sabra Moore, *Woodsman* (wall) 10. Close-up, Sabra drawing

were wakened by the heat of fire crackling her windows and barely escaped with their lives as the wildfire swept through the canyon and the cluster of houses. All of his artworks were destroyed.

I seldom wear makeup, but I bought pancake makeup for the opening. I discussed the problem with Aissa, my designer neighbor; we agreed: either wear makeup or a veil. The dentist had clipped a blood vessel during my gum surgery. My face swelled; I developed a black eye and purple splotches dotted my cheeks. The last day I was drawing on the wall, students would approach and then quickly turn away once they saw my face. The opening was all afternoon to allow visitors to go to both Pratt campuses. "People hesitated and then entered under the arch," Roger observed. "They made a choice." The opening was crowded with friends who had been in New Mexico; the borders are porous between these two distant places. Robin, Sydney, Mary, Owen, Sue, Alan, and Ed all came to see the completed installation they had already glimpsed in part. Few Heretics appeared. I rushed over to stop a child from climbing a ladder in the adjacent installation. It was Lisa Maya Knauer's daughter. REPOhistory was starting a project about abortion, she told me. "We should interview you." The creative writing teacher at Pratt, Rosemarie Santini, came over. "I love the stories; I've brought my class to see the show." Sylvia spilled wine on *Arrowhead*. "I've anointed it." May appeared, "You look more Native American each time I see you."

I dream that Daddy is coming to my exhibit. Someone asks me about him, so I tell how he worked for the railroad and organized for the union. "I don't know where he lives now." I am feeling upset because someone has painted over my wall drawings. Now, Daddy is coming and my show is incomplete.

A group on race and class was meeting to develop ideas for *Choice Histories: Framing Abortion*, the REPOhistory project Lisa Maya had mentioned to me. Greg invited me to join. This was the only the second exhibition that I can recall on this core subject since our *Choice Works*

11. Sabra Moore, *Place/Displace* (all), *Woodsman* (tent floor) 12. *Directions* 13. *Arrowhead* (view into text box)

project at Central Hall Gallery in 1985. They were developing a time line about reproductive rights. "It's easy to be right about the past, but what about the present and what about feelings?" I wondered. I felt like an "expert" in this room of younger artists because of my work at the clinic and my life experiences, but Greg was enthusiastic. "You should go to all the committees; you have such a connected way of seeing this issue." Later, I wrote in my journal: "I've been loyal and idealistic about our art movements. I don't regret any of that. But, now, I feel I have to focus more clearly on my own art."

I dream that I go to a Heresies *meeting. The room is filled with women and a scattering of men. Avis is chairing the meeting. I say, "I've only come to visit, not to join again." I wonder how men could also be part of the Collective. Then, I am in a room with closets. I have left things there and start pulling objects off a shelf. I take back an African doll.*

Ora was supposed to meet me at the installation; I had been meeting many friends there. Benita and Brooke had come at different times; both were interested in the idea of my recreating an unacknowledged history. Marilyn had visited from Texas. She liked that the "woods wasn't a real woods; you made it into something else." She hadn't seen the hidden guns. Elizabeth Riley had been taking computer classes and passed through the installation each day. She hadn't seen Ora. I wandered down the street to Miriam Schapiro's show at Bernice Steinbaum Gallery. She had appropriated a series of Freda Kahlo's artworks, inserting herself into the paintings. I thought of my experience with the drawings for the *Bulfinch* book; "You trace their lines, you 'claim' them, but they've already solved the bigger problems of space and form." It was hard to separate Miriam's paintings from her personality. Lawrence called her "the General." "But she's lost her army," Ora had added. This show felt more like an attempt at conquest. I looked up and there was Ora. We went around looking at the paintings, whispering to each other. Then,

14. Completed installation, *Place/Displace* with *Lillie's Peaks* in center 15. Laser transfer *Curtains* frame window

we saw Miriam, dressed Navajo style in a velvet blouse and silver belt, seated next to Bernice at the desk. She clearly didn't recognize me. "Oh, Sabra, it's you," she said, mispronouncing my name. We went next door to a show at Phyllis Kind Gallery, which featured intensely felt artwork made by mental patients in an Austrian institution. I was drawn to the obsessive signs one artist had painted with words bulging off the borders. "It's always important to know what is authentic," Ora added as we left.

Ora thought my installation was "beautiful, dense, and authentic"; none of the shows had been reviewed. "You should document the installation, you should get a good record, and then figure out the ten people you need to see the show and concentrate on getting them to come over." Her still life paintings often incorporated wooden figures from Mexico. She considered them to be metaphors for the displacement of rural culture, so she understood my title for the cemetery series.

I dream that I uproot my narcissus plant and replant it. Have I been foolish and damaged the blooms?

Faith Ringgold was having a show, and Roger and I went to her opening. I ran into Faith Wilding. A new women's group focused on action was forming, she told me. They were meeting at the Drawing Center in SoHo; I promised to go. Vivian came up; she hadn't made it to my installation. "You're not off the hook yet. It's up for two more days." Marina joined us, and we wandered down the street to see Clarissa Sligh's show at Art in General. She had asked various friends and colleagues to send their recollections about when they first became aware of race. It had been difficult for me to write, but I had sent her a page. Ayisha came over. "I'm wanting to make artworks about my grandmother." She told me that my show had given her some ideas. I hadn't seen Emma since my final *Heresies* meeting in the spring; she had signed my visitors'

16. Faith Ringgold show card 17. Ayisha Abraham, *The Migration of Memory* 18. Grace Williams, *Ceremonial Vessels*

book. "I sent all of the Fabulous Women [a group she was in] to see your show." "We saw Faith's painting of you." "Don't tell me! That's what I'm going to see." She headed for the elevator. All of our statements were on the wall—testimonials to the civil rights struggle and the ongoing issues of racism. Mine was there too.

Ed Swift called to tell me about a show at Roger Arthur Gallery, a new gallery that featured artists from the South. Clyde Connell was a ninety-one-year-old artist from Louisiana who made totemic sculpture evocative of African art. "You've got to go see her work!" A few days later, Alan called with news. Henry had prostate cancer. Melvyn was in Taos. Henry had opened one of the Wurlitzer studios for him to work during the winter and recover from the devastating fire in California.

The action group Faith had described chose the name WAC for Women's Action Coalition. I started going to the weekly meetings; each week, a larger group gathered. We planned to be militant—thus, the evocation of the acronym. The meetings were open, but its core came from women connected to various alternative spaces, such as Franklin Furnace, Exit Art, Art Matters, and the Drawing Center. Many well-known performance artists including Laurie Anderson, Rena, Holly Hughes, Theodore Skipitares, and the radio journalist Laura Flanders had joined along with the usual mix of visual artists with various levels of art world acceptance. A lot of us former *Heretics* were there, including Betsy, Faith, May, Mary Beth, Su Friedrich, and Ida Applebroog, and many so-called anonymous women from Guerrilla Girls and others from Act Up. There was a notable absence of women of color. The meetings were a peculiar blend of downtown art world power centers and heartfelt reaction to ongoing violence against women and the rightward shift in national politics.

19. WAC flier, Santa Fe 20. WAC card 21. *Domestic Violence: The Facts Are In show* in conjunction with *Combat Zone*

On Groundhog Day, I stayed up making a banner for a WAC support demonstration at a rape trial in the Bronx. A black woman had accused five white fraternity men from St. John's College of raping her. I painted scribbled faces of women shouting "Justice!" across a cloth banner. Mine was the only expressive one. Laurie Anderson had printed elegant blue dot fans, echoing the news photos of dotted-out faces of the accused rapists, and others carried printed headlines about the story. Barbara Kruger led a group of women wearing black judges' robes. This was our first demonstration, so we took the court by surprise as we filed inside to witness the trial. I saw Ida, Faith, and May and joined them as we entered the courthouse. Hearing the prosecutor read the charges against the accused focused me. "I'm here because this happened to me," I thought, "because of the violence with C, which I endured alone. I'm here because of sex to which I unwillingly submitted. I'm here in debt to the person of my young adult years and for this woman as well." I wasn't sure what I thought a fair punishment should be for the rapists, but I felt a visceral sense of empowerment that a judge and jury would be hearing her story.

I dream that I meet Clyde Connell at the base of an icy field. She seems awestruck about the standing ovation she has just received for her artwork. I say, "I want you to see my work." We head over to a kind of shed or concession stand inside a vast interior room. My work is stored in two long rows. I say. "This is my work, you can see it now." Then, Faith Wilding comes over to us. She tells me that my show was wrong; I painted the tombstones with the wrong colors.

The Guggenheim Museum was opening a satellite branch downtown on Broadway in the summer. Word quickly spread that the inaugural show would feature four minimalists, all men, including Carl Andre. Guerrilla Girls came to a WAC meeting in full gorilla suit to pass out pink cards for us to sign. The text read something like this: "We hear that you are planning to open a museum with a show featuring four white boys. . . Welcome to Downtown." The next week, the

22. Su Freidrich, *The Ties That Bind* film announcement 23. Guerrilla Girls book publication announcement

museum sent a woman curator to explain that the artists were all male because the first show would reflect "the depth of their collection." Some members of the museum staff were "sympathetic" to our concerns, she added. "The director would be willing to meet with WAC." "Why? To see what a woman artist looks like?" someone quipped.

The demonstrations at the rape trial broadened. The press we had generated garnered support groups, including women from a battered women's shelter in Queens. We exchanged stories while marching together. I stood next to Su Friedrich as we shouted, "No Means No!" "We've got to get better slogans," Su said. The accused rapist unexpectedly decided to plead guilty, avoiding the judgment of a jury. A few days later, the judge meted out punishment—a suspended sentence and mandated community service.

I had written a proposal for traveling *Place/Displace* to Women & Their Work in Austin for a double installation with Marilyn Lanfear. Benita read my draft. "It's very beautifully written," she told me, "the perfect length, evocative, and suggestive." She showed it her husband, Colin, an art historian. "He thinks it's got a lot going for it—it has populism." Benita offered to write the Menil Collection to try to fund a catalogue.

Barbara and I were researching a baseball calendar for Workman Publishing; we drove out to Larchmont to look at a collection of baseball memorabilia. I rushed back for Liliana Porter's retrospective at the Bronx Museum. Zarina Hashmi had a show opening there the same evening. Neither had made it my installation, but Zarina had tried. She was still suffering a kind of agoraphobia after the Gulf War; she got to the door of the Puck Building, but then was afraid to enter. Liliana's show was "huge and impressive." I especially loved the earlier works with her silkscreened hands superimposed over geometric forms. Zarina's show was intimate with wonderful sculptural houses in many shapes and materials—some spirals, some on wheels, and some in

24-25. Liliana Porter, *Two Mirrors* (diptych) 26. Zarina Hashmi, *House on Wheels*, exhibit card for *House with Four Walls*

the form of books. Catalina came over. She had just gotten back from Canada, and handed me a card Lani Maestro had sent with her. Catalina was having a show at Lehman College. I promised to go. Then, I saw Emma talking to Nancy Azara. "Did anything happen with your show?" Emma asked. "Friends liked it; the students and teachers were excited. I may travel it to Texas." "I did get over to the Puck Building and I saw your work," Susana Leval told me without commenting further. She was surprised to learn that I had done the photo research on the O'Keeffe book for her old friend Benita. "You're building a house in Abiquiu! It's a mythic place." I opened Lani's card when I got home. A joint trip to the Philippines had ruptured her friendship with Freda. "Your stories about Josely brought back a lot of similar difficult memories."

I dream that I am moving through rooms built like boxcars; Sunday Dog is with me. There has been some kind of calamity; a river nearby is boiling and churning. Maybe there was an earthquake. I try to retrieve my journals.

Ayisha invited me to her studio. Both she and Lisa Maya Knauer were working with the REPOhistory group on class, race, and abortion. I felt more at ease about joining, thinking of ideas for small artworks related to Guinea. WAC was also debating formats for actions about abortion. Most of the earlier demonstrations for reproductive rights had involved violent imagery—women wailing in chains or a poster from a terrible crime scene showing the nude back of a woman keeled over on her knees after bleeding to death from an illegal abortion. I spoke against the symbol of the coat hanger. "It equates abortion with violence." Lenora Champagne left a message on my phone. She wanted to talk about why the WAC meetings made her mad. "Your comments reflected an intelligence I thought was urgently missing in the meetings."

We were all getting consumed by these weekly meetings; their scale and energy made anything seem possible. Artelia had started coming to WAC. She proposed an action for

27. Lenora Champagne, *Red Light District* performance 28. Artelia Court, Halloween party invitation

economic justice, thinking about the thousands of single mothers like her trying to collect delinquent child support payments. Mother's Day was coming up, presenting a perfect occasion for an action. I proposed making memorials or shrines in subways to women killed by their partners, remembering the symbolic power of the New Mexico roadside *descansos*. The lawyer Mary Dorman, splendid in a tailored suit, electrified the room with her call for a revival of the Equal Rights Amendment (ERA), a struggle we narrowly lost years ago.

Diana Kurz, Theodore Skipitares, and others signed up to work with me on the subway memorials. We met at Diana's studio. She was worried about Sylvia's infatuation with Robert. "There's something nineteenth century and European about it, grooming a young man." I wanted to talk about the shrines. We were thinking of using a repeated slogan: "This Is Not For Love."

People continued to wrangle at the WAC meetings over the lack of diversity. Roma Baran proposed bilingual leaflets; Barbara Yoshida offered to find translators for Spanish, Chinese, Korean, and Japanese. About a third of the room felt this was "too complicated." Su Friedrich voiced, for many people uncomfortably, why there were so few women of color at the meetings. "People are bringing their friends." I went home and called Kazuko and Patricia Spear Jones. "I'm not sure this group can transcend its white origins," I wrote in my journal.

Roger and I walked into Carol Bayard's dense installation at Art in General. One hundred babies made of mud and rags floated across the ceiling and twenty-five male torsos made of mud were planted below in a field of dirt, reflecting on the daunting statistic that only twenty-five black men out of one hundred births survive into adulthood. Seventy-five empty shoes lined the room. I ran into Willie Birch. "Hi, Sabra, best friend of Marina. She sends a note saying, 'Come tomorrow and see my show.'" He asked if I'd ever shown those pieces he saw in my studio when Lamidi was visiting. "They were in my installation at the Puck Building." "I told Marilyn Griffin of

29. Carole Byard, *The Perception of Presence* 30. Alison Saar, *Tattooed Lady* for Howardena Pindell's *Autobiography...*

the SculptureCenter about you several times. You should call her while I am still in good. They like all this minimalist stuff, but wait until she sees your work . . . the intensity of that piece . . . she won't even get to the content." Willie had a show coming up at Exit Art and another show in the fall at Roger Arthur Gallery. Both he and the dealer were from New Orleans. Roger came over with Crystal, a writer friend of Willie's. "I'm going to have a party, but I know about six hundred people and I can only invite two hundred." "Well, you've already invited three." How soon was our place in New Mexico going to be finished and when could they come visit? "You can come this summer," Roger said. "No, he wants to wait until it's like *House & Garden* magazine," Crystal said. We laughed. Willie told her we were building the house ourselves. "I'll think of you when I lay the adobes."

Marilyn Griffin asked me to send slides "right away," promising a studio visit. "I owe Willie a debt; he obviously paved the way," I thought contentedly, wandering along Canal Street on my way to the weekly WAC. I ran into Linda Cunningham and Artelia going to the same place. We were planning actions for a march on Washington with other labor and rights groups in April. Mary Beth presented some well-thought-out ideas for the march, but Laurie Anderson criticized them as "poor" and "going backwards." It was difficult to propose competing concepts with Laurie in the room. I kept out of it. Roma asked me if I would be one of the facilitators. The meetings were getting delicate, but I agreed.

I dream that Roger and I are in New Mexico with Mother. I see an exquisite palm-sized object made of glittery quartz and call them to come look. The dirt caves in, exposing potshards with fine drawings. Another oval opens in the ground revealing dark blue and silver objects. Suddenly, I feel the earth pushing against my hand; the openings close.

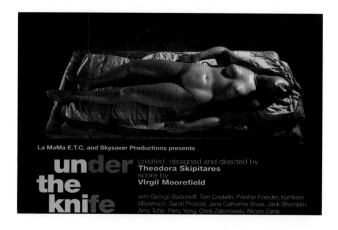  

31. Theodora Skipitares, *Under the Knife* performance 32. WAC ribbon 33. Catalina Parra, *Nubian Shield*

Irish American gay and lesbian activists had been trying to join the St. Patrick's Day Parade down Fifth Avenue for several years; often, their participation had been met with police repression. Irish heroine Bernadette Devlin McAliskey was in town for these events and came to speak to us at one of our weekly WAC meetings. She welcomed us to the struggle to "control your own life. . . . We have a saying in Ireland: just because you didn't win it, doesn't mean you lost it." She shared stories about the efforts in Ireland for reproductive rights. "We women have a common oppression as women that transcend culture, class, and ethnicity. . . . If you get close enough to sniff power like the smell of bread, you'll learn why the police, the church, and the state are there." It shocked her that such a small percentage of Americans voted in elections, a right "paid with so much blood." Twenty years ago, the feminists she met here were women with "small dogs and tanned husbands." An activist from the St. Patrick's Day Parade raised her hand: "I've never heard you speak before." "And you're wondering if I'm ever going to stop."

All afternoon, the actor Al Pacino drove a red Ferrari back and forth beneath our loft windows as they kept filming him for the perfect take. The film crew made trash swirl around to add an aura of dysfunction to the subway rattling along the train tracks. I was working on a sub-mission for International Society of Copier Artists (ISCA); the theme was environmental mayhem and I kept trying out word combinations—"may hem/may hymn/may him/may hen"—repeated against photos of my feet on our land. I had learned a new word from the REPOhistory meetings: straight-lacing, describing the same failed attempt at abortion that my sixteen-year-old aunt had used when she wrapped her stomach tightly with tape.

Carol Sun called me for a studio visit. She wanted to recommend me for a small grant cofunded by the Pyramid Art Center and Lower Manhattan Cultural Council. They were looking for

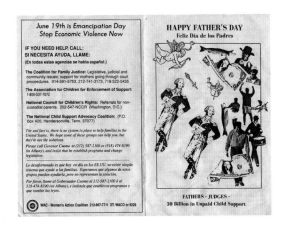

34. *The June Wedding*, WHAM!/Act Up 35. *Happy Father's Day*, WAC action flier, re-delinquent child support payments

"hidden artists who haven't gotten much funding." She had planned to only recommend minority artists, but then decided to include me.

Many friends from my projects were having shows. Roger went with me to Catalina's show at Lehman College, replete with word/image analyses and puns. My favorites were the early, more obscure works done in a sort of code during the Pinochet repression. Then, we headed downtown to Willie's Exit Art opening party. I was looking forward to dancing. We all followed Willie prancing in a circle as he waved a handkerchief. He kept chanting to me: "You're going to have a show at SculptureCenter." "They haven't called me yet, Willie." "I'm telling you, girl, you're going to have a show! They're finally beginning to understand this Texas, Louisiana, New Mexico thing."

It had been twenty years since the 1972 Corcoran Conference for Women in the Visual Arts that some art historians believe launched the feminist art movements. I had my doubts about its significance, but Mary Beth called to ask me to speak about *Heresies* and WAC for the upcoming twentieth-anniversary celebration at the same institution. A few days later, the art historian and conference organizer, Mary Garrard, called me. Would I speak about *Heresies*, not WAC, unless Ellen Lanyon preferred to speak for *Heresies*? "That's fine," I replied, "but Ellen was only in *Heresies* about a year and I worked for twelve years." I called Mary Beth to complain. We talked about enemies and friends. "You can't tell Mary anything." I thought I was making Mary Beth nervous with my stories, so I refrained from mentioning the old conflict with Elsa Honig Fine, who would speak about the *Woman's Art Journal* just before *Heresies*.

The Corcoran conference was not the only occasion to delve into our recent past. Cindy Carr called me to ask about the 1984 Let MoMA Know demonstration. She was writing an article on Guerrilla Girls. The Guerrilla Girls had named that demonstration as the pivotal action that had led to their formation. Someone said I had organized it. There were three of us organizers,

36. *Bea is 60*, flier to benefit *Kitchen Table: Women of Color Press* 37. Willie Birch, *Wake Up*

including me, Betsy Damon, and Annie Shaver-Crandell. I named all three and told Cindy about the slogans, the boxes with ribbons and names, and the *Model MoMA* I had kept stored in my studio. "They should go to some archive."

Arlene Raven was bringing a group she called her "ladies" for a studio visit; they would also visit the lofts of Carol Sun and Linda Peer. I had followed Ora's advice and called her during my show. Nine elegant women, some dressed in furs, filed into our loft. Sunday Dog was banished to the bedroom; she protested by furiously scratching the door. "Sabra's work is all about the place she comes from; it relates to a specific place in Texas and it's made here, in New York, in another place." She asked me to comment; I could hear that the dog was shredding the door. I went through a quick time line—the splits in my family due to the Civil War, the two types of farming, my being able to see both sides of my family's cultural divide, the sad towns my parents chose in place of the farms, my preference for the country, my grandmothers' quilting, and how I left Texas and went to Africa. "I was either going to graduate school or join the Peace Corps," I explained. Arlene added in response to my story, "I still want to go to the Peace Corps." We moved over to look at *Lillie's Peaks*. "Many people work with these materials—beads, strings, and sticks—and work with these sorts of 'outsider' ideas and ideas about multiculturalism, but your artwork feels authentic. It's the first time I've seen it done in an authentic way," Arlene commented. "It's the way I worked as a child." She picked up one of the *thirteen houses*. "Look at this . . . I feel like, if I even had one of these in my apartment, it would fill the whole space; it would demand so much attention. I mean this as high praise." She asked how I relate to museums and galleries. "I don't relate well," I thought, "it's why I've had to create all those shows." But I said, "I am obviously not a modernist. The people who relate best to my artwork are so-called minority artists who come from a craft tradition."

38. Sabra Moore, *Running Out of Time: 13 House Count* (all), *Corn* 39. *Cloud* 40. *Deer*

WAC now had a multicultural committee that included many familiar faces: Emma, Jose-ly, Lorraine O'Grady, Patricia, and Linda Cunningham. Laura Flanders and I cochaired the meeting where they presented ideas addressing the lack of diversity. I hesitated to join.

I was working on a small card about the size of a calling card for Ana with one of her *siluetas* printed on both sides and a text in English and Spanish: "We remember Ana Mendieta." I wanted to be ready for our demonstration in late June. Her death remained an open wound for many of us. There had been no real justice, and without justice, there could be no reconciliation. The trial of the St. John's rapist was an example of that. Carl had been able to waive his right to a jury trial, so he never had to face a jury that might have included women and Hispanics. A single white man, like Carl, had decided his fate. Ana's art, her anger, her drinking, and her sense of displacement had all been used against her in the trial. While Carl had been forced to isolate himself after the trial and seldom appeared at openings, his work was still shown in prestigious venues and collected. He had never publicly admitted responsibility for her death or offered re-gret. I thought of Grandmother, who had been marked by the murder of her second husband as if she had caused the violence and abuse of the murderer by leaving him for another.

The Guggenheim was scrambling to contain the damage to its image as their opening date neared. We heard that they had bought some of Louise Bourgeois's sculptures in order to include a woman in the inaugural show. Our outrage had already had an impact. If Ana had be-come an unintended symbol, so had Carl.

The philosophy committee met at Kathryn LaRoche's loft, a whimsical place with a big ladder near the door, decorated like a Christmas tree. WAC was swelling at each meeting with hundreds of women now in attendance. We were debating how to structure the meetings so everyone continued to be heard. I loved the unpredictable power of the whole group in the big

41. Sabra Moore, *Running Out of Time: 13 House Count* (all), *Straw* 42. *Straw* 43. *Continent*

room despite the potential for chaos. Phyllis Kind agreed with me, but others thought we might function better by meeting in smaller groups with one member reporting to the whole. Roma described her own clear vision—all decisions should be made from the floor with temporary groups in authority for specific issues and, perhaps, a pool of elected facilitators that would change every few months.

It was getting warm. I spent an afternoon working in the triangular Pearl Street garden, tying strings to the fence so the wild rose could climb. I wanted to get the garden in order before we left for Abiquiu in July. It was exciting to find buds on the plants. The hollyhocks, honeysuckle, wisteria, clematis, and althea had all wintered over safely. Obie and Barry stopped by; Barry had a pine tree sapling he wanted to plant. I had finished the proposal for the Pyramid Art Center and Lower Manhattan Cultural Council grant with Carol's recommendation. The selection committee was comprised of people I knew, Robbie McCauley, Susana Leval, and Yong Soon Min, opening the door to either hurt or gratification. I planned to send Emma the *Heresies* statement I had read at the Corcoran conference, a storytelling event. Elsa had refused to speak to me.

Sylvia came for dinner; she wanted to select one of my artworks for her burgeoning collection of women's art, but fell asleep after eating as she always did. When Roger went to wash the dishes, Sylvia roused, so we went into my studio to look through my artworks. Sydney Hamburger had come over one afternoon and helped me figure out prices; I was trying to find ways to make sales without feeling robbed. I pulled out small works first, but Sylvia said, "Do you still have that kimono piece?" She was thinking about *Door*, the ozone-hole work I had made in Taos that she had admired at Roger's birthday party. "But it's very expensive." "How much?" "Five thousand dollars." "Well, it's worth it. I assume you would take payments." "Sylvia, I had assumed you would want something small." "Not necessarily. I want an important piece. I like

44. Sylvia Sleigh, *Invitation to a Voyage: The Hudson River at Fishkill* (four panels of 5)

the clothes and this was your first use of wood." We poked around some more. She asked about the wardrobe piece. "It's been hard to get back to it." I still had not painted the interior side with the story of Opal's dead baby. "I'm having trouble getting back to my room," Sylvia said, referring to the *Invitation to a Voyage* series she had been painting when Lawrence had died, "I've needed to be selfish for a while. These trips have helped me immensely." It surprised me that she had given Robert the wonderful *Three Graces* painting I used to pass at the entry to her studio. We gossiped about May. "You're a little wild," she said, meaning I was too much for May's New England rigidity.

I dream that I plunge into a pond wearing my clothes. I know I'll get wet, but I don't seem to get wet. I swim like a porpoise. Then, I navigate a narrow channel, like an irrigation ditch. The water is thick with vegetation and dirt. I turn around and swim back where people are waiting.

Los Angeles was on fire with people rioting after the videotaped beating of Rodney King by police. It was almost Mother's Day, and WAC had galvanized around Artelia's ideas for economic justice. I was making a single-fold flier with collaged flowers surrounding my fist gripping a wadded-up dollar bill; inside were chants and statistics about the failure of millions of men to pay child support. Meika Angleo and her partner, the lawyer Berta Hernandez, were printing three thousand copies. We now had a drum corps with drummers of all ages. Su's concern about the quality of our chants had been amply met by the rock musician Barbara Barg and others. WAC was now "wired"; many of us had no idea what this meant when a group of women in their twenties stood up to announce the creation of a website, attracting a phalanx of young women activists who had not participated in our years of intricate meetings, shows, events, collaborations, arguments, reconciliations, and actions.

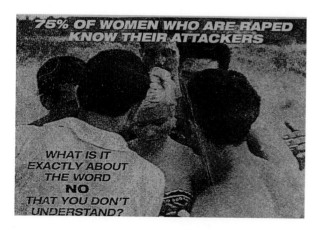 

45. WAC pink card mailed to Judge R. Benjamin Cohen 46. *Can We Get Along Here?*, Rodney King button

Grace Paley and Bea Kreloff came one evening to give us civil disobedience training in anticipation of the various marches being planned for the national conventions. A group was going to the Republican National Convention in Houston and planning an action called "Women Ignite." The Democrats were meeting in New York, and WAC would be there too. I ran into May; she had asked me to recommend her for a residency at the Wurlitzer. "Are you going to Taos soon?" "No, we didn't like him [Henry]; he's too rich, and the place is too small." "Did you cancel? Someone else may want to go." "I never thought of doing that." The room was packed as Grace spoke. Suddenly, a small yellow warbler flew into the room, circling in ever widening arcs. A hum of reaction followed the bird. I hurried to the back of the room and climbed a ladder; I had caught birds before. Annie Philbin, the director of the Drawing Center, and Ana Blum rushed back with me, all of us trying to catch the bird. The warbler flew into the back hall, frantic to find an exit. I raised my cupped hands and caught it, feeling the soft burr of its wings against my palms. We three ran outside, closing the door, and released it at the base of a tree. It lay there exhausted, and then opened its eyes and bolted off. "You saved the bird!" "Oh, these Mother Earths, I'm not surprised," Linda Matalon told Annie later.

We assembled in the big rotunda at Grand Central Station on the Friday before Mother's Day, armed with our fliers. Ana Blum and three other agile women had managed to climb onto the narrow rail walkway above the ticket windows without attracting notice. Drumming would be their signal to unfurl a huge pink banner reading: "30 Billion Dollars Owed to Mothers." When the drums echoed throughout the cavernous chamber, we started dancing, chanting, and waving dollar bills. Commuters reached out eagerly for the fliers; our action an asterisk across the rush for trains. "Mom's in a rage/We want a living wage/We took it to the courts/But still there's no support," we chanted. Police soon poured into the room, but it took them a while to find an officer

47. Susanna Cuyler flier, *Patriarchy's Demolition: A Year of WACtion* 48. Sabra, Artelia, and India at a WAC demonstration

adept enough at scaling the wall to make the women lower the banner. It was embarrassing for the police to take a stand against mothers, especially since one of the drummers was visibly pregnant, but they made us leave the building. We reassembled outside; our energy level was high. We kept drumming and chanting until the four women who had been detained reappeared with a court summons in hand; they unfurled the banner along the sidewalk. The television crews arrived as we were leaving. One of the cops watching us said, "Get back together, the television is here." But we didn't. "It wouldn't be good. We've dispersed; we can't make it up for the cameras."

I dream that a new landlord has bought our Pearl Street building. He is going to make a kind of corporate garden in place of my pretty triangular one. It's night. I watch him cut down a big palm tree I have planted and then he cuts a smaller flowering tree. I feel wounded and distraught. I am trying to plead my case to a court, begging him to not uproot my garden.

Patricia and I sometimes facilitated meetings as a team. It was nice to work together after our years of collaboration at *Heresies*. Sometimes, it felt like every possible cause was represented at these gatherings. One night, Geraldine Ferraro and Liz Holtzman, both candidates for United States Senator, came to make short presentations. Then, a blond, heavyset policewoman from Gulfport, Mississippi, appeared to tell her story; she had blown the whistle on police brutality. She was afraid her fellow police officers would retaliate: "They're going to kill me!" Women firefighters from the Fire Department of New York City came to present their grievances. There was another argument about pornography and censorship. The multicultural committee and the lesbian coalition made their reports. We debated whether or not to allow photography and filming at the meetings. Kate Millet stood up and said, "This is a meeting of eagles." A woman from La Madre declared, "It's been years since I've been in a room with such political energy."

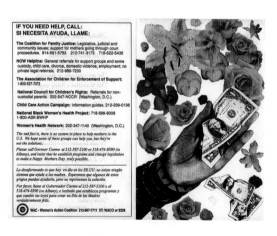

49-50. Flier designed by Sabra Moore for *WAC Mother's Day Action* at Grand Central Station

Patricia and I were exhausted when the meeting ended; we went out for coffee to wind down. "I was scared going into that meeting," she told me. "That was a damned difficult meeting; you did a fantastic job!" "So did you! We let everyone be heard, but I don't think we resolved anything." "There's nothing like a Southern woman who's made up her mind," Patricia said, referring to the Gulfport policewomen. Patricia was from Arkansas; she and the drummer, Barbara Barg, who was twenty years younger than Patricia, had gone to the same high school. The next day, Barbara Yoshida called me to talk about the meeting; she thought we had handled it well. I called Betsy and left a message. "Patricia can't facilitate next week and, obviously, I won't be doing it again so soon." We had some suggestions for facilitators. There was a message when I got home from work. "I've had so many complaints about how bad the meetings have been; Linda Matalan and I are going to do it." "Two little slaps on the back and then one on the front," I wrote in my journal.

I noticed a man in the subway as we both entered the car one evening coming home. He was a light-skinned black man in his sixties dressed in khaki like a workman. There was something familiar about his face and his full mustache; I couldn't place what attracted me. I glanced at his hands and saw a broad gold band on his index finger; it was not the milky cat's eye ring C used to wear. I got up and moved towards the door, exiting at the next stop to wait for another train. How strange that I wasn't sure, but it made me uneasy.

Choice Histories was opening at Artists Space. I only invited Ora and Sydney, but the room was full of friends from WAC and REPOhistory. Janet Henry and Janet Goldner were there from the multicultural committee. Tomie Arai invited us to her show at the Alternative Museum. We had built a big table with drawers filled with artworks that could be pulled out that was similar to the ones in the old installation at the National Museum of the American Indian with small glass-topped oak drawers that you could open, revealing stunning artifacts. Ours were a bit

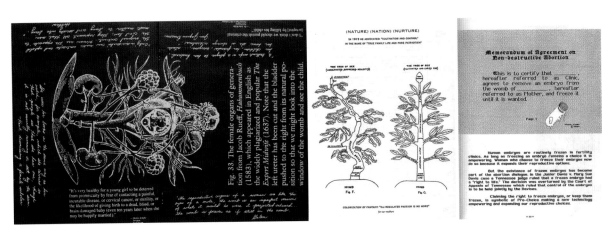

51. *Choice Histories Chronology*, Todd Ayoung/Megan Pugh 52. *Chronology*, Sarah Vogwill, Flash Light

rougher; each drawer secreted hidden stories and images. I had made a drawer that opened by grasping a painted mannequin's hand. It contained a sewn cloth calendar related to my abortion in Guinea and a hot pad shaped like a glove telling Opal's story through text and laser transfer prints. There was an illustrated timeline along the table and other objects. The filmmaker Lisa Maya Knauer made a video for this exhibit and had asked me to talk about my experiences working at the abortion clinic. She had read my interview in *Heresies*. I had not mentioned my own abortion, but, suddenly, I was telling that story as well. I was astonished to find myself crying without relief as Lisa kept filming. Her three-part video was running from a monitor on the wall during the opening. She had paired my interview with a woman reading an Audre Lorde text and another woman whose story was similar to mine. Ayisha asked Lisa about my crying. Had I been acting? No, I was ambushed by raw emotions the moment I mentioned that day in Kankan when I went alone to find the Czech doctor and thought I might die.

Antiabortion activists were trying to block patients' access to Eastern Women's Services and had organized a march from a nearby Catholic church to the clinic. WAC organized a counter demonstration. I usually resent the massive police presence at marches, but, this time, I was glad for the barriers separating our two groups. A deep rage engulfed me as I stood with others chanting against the rows of men gesturing towards us with their crosses and rosaries as if our bodies were unclean. In their eyes, we were murderers; their signs grotesquely magnified aborted fetuses. The painter Elizabeth Murray, normally quiet and gentle, was standing next to me. "I felt like punching them in the face; I had to control my anger," I said, tears stinging my cheeks. "So did I; everyone felt that. I wanted to snatch that man off the cross and be done with it."

53. Sabra Moore, artworks for *Choice Histories: Framing Abortion* (all), *Calendar* 54. *Hot Pads with Opal Story, Calendar*

I was worried about money; this year, I hadn't been offered any big projects, but I was doing many small jobs: the calendars, Marshall De Bruhl's book, *A Life of Sam Houston*, with Random House, and a few book covers for Peter. I kept running into Fred; he seemed apologetic. Sylvia's purchase of *Door* would save us for the summer; we had applied for a building loan from a bank in Española.

I had sent my slides to Jeannette Ingberman at Exit Art, following Willie's advice. I ran into her at another WAC action. "I've had your slides for weeks; I haven't looked at them." "We're leaving in a week and will be gone for three months." "Call me when you get back, and I'll make a studio visit." Someone said, "Hi!" I turned around; it was Lucy, just back from her spring teaching at Boulder. She had been visiting Harmony in Galisteo and may have found land nearby. We hugged and wandered over to see the *Choice Histories* show. Patricia was there. She had been elected as one of the facilitators; I had encouraged her to run. WAC had adopted Roma's idea. All of the chosen facilitators were members of the multicultural committee—Tracy Gossolu, Janet Henry, Joy Silverman, Patricia, Laura Flanders, and Linda Matalan. Betsy had withdrawn her name; I wasn't elected. Patricia said, "We think it's not the multicultural committee anymore; it's the leadership committee."

I dream that Roger and I are in a big field. I see two white deer, a fawn and very small doe. I say, "Look at those deer." He says, "Look at that deer." A huge white buck is trotting towards us. I try to avert my eyes and turn slightly to block his attention, but he trots right over to me and starts licking my hand.

Mark O'Brien was curating *Homeplace*, a show for Henry Street Settlement on the theme of home. He knew my work from REPOhistory and came to my studio. Mark's blue eyes never looked quite at you, always focusing a bit to the side, but he looked carefully at my artworks.

55. *Operation Rescue* action flier 56. WAC cloth banner 57. *Homeplace* exhibit card, Mark O'Brien curator

He felt that my sculptures were "intense and obsessive" and "one" with the concept of nature as a home. "They're not separate ideas as people think here." He wanted to interview me for a video for *Homeplace*, but we were leaving in a week. Another day, Xiu Yuan Lu, an anthropologist from Beijing, came to interview me about *Heresies*—a happy reversal of the usual "first world" anthropological gaze.

Guerrilla Girls had printed white paper bags with gorilla faces for us to wear as hats at the Guggenheim demonstration. They were small for our heads; we looked like medieval bakers marching around, but everyone chose to wear them. Roger came with me to photograph. We gathered first at the back of the new museum. I had a stack of Ana's cards in my purse and passed some out to Barbara Yoshida, Edith, Linda, Meika, and other friends nearby. Then, Josely and Janet appeared hoisting a beautifully printed banner with Ana's repeated face and the words, "Carl is in the Guggenheim/Where is Ana Mendieta?" We started chanting, "Where is Ana?/Ask Carl/Where is Ana?/Ask Carl." The police started massing and placing more serious barricades as our numbers grew. I gave some more cards to Josely. Richly dressed people were passing the barricades to go inside—some defiant and some hurrying past with sheepish faces. I looked around and saw Lucy. Then, we heard the drums approaching from a narrow side street, the sound echoing against the brick facades. The beat was somber and measured. The drummers were all wearing dark glasses and T-shirts with Ana's face printed on the front. We become silent. The dirge built. The drummers formed a circle in front of the barricades and starting a wailing chant: "a-n-a-a-a-n-a-n-a-a-n-a-a-n-a." We joined and repeated the wail, evoking her spirit. Then, the drums grew angry and we grew angry; the police grew tense. I looked for Lucy. To her credit, she stayed outside, leaning against a car. Her ex-husband, Robert Ryman, was in the show; her son, Ethan, was going to the opening. She told him she was going to the

58. Sandra Lee-Phipps, WAC demonstration, Downtown Guggenheim 59.-60. *Guerrilla Girls sack*, both sides

demonstration. We started chanting against people entering the show. "Shame! Don't go in!" Robert Rauschenberg pushed past us and went inside. Then, some WAC activists went inside, carrying my cards and fliers with Ana's face. Ela Blum was inside, watching us from the big glass façade; Betsy was taking notes like a girl reporter, making faces at us on the street and rolling her eyes. Josely came over to ask me for more cards: she and Joy Silverman went in. "Carl's work is covered with her images and everyone is guarding it, not letting them touch the cards." Lucy turned to me, "What are they doing?" Reluctantly, I said, "They're dropping my cards on Carl's work." I gave her my last card. "I'll save this and keep it in my archive. I try to save things so people will know what we've done." Lorraine O'Grady and I tried to go inside, holding hands; people cheered as we mounted the steps. The guards wouldn't let us past. Leo Castelli came out; we whistled and shouted at him, but he was undisturbed. He turned and gestured towards us like the pope. Artelia and I went around to the front Broadway entrance. People had started gathering there, chanting loudly. Our good lawyer, Berta, was at the barricades, trying to keep us on the sidewalks. "No arrests." "We have passed a threshold," Artelia said, "we no longer have to prove ourselves; there is only confidence and anger left." I saw Josely. "Your cards were great; you can see them after they fall. Everyone was stooping to pick them up." Louise Bourgeois passed us accompanied by her tall studio assistant, his dreadlocks covered with a cap. She was in the show. I raised my fist and smiled at her. She smiled back and raised her fist; the undiminished militancy of a stalwart eighty-year-old woman.

We had one more parade to attend, and then we headed the next day for Abiquiu. We had found two women to sublet our loft—a glamorous Russian mother/daughter pair. I felt a bit uneasy. Barbara Pollack had told me, "You're going to be famous." The *New York Times* might be printing a photo of my Pearl Street sign for an article about the Lower Manhattan Sign Project.

61. Sandra Lee-Phipps, WAC action 62. Ana Mendieta, *El Laberinto de Venus* 63. Sandra Lee-Phipps, WAC action

Our signs were finally installed and REPOhistory was celebrating with a history parade replete with performers. I had sewn a shell garment to wear, tying a hundred shells cut out of opalescent plastic mesh onto a flimsy beige cloth that looked like an African robe. My sign's photo didn't appear in the newspaper, but it didn't matter. I was still feeling buoyed by the intense solidarity of the Guggenheim demonstration. I marched next to Leela Ramotar and Ayisha Abraham. We chanted, "What is history? Whose history is it?" as we passed by each sign. The performers answered with various responses—sometimes reading texts and sometimes dancing or acting out parts of the stories printed on each sign. It felt like a people's circus. Marithelma and Fabio joined Roger. "I couldn't understand what REPOhistory was," Marithelma said, "it's great." At my sign for Pearl Street, the dancer Yekk pranced like a deer, miming "sacred symbols" and "walk softly." Ayisha turned to me, "Do you have Indian heritage?" "Yes, some." "I've always wondered. You can see it." Lucy was giving a REPOhistory party that evening, but we had promised to go with Sylvia to eat with Catherine Stimpson and Liz Wood at their house on Staten Island. "We had looked forward to laughing with you," Marina and Willie said. We hugged goodbye. I fell asleep in the truck after we drove Sylvia home.

64. Lower Manhattan Sign Project (all), Sabra with Ayisha Abraham 65-66. Pearl Street sign 67. Shell robe

Epilogue

I have recently flown twice to New York City; the plane banks as it ascends along the jagged ridge of Sandia Peak near Albuquerque. The Spanish settlers saw the ragged edge as a bitten slice of watermelon in the pink glow of sunset, but the Pueblo people mark this peak as one of the four sacred boundaries. It is the sentinel that marks the way home for me now as well.

I traveled to be with two friends who were dying—the first trip was a promise to Frankie Buschke that I would return to New Mexico with her ashes and bury them on our land in Abiquiu. I also returned with boxes of her layered and singed artworks, which I rescued with another friend from the chaos of her Brooklyn apartment. The second trip was to sit with Sylvia Sleigh as she died peacefully at home. Sylvia was ninety-four and had continued to paint until she fell down in her sitting room from a stroke two weeks earlier. The Museum of Modern Art (MoMA) had just arranged to purchase her 1977 painting of the women in A.I.R. Gallery, confirming again Alice Neel's advice that women artists need to live long lives, success comes late. Five of us were with her as she died, lightly touching her arms, her hands, and her soft hair. Sylvia's neighbor down the block, Louise Bourgeois, had died a few months earlier; Nancy Spero, the previous winter. It had been many years since any of us had pinned Nancy's work to a gallery wall with push pins.

 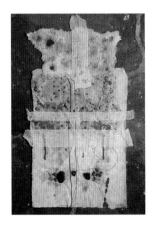 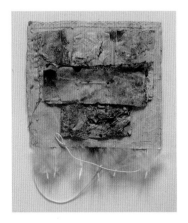

1. Sylvia Sleigh, *A.I.R Group Portrait*. 2. Frances Buschke, *Untitled* 3. Frances Buschke, *Untitled*

Heresies published its last issue, Latina, in 1993. In the four years after Kay's embezzlement, only three issues were published, including Art of Education and IdiomA. The magazine won the lawsuit, *Heresies v. Kenny, et al.*, in June of that same year. Kay was forced to return most of the money she had taken; she had already returned materials for the Women on Men issue. That issue was still listed as "upcoming" in Latina, but it was never published; the format change stayed as an idea only. Our lawyers, Arlene Boop and Daniel Alterman, waived their $21,000 accumulated legal fees "to protect and preserve the integrity of the Collective." *Heresies* folded shortly afterwards.

In the winter of 1995, our Pearl Street landlord destroyed the pocket flower garden I had nurtured next to the Manhattan Bridge, coming in the night with a dumpster and scraping the lot clean. Our friend, Obie, called me in Abiquiu where Roger and I were working on finishing our house. I returned before the landlord had covered the site with asphalt, just in time to dig up the bones of my three cats for reburial in New Mexico. I located them from the stumps of Sylvia's wisteria vine, Ora's wild rose bush, and Mother's althea. The following winter, we moved to New Mexico full time, leaving New York City on a cold rainy day in December. I was crying as we finished packing the two moving vans we were driving. "Isn't this a terrible time to be moving?" I said to a neighbor, standing in the gray light between the stone bridge buttresses that framed our street. "Look at it this way. Isn't this a great time to be leaving New York?" I didn't dream until we reached Oklahoma; my hands still aching from the labor of tying and packing.

I dream that I am in a deserted department store, carrying a heavy package. I find the store archaeologist and hand the box to him. Then, I mount a huge metal horse, shiny and silver, and lower my head as I depart through an improbably narrow door, riding on its wide back.

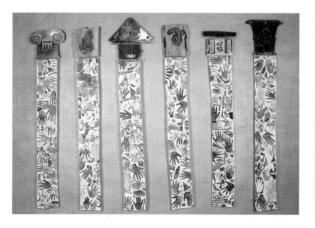  

4. Sabra Moore (all), *Palm Trees with Capitals* 5. *Palm Trees* (detail) 6. *Palm Trees* (detail)

A few years ago, Joan Bradermann came out to film former *Heresies* collective members living in New Mexico for her documentary, *The Heretics*. May and I rehashed the same argument about founders and followers until Joan agreed to expand her concept beyond the founding members to include Emma Amos, Cecilia Vicuña, Sue Heinemann, me, and a few others who had nurtured the magazine over its seventeen years of publication.

We are all working, our lives spiraling out from our collective experience to find our many points of true north. I have been making sculptures in the shape of boats, echoing Candace Hill-Montgomery's landlocked yacht moored inside a tightly fenced backyard in the Bronx as a symbol of hope. I recently installed a five-piece artwork called *Palm Trees* for a museum show in Taos; each eight-foot wooden post is engraved with the wood-burned palm prints drawn from the photocopied hands of eighty-two friends, my quixotic forest of support. My artwork is still centered on our flawed relationship to nature and my efforts to make hidden stories visible.

I have worked with farmers for the past sixteen years, managing the Española Farmers' Market. Each year, we host a Biggest Vegetable & Best Poem Contest, and I make a postcard and artist's book with children's poetry that I distribute for free. "Would you call your work with the farmers a form of art?" someone asked. "The growers certainly wouldn't call it art." My postcards made them visible and helped us secure funding for a permanent site. Now, we have a shaded market plaza, a community flower garden, and fields for planting vegetables. One winter, I hosted a season's end potluck and invited the farmers to visit my studio. Nicolas Romero, who grows sugar beets in a nearby mountain village, was looking at *A Warhead Doesn't Have a Heart*, an eight-foot sculpture I had made in response to the Iraq War. It is shaped like a tipi with forty small paintings sewn with wire inside its conical structure. "Sabra, do you make this just for pretty?"

7. Sabra Moore (all), Sabra installing *Three Boats*, Santa Fe Roundhouse 8. *We Are All in the Same Boat*

Lucy and I still talk about *Heresies* and its dissolution. "I used to have an art community," she said. Something ended and other things began, but the residue of what we tried to do together remains as a thorn and a seed. Greg Sholette recently came to visit with Lucy and her partner Jim Farris. I had not seen Greg since the REPOhistory parade. We stood outside talking, looking across the canyon as the light turned the cliffs golden. "After *Committed to Print*," Greg said, "we thought things would just keep going, but the art world took a different turn."

Many of us are working as artists in our communities. Marina has directed the Saturday program at Cooper Union for minority high school students since I first saw her clothesline work at the Arsenal in Brooklyn. Lucy still combines social activism with her rapidly multiplying books and lectures. She recently published a land-based history of the Tano culture in Galisteo where she lives; my drawings of petroglyphs dot the margins. Harmony has retired from teaching in Arizona and works full time in her studio near Lucy's place. Janet Goldner has deepened her ties to Africa and works in Mali for part of each year. She was in a group show I organized in 2008 at gallery onetwentyeight, the Rivington Street venue that Kazuko still directs. Janet called this women's exhibition "an old timey" project. Howardena and I discuss chickens when we talk on the phone; she teaches art at State University of New York at Purchase. Gertrude is in her eighties and still lives in Houston, making her welded gates and installations. Cecilia recently sent me photos from her video of red cloth lines undulating in the ocean waves that was included in a drawing exhibition at MoMA. Bibi teaches art to children in Manhattan and was planning a visit with Sylvia to select paintings for a show on the day of her stroke. I make painted tile mosaics with children in the Española Public School District, leaving glistening patterns on the exterior walls of the schools. Marilyn lives in San Antonio and continues to make installations about her kin; she found lightning stones on our land during one of her many visits. Faith is famous; her

9. Sabra working on *Carreta Boat* 10. Sabra Moore, *A Warhead Doesn't Have a Heart* (detail)

story quilts hang in many museums. May is famous too. You can visit her 1974 painting *The Artist's Studio (After Courbet)* at the University of Missouri and see the young May in front of one of her *Big Daddy* paintings. Sylvia, Lawrence, Rudolf, Nancy, and Leon cluster nearby, each frozen in introspection. Ora died unexpectedly in 1997 while recovering from surgery in her Westbeth loft the same week my book of petroglyph drawings was published. Patricia still lives in Brooklyn writing poetry. Lamidi was named a UNESCO Living Human Treasure in 2006. Obie died of HIV-related lymphoma a few years after our move; he was buried in an unmarked grave in New York City's potter's field on Hart Island. I keep his silver miniature teapot near a plateful of potshards in our house. Catalina moved to Argentina as cultural attaché for Chile when the Pinochet regime was replaced by democracy. She started studying tango.

The personal is political.

Mother died just before dawn on Mother's Day in 2009, a few weeks past her ninetieth birthday. In her old age, she suffered from the same afflictions as her mother, spending her last four years in a nursing home severely brain damaged from repeated strokes. She gave her house and all its contents to my nephews; I received nothing. She dunned me in her will for the money she had given us when we were building our house. My sister Nancy abruptly presented me with all the show cards, catalogues, and reviews that Mother had carefully preserved, but she kept my artworks for her sons. I last saw Mother on her ninetieth birthday, and we sang together the song she had sung to me in childhood, "Let Me Call You Sweetheart, I'm in Love with You." I brought her a birthday present, but she said in her halting intonation, "You . . . are . . . my . . . best . . . present." She asked to be buried with the ring I gave her. I agreed.

The political is personal.

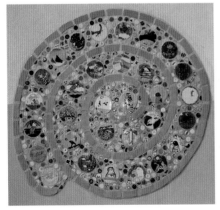

11.-12. Sabra Moore, mosaics with elementary school students (all), *Eagle/Bird* (details), El Rito 13. *Leopard/Sunflower*, Alcalde

Endnotes

Chapter 1

1. Henri Ghent, "An Experiment Thrives in Brooklyn," *ART Gallery Magazine* (April 1970): 52–55.
2. Robert Frost, "The Death of the Hired Man," in *North of Boston* (New York: Henry Holt and Company, 1915), lines 122–3.
3. Yippies were members of the Youth International Party.
4. The Chicago Eight were anti-Vietnam War protestors indicted for conspiracy to disrupt the Democratic Convention in Chicago in August 1968 and included David T. Dellinger, Rennard C. Davis, Thomas E. Hayden, Abbot H. Hoffman, Jerry C. Rubin, Lee Weiner, John R. Froines, and Bobby G. Seale.
5. Lucy R. Lippard, "Changing since *Changing*," in *The Pink Glass Swan: Selected Feminist Essays on Art* (New York: The New Press, 1995), 34–5.
6. Weather Underground, known colloquially as the Weathermen, was formed in 1969 when activists formerly associated with Students for Democratic Society (SDS) tired of peaceful demonstrations as a method for ending the Vietnam War and changing the political situation in America. Those who wanted direct action, including violent direct action with bombings of government buildings and banks, chose to go underground. The name Weatherman comes from Bob Dylan's lyric, "You don't need a weatherman to know which way the wind blows," from the song "Subterranean Homesick Blues."
7. The forest people in Guinea were called Guerzé, a tribal name written as Kpelle in English.
8. Criticism/self-criticism was a technique adapted by many women's groups from poorly understood practices in the Chinese Cultural Revolution. The intent was to insure that every woman in the group have an opportunity to speak. At the end of a meeting, someone could suggest that we do criticism/self-criticism and each member of the group would then evaluate in turn the effectiveness of the meeting and offer criticism if appropriate.
9. Lucy R. Lippard, "A Note on the Politics and Aesthetics of a Women's Show," in *Women Choose Women* (New York: The New York Cultural Center, 1973), 7.

Chapter 2

1. Barbara Zucker, "Making A.I.R," *Heresies* 2, no. 3 (1978): 81.

Chapter 3

1. Colette, *The Collected Stories of Colette*, ed. Robert Phelps (New York: Farrar, Strauss & Giroux, 1983).
2. Hilton Kramer, "Does Feminism Conflict with Artistic Standards?" *New York Times*, January 27, 1980.
3. Vivien Raynor, "Art: Rosalind Browne, a Feminist Lesson," *New York Times*, March 6, 1981.
4. Mel Watkins, "James Baldwin Writing and Talking," *New York Times Book Review*, September 23, 1979.

Chapter 4

1. Yukio Yashiro, *2,000 Years of Japanese Art* (New York: Harry N. Abrams, Inc., 1958), 26.
2. Sabra Moore, "A Note about the Shows," *Views by Women Artists* (New York: New York Chapter of the Women's Caucus for Art, 1983), 3. Exhibition catalogue.
3. Elsa Honig Fine, "On Point Perspective," *Women's Art Journal* 3, no. 1 (1983): ii.
4. Samuel Noah Kramer, *The Sumerians: Their History, Culture, and Character* (Chicago: University of Chicago Press, 1963), 79.

5. Lucy Lippard, *Events* (New York: The New Museum, 1983), 26. Exhibition catalogue.
6. Lucy Lippard, *All's Fair: Love & War in New Feminist Art* (Columbus, Ohio State University, 1983). Exhibition catalogue.

Chapter 5

1. Daisy Zamora, "I Had to Break with All That. . . By Going to Fight," interviewed by Margaret Randall, *Heresies* 4, no. 1 (1981): 67–70.
2. In 1972, there was a devastating earthquake in Managua, the capital city of Nicaragua, that left thousands homeless and without aid as the US-backed Somoza regime stockpiled earthquake relief funds for its own benefit.
3. Friar Diego de Landa, *Yucatan Before and After the Conquest* (New York: Dover Publications, Inc., 1978), 82.
4. Grace Glueck, "Art: 'Interventions,' on U.S. Latin Role," *New York Times*, February 3, 1984.
5. Ibid.
6. Mary Beth Edelson, "Success Has 1,000 Mothers: Art and Activism," in *Women's Culture in a New Era: A Feminist Revolution*, ed. Gayle Kimball (Lanham, MD: The Scarecrow Press, Inc., 2005), 59.
7. Susan Heller Anderson and David Bird, "Protest at the Modern for More Women's Art," *New York Times*, June 15, 1984.
8. Gerald Marzorati, "Your Show of Shows," *ARTnews*, September 1984, 65.

Chapter 6

1. Melinda Wortz, *1 + 1 = 2* (New York: Bernice Steinbaum Gallery, 1984), 7. Exhibition catalogue.

Chapter 7

1. Ronald Sullivan, "Greenwich Village Sculptor Acquitted of Pushing Wife to Her Death," *New York Times*, February 12, 1988.

Chapter 8

1. Sarah Williamson, "Reconstruction Project," *Women Artists News* 9, no. 4 (1984): 8–9.

Illustration Notes and Photo Credits

Cover

Sabra walking past her window installation, *Gladys Apron*, Windows on White, New York City, 1985. Photo Credit: Roger Mignon

Frontispiece

Opening of Sabra's window installation, *House Dress/ Gladys Story*, 1984, with Frankie Buschke talking inside Printed Matter Inc. and Sabra outside laughing, 1984, black-and-white photo, 8 x 10 in. Photo Credit: Roger Mignon

Facing Table of Contents

Sabra working on a pastel, circa 1979, in her Warren Street studio in Brooklyn, color photograph, 8 x 10 in. Photo Credit: Courtesy of Sabra Moore

Facing Foreword/ Lippard

Artists gathering at *Heresies* benefit exhibit, *Issues That Won't Go Away*, PPOW Gallery, 1987, to read dedications honoring Lucy R. Lippard, 1987, black-and-white photo, 8 x 10 in. Photo Credit: Roger Mignon

Facing Foreword/ Randall

Activists with Women's Action Coalition (WAC) and Guerrilla Girls demonstrate against the opening of the Downtown Guggenheim, 1992, black-and-white photo. Photo Credit: Sandra Lee-Phipps

Facing Preface

Sylvia Sleigh, *Sabra Moore: My Ceres*, 1982, oil on canvas, 36 in. diameter. Photo Credit: Sylvia Sleigh

Preface

1. Caroline Moore, *door stop doll*, circa 1950, gourd, bottle, nylon stocking, doll dress, field cotton, 14 ½ in., width varies. Photo Credit: Sabra Moore

2. Mimi Smith, *Knit Baby*, 1968, yarn, undershirt, thread, 21 x 10 x 4 in. Photo Credit: Mimi Smith
3. Zarina Hashmi, *Untitled*, undated, 11 x 8 ½ in. One of ten woodcuts reproduced in Hashmi's artist's book illustrating ten proverbs from *101 Urdu Proverbs* with proverbs translated by Rani Kishwar Chishti. Photo Credit: Zarina Hashmi
4. Guerzé gris-gris, N'Zérékoré, Guinea, circa 1965, wood, 5 ⅛ x 2 ⅞ in., depth varies. Photo Credit: Sabra Moore
5. Malekeh Nayiny, *Mask*, 1980, Atlantic Gallery exhibit card, 5 ½ x 8 in. Photo Credit: Malekeh Nayiny
6. Emma Amos, *Will You Forget Me?*, 1991, acrylic on canvas with African fabric borders, 64 x 33 in. Photo Credit: ©Emma Amos, Licensed by VAGA, New York, NY/photo by Becket Logan
7. Vivian E. Browne, *Benin Equestrian*, 1973, acrylic on canvas. Photo Credit: Estate of Vivian E. Browne/ Courtesy of Adobe Krow Archives
8. Ora Lerman, *Make a Wish, If Birthday Boxes Only Bore New Persona*, 1975–1976, hand-ground oil on canvas, 30 x 40 in. Photo Credit: Ora Lerman Charitable Trust/ photo by Malcolm Varon
9. Sabra inside Printed Matter with *House Dress/Gladys Story* window installation, 1984. Photo Credit: Roger Mignon

Chapter 1

Sabra Moore, colored pencil drawings, 1964–1966 (all). 1. *A Neighbor*, 11 ⅞ x 8 ⅞ in. 2. *Cows in the Yard*, 8 ⅞ x 8 ¾ in. 3. *Forest near N'Zérékoré*, 7 ¾ x 6 in. Photo Credit: Sabra Moore
4. *African-American Artists: Since 1950*, Brooklyn College catalogue cover with Romare Beardon painting. Photo Credit: Collection of Sabra Moore
5. January 24–30, 1969 cover of *RAT* with illustration by Driggs, newsprint, 17 x 11 ½ in. Photo Credit: ©1969 RAT: Subterranean News, art by Driggs/ Collection of Sabra Moore
6. *Museum* magazine's first year issue, 1970. Photo Credit: Courtesy of Sabra Moore New York City Women's Art Movement Archive, Barnard College
7. Sabra Moore, *Squeezed?*, 1969, photocopy, 11 x 8 ½ in. Antiwar flier made for Fifth Avenue Vietnam Peace Parade Committee. Photo Credit: Sabra Moore/ Courtesy

of Sabra Moore New York City Women's Art Movement Archive, Barnard College

8. Sabra Moore, *Imperialism Sucks*, 1969, silkscreen, 35 x 23 in. Poster made for Fifth Avenue Vietnam Peace Parade Committee for the 1969 March on Washington, DC. Photo Credit: Sabra Moore/ Courtesy of Sabra Moore New York City Women's Art Movement Archive, Barnard College

9. Sabra Moore, *RAT* cover, Chicago Conspiracy, 3/28/1969, newsprint, 17 x 11 ½ in. Photo Credit: Sabra Moore/ Courtesy of Sabra Moore New York City Women's Art Movement Archive, Barnard College

10. Anonymous flier for Kunstler/Kennedy event, photocopy, 11 x 8 ½ in. Photo Credit: Courtesy of Sabra Moore New York City Women's Art Movement Archive, Barnard College

11. Art Workers' Coalition and Peter Brandt, *And Babies? And Babies*, 1970, color photo, offset poster, 25 x 38 in. Photo by © R. L. Haeberle. The quote is taken from an interview with Paul Meadlo by Mike Wallace. Photo Credit: Courtesy of Sabra Moore New York City Women's Art Movement Archive, Barnard College

12. Faith Ringgold, *The Flag is Bleeding*, 1967, oil on canvas, 72 x 46 in. Photo Credit: Faith Ringgold © 1967, Collection of Artist/ACA Galleries, NYC

13. Nancy Spero, *Artaud Painting—Me, Antonin Artaud, born September 4, 1886*, 1969, cut-and-pasted paper, gouache, and ink on paper, 25 x 19 ¾ in. Photo Credit: ©The Nancy Spero and Leon Golub Foundation for the Arts Licensed by VAGA, New York/ Courtesy Galerie Lelong, New York

14. Black-and-white photo of Catalina Parra in Germany, circa 1970s. Photo Credit: Courtesy of Catalina Parra

15. Sylvia Sleigh, *Philip Golub Reclining*, 1971, oil on canvas, 42 x 60 in. Photo Credit: Estate of Sylvia Sleigh/ Private collection, Dallas, TX

16. WAC protest honoring Ana Mendieta and against the inclusion of Carl Andre in the inaugural exhibit of the Downtown Guggenheim, 1992. Photo Credit: Sandra Lee-Phipps

17. Anonymous WAR leaflet, *Museums Are Sexist!*, circa 1970, photocopy, 11 x 8 ½ in. Photo Credit: Courtesy of Sabra Moore New York City Women's Art Movement Archive, Barnard College

18. Jacqueline Wray, *Views by Women Artists* cover design, 1982, 8 ½ x 11 in. Photo Credit: Courtesy of Sabra Moore New York City Women's Art Movement Archive, Barnard College

19. Anonymous WAR leaflet, *You Trust Your Mother But. . .*, circa 1970, photocopy, 11 x 8 ½ in. Photo Credit: Courtesy of Sabra Moore New York City Women's Art Movement Archive, Barnard College

20. Anonymous, *button*. Photo Credit: Collection of Sabra Moore

21. Call for demonstration against MoMA, 1972, photocopy with red stamp, 14 x 8 ½ in. Photo Credit: Courtesy of Sabra Moore New York City Women's Art Movement Archive, Barnard College

22. *Kate Millett Reads*, offset poster, design by Rachel Ackerman Late Night Fantasy Graphics, 17 x 11 in. Reading a benefit for sister artist at Rachael Ackerman's studio. Photo Credit: Courtesy of Sabra Moore New York City Women's Art Movement Archive, Barnard College

23. Kate Millet, *Madhouse, Madhouse*, 1989, photo offset, 11 x 8 ½ in. Page art for *Heresies* issue #24: 12 Years, page 14. Photo Credit: Kate Millet

24. Poster for Pratt Faculty Exhibition, photo offset, 11 x 8 ½ in. Photo Credit: Courtesy of Sabra Moore New York City Women's Art Movement Archive, Barnard College

25. *Women's Open Art Show*, Women's Interart Center, 1972, photocopy, 11 x 8 ½ in. Photo Credit: Courtesy of Sabra Moore New York City Women's Art Movement Archive, Barnard College

26. Lamidi Fakeyeh, black-and-white photo of Sabra next to Lamidi's carved doors for the Catholic church in Ibadan, Nigeria, 1965, 5 ¾ x 5 ⅝ in. Photo Credit: Lamidi Fakeye/ Collection of Sabra Moore

27. Demonstration in N'Zérékoré, Guinea, in support of the Union of African States, snapshot. Photo Credit: Sabra Moore

28. Traoré Sekou, drawing of a *niamou*, circa 1965, color pencil on paper, 11 x 8 ½ in. Photo Credit: Collection of Sabra Moore

29. Sabra Moore, *Untitled*, drawing of ibeji, circa 1965, blue ink on paper, 11 ¾ x 9 in. Photo Credit: Sabra Moore

30. Sabra Moore, *Untitled*, drawing of Guerzé mask, circa 1965, black ink on paper, 9 x 11 ¾ in. Photo Credit: Sabra Moore

31. Sabra Moore, *Untitled*, drawing of ibeji, circa 1965, blue ink on paper, 11 ¾ x 9 in. Photo Credit: Sabra Moore

32. Marta Maria Perez, *To Conceive/Para Concebir*, detail from a three-page text and photo article that included some of the photos Perez made between 1985 and 1986 exploring superstitions and beliefs about conception and motherhood from her native Cuba. The article was published on pages 54–56 of *Heresies* issue #24: 12 Years. Photo Credit: Maria Marta Perez

33. Sabra Moore, *Choice Histories*, photocopier montage page art, 11 x 8 ½ in. From *Choice Histories: Framing Abortion*, an artists' book by REPOhistory produced in conjunction with the collaborative exhibition of the same name, page 31, 1992. Photo Credit: Sabra Moore

34. Kazuko Miyamoto's 1981 installation at Kenkeleba House, *Heresies* issue #14: Women's Pages. Photo Credit: Akira Hagihara/ Courtesy of Kazuko Miyamoto

35. *Choice Histories: Framing Abortion*, cover of an artists' book by REPOhistory in conjunction with exhibition of the same name, 1992. Photo Credit: Courtesy of REPOHistory

36. Suzanne Opton, *Four Women, Vermont*, 1980, photo, reproduced in *Heresies* issue #18: Mothers, Mags & Movie Stars. Photo Credit: Suzanne Opton

37. Sabra Moore, *Make It New*, 1969, collage on paper, 10 ¼ x 8 in., created for distribution via Liberation News Service (LNS). Photo Credit: Sabra Moore

38. Mimi Smith, *Don't Turn Back*, 1985, acrylic, paper, Xerox, ink, on clock; 14 (diameter) x 3 in. Photo Credit: Mimi Smith

39. *Support 1st Amendment*, NY/ACLU Artists' Benefit poster designed by Louise Bourgeois, 3/11/1972, black-and-white photo offset on card stock, 17 x 27 ¼ in., for show at Castelli's Gallery. Photo Credit: Courtesy of Sabra Moore New York City Women's Art Movement Archive, Barnard College

40. Sabra Moore, *Women Act Now*, 1969, 11 ¾ x 5 ½ in., created for distribution via Liberation News Service (LNS) Photo Credit: Sabra Moore

41. Call for *Flags* show, 1970, black-and-white photocopier leaflet, 11 x 8 ½ in. Photo Credit: Courtesy of Sabra Moore New York City Women's Art Movement Archive, Barnard College

42. Sabra in Warren Street garden and Saskia cat in kitchen window. Photo Credit: Roger Mignon

43. Sabra's Pearl Street Studio showing wall. Photo Credit: Sabra Moore

44-47. Sabra Moore, *Untitled*, 1970, pencil on paper, 11 x 8 in. (all). Photo Credit: Sabra Moore

48. Artists collect hundreds of signatures at second demonstration to protest the use of John D. Rockefeller's collection in the Whitney Bicentennial exhibit, March, 1976. Cynthia Mailman is center with beret. Photo Credit: *Art Workers News*, Vol.5, No.10, Feb-March 1976/ Montage from photos by Laima Druskis

49. *Women Chose Women* cover, catalogue, 1973, 9 x 7 ¼ in., design by Bob Crosier, Inc. for an exhibition of works by 109 women artists organized by Women in the Arts and presented by the New York Cultural Center, New York City. Photo Credit: Women in the Arts

50. Georgia Matsumoto, *Untitled*, circa 1970, engraving, 5 ⅜ x 5 in. Photo Credit: Collection of Sabra Moore

51. Sylvia Sleigh, *Working At Home*, 1969, oil on canvas, 56 x 32 in. Photo Credit: Hauser & Wirth Collection, Switzerland

52. May Stevens, *Big Daddy With Hats*, 1971, color lithograph, 23 x 24 ½ in. Photo Credit: May Stevens, Courtesy of Ryan Lee Gallery, New York

53. Sabra's parents, Christine and Frank Moore, at the Red River Bridge with sister Nancy, circa 1940, snapshot taken near Clarksville, Texas. Photo Credit: Collection of Sabra Moore

54. Lillie Parks's morning star quilt hanging on her daughter-in-law Gladys's clothesline, quilt circa 1950s. Photo Credit: Sabra Moore

55. Ruth Gray, *Monkeys in Moonlight*, undated, card, 4 ¼ x 6 in. Photo Credit: Ruth Gray/ Collection of Sabra Moore

56. Linda Peer, *Avalokiteszara, the Bodhisattva of Compassion, as a Person with Karposi's Sarcoma*, 1995, wood and mixed media, 12 ¾ x 2 ¾ x 1 ¼ in., reproduced on exhibit card for *Passion & Compassion: Five Artists reflect on Buddhism*, Asian American Arts Center. Photo Credit: Linda Peer

57. *Guerrilla Girls Speak Back to the Whitney*, 1987, exhibit card, the Clocktower, the Institute for Art and Urban Resources, Inc. Photo Credit: Guerrilla Girls/ Collection of Sabra Moore

58. Sabra Moore, *From Bandelier*, 1972, colored pencil on paper, 11 ½ x 8 ½ in. Photo Credit: Sabra Moore

59. Sabra Moore, *Untitled*, 1970, acrylic on Masonite, 30 x 30 in. Photo Credit: Sabra Moore

60-61. Sabra Moore, *Journal pages with ink drawings*, Book #48, black ink on paper, 9 ¾ x 7 ½ in. Photo Credit: Sabra Moore

Chapter 2

1. *Artists Day* leaflet, May 1978, celebrating artists-run galleries on Atlantic Avenue and Park Slope in Brooklyn with a proclamation by Borough President Howard Golden. Photo Credit: Courtesy of Sabra Moore New York City Women's Art Movement Archive, Barnard College

2. Drewann Rodney and Sabra install the logo designed by Drewann at 81 Atlantic Gallery window. Photo Credit: Collection of Sabra Moore

3. Drewann Rodney, *Works on Paper Membership Group Show*, June 14–July 10, year undated, circa 1975–1977, offset, 11 x 8 ½ in. Photo Credit: 1981

4. Kate Correa, *Untitled*, back reads: "Greetings from Taos," 1982, earth pigments, cloth glue, thread, string, 5 ¾ x 3 ½ in. Kate and Sabra exchanged numerous art postcards during this period. Photo Credit: Kate Correa

5. Malekeh Nayiny, *Untitled*, undated, solarized photo, 5 ½ x 7 ¾ in. Photo Credit: Malekeh Nayiny/ Collection of Sabra Moore

6. Rebecca Leonard, *Seeraubel-Jenny (Pirate Jenny) dedicated to Lotte Lenya*, 1981, mixed media, 37 x 28 x 4 in. Photo Credit: Rebecca Leonard/ Courtesy of Sabra Moore New York City Women's Art Movement Archive, Barnard College

7. Emily Barnett, *Life and Art in the Studio*, 1986–1988, oil on canvas, triptych, 92 x 188 in. This painting pays homage to Courbet's *The Painter's Studio* and to Velasquez's *Las Meninas*. Emily was a member of NoHo Gallery. Photo Credit: Emily Barnett

8. *Artists-Owned Spaces* flier with David Cole drawings, undated, photocopy, 11 x 8 ½ in. Photo Credit: David Cole/ Courtesy of Sabra Moore New York City Women's Art Movement Archive, Barnard College

9. Drewann Rodney, *Massachusetts/Maine*, 1976, photocopier print on paper show card, 11 x 8 ½ in. Photo Credit: Drewann Rodney/Collection of Sabra Moore

10. Stephanie Rauschenbusch, *Breakfast With Cezanne, Utamaro and Van Gogh*, 1978, oil on linen, 46 x 50 in. Photo Credit: Stephanie Rauschenbusch

11. Roger Mignon, *Waiting for a Phone Call*, 1980, oil on canvas, 72 x 66 in. This painting is an homage to Andy Trompetter, founder of Blackbird Theater, former Bread and Puppet performer, and Jewish child survivor of the Nazi occupation of Amsterdam that took the lives of his parents. Andy died suddenly at the age of 37. Photo Credit: Roger Mignon

12. Kazuko, *Woman in Blue Blanket*, performance at Sarah Delanore Roosevelt Park, undated, paper rope with sticks, size varies. Photo Credit: Kazuko Miyamoto

13. Dumbo from Pearl Street Studio window showing Manhattan Bridge, undated, color photo, 4 x 6 in. Photo Credit: Roger Mignon

14. Judith D. Fox, *Person who is a woman and old, leaning*, 1976–1977, terra cotta, 13 ¼ x 5 ¼ x 6 in. Photo Credit: Judith D. Fox/ Courtesy of Sabra Moore New York City Women's Art Movement Archive, Barnard College

15. Artists-collaborators for Atlantic Gallery banner at opening of cooperative gallery, January 12, 1974. Left to right: Linda Smith, Sabra Moore, Suzanne Stanley, Barbara Spiller, and Drewann Rodney. Twenty-five members participated in the inaugural group show of the second gallery on Atlantic Avenue; Gallery 91 had opened three years earlier. According to an article by Eileen Blair, 1,200 people attended opening day. Photo Credit: Linda Barber Hall photo, *The Phoenix*

16. Ruth Gray, *Untitled*, 1981, altered Polaroid, 4 ¼ x 3 ½ in. Photo Credit: Ruth Gray, Collection of Sabra Moore

17. Roger Mignon, *Atlantic Gallery moves to 458 West Broadway in SoHo*, 1980, black-and-white photo, 5 x 7 in. The new banner is visible hanging from the fire escape adjacent to the gallery's second-floor windows. Photo Credit: Roger Mignon

18. *Festival of Artists' Co-Op Galleries* flier, celebrating cooperatives in SoHo, Uptown Manhattan, and Brooklyn, June, year undated, photocopy, 14 x 8 ½ in. Photo Credit: Courtesy of Sabra Moore New York City Women's Art Movement Archive, Barnard College

19. Roger Mignon, *Ira Rappaport exhibit at Atlantic Gallery in Brooklyn*, showing his wooden sculptures, undated, black-and-white photo, 8 x 10 in. Co-op member Kate Correa is near the left-hand wall in light-colored shirt and jeans. Photo Credit: Roger Mignon

20. Sally Brody, *Paintings & Prints*, April, year undated, red-and-green silk screen poster, 10 x 7 in. Photo Credit: Sally Brody

21. Roger Mignon, *Atlantic Gallery first opening at 458 West Broadway site. Sabra (center) is talking to three women friends. Rebecca Leonard is in foreground to right.*, 1980, black-and-white photo, 4 x 6 in. Photo Credit: Roger Mignon

22. Rich Samuelson, *Sea Gull & Wax, encaustic paintings*, May 1980, exhibit card, color offset, 9 x 6 in., Atlantic Gallery. Photo Credit: Rich Samuelson

23. Lamidi Fakeye, *Carving*, most likely in his house in Ibadan, circa 1960s, black-and-white print, 5 ⅜ x 3 ¼ in. Photo Credit: Collection of Sabra Moore

24. *Day of Solidarity with Zimbabwe, March 17* Cuban poster, year undated, color offset on paper, 20 ¾ x 12 ⅞ in. Photo Credit: Organization of Solidarity with the People of Asia, Africa, and Latin America (OSPAAAL), Collection of Sabra Moore

25. Sabra Moore, *Untitled*, drawing, circa 1965, pencil on paper, 9 x 6 ⅞ in. Photo Credit: Sabra Moore

26. Lamidi Fakeye, *Post Carvings*, undated, black-and-white photo, 5 ⅜ x 3 ¼ in. Photo Credit: Lamidi Fakeye/ Collection of Sabra Moore

27. Sabra Moore, *Niamou drawing*, circa 1964–1965, black ink on paper, 11 ¾ x 9 in. Photo Credit: Sabra Moore

28. Sabra Moore, *Mask drawing*, circa 1964–1965, black ink on paper, 11 ¾ x 9 in. Photo Credit: Sabra Moore

29. Sabra Moore, *Two Niamou masks*, circa 1964–1965, black ink on paper, 11 ¾ x 9 in. Photo Credit: Sabra Moore

30. Sabra walking to the school truck from her backyard in N'Zérékoré, circa 1965, color snapshot, 4 x 6 in. Photo Credit: photo by Sally Banks/ Collection of Sabra Moore

31. Lillie Parks's crazy quilt on Gladys Parks's clothesline, undated, color snapshot, 4 x 6 in. Photo Credit: Sabra Moore

32. Caroline and Harry Moore in their yard near Clarksville, Texas, with baby Nancy, Sabra's older sister, on blanket, circa 1939, black-and-white snapshot, 6 x 4 in. Photo Credit: Collection of Sabra Moore

33. Sole remaining quilt of Gladys's mother, May Greer, who died when Gladys was twelve, undated, color photo, 4 x 6 in. When the red-and-white zigzag quilt wore thin, Gladys quilted a plain white cover with intricate white stitching to preserve it like a palimpsest. Photo Credit: Sabra Moore

34. Sabra Moore, *4/TELLS #3*, one artist's book of the four-part *AKIN* series of dark family stories, 1989, color Xerox on archival paper with translucent cover and ribbon, 10 ¼ x 7 ¼ in., unfolds to 51 ¼ in. Photo Credit: Sabra Moore

35. Caroline Bryant (center, third from left) during her second marriage, circa 1910, black-and-white photo, 3 ⅜ x 5 ½ in. Photo Credit: Collection of Sabra Moore

36. Grandfather Harry Moore (left) with mules standing next to Charlie Westbrook, undated, black-and-white snapshot, 4 x 6 in. Photo Credit: Collection of Sabra Moore

Chapter 3

1. Tomie Arai and others, *Wall of Respect for Women*, New York City, 1974. Photo Credit: Tomie Arai in collaboration with Mercedes Colon, Harriet Davis, Eleanor Gong, Cami Homann, Nadine Jannuzzi, Phyllis Seebol, Carol Taylor and Harriet Williams. Sponsored by Cityarts Workshop, New York. Photo courtesy of Tomie Arai

2. *Keeping '85 Cool. . . and Loose!*. First panel, standing, left to right: Arlene Raven, Clusuf, T-shirt mannequin "The Girls," and Jerri Allyn. Bottom row, seated, left to right: Adrienne Weiss, Geraldine Hanon, and Nancy Fried. This postcard was sent to Sabra on July 25, 1986 with a note from Jerri Allyn concerning her entry for the *150 Artists Book, Connections Project/Conexus*: "Sabra! I've been away. . . and for the last three days have been calling all over to get a number for you. . . . Anyway, I am almost finished with a Waitress entry if it's not too late." Photo Credit: Courtesy of Jerri Allyn, photos by Sarah Conklin/ Connections Project/ Conexus Archive, Barnard College

3. *ABC NO RIO: The First Five Years*, anniversary exhibit card for ABC NO RIO, 156 Rivington Street, a program of the Cultural Council Foundation, year undated, photo offset, 4 ¾ x 6 in. Photo Credit: Collection of Sabra Moore

4. *Greetings from the New York City Women's Caucus for Art* (NYC/WCA), montage by Sabra Moore for *WCA Newsletter*, Winter 1981, page 11, photo montage on poster board, 7 x 10 in. Pictured left to right: Selina Trieff is standing; Debbie T. Barbaro is directly in front of Selina; Sabra Moore is seated wearing vest and gesturing; Nancy Hagin is in front of a curtain with the head of Annie Shaver-Crandell over her shoulder; the small figure of Arlene Raven is next to Annie, which followed by the bust of Ora Lerman; Sharon Gilbert is wearing the stripped shirt; Kathie Schnapper is centered below Sharon and Ora; the heads of Bibi Lenĉek and Annette Weintraub are to the far right; Joan Marter is in foreground on the right; and the woman in the white vest is unidentified. Photo Credit: Sabra Moore/ photos by Bibi Lenĉek

5. *Chrysalis* issue #10 cover, 1980. Cover image from article by Ruthe Winegarten, "I Am Annie Mae. The Personal Story of a Black Texas Woman." Photo Credit: © 1980 *Chrysalis: A Magazine of Women's Culture*

6. *Chrysalis* issue #3 cover, 1977. Cover image of a chrysalis is by Ellen Lanyon. Photo Credit: © 1977 *Chrysalis: A Magazine of Women's Culture*

7. Amy Zerner, *A Woman's Web (Is Never Done)*, 1979, fabric and mixed-media collage tapestry, 30 x 31 ½ in. Photo Credit: Amy Zerner/ Courtesy of Sabra Moore New York City Women's Art Movement Archive, Barnard College

8. Sabra Moore, *The Rio Grande as Viewed from the Ridge of Alamo Canyon, Bandelier National Monument, New Mexico, with Texas Deer Antler*, 1982, casein, gesso, Xerox transfer, on watercolor paper, 22 ½ x 30 in. Photo Credit: Sabra Moore

9. Sabra working on pastel, circa 1979, color photo, 8 x 10 in. Photo Credit: Courtesy of Sabra Moore

10. Sabra Moore, *notes, notes*, 1980, accordion-folded color Xerox book in the form of an unfolding journal meditation, 8 ½ x 7 ¼ in., unfolds to 21 ¾ ft. Photo Credit: Sabra Moore

11. (Top) Sabra Moore, *Flowers* (AKIN series), 1988, black-and-white red Xerox-folded book with ribbon in the form of a letter with cemetery photo, 3 ½ x 4 in. (Bottom) Sabra Moore, *Wash & Iron* (AKIN series), 1986, black-and-white accordion-folded photocopier book with cloth ties and sewn acetate cover, 3 ½ x 4 in., unfolds to 42 in. Images from two clotheslines connected to Moore's childhood and texts related to washing and ironing. Photo Credit: Sabra Moore

12. Sabra Moore, *Gladys Sad Box* (AKIN series), 1991, black-and-white accordion-folded book with red pages and color Xerox covers, 7 ½ x 7 ⅛ in., unfolds to 31 ½ ft. Visual meditation on Moore's kin visiting cemetery with text listing items inside what her grandmother called her *Sad Box*. Photo Credit: Sabra Moore

13. Chris Millon, *Death Drawings: Hunting in Suburbs*, 1980, from a photo series on hunting begun in 1976. The "spoils" form a family hunt documented annually on Thanksgiving Day only. Reproduced in *Heresies* issue #13, page 78, 1981. Photo Credit: Estate of Chris Millon

14. Pat Ralph, *Flying High (Icarus series)*, 1980, oil on canvas, 68 x 48 in. Photo Credit: Pat Ralph

15. Selina Trieff, *Pink Bird on Her Shoulder*, 1991, oil on canvas with gold leaf, 72 x 60 in. Photo Credit: Estate of Selina Trieff

16. Sylvia Sleigh, *Selina Trieff*, 1984, oil on canvas, 36 x 24 in. Photo Credit: Estate of Sylvia Sleigh

17. Sabra (left) and Nancy Hagin (right) at a NYC/WCA meeting, 1980. Photo Credit: Bibi Lenĉek

18. Nancy Hagin, *Early April*, 1997, acrylic on canvas, 36 x 30 in. Photo Credit: Nancy Hagin

19. Alice Neel being filmed, 1976. Reproduced in *Art Workers News*, Vol. 6, No. 5, page 2, October 1976, the Foundation for the Community of Artists. Photo Credit: Photo Courtesy of the Festival of Women's Films

20. Bibi Lenĉek, *Ora Lerman at NYC/WCA*, undated, circa 1979, black-and-white photo. Photo Credit: Bibi Lenĉek

21. Sylvia Sleigh, *Aphrodite: Annie Shaver Crandell*, 1982, oil on canvas, 50 x 20 in. Photo Credit: Estate of Sylvia Sleigh/ Private collection, Paris

22. Anita Steckel, *Giant Woman on Empire State, Giant Woman series*, 1973, black-and-white photo collage and pencil on paper, 3 x 4 ft. Photo Credit: Estate of Anita Steckel

23. Muriel Castanis, exhibit card with photo of Castanis carrying artwork, Maurice M. Pine Free Public Library, New Jersey, March 1982, 10 x 4 ½ in., unfolds to 14 in. Photo

Credit: Courtesy of Sabra Moore New York City Women's Art Movement Archive, Barnard College

24. Muriel Castanis, exhibit card, *Sculpture*, Tweed Courthouse, black-and-white-on-beige cardstock, 5 ½ x 4 ¼ in., showing *Spirit of Liberty*, 1985, cloth and epoxy, 8 x 4 ft. Photo Credit: Collection of Sabra Moore

25. Nancy Deffenbach, *an ofrenda * for Frida Kahlo*, show card, Bry Art gallery, Northeast Louisiana University, Monroe, Louisiana, 1984, color offset, 6 x 5 in. Photo Credit: Collection of Sabra Moore

26. Linda Peer, *Woman on a Couch*, 1983, acrylic on plaster. Photo Credit: Linda Peer

27. Linda Peer, *Installation at Windows 462*, show card, 462 Broadway, New York City, 1985, photocopy on cardstock, 6 ¼ x 4 ¼ in. Photo credit: Linda Peer

28. Joyce Kozloff, *Vestibul, Amtrak Station, Wilmington, Delaware*, 1984, hand-painted ceramic tiles, 360 x 240 x 180 in. Photo Credit: Joyce Kozloff, photo by Eugene Mopsik

29. Janet Goldner, *studio with Malian-influenced sculptures*, 1988. Photo Credit: Janet Goldner, photo by Larry Wheelock

30. Phyllis Janto, *Shadow House, Light House, Long House*, 1982, wood, left to right: 8 x 8 x 5 ft., 10 x 10 x10 ft., and 8 x 10 x 5 ft. Installed at the Maine Festival, Bowdoin College, Brunswick, Maine. Photo Credit: Phyllis Janto

31. Merle Temkin, *Merle's Daytime: Sundial*, 1987, wood, mirrors, paint. Site specific installation at Snug Harbor, Staten Island, New York. Relates to century-old sundial near site. The viewer's shadow marks the time. Photo Credit: Merle Temkin

32. *Heresies* issue #1 cover, 1977, photo offset, 11 x 8 ½ in. Photo Credit: © 1977 *Heresies: A Feminist Publication on Art and Politics*

33. Marion Lerner Levine, *The Ghost's Cup*, 1995, watercolor on paper, 22 x 30 in. Photo Credit: Marion Lerner-Levine

34. Donna Henes, *Vernal Equinox ceremony*, South Street Seaport, March 20, 1988, announcement card for *Standing Eggs on End Ceremony*, 6 x 3 ¾ in. Photo Credit: Reprinted by permission of Donna Henes

35. Janet Culbertson, *Shelter Island Trees at Night*, 1987, ink, paint, charcoal on rag paper. Photo Credit: Janet Culbertson

36. Harmony Hammond, *Sneak*, 1977–1979, cloth, wood, acrylic paint, foam and latex rubber, Rhoplex, 13 units each approximately 39 x 36 in. Photo Credit: Courtesy of Alexander Gray Associates. Art ©Harmony Hammond/ Licensed by VAGA, New York

37. *Ionizing Radiation* flier, Clamshell Alliance/Stop Nuclear Power, October 1976, photocopy, 11 x 8 ½ in. Photo Credit: Courtesy of Sabra Moore New York City Women's Art Movement Archive, Barnard College

38. Science for the People, *Three Mile Island Nuclear Disaster*, April 1979, printed brochure, 8 pages. Photo Credit: Courtesy of Sabra Moore New York City Women's Art Movement Archive, Barnard College

39. Ana Mendieta, *Untitled* (*Silueta* series), 1978, gunpowder and burning images on earth and grass, color photo, 8 x 10 in. Photo Credit: © The Estate of Ana Mendieta Collection. LLC, Courtesy of Galerie Lelong, New York

40. Jenkins photo, Donna Henes's *Spring Equinox celebration*, Jeannette Park World Trade Center, 1980, color transparency. Photo Credit: Sarah Jenkins photo, Reprinted by permission of Donna Henes

41. Ann Marie Rousseau, *Women's Pentagon Action*, November 17, 1980. Two thousand women encircled the Pentagon to protest the American war machinery. This photo was printed on page 1 of *Heresies* issue #13: Feminism & Ecology, 1981. Photo Credit: © Ann Marie Rousseau

42. Discussion at *Women & Life on Earth* installation, Amherst College. Celeste Wesson (center) is next to Sabra and Chris Costan (right). Photo Credit: Chris Costan/ Courtesy of Sabra Moore New York City Women's Art Movement Archive, Barnard College

43. Sabra working on *Women & Life on Earth* installation. Photo Credit: Chris Costan/ Courtesy of Sabra Moore New York City Women's Art Movement Archive, Barnard College

44. Lyn Blumenthal at Coney Island, dedication page of *Heresies* issue #24: 12 Years, 1989. In memory of Lynn Blumenthal, 1948–1988, who was an associate member of *Heresies*. Photo Credit: Reprinted from *Heresies* Issue #24, *12 Years* ©1989

45. Invitation, *Feminism in Ecology*, Craft Students League show with members of the *Heresies* issue #13 editorial collective, color offset card, 5 ½ x 8 ½ in. Photo Credit: Collection of Sabra Moore

46. Racism Is the Issue leaflet, photo offset on brown paper, 11 x 8 ½ in. Photo Credit: Courtesy of Sabra Moore New York City Women's Art Movement Archive, Barnard College

47. Michele Godwin, *Heresies* issue #15: Racism Is the Issue cover, 1982, 12 x 9 ¾ in. Photo Credit: © 1982 *Heresies: A Feminist Publication on Art and Politics*

48. *Heresies* issue #9: Women Organized/Women Divided cover, graphic by Lucy R. Lippard, 1980, photo offset, 11 x 8 ½ in. Photo Credit: © 1980 *Heresies: A Feminist Publication on Art and Politics*

49. Ora Lerman, *Who Are We? Where Are We Going?*, 1991, hand-ground oil on canvas, 27 x 54 in. Photo Credit: Ora Lerman Charitable Trust/ photo by Malcolm Varon

50. Helen Aylon, *The Earth Ambulance*, Brooklyn Bridge Anchorage, 1992, photo offset flier, 11 x 8 ½ in. Celebrating the finale performance within a ten-year installation called *Terrestri: Rescued Earth*. Aylon's quote on the flier reads: "And the women carried the earth in sacs for they fearing the S.A.C. of the military." Photo Credit: Courtesy

of Sabra Moore New York City Women's Art Movement Archive, Barnard College

Chapter 4

1. Camille Billops, *KKK Boutique Ain't Just Rednecks*, card announcing First Prize for Best Docu/Fantasy 1994, awarded by the National Black Programming Consortium to Camille Billops and James Hatch and also celebrating the twentieth anniversary of the Hatch-Billops Collection, 1994, photo offset, 6 ¼ x 4 ½ in. Photo Credit: © Camille Billops
2. Opening of Sabra Moore's *House Dress/Gladys Story* window installation at Printed Matter, Inc., 1984, black-and-white photo, 8 x 10 in. Left to right: Sylvia Sleigh facing Bibi Lenĉek, Linda Peer, Marithelma Costa, Fabio Salvatore, and unidentified woman. Photo Credit: Roger Mignon
3. Lenora Champagne, *Manna*, a performance piece performed in 1985. The script for *Manna* was reproduced in *Heresies* issue #18: Mothers, Mags & Movie Stars, pages 68–72. Photo Credit: Photo by Mary Mallot, Courtesy of Lenora Champagne
4. Tak Inagaki (left) with crew filming Sharon Gilbert installing art at *Know Peace/No Piece*, 1991, black-and-white photo, 8 x 10 in. Photo Credit: Roger Mignon
5. Bibi Lenĉek, *Domestic Scenes: A Cup of Coca*, 1976–1977, oil on canvas, 40 x 62 in. Photo Credit: Bibi Lenĉek
6.–8. NYC/WCA board meeting at Sabra's Warren Street apartment in Brooklyn, circa 1981, color photos, 4 x 6 in. Left to right: Sharon Gilbert, Joan Turken, Ora Lerman, Jacqueline Wray, Joan Turken, and Sabra Moore. Photo Credit: Bibi Lenĉek
9. Ora Lerman, *Which Side of the Door of Dreams Do We Enter?*, center panel of trilogy, 1978–1980, hand-ground oil on canvas, 180 x 30 in. Photo Credit: Ora Lerman Charitable Trust/ photo by Malcolm Varon
10. Faith Ringgold, *The Ringgold Doll Kit*, 1981, black-and-white photo, 8 x 10 in. Photo Credit: Faith Ringgold/ Courtesy of Sabra Moore New York City Women's Art Movement Archive, Barnard College
11. Ora Lerman, *Which Side of the Door of Dreams Do We Enter?*, right side panel of trilogy, *Sea Light Strokes Me and I Surrender Softly to Memory*, 1978–1980, hand-ground oil on canvas, 180 x 30 in. Photo Credit: Ora Lerman Charitable Trust/ photo by Malcolm Varon
12. Flier for Greatness: A Re-Evaluation panel, sponsored by Coalition of Women's Art Organizations (CWAO), New York Feminist Art Institute, November 14, 1980, offset, 11 x 8 ½ in. Linda Cunningham (chair), Harmony Hammond, Sabra Moore, Lorraine O'Grady, Kathy Schnapper, Elizabeth Weatherford, Catharine Stimpson, and discussant. Photo Credit: Courtesy of Sabra Moore New York City Women's Art Movement Archive, Barnard College
13. Roger Mignon, *Sabra in her studio next to her recent artworks*, Atlantic Gallery solo exhibit, 1981, black-and-white photo, 8 x 10 in. Photo Credit: Roger Mignon
14. Nigerian ibeji doll, color snapshot, 6 x 4 in. Photo Credit: Sabra Moore
15. The American Quilt: An Innovative Art Form NYC/WCA panel, 1981, black-and-white photo, 5 x 7 in. Left to right: Faith Ringgold, Elyse Taylor, Pat Mainardi, and Susan Hoffman. Photo Credit: Bibi Lenĉek
16. Susan Hoffman and Sabra Moore holding up Hoffman's quilt during panel discussion, 1981, black-and-white photo, 5 x 7 in. Photo Credit: Bibi Lenĉek
17. Faith Ringgold, *Echoes of Harlem*, 1980, acrylic on canvas, 96 x 84 in. Photo Credit © 1980 Faith Ringgold, Collection of Studio Museum in Harlem, NYC
18. *Women Artists News* cover, March 9, No. 3, Spring 1984. Photo Credit: © 1984, Women Artists News
19. Marilyn Lanfear, *A Quilt Is a Cover*, 1981, silk, cotton, buttons, 80 x 87 in. Photo Credit: Marilyn Lanfear
20. Susan Kaprov, *Precambrian Waltz*, commissioned for the Port Authority Technical Center, 1987, acrylic photomontage on Hexcel aluminum, 8 x 40 ft. Photo Credit: © Susan Kaprov
21. Jacqueline Gourevitch, *Cloud Painting #101, 1985, diptych,* oil on canvas, 68 x 54 in. each. Photo Credit: Jacqueline Gourevitch
22. Diana Mara Henry, *Women's Pentagon Action*, showing activists panting gravestones in front of the Pentagon for women victims of militarism, 1981. Detail of page layout including type montage by Sabra Moore, *Heresies* issue #13: Feminism & Ecology, page 1. Photo Credit: © Diana Mara Henry/ www.dianamararhenry.com
23. *Heresies* issue #13: Feminism & Ecology cover, 1981. Photo Credit: © 1981, *Heresies: A Feminist Publication on Art and Politics*
24. Ellen Lanyon, *Mount St. Helens May 18, 1980*, 1981, lithograph on paper, 11 ¼ x 9 in. Ellen's hand lettering in pencil describes how to create a "wind-agitated volcanic eruption" in a small vessel with sand and wine; she gave each member of the editorial collective of *Heresies* issue #13 one of these lithographs. Photo Credit: Estate of Ellen Lanyon
25. Judy Simonian, *Wall Exposure No. 1*, photo of 1978 project in which Simonian sandblasted a concrete retaining wall in Los Angles to expose its original construction materials. Detail of page layout including type montage by Sabra Moore, *Heresies* issue #13: Feminism & Ecology, page 88, 1981. Photo Credit: Judy Simonian artwork with type montage by Sabra Moore
26. Sarah Jenkins, photo of Hattie Carthan and Ruth Mitchell, Magnolia Earth Tree Center, Brooklyn. Detail of page layout including type montage by Ellen Lanyon, *Heresies* issue #13: Feminism & Ecology, page 32, 1981. Photo Credit: Sarah Jenkins (photo)/ Estate of Ellen Lanyon

(type montage)/ Reprinted from *Heresies* Issue #13, *Feminism & Ecology*, p. 32, 1981

27. Patricia Johanson, *Leaf Fountain/ 3/8 Phyllotaxy*, 1974, ink and charcoal, 30 x 30 in. This was also reproduced in *Heresies* issue #13: Feminism & Ecology, page 89, 1981. Photo Credit: © Patricia Johanson, Collection of Museum of Modern Art, gift of R.L.B. Tobin

28. Jacqueline Wray, *Views by Women Artists* invitation poster for sixteen independently curated shows, 1982, photo offset, unfolds to 22 x 16 in. Photo Credit: Jacqueline Wray (design)

29. *Women and Art in Society* poster, Women's Caucus for Art Tenth Annual Conference, 1982, photo offset, unfolds to 22 x 16 in. Photo Credit: Jacqueline Wray (design)

30. Sharon Gilbert, *Waste*, 1980, photocopier artist's book, 4 ¼ x 2 ¾ in. Includes statistics related to nuclear waste. Photo Credit: Estate of Sharon Gilbert

31. Donna Henes, *Invitation, Wild Art Show*, 1982, photocopier, 8 ½ x 11 in. One of sixteen independently curated shows that comprised *Views by Women Artists*. Photo Credit: Reprinted by permission of Donna Henes

32. Linda Cunningham, *Like Time, Like Light, Yet, In a Grave Hour*, 1983, experimental bronze castings, 4 x 15 ft. Photo Credit: Linda Cunningham

33. Maureen Connor, *Count Orgaz Comes Again*, 1979, fabric, 12 x 6 ft. This artwork was included in *Pieced Work*, curated by Sabra Moore, which was one of sixteen independently curated shows that comprised *Views by Women Artists*. Photo Credit: Maureen Connor

34. Lorna Simpson (with Irene and Rejendra), *Untitled*, 1982, mixed media installation, size varies. This artwork was included in *Working Women/Working Artists/Working Together*, curated by Lucy R. Lippard and Candace Hill-Montgomery, which was one of sixteen independently curated shows that comprised *Views by Women Artists*. Photo Credit: Lorna Simpson

35. Eileen Spikol, *Shades of Venus*, 1979, polychrome plaster, 60 x 25 x 2 ¼ in. This artwork was included in *Pieced Work*, curated by Sabra Moore, which was one of sixteen independently curated shows that comprised *Views by Women Artists*. Photo Credit: Estate of Eileen Spikol

36. NYC/WCA board, 1982. Front row, left to right: Sabra Moore, Linda Cunningham, Jacqueline Wray, and Annie Shaver-Crandell. Back row, left to right: Bibi Lenĉek, Sylvia Sleigh, and Kathy Schnapper. Photo Credit: Bibi Lenĉek

37. Sylvia Sleigh, *The Turkish Bath*, 1973, oil on canvas, 76 ½ x 102 ½ in. Photo Credit: Estate of Sylvia Sleigh/ The David and Alfred Smart Museum of Art, The University of Chicago, Chicago, IL

38. Anne Pitrone (with Nancy Cheng), *The Revolutionary Scale: Masks for the Office*, 1982, 5 silhouettes, 11 in. wide. This artwork was included in *Working Women/Working Artists/Working Together*, curated by Lucy R. Lippard and

Candace Hill-Montgomery, which was one of sixteen independently curated shows that comprised *Views by Women Artists*. Photo Credit: Anne Pitrone/ Courtesy of Sabra Moore New York City Women's Art Movement Archive, Barnard College

39. Nancy Azara, *Blue Ritual*, detail, 1988, carved and painted wood with gold and silver leaf, 39 x 14 x 8 in. Photo Credit: Nancy Azara

40. Mimi Smith, *Travel Clock*, 1977, pencil, ink on paper, 4 x 6 in. Photo Credit: Mimi Smith

41. Howardena Pindell, *Autobiography: India (Lakshmi)*, 1984, mixed media on board, 33 x 19 x 20 in. Photo Credit: Courtesy of Howardena Pindell and Garth Greenan Gallery, New York

42. Mierle Laderman Ukeles (with Cayo Sexton of CLU and NYU), *Walls of Stress/Bowls of Devotion: Ode to the New Nightingales*, 1982, mixed media installation, size varies. This artwork was included in *Working Women/Working Artists/Working Together*, curated by Lucy R. Lippard and Candace Hill-Montgomery, which was one of sixteen independently curated shows that comprised *Views by Women Artists*. Photo Credit: Mierle Laderman Ukeles, Courtesy of Ronald Feldman Fine Arts, New York

43. Elyse Taylor, *Ingrid*, 1981, acrylic on canvas strips, 48 x 52 in. This artwork was included in *Pieced Work*, curated by Sabra Moore, which was one of sixteen independently curated shows that comprised *Views by Women Artists*. Photo Credit: Elyse Taylor

44. Marina Gutierrez, *Mut with Stars*, detail, 1992, graphite and acrylic on paper, 72 x 30 in. Photo Credit: Marina Gutierrez

45. Bibi Lenĉek, *TV Couple*, 1978–1980, oil on canvas, 48 x 50 in. Photo Credit: Bibi Lenĉek

46. Nancy Spero, exhibit card for *Woman as Protagonist: The Art of Nancy Spero, A Video Documentary by Irene Sosa*, Exit Art/The First World, 1993, offset on green card stock, 5 ½ x 4 ¼ in. Photo Credit: Art © The Nancy Spero and Leon Golub Foundation for the Arts/ Licensed by VAGA, New York, NY

47. Pamela McCormick, *Suspended Stone Sculpture*, 1981, blue stone, Plexiglas, hardware cloth, thread, 60 x 36 x 35 in. This artwork was included in *New Sculpture: Icon and Environment*, curated by Susan Sollins, which was one of sixteen independently curated shows that comprised *Views by Women Artists*. Photo Credit: Pamela McCormick

48. Tania Kravath, *T-shirt Women Artists Take over New York* flier, design for *Views by Women Artists* events, 1982, photocopy on paper, 11 x 8 ½ in. Photo Credit: Courtesy of Sabra Moore New York City Women's Art Movement Archive, Barnard College

49. Ana Mendieta, *Cahubaba (Escultras Rupestres)* [*Old Mother Blood (Rupestrian Sculptures)*], 1981, black-and-white photo, 53 ¾ x 39 ⅞ in. Photo Credit: © The Estate of Ana

Mendieta Collection, LLC, Courtesy of Galerie Lelong, New York

50. Candace Hill-Montgomery, *Juggling Picture Show*, exhibition with Hung Tang and Chiyang Liu at Eric Turner Gallery, card, 1984, photo offset on cardstock, 6 x 9 in. Photo Credit: Candace Hill-Montgomery, Collection of Sabra Moore

51. May Stevens, *Ordinary-Extraordinary*, 1980, printed book, 11 x 8 ½ in. This artwork was included in *Women Artists' Books*, catalogue statement by Nancy Linn, which was one of sixteen independently curated shows that comprised *Views by Women Artists.* Photo Credit: May Stevens

52. *Woman's Art Journal* cover, Vol. 3, No.1, Spring/Summer 1982, pages 11–28, with sixteen catalogue essays from *Views by Women Artists.* Photo Credit: © 1982 *Woman's Art Journal*

53. A to Z: An Intensive Workshop flier on painting, performance, and politics with Jerri Allyn, May Stevens, and Holly Zox, New York Feminist Art Institute (NYFAI) Center for Learning, circa 1986, poster, 9 ¼ x 14 ¾ in. Workshop focused on "goals and strategies to accomplish what we'd like in our work and define audience we'd like to reach." Photo Credit: Courtesy of Sabra Moore New York City Women's Art Movement Archive, Barnard College

54. Donna Henes, *Reverence to Her Winter Solstice* poster, 1983, photocopy, 11 x 11 in. Photo Credit: Reprinted by permission of Donna Henes, poster design by Sue Turner

55. NYC/WCA board seated on Sylvia Sleigh's front steps, 1985. Top row, left to right: Selina Treiff, Annie Shaver-Crandell, Susan Gill, and Carol Grape. Second row, left to right: Ora Lerman, Sylvia Sleigh, and Jacqueline Wray. Bottom row, left to right: Sabra Moore, Bibi Lenĉek with baby Nikko, and Joan Watts. Photo Credit: Courtesy of Bibi Lenĉek

56. May Stevens, *Soho Women Artists*, 1977–1978, acrylic on canvas, 78 x 144 in. Harmony Hammond is in white talking to Marty Pottenger; May Stevens is painting and Louise Bourgeois is wearing her multi-breasted artwork near Buffie Johnson straddling a bicycle; Miriam Schapiro is in blue with her eyes closed. Photo Credit: May Stevens, Courtesy of Ryan Lee Gallery, New York/ Collection, National Museum of Women in the Arts

57. Roger Mignon, *Oh Grandma. . .*, 1983, oil on canvas, 62 x 120 in. Photo Credit: Roger Mignon

58. Sabra Moore, *Caroline's Songbook (My Version)* cover, 1983, color Xerox with sewn bindings, 14 x 8 ½ in., 42 pages. Photo Credit: Sabra Moore

59. *Dangerous Works* flier, Artists Against Nuclear Madness, 1982, 11 x 8 ½ in. Photo Credit: Courtesy of Sabra Moore New York City Women's Art Movement Archive, Barnard College

60. Sylvia Sleigh, *Sabra Moore: My Ceres*, 1982, oil on canvas, 36 in. diameter. Photo Credit: Sylvia Sleigh

61. Gladys Parks, *String quilt*, made in strips with Sabra's old dresses, circa 1970, cotton, 70 x 69 in. Photo Credit: Collection of Sabra Moore

62. Ellen Lanyon, *Chromes: II Autumn, III Spring*, detail, 1982–1983, acrylic on canvas, 68 x 204 in. overall. Photo Credit: Estate of Ellen Lanyon

63. *Heresies* Dire Need Emergency Benefit dance, graphic artist unidentified, undated, photocopy, 11 x 8 ½ in. Photo Credit: Courtesy of Sabra Moore New York City Women's Art Movement Archive, Barnard College

64. Cecilia Vicuña, *Con cón, Chile*, Casa Espiritu, 1966, black-and-white photo. Photo Credit: Cecilia Vicuña

65. Sue Heinemann, *Keep Out*, 1984, color pencil on paper, 5 ⅛ x 3 ⅛ in. Sue sent this drawing for Sabra's collective artist's book *Making/Making Art/Making Sex/Making Baby* for the *Carnival Knowledge* show at Franklin Furnace, New York City. Photo Credit: Sue Heinemann

66. Photo of Cindy Carr, Lenora Champagne, and Patricia Spear in performance of *Women in Research*. Photo Credit: Photo by Hali Breindel, Courtesy of Lenora Champagne

67. Emma Amos, *Diagonal Diver*, 1985–1987, acrylic on canvas with Burkina Faso border, 75 x 59 in. Photo Credit: ©Emma Amos, Licensed by VAGA, New York, NY/photo by Becket Logan

68. Heretics installing the third Heresies Benefit at Frank Marino Gallery to celebrate its sixth year of publication, 1982. Left to right: K. Webster, Cindy Carr, and Patricia Spears Jones. This photo appeared in Guy Trebay's September 22–28 "Opinionated Survey of the Week's Events," *The Village Voice*. Photo Credit: © 1982 Sharon Pryor-Carter, *The Village Voice*

69. *Heresies Benefit, 50 Women Choose 50 Women* exhibit card, Bess Cutler Gallery, 1983, black-and-white photo offset on card stock, 17 x 22 in. Photo Credit: Courtesy of Sabra Moore New York City Women's Art Movement Archive, Barnard College

70. Linda Peer, *I Make Myself*, 1984, photo montage and text by Linda, color Xerox background by Sabra, 8 ½ x 8 ½ in. Linda sent this montage for Sabra's collective artist's book *Making/Making Art/Making Sex/Making Baby* for the *Carnival Knowledge* show at Franklin Furnace, New York City. Photo Credit: Linda Peer

71. *Protective Devices* poster, designed by Sabra Moore for window installation at Windows on White, New York City, with thirty artists responding to the concept, 1983, photocopy with stamp, 11 x 8 ½ in. Photo Credit: Sabra Moore

72. Vanalyne Green, *Trick or Drink*, 1984, still photo from video based on live performance exploring various forms of addiction. Photo Credit: Courtesy of Vanalyne Green

73. Sharon Gilbert, *Mask of Opinion*, 1983, rag paper, Xerox, 20 x 30 x 5 ½ in. This was the artwork Sharon made for *Protective Devices* at Windows on White. Photo Credit: estate of Sharon Gilbert

74. Hannah Wilke, *And I Played/& I Stayed 'Till Heaven*, book page for *Protective Devices* artist's book, 1983, photocopy, 8 ½ x 7 in., based on 8 x 10 in. photo. Back of the book dedication by Wilke reads: "In Memoriam: Selma Harriet Fabian Butter, wife of Emanuel Butter; Daughters, Marsha Leslie Scharlatt, Arlene Hannah Wilke; Grandchildren, Emmanuelle, Damon and Andre W. Scharlatt. December 31, 1909–April 28, 1982." Photo Credit: Estate of Hannah Wilke, Courtesy of Ronald Feldman Fine Arts, New York

75. Sylvia Sleigh, *Lorica for Athena as Daddy's Little Girl: The Gorgon Lobby Protest*, 1982, iridescent acrylic on paper with insulated wire, 10 ½ x 6 x 4 in. This was the artwork Sylvia made for *Protective Devices* at Windows on White, 1983. Photo Credit: Estate of Sylvia Sleigh

76. Sabra Moore, *Caroline Had a Beautiful Garden/Swept Dirt/ She Planted Flowers in Circles/In Front of Her House/ Like They Do in Africa*, 1982, oil on gessoed paper, photo transfer print, Xerox, gold leaf, 61 x 102 in. Photo Credit: Sabra Moore

77. Sabra Moore, *House Book*, 1983, covers, photo transfer and oil on gessoed paper with hand-sewn wax-linen binding, 10 double-sided color Xerox pages on archival paper with cutouts, gessoed center page with cutouts and photo transfer prints, 12 x 13 ¾ in. Photo Credit: Sabra Moore

78. Sabra Moore, *Pieced for Opal*, 1983, color Xerox on archival paper, glue, 55 x 66 in. Photo Credit: Sabra Moore

79. Sabra Moore, *Caroline's Songbook (My Version)*, interior double page, 1983, color Xerox with sewn bindings, 14 x 8 ½ in., 42 pages. Photo Credit: Sabra Moore

80. Sabra Moore, *Pieced for Caroline*, 1983, color Xerox on archival paper, oil on gessoed wood, string, 60 x 45 in. Photo Credit: Sabra Moore

81. *Classified: Big Pages from the Heresies Collective* installation, 1983, the New Museum. Artworks left to right: *A Roomful of Mothers*, Sabra Moore; *Devotion Procession. Or We're #1*, Sandra De Sando; *Mobility: A Game of Chance and Ambition*, Lyn Hughes; *Aspirella: Cinderella's Unfortunate Stepsister*, Kay Kenny. Photo Credit: ©1983, The New Museum, photo by David Lubarsky

82. Sue Heinemann, Nicky Lindeman, Sabra Moore, and Holly Zox, *Dream Kitschen*, one of the "big pages" for the *Classified: Big Pages from the Heresies Collective* exhibition at the New Museum, 1983, miscellaneous found and crafted materials, 8 x 12 ft. Photo Credit: Courtesy of Sabra Moore

83. Lenora Champagne performance at Franklin Furnace using Sabra's window with curtain and text about Mother Gladys's kitchen window and Sue Heinemann's ironing board with X-ray, both objects borrowed from the *Dream Kitschen* installation at the New Museum, 1983. Photo Credit: Photo by Darlene Delbecq, Courtesy of Lenora Champagne

84. Sabra Moore, *A Roomful of Mothers*, *Classified: Big Pages from the Heresies Collective* exhibition at the New Museum, 1983, 8 x 6 ft. each. Left: oil on gessoed paper with color Xerox montage of photos and photo transfer print. Right: color Xerox on archival paper with glue. Photo Credit: Sabra Moore/ Courtesy of The New Museum, photo by David Lubarsky

85. Sabra Moore, *Gladys Apron (Pink Version)*, 1983, oil on gessoed paper with color Xerox and photo transfer, 35 ½ x 24 in. This was included in the *Dream Kitschen*. Photo Credit: Sabra Moore

86. Sabra Moore, *A Roomful of Mothers*, detail, *Classified: Big Pages from the Heresies Collective* exhibition at the New Museum, 1983, color Xerox on archival paper. Photo Credit: Sabra Moore

87. Sabra with *Heresies* raffle sign board in effort to fundraise for the magazine on a Lower Manhattan street, undated. Photo Credit: Lucy R. Lippard

88. *All's Fair: Love & War in New Feminist Art*, postcard packet catalogue for exhibition curated by Lucy R. Lippard, the Ohio State University Gallery of Fine Art, Kimberly Elam design, 1983, color offset, 4 ¾ x 6 ¼ x ¼ in. Photo Credit: Courtesy of Sabra Moore

89. Marina Gutierrez, book page, *150 Artists Book (Race), Connections Project/Conexus*, 1987, pencil on paper, 8 x 3 in. Photo Credit: Marina Gutierrez/ Courtesy of Connections Project/ Conexus Archive, Barnard College

90. Mother Gladys in bed, undated, color snapshot, 4 x 6 in. Photo Credit: Courtesy of Sabra Moore

91. Sabra Moore, *Gladys Place*, 1988, laser transfer on curtain, oil on gessoed wood, curtain rod, 21 x 15 ½ in. Photo Credit: Sabra Moore

92. Sisters of Survival, *Shovel Defense Documentation, 1982* performance to dramatize the absurdity of civil defense planning to survive nuclear war. Reproduced from *All's Fair: Love & War in New Feminist Art*, postcard packet catalogue, 1983, color offset card, 6 x 4 ½ in. Photo Credit: Courtesy of Sisters of Survival: Jerri Allyn, Nancy Angelo, Anne Gauldin, Cheri Gaulke, Sue Mayberry, Marguerite Elliot

93. *Carnival Knowledge* poster inviting artists and writers to participate in a NY Coalition for reproductive rights and "The Most Magnificent Winter Carnival given in celebration of the ninth anniversary for the 1973 Supreme Court decision for abortion rights," 1982, three-fold poster opens to 11 x 17 in. Photo Credit: Courtesy of Sabra Moore New York City Women's Art Movement Archive, Barnard College

94. *Working Woman's Wheel of Misfortune*, 1981, photo by Anton Van Dalen from Carnival Knowledge, a traveling educational show about reproductive rights comprised of photos, text, and fabric documentation. Reproduced from *All's Fair: Love & War in New Feminist Art*, postcard packet

catalogue, 1983, color offset card, 6 x 4 ½ in. Photo Credit: Carnival Knowledge/ Courtesy of Sabra Moore

95. Sabra Moore, *end page, Making/Making Art/Making Sex/ Making Baby*, collective artist's book in which Sabra incorporated images from nine artists and friends into nine separate page designs, 1984, color Xerox on archival paper,15 pages, 8 ½ x 8 ½ in. This book was created for the *Carnival Knowledge* show at Franklin Furnace, New York City. Photo Credit: Sabra Moore

96. Sabra Moore, *Daddy's Gun (box)*, 1983, cloth, gesso, oil, color Xerox, found drawer, 3 x 6 x 5 ½ in. Photo Credit: Sabra Moore

97. Sabra Moore, *Daddy's Gun (book)*, 1983, color Xerox on archival paper, gesso, heat transfer print, string, 10 ¾ x 8 ½ in., book is 5 ¼ x 4 ½ in. Photo Credit: Sabra Moore

Chapter 5

1. Roger Mignon, *Roger and Sabra under the Manhattan Bridge in Dumbo*, circa 1984, black-and-white photo, 5 x 7 in. Photo Credit: Roger Mignon

2. *5 & Dime Artists' Holiday Store*, 1985, card design by Isabelle Drevaux, photo offset, 4 ¼ x 6 ¼ in. Photo Credit: Collection of Sabra Moore

3. Card listing events to celebrate six weeks of *Artists Call Against US Intervention in Central America*, 1984, photo offset, 5 ¼ x 3 ¼ in. Photo Credit: Collection of Sabra Moore

4. Roger and Sabra pose in front of wooden doors down the street from their loft at 81 Pearl Street in Dumbo, circa 1984, black-and-white photo, 7 x 5 in. Photo Credit: Roger Mignon

5. *Todas Las Americas*, announcement card for poetry reading by Claribel Alegria, Ariel Dorfman, and others as part of *Artists Call Against US Intervention in Central America*, 1984, photo offset, 6 x 4 ¼ in. Photo Credit: Collection of Sabra Moore

6. *Nicaraguan Painters*, card announcing slide show and reception benefit for two Nicaraguan painters sponsored by Ventana, 1985, photo offset, 5 ½ x 4 ¾ in. Photo Credit: Collection of Sabra Moore

7. *Artists Call Against US Intervention in Central America* flier with Claes Oldenburg graphic, 1984, color offset, 36 ¾ x 24 in., production by Sara Seagull. Photo Credit: Courtesy of Sabra Moore New York City Women's Art Movement Archive, Barnard College

8. Sabra Moore, *Reconstructed Codex*, opening pages, Xerox version, limited edition of 30, 1984, color Xerox on archival paper with hand-cut edges, 8 x 3 in. each. One page from the Dresden Codex on which this project was based is on the right-hand side. Photo Credit: Sabra Moore

9. *Reconstruction Project* flier, designed and conceived by Sabra Moore, 1984, hand-stamped photocopy, 11 x 8 ½ in. Photo Credit: Sabra Moore

10.–12. *Reconstructed Codex* in sewn double-page sequence, central artwork for *Reconstruction Project*, Artists Space, 1984, media varies, 8 x 3 in. each, book extends to 13 ft.

10. Frances Buschke, mixed media and burning on paper. Photo Credit: Frances Buschke/ Courtesy of Sabra Moore New York City Women's Art Movement Archive, Barnard College

11. Nancy Spero, cutout painted papers on gessoed watercolor paper. Photo Credit: Art © The Nancy Spero and Leon Golub Foundation for the Arts/ Licensed by VAGA, New York, NY/ Courtesy of Sabra Moore New York City Women's Art Movement Archive, Barnard College

12. Liliana Porter, lithograph and pencil on gessoed watercolor paper. Photo Credit: Liliana Porter/ Courtesy of Sabra Moore New York City Women's Art Movement Archive, Barnard College

13.–15. *Reconstructed Codex* in sewn double-page sequence, central artwork for *Reconstruction Project*, Artists Space, 1984, media varies, 8 x 3 in. each, book extends to 13 ft.

13. Josely Carvalho, silkscreen on gessoed paper. Photo Credit: Josely Carvalho/ Courtesy of Sabra Moore New York City Women's Art Movement Archive, Barnard College

14. Virginia Jaramillo, mixed media on paper. Photo Credit: Virginia Jaramillo/ Courtesy of Sabra Moore New York City Women's Art Movement Archive, Barnard College

15. Emma Amos, acrylic on paper. Photo Credit: ©Emma Amos, Licensed by VAGA, New York, NY/ Courtesy of Sabra Moore New York City Women's Art Movement Archive, Barnard College

16. *Reconstruction Project* installation, red (east), yellow (south) directional color walls, Artists Space, 1984, 7 x 3 ft. average. Left to right: Kazuko Miyamoto and Linda Peer (red, both), Sabra Moore, Marina Gutierrez, Liliana Porter, and Emma Amos (yellow, all). Photo Credit: Roger Mignon

17. *Reconstructed Codex* double pages continue in sequence: Kathy Grove, 1984, mixed media and paint, 8 x 3 in. each. Photo Credit: Kathy Grove/ Courtesy of Sabra Moore New York City Women's Art Movement Archive, Barnard College

18. Sewn *Reconstructed Codex* on 13 ft. platform painted in the Mayan directional color for center, turquoise, 1984, 35 mm color slide. Photo Credit: Roger Mignon

19. *Reconstruction Project* installation, red wall (east), Artists Space, 1984, black-and-white photo, 8 x 10 in. Left to right: Kathy Grove, Catherine Correa, Camille Billops (above door), Kazuko Miyamoto, and Linda Peer. Photo Credit: Roger Mignon

20. *Reconstruction Project* Installation, black wall (north), Artists Space, 1984, black-and-white photo, 8 x 10 in. Left to right: Helen Oji, Frances Buschke, Josely Carvalho, Christine Costan, and Catalina Parra. Photo Credit: Roger Mignon

21.–22. *Reconstructed Codex* double pages continue in sequence, 1984, 8 x 3 in.

21. Camille Billops, oil stick on gessoed paper. Photo Credit: Camille Billops/ Courtesy of Sabra Moore New York City Women's Art Movement Archive, Barnard College

22. Linda Peer, mixed media collage. Photo Credit: Linda Peer/ Courtesy of Sabra Moore New York City Women's Art Movement Archive, Barnard College

23. Sabra Moore, *Reconstructed Codex*, 1984, front and back gessoed covers with transfer prints and paint, Xerox version, limited edition of 30, 8 x 3 in. each. Photo Credit: Sabra Moore

24. Sabra with Mother Gladys and Daddy Chess on the front porch of their house in Clarkesville, Texas, circa early 1980s, black-and-white photo, 8 x 10 in. Photo Credit: Roger Mignon

25. Sabra Moore, *Generate* (*AKIN* series), artist's book page with Chester, his mother's morning star quilt pattern, and woods, 1990, photocopy on archival paper, 4 ¼ x 7 in. Photo Credit: Sabra Moore

26. Sabra Moore, *Generate* (*AKIN* series), artist's book page with Gladys, Lillie's morning star quilt pattern, cemetery, and woods, 1990, photocopy on archival paper, 4 ¼ x 7 in. Photo Credit: Sabra Moore

27. Sabra sitting with Mother Gladys on her living room couch, circa 1985, 35 mm slide. Photo Credit: Roger Mignon

28.–30. *Reconstructed Codex* double pages continue in sequence, 1984, 8 x 3 in.

28. Helen Oji, acrylic on gessoed paper. Photo Credit: Helen Oji/ Courtesy of Sabra Moore New York City Women's Art Movement Archive, Barnard College

29. Kazuko, mixed media, includes felt toy hat and straw, paint. Photo Credit: Kazuko Miyamoto/ Courtesy of Sabra Moore New York City Women's Art Movement Archive, Barnard College

30. Marina Gutierrez, acrylic on gessoed paper with stamped figures. Photo Credit: Marina Gutierrez/ Courtesy of Sabra Moore New York City Women's Art Movement Archive, Barnard College

31.–34. Sabra Moore, Journal #37 drawings, 1984, ink on paper, 9 ¾ x 7 ½ in. (all). Images on pages: *Chichen Itza temples* (31), *Tulum* (32), *Chichen Itza* (33), and *Chichen Itza cenote* (34). Photo Credit: Sabra Moore

35. Betsy Damon, *7,000 Year-Old Woman*, performance #2, a street event, "claiming a space on Prince Street near West Broadway, New York, May 21, 1977," as described in *Heresies* issue #3: Lesbian Art and Artists, 1977, pages 10–13. Photo Credit: Su Friedrich (photo)/ Betsy Damon (performance)

36. Betsy Damon, *Meditation and Chanting for the survival of the planet*, photo by Pam Duffy, card, year undated, photocopy, 5 x 7 in. Photo Credit: Courtesy of Betsy Damon

37 "Let MoMA Know" flier announcing demonstration against the Museum of Modern Art (MoMA) for June 14, 1984

and inviting participants to bring names and show cards to insert into the *Model MoMA*, designed by Sabra Moore, 1984, photocopy, 14 x 8 ½ in. Photo Credit: Courtesy of Sabra Moore New York City Women's Art Movement Archive, Barnard College

38. "MoMA Opens" demonstration flier with three demands to address the dominance of "white male artists" in shows and collections, 1984, photocopy, 14 x 8 ½ in. Photo Credit: Courtesy of Sabra Moore New York City Women's Art Movement Archive, Barnard College

39. "The Museum of Modern Art OPENS But Not to Women Artists" badge, 1984, silver-coated cardboard, ⅞ x 2 ⅞ in. This mimics the official "Museum of Modern Art OPENS" aluminum badge. Photo Credit: Courtesy of Sabra Moore New York City Women's Art Movement Archive, Barnard College

40. "Let MoMA Know" demonstration flier calling for activists to bring cards to attach to the ribbon suspenders that the organizers had created, designed by Kathie Brown, June 14, 1984, photocopy, 14 x 8 ½ in. Photo Credit: Courtesy of Sabra Moore New York City Women's Art Movement Archive, Barnard College

41. Joyce Kozloff holds "MoMA Dearest" sign while parading in front of the Museum of Modern Art, 1984, black-and-white photo, 4 x 6 in. Photo Credit: Carol Bruns/ Courtesy of Sabra Moore New York City Women's Art Movement Archive, Barnard College

42. Unidentified man crossing street away from the protestors marching in front of the museum, 1984, black-and-white photo, 4 x 6 in. Photo Credit: Carol Bruns/ Courtesy of Sabra Moore New York City Women's Art Movement Archive, Barnard College

43. Sabra and Linda Cunningham wearing their ribbon suspenders with artists' show cards attached, MoMA is in the background, 1984, color Polaroid, 3 ½ x 3 ½ in. Photo Credit: Collection of Sabra Moore, photo by Sharon Smith

44. Cover featuring images from the protest against MoMA, *Women Artists News* (*WAN*), Summer 1984, article by Gladys Osterman, pages 1 and 10–11, with double-page photo montage. Photo Credit: © Women Artists News/ Courtesy of Sabra Moore New York City Women's Art Movement Archive, Barnard College

45. Frankie Bushke holds a protest banner reading "Women's Visibility Event (W.A.V.E.)" in front of MoMA, June 14, 1984, 35 mm photo. Photo Credit: © 2015 Clarissa Sligh/ Collection of Sallie Bingham Archives, Duke University

46. Male supporter holding printed and enlarged copy of protest badge at demonstration against MoMA, 1984, black-and-white photo, 4 x 6 in. Photo Credit: Carol Bruns/ Courtesy of Sabra Moore New York City Women's Art Movement Archive, Barnard College

47. Lucy R. Lippard and May Stevens walking together, wearing white, at MoMA protest, June 14, 1984, 35 mm photo. Photo Credit: © 2015 Clarissa Sligh/ Collection of Sallie Bingham Archives, Duke University

48. Sabra Moore, *House Dress/ Gladys Story* with printed text, reverse side, 1984, oil on gessoed paper and wood, string, color Xerox on archival paper, 60 x 45 in. This side was visible inside Printed Matter bookstore. Photo Credit: Sabra Moore

49. Sabra Moore, *Sixteen Houses*, detail, 1984, oil on gessoed wood, color Xerox cuts printed on archival paper, string, 60 x 45 in. Photo Credit: Sabra Moore

50. Sabra standing on the sidewalk in front of Printed Matter with window installation, *House Dress/Gladys Story* and *Sixteen Houses* in double windows, 1984, black-and-white photo, 8 x 10 in. Photo Credit: Roger Mignon

51. Sabra Moore, *Sixteen Houses*, window installation, 1984, oil on gessoed wood, color Xerox cuts printed on archival paper, string, 60 x 45 in. Color 35 mm slide. Photo Credit: Roger Mignon

52. Printed Matter interior with Moore's double window installation visible in the background, 1984, black-and-white print, 8 x 10 in. Photo Credit: Roger Mignon

53. View outside SOHO20 Gallery of one window of Sabra Moore's installation, *Selling the Bed*, with color Xerox text describing her parents selling the old wooden poster bed in trade for a modern Formica bedroom suite, four small houses are in front, 1984, color 35 mm slide. Photo Credit: Roger Mignon

54. Sabra near her window installation, *Selling the Bed*, adjacent to a homeless woman with her cardboard box shelter and umbrella, 1984, black-and-white photo, 8 x 10 in. Photo Credit: Roger Mignon

55. Sabra Moore, *Gesso Bed #3*, 1984, oil on gessoed paper and wood, color Xerox cutouts, string, twigs, roots, 14 x 12 x 12 in. Photo Credit: Sabra Moore

56. Sabra Moore, *Selling the Bed*, 1984, oil on gessoed paper and wood with curtain, 84 x 45 in. Photo Credit: Sabra Moore

57. Sabra Moore, *Gladys Place (view under curtain)*, 1988, laser transfer on curtain, oil on gessoed wood, curtain rod, 21 x 15 ½ in. Photo Credit: Sabra Moore

58. Gladys Parks's quilt hanging on her backyard clothesline in Clarkesville, Texas, undated, color snapshot, 4 x 6 in. Quilt is cotton, 66 x 70 in. Photo Credit: Courtesy of Sabra Moore

59. *Art Against Apartheid* protest flier, planning meeting at Central Hall Gallery, 1984, photo offset, 11 x 8 ½ in. Photo Credit: Collection of Sabra Moore

60. *Art Against Apartheid/The Year of the South African Woman* poster, designed by Nancy Spero, 1984, red and black on white, color offset, 22 x 17 in. Photo Credit: Courtesy of Sabra Moore New York City Women's Art Movement Archive, Barnard College

61. *Celebrate Nelson Mandela's Birthday* flier sponsored by *Art Against Apartheid*, 1984, photo offset, 11 x 8 ½ in. Photo Credit: Courtesy of Sabra Moore New York City Women's Art Movement Archive, Barnard College

62. *Artist Street Action Against Apartheid* leaflet, 1984, photo offset, 14 x 8 ½ in. Photo Credit: Collection of Sabra Moore

63. *Emma Amos and "X Flag"*, card for a presentation by Emma Amos at Hatch-Billops Collection, New York City, 1994, photo offset, 4 ¼ x 6 in. Photo Credit: ©Emma Amos, Licensed by VAGA, New York, NY/photo by Becket Logan

64. Vivian E. Browne, *Versitile Source*, detail, 1987, acrylic on canvas, 14 x 20 in. Photo Credit: Estate of Vivian E. Browne, Courtesy of Adobe Krow Archives

65. Camille Billops dancing, card for Hatch-Billops Collection Christmas sale, 1987, photo offset, 6 x 4 ¼ in. Photo Credit: Camille Billops

66. NYC/WCA board meeting in Bibi Lenĉek's loft on the occasion of Annie Shaver-Crandall's final meeting as president, 1984, black-and-white photo, 4 x 6 in. Back row, left to right: Unidentified woman, Annette Weintraub, Carol Grape, Ora Lerman, Sylvia Sleigh, and Sabra Moore. Front row seated, left to right: Bibi Lenĉek, Linda Selvin, Annie Shaver-Crandall, Linda Cunningham, and Jacqueline Wray. Photo Credit: Bibi Lenĉek/ Courtesy of Sabra Moore New York City Women's Art Movement Archive, Barnard College

67. The group five minutes later: Annie is holding the book she was awarded as a gift and Linda is holding the Let MoMA Know flier from our successful demonstration, 1984, black-and-white photo, 4 x 6 in. Photo Credit: Bibi Lenĉek/ Courtesy of Sabra Moore New York City Women's Art Movement Archive, Barnard College

68. *Speaking Volumes: Women Artists' Books*, curated by Lucy R. Lippard at AIR Gallery, card drawn by Lucy R. Lippard, circa 1984, Xerox on cardstock, 4 x 6 in. Photo Credit: Collection of Sabra Moore

69. Marithelma Costa reading poetry, galleryonetwentyeight, 1991, black-and-white print, 8 x 10 in. Photo Credit: Roger Mignon

70. *Earth/Air/Fire/Water* show card, Bernice Steinbaum Gallery, *Heresies* Benefit, 1984, color offset. Photo Credit: Courtesy of Sabra Moore New York City Women's Art Movement Archive, Barnard College

Portfolio A

1. Sabra Moore, *House Dress/Gladys Story*, one of a two-part window installation, Printed Matter, 1984, oil on gessoed paper and wood, string, color Xerox on archival paper, 60 x 45 in. Photo Credit: Sabra Moore

2. Great-grandmother Lillie Parks's crazy quilt, circa 1950s, recycled cloth, embroidery, 80 x 72 in. Photo Credit: Courtesy of Sabra Moore

3. Sabra Moore, *Pieced for Caroline & Harry*, 1982, photocopier images created in Xerox machine and printed on archival paper, 38 ½ x 35 ¼ in. Photo Credit: Sabra Moore

4. Faith Ringgold, *Echoes of Harlem*, 1980, acrylic on canvas, 96 x 84 in. Photo Credit © 1980 Faith Ringgold, Collection of Studio Museum in Harlem, NYC

5. Diana Kurz, *Children (An Artist's Response to the Holocaust)*, series related to her murdered Viennese kin, 2002, oil on canvas and mixed media, 79 x 61 ½ x 4 in. Photo Credit: Diana Kurz

6. Sylvia Sleigh, *Working At Home*, 1969, oil on canvas, 56 x 32 in. Photo Credit: Hauser & Wirth Collection, Switzerland

7. Ora Lerman, *Red Comes to Wolf's Bed and Transforms His Appetite*, early 1980s, hand-ground oil on canvas, 36 x 24 in. Photo Credit: Ora Lerman Charitable Trust, photo by Malcolm Varon

8. Sabra Moore, *Selling the Bed*, 1984, oil on gessoed paper and wood with curtain, 84 x 45 in. Created for a two-part window installation at SOHO20 Gallery with texts relating to Sabra's family selling the hand-made wooden bed for a mass-produced Formica bedroom suite. Photo Credit: Sabra Moore

9. Bibi Lenĉek, *From an Interior, 4 (Green)*, 1975, oil on canvas, 48 x 50 in. Photo Credit: Bibi Lenĉek

10. Sabra Moore, *A Roomful of Mothers*, 1983, oil on gessoed paper with color Xerox montage of photos and photo transfer print, 8 x 6 ft. Mothers of members of the *Heresies* collective, left to right, naming the daughters: Lucy R. Lippard, Sue Heinemann, Michelle Godwin, Vanalyne Green, Sandra De Sando, Sabra Moore, Patricia Spears Jones, and Josely Carvalho. Lower right, left to right: Kathie Brown, Kay Kenny, and Holly Zox. Upper left in wedding dress: Lyn Hughes. Photo Credit: Sabra Moore

11. Sabra Moore, *A Roomful of Mothers*, 1983, color Xerox on archival paper with glue, 8 x 6 ft. each. This double "page" was made for *Classified: Big Pages from the Heresies Collective* exhibition at the New Museum, 1983. The "quilt" is pieced with fragments of the handwritten stories exploring our class backgrounds overlaid with lace, cloth, and cutouts from our mothers' snapshots. Photo Credit: Sabra Moore

12. Marilyn Lanfear, *Every Night She Latched All The Windows & Locked All The Doors & Put The Babies In Her Bed*, 1997, mother-of-pearl buttons, linen, 95 x 95 in. Photo Credit: Marilyn Lanfear

13. Sabra Moore, *Opening Doors Work*, 1985–1995, oil on gessoed paper and wood, string, light bulb, color Xerox cutouts, metal speculum, 88 x 48 x 21 in. Double doors open to two stories related to reproductive rights; this view opens to Sabra's story. The closed door opens to Opal's story, Sabra's paternal aunt. Photo Credit: Sabra Moore

14. Emma Amos, *Will You Forget Me?*, 1991, acrylic on canvas with African fabric borders, 64 x 33 in. Photo Credit:

©Emma Amos, Licensed by VAGA, New York, NY/photo by Becket Logan

15. Mimi Smith, *Knit Baby*, 1968, yarn, undershirt, thread, 21 x 10 x 4 in. Photo Credit: Mimi Smith

16. Kazuko Miyamoto, *Woman on Stepladder*, laser transfer on silk. Photo Credit: Kazuko Miyamoto

Chapter 6

1. *Heresies* issue #18: Mothers, Mags & Movie Stars cover, 1985. Photo Credit: © 1985, *Heresies: A Feminist Publication on Art and Politics*

2. Carol Sun, *China Mary Series: Herstory*, 4 panels, 2002, acrylic on canvas, 76 x100 in. Objects include abaci, books, chains, chopsticks, teapots. Photo Credit: Carol Sun

3. Patricia Spears Jones, *Mammies*, page art for *Heresies* issue #18: Mothers, Mags & Movie Stars, 1985, black-and-white Xerox, 11 x 8 ½ in. Photo Credit: Patricia Spears Jones

4. Marilyn Lanfear, *Table with Ink Paintings*, 2001, ink paintings in vintage frames on antique wood table, 42 x 60 x 20 in. Photo Credit: Marilyn Lanfear

5. Marilyn Lanfear, *Sara Crew*, 1999, lead, antique chair, 23 x14 x 18 in. Photo Credit: Marilyn Lanfear

6. Diana Kurz, *Freedom Fighters (Portrait of Remembrance* series), 1999, oil and paper on canvas with wood, 75 ½ x 57 in. Photo Credit: Diana Kurz

7. May Stevens, *Forming the Fifth International*, 1985, acrylic on canvas, 78 x 120 in. Photo Credit: May Stevens, Courtesy of Ryan Lee Gallery, New York

8. Lorraine O'Grady, *Miscegenated Family Album (Sisters IV). L. Devonia's sister Lorraine. R. Nefertiti's sister Mutnedjmet*, 1980/1994, Cibachrome prints, 26 x 37 in. Photo Credit: Courtesy Alexander Gray Associates, © 2015 Lorraine O'Grady/Artists Rights Society (ARS), New York

9. Sharon Gilbert, *Etymography*, 1983, paper and glue, 35 x 31 x 5 ½ in. Photo Credit: Estate of Sharon Gilbert

10. Emma Amos, *The Gift*, forty-four paintings of sister artists and friends, 1990–1991, watercolor on paper, 26 x 20 in. each. Photo Credit: ©Emma Amos, Licensed by VAGA, New York, NY/photo by Becket Logan

11. Mary Beth Edelson, *Some Living American Women Artists/Last Supper*, 1972, cut-and-pasted gelatin silver prints with crayon and transfer type on printed paper with typewriting on cut-and-taped paper, 28 ¼ x 43 in. Photo Credit: Mary Beth Edelson

12. Kathy Grove, *The Other Series: After Durer*, 1988, gouache and watercolor on C-print, 25 ½ x 20 ¾ in. Photo Credit: Kathy Grove

13. Catalina Parra, *Let the Pope Pay THE E(X)TERNAL DEBT/ LA DEUDA E(X)TERNA que la pagne el Papa* (series #1 of 5), 1991, mixed media collage, photograph, text, white

board, transparent thread, 40 x 30 in. Photo Credit: Catalina Parra

14. May Stevens, *Big Daddy & George Jackson*, 1972, collage on paper, 22 x 27 ¾ in. Photo Credit: May Stevens, Courtesy of Ryan Lee Gallery, New York

15. Kazuko, *Body, Connections Project/Conexus*, book page, 1987, photo, 8 x 3 in. Photo Credit: Kazuko Miyamoto, Courtesy of Connections Project/Conexus Archive, Barnard College

16. Sylvia Sleigh, *Invitation to a Voyage: The Hudson River at Fishkill*, detail, *Riverside*, Panel 6, 1979–1999, oil on fourteen canvases, 96 x 60 in. each. Photo Credit: Sylvia Sleigh/ Hudson River Museum, Yonkers, NY

17. Miriam Schapiro, *Love's Labor*, 1991, acrylic and fabric on canvas, 90 x 72 in. Photo Credit: Estate of Miriam Schapiro

18. Kathy Grove, *The Other Series: After Delacroix*, 1988, gouache and watercolor on C-print, 24 ½ x 21 ½ in. Photo Credit: Kathy Grove

19. Faith Ringgold, postcard invitation for *The French Collection* exhibit at Bernice Steinbaum Gallery with key to people shown in painting, 1992, color offset on cardstock, 6 ½ x 7 ½ in. Photo Credit: Faith Ringgold/ Courtesy of Sabra Moore

20. Faith Ringgold, *Sunflower Quilting Bee at Arles: French Collection Part 1 #4*, 1991, acrylic on canvas, tie-dyed pieced fabric border, 74 x 80 in. Photo Credit: © Faith Ringgold/ Private Collection

21. Clarissa Sligh, *Reframing the Past* card for lecture at Hillwood Art Museum, 1991, photo offset, 5 ½ x 8 ½ in. Photo Credit: Clarissa Sligh, photo by Ellen Eisenman

22. Grace Graupe-Pillard, *The Wonder Women Wall*, installation at Port Authority Bus Terminal, North Terminal, March–December 1992, individual pastel cutout canvas drawings affixed directly to way with map tacks and staples, 20 x 20 ft. Photo Credit: Grace Graupe-Pillard

Chapter 7

1. *Heresies* issue #20: Activists/Organizers. . . cover, 1985. Photo Credit: © 1985 *Heresies Magazine: A Feminist Publication on Art and Politics*

2. Martha Wilson, *Nancy Reagan at the Inauguration*, performance, 1985, black-and-white print reproduced in *Heresies* issue # 19: Satire, page 7. As Martha states in her permission letter to Sabra: "This image was a black-and-white print that was used in the layout of *Heresies*, and destroyed in the process, so it no longer exists—or it's deep in a pile of *Heresies* layout materials somewhere! To create an electronic image, I would have scanned the magazine, as you did." Photo Credit: Courtesy of Martha Wilson and P.P.O.W Gallery, New York

3. Janet Pfunder and Janey Washburn, *Paintings*, Esta Robinson Gallery, 1983, photo offset card, 8 ½ x 5 in. Photo Credit: Courtesy of Sabra Moore New York City Women's Art Movement Archive, Barnard College

4. Chris Costan, solo exhibit at Avenue B Gallery showing Chris Costan next to one of her large paintings, 1985, color offset card, 6 x 4 ½ in. Photo Credit: David Cox, 1986/ Courtesy of Chris Costan

5. *Avenue B Basement*, Avenue B Gallery group show, 1984, color offset poster, 9 x 8 ½ in. Photo Credit: Collection of Sabra Moore

6. Linda Peer, *Untitled*, 1986, oil on wood, 14 x 12 x 10 in. Photo Credit: Linda Peer

7. Kathie Brown, *Choice Works: Artists Speak Out on Reproductive Rights* poster design, Central Hall Gallery, cosponsored by Political Art Documentation/Distribution (PADD) in conjunction with *State of Mind/State of the Union*, 1985, color offset, unfolds to 17 x 11 in. Photo Credit: Courtesy of Sabra Moore New York City Women's Art Movement Archive, Barnard College

8. *We the People, Counter Inaugural Cabaret* poster, New Heritage Theater, organized by *Artists Call Against US Intervention in Central America*, 1985, photo offset, 11 x 17 in. Photo Credit: Collection of Sabra Moore

9. *State of the Mind/State of the Union* performance series, Central Hall Gallery, cosponsored by Political Art Documentation/Distribution (PADD), 1985, offset, 11 x 8 ½ in. Photo Credit: Collection of Sabra Moore

10.–12. Sabra Moore, *Opening Doors Work*, 1985–1995, oil on gessoed paper and wood, string, light bulb, color Xerox cutouts, metal speculum, 88 x 48 x 21 in. (all). Double doors open to two stories related to reproductive rights; this view opens to Sabra's story. The closed door opens to the story of Opal, Sabra's paternal aunt. See 10–12 to identify various details. Photo Credit: Sabra Moore

10. Sabra Moore, *Opening Doors Work*, beaded speculum next to one of three additional versions of the speculum in various materials, 1985, metal speculum, string, papier-mâché, gesso, oil, size varies, located inside draw on right side of sculpture. Photo Credit: Sabra Moore

11. Sabra Moore, *Opening Doors Work*, detail showing hand cutout in right side of sculpture over drawer with four speculums. Photo Credit: Sabra Moore

12. Sabra Moore, *Opening Doors Work* with both doors closed. Photo Credit: Sabra Moore

13. Sabra Moore, *Opening Doors Work*, detail from Opal's story side with door open to reveal part of text and the laser transfer print dress inside. Photo Credit: Sabra Moore

14. Sharon Niemeczyk, page art for *Heresies* issue #14: The Women's Pages, 1982, page 4. Photo Credit: Sharon Niemeczyk

15. Sabra at work on *Opening Doors Work* in her Warren Street studio, 1985. Photo Credit: Roger Mignon

16. Roger Mignon, *Keep On Trucking*, 1985, colored pencil and ink on paper, 8 ¾ x 12 in., made for Sabra's 42nd birthday. Photo Credit: Roger Mignon

17. Ilona Granet, *Curb Your Animal Instinct*, 1986, metal sign, silkscreen enamel on metal, 24 x 26 in. Photo Credit: Ilona Granet

18. Sabra's poetry reading/performance during *Choice Works* exhibit, Central Hall Gallery, 1985, black-and-white photo, 8 x10 in. Photos of Sabra's grandparents were projected onto the curtain/window she made for the *Dream Kitschen* at the *Heresies* New Museum show. Photo Credit: Roger Mignon

19. Sabra Moore, *Gladys Apron #2 with Nest* (series of four), 1985, oil on gessoed paper with wood, 24 x 24 in. Photo Credit: Sabra Moore

20. Sabra Moore, *Gladys Apron #1* (series of four), 1985, oil on gessoed paper with wood, 24 x 24 in Photo Credit: Sabra Moore

21. Sabra Moore, *Gladys Apron* installation showing window with four aprons, Windows on White, 1985, black-and-white print, 10 x 8 in. Photo Credit: Roger Mignon

22. Sabra Moore, *Gladys Apron* installation showing triple windows, 1985, color slide. Photo Credit: Roger Mignon

23. Sabra Moore, *Xerox Book Pages with Gladys Apron*, 1980, color Xerox on archival paper, glue, 76 x 60 in. Photo Credit: Sabra Moore

24. Catalina Parra, *Welcome Home*, 1983, mixed media collage, photograph, text, brown tape, blue thread, white paper board, 28 x 22 in. Photo Credit: Catalina Parra

25. Bibi Lenĉek, *Untitled*, 1980, pastel on canvas mounted on folding screen, 50 x 82 in. Photo Credit: Bibi Lenĉek

26. Catalina Parra, book page, *Race, Connections Project/Conexus*, 1987, newspaper clipping with gauze on paper, 8 x 3 in. Photo credit: Catalina Parra, Courtesy of Connections Project Conexus Archive, Barnard College

27. Sharon Gilbert, birth announcement for Elena Floris, daughter of Sharon Gilbert and Vyt Bakaitis, 1982, color Xerox on card, 4 ¼ x 5 ½ in. Photo Credit: Estate of Sharon Gilbert

28. *Latitudes of Time* curated by Sharon Gilbert, Bibi Lenĉek, and Sabra Moore, two-fold announcement card, City Gallery, 1985, photo offset, unfolds to 7 ¼ x 8 ½ in. Photo Credit: Courtesy of Sabra Moore New York City Women's Art Movement Archive, Barnard College

29. Sabra at Chaco Canyon doorway, circa 1985, 35 mm color slide. Photo Credit: Roger Mignon

30. Ana Mendieta, *Untitled* (Silueta series), 1978, color photo, 8 x 10 in. Photo Credit: © The Estate of Ana Mendieta Collection, LLC, Courtesy of Galerie Lelong, New York

31. Ana Mendieta, *Untitled (Earth-Body Works)*, 1982, Caumsett State Park, Long Island, 35 mm color slide. Photo Credit: © The Estate of Ana Mendieta Collection, LLC, Courtesy of Galerie Lelong, New York

32. Ana Mendieta, *Untitled (Earth-Body Works)*, 1982, Caumsett State Park, Long Island. 35 mm color slide. Photo Credit: © The Estate of Ana Mendieta Collection, LLC, Courtesy of Galerie Lelong, New York

33. Ana Mendieta, *Untitled*, 1984, ink and wash on handmade paper, 24 ½ x 18 ¼ in. Photo Credit: © The Estate of Ana Mendieta Collection, LLC, Courtesy of Galerie Lelong, New York

34. *Heresies* issue #18: Mothers, Mags & Movie Stars dedication page to Ana Mendieta, written by the editorial collective with photos by Mary Beth Edelson, 1985. Photo Credit: © 1985, Reprinted from *Heresies* issue #18, Mothers, *Mags & Movie Stars*

35. Ana Mendieta, *Untitled*, 1982, design on leaf, approximately 5 ½ x 3 ¾ in. Photo Credit: © The Estate of Ana Mendieta Collection, LLC, Courtesy of Galerie Lelong, New York

36. Guerrilla Girls postering, *What Do These Artists Have in Common?*, 1985, black-and-white photo. Photo Credit: © Lori Grinker/ Contact Press Images

37. Mary Beth Edelson, *Coming Round*, 1983, oil on two (2) 8 x 6 ft. canvas panels, total dimensions 8 x12 ft. Photo Credit: Mary Beth Edelson

38. Guerrilla Girls Palladium exhibit card, October 7, 1985, color offset, 7 x 3 ½ in. Card reads: "Please Join Guerrilla Girls The Women Artists Terrorist Organization. . ." Photo Credit: Guerrilla Girls/ Courtesy of Sabra Moore

39. Sabra Moore, *Give & Take* (box), part one of a two-part installation in which visitors could "take a book" from the box marked "take" and then "give" a word or a coin, 1985, oil on gessoed wood, *Wash & Iron* books, 5 x 4 ½ x 3 ½ in. Photo Credit: Sabra Moore

40. Sabra Moore, *Give & Take* (hand/bag), part two of a two-part installation in which visitors could leave a word or a coin in the wire net bag in return for taking a book, 1985, oil on gessoed wood, painted mannequin hand, net bag with cloth string, 15 ¼ x 4 x 7 ½ in. Photo Credit: Sabra Moore

41. Sabra Moore, *Wash & Iron*, 1985, accordion-folded artist's book inside translucent cover, photocopy on archival paper, cloth tie, color Xerox on translucent paper with thread, 5 x 4 ⅛ in. Photo Credit: Sabra Moore

42. Marilyn Lanfear, *Pink Organdy Blouse*, 1987, lead, cast iron stand on wood shoulders, blouse, 32 x 12 in., overall height: 45 in. Photo Credit: Marilyn Lanfear

43. Ora Lerman, *Geese Lay Golden Eggs in the Attics of Sidilkow*, 1986, watercolor, 18 x 24 in. Photo Credit: Ora Lerman Charitable trust/ Photo by Malcolm Varon

44. Marilyn Lanfear, *Diana's Huipil with Una Talla and Hand-woven Labels*, 1987, lead, cast iron stand on wood shoulders, blouse, 32 x 12 in., overall height: 45 in. Photo Credit: Marilyn Lanfear

45. *Heresies* issue #19: Satire cover, 1985. Photo Credit: © 1985 *Heresies Magazine: A Feminist Publication on Art and Politics*

46. Sabra Moore, *A Roomful of Mothers* montage, *Heresies* issue #18: Mothers, Mags & Movie Stars, page 3, 1985, photo montage, size variable. The mothers of editorial

collective members right to left: Lucy R. Lippard, Penelope Goodfriend, Kathie Brown, Josely Carvalho (in hat), Sandra de Sando (crouching), Michelle Godwin, Kay Kenny (in nurse's cap) Chris Costan (above Kay), and Sabra Moore. Photo Credit: Sabra Moore

47. *Heresies Speaks Up* flier for performance and talk for the double issue *Heresies* issue #18 and issue #19, Franklin Furnace, 1985, photocopy, 11 x 8 ½ in. Photo Credit: Courtesy of Sabra Moore New York City Women's Art Movement Archive, Barnard College

48. Cecilia Vicuña, *Cementerio*, New York, 1982, found objects, size varies. Cecilia describes these constructions as "basuritas Chileanas in New York," or "little pieces of Chilean garbage," to explore the idea of "throwaways" in a text/visual page for *Heresies* issue #24: 12 Years, page 92. Photo Credit: Cecilia Vicuña

49. Carol Sun, *Maternity*, 1990, 4 panels, acrylic on canvas, 76 x 100 in. Photo Credit: Carol Sun

50. Cecilia Vicuña, *Precario/Precarious*, invitation card for exhibit at Exit Art Gallery, New York, 1990, photo offset, 6 x 6 in. Photo Credit: Cecilia Vicuña

51. Virginia Maksymowicz, *The History of Art*, 1988, cast paper and acrylic paint, cast from life. This one depicts cave art. Photo Credit: Virginia Maksymowicz

52. Virginia Maksymowicz, *The History of Art*, 1988, cast paper and acrylic paint, cast from life. This one depicts Byzantine mosaics. Photo Credit: Virginia Maksymowicz

53. *Liberty. . . And The Pursuit of Liberty*, NYC/WCA poster for the 1985 Annual National Conference, 1986, color offset, 12 x 9 ½ in., unfolds to 24 x 19 in. Photo Credit: Courtesy of Sabra Moore New York City Women's Art Movement Archive, Barnard College

54. Announcement card for *Costumes, Masks and Disguises* and two other exhibits at the Clocktower organized by the NYC/WCA for the 1986 Annual National Conference, 1986, color offset, 5 x 7 in. Photo Credit: Courtesy of Sabra Moore New York City Women's Art Movement Archive, Barnard College

55. Annie Shaver-Crandell, tenure/birthday card, 1986, photocopy on orange paper, 8 ½ x 11 in. Card reads: " I know she's having another birthday, but she looks younger somehow. . ." "Oh, that's because she finally got tenure." Photo Credit: Courtesy of Sabra Moore New York City Women's Art Movement Archive, Barnard College

56. Sylvia Sleigh, *Arlene Raven and Nancy Grossman*, 2004, oil on canvas, 21 x 30 in. Photo Credit: Estate of Sylvia Sleigh/ Private collection, Brooklyn, NY

57. Double portrait photo of Sylvia Sleigh and Lawrence Alloway, circa 1968, gelatin silver print. Photo Credit: Estate of Sylvia Sleigh, photo by Vivian Campbell Stoll

58. Sylvia Sleigh, *Howardena Pindell*, 1978, oil on canvas, 36 x 24 in. Photo Credit: Estate of Sylvia Sleigh/ Private collection

59. Donna Henes, *Dressing Our Wounds in Warm Clothes; Ward's Island Energy Trance Mission*, 1980, color, three-page foldout. Photo Credit: Reprinted by permission of Donna Henes

60. Donna Henes, *Mama Donna's Tea Garden & Healing Haven*, announcing new address "with great pleasure, relief and hope," 1989, photocopy, 3 ¾ x 6 in. Photo Credit: Reprinted by permission of Donna Henes

61. Sabra Moore, *Wash & Iron* (AKIN series), detail with text from "wash" side: "& rinse water. We washed by hand. I liked to put my hands inside the bluing water," 1985, accordion-folded book, photocopy on archival paper, 4 ¼ x 3 ½ in., unfolds to 42 in. Photo Credit: Sabra Moore

62. Sabra Moore, *Wash & Iron* (AKIN series), detail with text from "iron" side: "preferred the hand iron, I could do difficult clothes, like his railroad cap, sprinkle first," 1985, accordion-folded book, photocopy on archival paper, 4 ¼ x 3 ½ in., unfolds to 42 in. Photo Credit: Sabra Moore

Chapter 8

1. Sabra at her artist residency at the Helene Wurlitzer Foundation in Taos, standing in the yard with the neighbor horse, Chowpena, 1986, 35 mm color slide. Photo Credit: Roger Mignon

2. Looking for rock art inside caves at Tsankawi, pre-Puebloan site near Bandelier National Monument, New Mexico, 1986, 35 mm color slide. Photo Credit: Roger Mignon

3. Sabra Moore, journal drawings, rock art in Chaco Canyon, New Mexico, Books #40 and #42, 1986, black ink on paper, 9 ¾ x 7 ½ in. Photo Credit: Sabra Moore

4. Sabra Moore, journal drawings, rock art at Lyden, New Mexico, Books #40 and #42, 1986, black ink on paper, 9 ¾ x 7 ½ in. Photo Credit: Sabra Moore

5. Sabra Moore, journal drawings, rock art at painted cave, Bandelier National Monument, New Mexico, Books #40 and #42, 1986, black ink on paper, 9 ¾ x 7 ½ in. Photo Credit: Sabra Moore

6. Sabra Moore, journal drawings, rock art at Lyden, New Mexico, Books #40 and #42, 1986, black ink on paper, 9 ¾ x 7 ½ in. Photo Credit: Sabra Moore

7. Sabra Moore, *Door*, detail showing "ribs," 1986, oil on gessoed wood with fabric strips, sticks, string, and beads, 63 ½ x 36 x 7 ½ in. Photo Credit: Sabra Moore/ Rowan University Art Gallery, Sylvia Sleigh Collection

8. Sabra Moore, *Door*, 1986, oil on gessoed wood with fabric strips, sticks, string, and beads, 63 ½ x 36 x 7 ½ in. Photo Credit: Sabra Moore/ Rowan University Art Gallery, Sylvia Sleigh Collection

9. Sabra Moore, *Door*, detail showing right side "ribs," 1986, oil on gessoed wood with fabric strips, sticks, string, and beads, 63 ½ x 36 x 7 ½ in. Photo Credit: Sabra Moore/ Rowan University Art Gallery, Sylvia Sleigh Collection

10. Sabra Moore, *Land*, 1986, oil of gessoed paper and wood with twigs and Xerox cutout, 30 x 13 x 5 in. Cutout shows baby Sabra on raft. Photo Credit: Sabra Moore/ Collection of Linda Peer

11. Roger Mignon in front of his temporary mural painting of whales along a fence at the New York Aquarium in Brooklyn, 1986, 35 mm color slide. Photo Credit: Courtesy of Roger Mignon

12. Roger's mural in progress with paint buckets and scale model painted sketch resting along sidewalk, 1986, 35 mm color slide. Photo Credit: Roger Mignon

13. Frances Buschke, *Untitled* collage, circa 1978, rice paper, seeds, string, feathers, gum Arabic, earth pigments, oil pastel, 3 ½ x 3 ⅛ in. Photo Credit: Estate of Frances Buschke/ Courtesy of Sabra Moore

14. Handwritten letter from Louise Bourgeois to Sabra confirming participation in *Connections Project/Conexus*. Photo Credit: Courtesy of Connections Project/Conexus Archive, Barnard College

15. Frances Buschke, *Untitled* collage, Taos, April 1978, mixed media on rice paper, oil pastel, earth pigments, gum Arabic, 10 ¾ x 8 ¼ in. Photo Credit: Estate of Frances Buschke/ Courtesy of Sabra Moore

16. Christine Moore visiting Sabra at Wurlitzer Foundation studio in Taos, 1986, color snapshot, 4 x 6 in. Photo Credit: Roger Mignon

17. Sabra drawing rock art at Lyden, New Mexico, 1986, 35 mm color slide. Photo Credit: Roger Mignon

18. Jaune Quick-to-See Smith, *The Courthouse Steps*, 1987, oil on canvas, 72 x 60 in. Photo Credit: Jaune Quick-to-See Smith

19. Sabra Moore, *Left Over*, 1992, oil on gessoed wood, tin, photo, twig, 34 x 28 x 8 in. Photo Credit: Sabra Moore

20. Jaune Quick-to-See Smith, *Sunset on Escarpment*, 1987, oil on canvas, 72 x 60 in. Photo Credit: Jaune Quick-to-See Smith

21. Sabra Moore, *Woodsman*, artist's book, double page detail, 1997, Xerox on glossy paper with oil on gessoed paper, 38 accordion-folded pages, 6 ¾ x 4 ¾ in. Photo Credit: Sabra Moore

22. Emmadele Lewis, Daddy's cousin, and her mother Mitty in Grandmother's living room near Clarksville, Texas, circa 1950s, black-and-white snapshot. Photo Credit: Collection of Sabra Moore

23. *Now You See Us* flier produced by the NYC/WCA and billed as *Women Artists Visibility Event II* to protest lack of representation by women artists in exhibits at the Guggenheim Museum, 1986, photocopy, 11 x 8 ½ in. Photo Credit: Courtesy of Sabra Moore New York City Women's Art Movement Archive, Barnard College

24. Guerrilla Girls invitation to Guggenheim protest, June 28, 1986. Photo Credit: Courtesy of Sabra Moore New York City Women's Art Movement Archive, Barnard College

25. *Women's Caucus for Art Gala*, benefit for the NYC/WCA at the loft of Shirley Smith and Jeannette Murray, 1986, photocopy flier, 14 x 8 ½ in. Photo Credit: Courtesy of Sabra Moore New York City Women's Art Movement Archive, Barnard College

26. Harmony Hammond, *A Queer Reader*, 2003, archival digital print, 43 x 29 in. Photo Credit: Courtesy of Alexander Gray Associates. Art ©Harmony Hammond/ Licensed by VAGA, New York

27. Catalina Parra, *The Human Touch*, (series #1 of 6), 1989, mixed media collage, photograph, newspaper, text, red thread, white paper board, 28 x 22 in. Photo Credit: Catalina Parra

28. Vivian E. Browne, *The Chief's Attendant #102*, 1972, acrylic on canvas, 64 x 53 in. Photo Credit: Estate of Vivian E. Browne, Courtesy of Adobe Krow Archives

29. Roger Mignon, *Forces of Nature #2*, 1986, pastel of pastel cloth, 92 x 60 in. Photo Credit: Roger Mignon

30. Roger Mignon, *Large Drawings*, Halloween evening opening, Atlantic Avenue, October 31, 1986, 35 mm color slide. Ora Lerman and Sabra are in animated conversation in front of Roger's large-scale drawings of Carol Sun in Tai Chi poses. Photo Credit: Courtesy of Sabra Moore

31. Roger Mignon, *Forces of Nature #1*, 1986, pastel of pastel cloth, 92 x 60 in. Photo Credit: Roger Mignon

32. Daddy Chess closing the window in the guest bedroom while reflected in mirror during the lonely period of his wife's illness, circa 1986, black-and-white photo, 8 x 10 in. Photo Credit: Sabra Moore, print by Roger Mignon

33. Guest bedroom of Mother Gladys's house with mirror and spindle bed, circa 1986, black-and-white photo, 8 x10 in. Photo Credit: Sabra Moore, print by Roger Mignon

34. Mother Gladys and Daddy Chess walking into Briggins Cemetery with Christine Moore, their oldest daughter, Acworth, Texas, circa 1983, black-and-white photo, 8 x 10 in. Photo Credit: Roger Mignon

35. Gladys storytelling about the people named on the tombstones, Briggins Cemetery Acworth, Texas, circa 1983, black-and-white photo, 8 x 10 in. Photo Credit: Roger Mignon

36.–39. Covers, booklets for the photocopier edition of *150 Artists Book, Connections Project/Conexus* designed alternately by Josely Carvalho and Sabra Moore using the stamps and envelopes sent by the participating artists with their page art. Each booklet contains artworks on one of eight themes of social concern, Environment (36), Body (37), Race (38), Shelter (39), 1986, photocopy on archival paper, 8 ¼ x 5 ½ in. Photo Credit: Courtesy of Sabra Moore New York City Women's Art Movement Archive, Barnard College

40. *Birth* cover, booklet on that theme for the photocopier edition of *150 Artists Book, Connections Project/Conexus*, 1986, photocopy on archival paper, 8 ¼ x 5 ½ in. Photo

Credit: Courtesy of Sabra Moore New York City Women's Art Movement Archive, Barnard College

41. Louise Bourgeois, *La Belle Pendue (verso)*, book page for *150 Artists Book, Connections Project/Conexus* on the theme of body, 1986, ink on watercolor paper, 8 ¼ x 5 in. Photo Credit: Louise Bourgeois/ ©The Easton Foundation/Licensed by VAGA, New York, NY, photo by Christopher Burke

42. Louise Bourgeois, *La Belle Pendue (recto)*, book page for *150 Artists Book, Connections Project/Conexus* on the theme of body, 1986, ink on watercolor paper, 8 ¼ x 5 in. Photo Credit: Louise Bourgeois/ ©The Easton Foundation/Licensed by VAGA, New York, NY, photo by Christopher Burke

43. *War/Death* cover, booklet on that theme for the photocopier edition of *150 Artists Book, Connections Project/Conexus*, 1986, photocopy on archival paper, 8 ¼ x 5 ½ in. Photo Credit: Courtesy of Sabra Moore New York City Women's Art Movement Archive, Barnard College

44. *Food* cover, booklet on that theme for the photocopier edition of *150 Artists Book, Connections Project/Conexus*, 1986, photocopy on archival paper, 8 ¼ x 5 ½ in. Photo Credit: Courtesy of Sabra Moore New York City Women's Art Movement Archive, Barnard College

45. Silkscreen packet with ties for the nine-booklet photocopier edition of *150 Artists Book, Connections Project/Conexus* designed collaboratively by Josely Carvalho and Sabra Moore, 1986, silkscreen on archival paper, ribbon, 5 ½ x 8 ⅝ x ⅝ in. each. Photo Credit: Courtesy of Sabra Moore New York City Women's Art Movement Archive, Barnard College

46. *Spirit* back cover, booklet on that theme for the photocopier edition of *150 Artists Book, Connections Project/Conexus*, 1986, photocopy on archival paper, 8 ¼ x 5 ½ in. Photo Credit: Courtesy of Sabra Moore New York City Women's Art Movement Archive, Barnard College

47. Installation of *Connections Project/Conexus* at Museum of Contemporary Hispanic Art (MoCHA), New York, 1987, showing wall with artworks on themes of body and shelter with house-shaped stands for original book pages of *150 Artists Book* in the foreground, 1987, 35 mm color slide. Photo Credit: Courtesy of Connections Project/Conexus Archive, Barnard College

48. Installation at MoCHA showing the large-scale artworks of Kazuko and Iole de Freitas on the theme of body with some of the original book pages in the foreground on house-shaped stands, 1987, 35 mm color slide. Photo Credit: Courtesy of Connections Project/Conexus Archive, Barnard College

49. Installation at MoCHA showing the large-scale artworks of Sabra Moore and Maria do Carmo Secco on the theme of shelter, 1987, 35 mm color slide. Photo Credit: Courtesy of Connections Project/Conexus Archive, Barnard College

50. Sabra, Sharon Gilbert, and Kathie Brown at the opening of *Connections Project/Conexus* at Museum of Contemporary Hispanic Art (MoCHA), New York, January 15, 1987, black-and-white photo, 8 x 10 in. Kathie was one of the 32 principal artists with her theme of food and Sharon made a book page on the theme of environment. Photo Credit: Roger Mignon

51. Installation at MoCHA showing (left to right) the large-scale artworks of Maria Lidia Magliani, Marina Gutierrez, Sophie Tassinari, and Jaune Quick-To-See Smith on the theme of race, 1987, 35 mm color slide. Photo Credit: Courtesy of Connections Project/Conexus Archive, Barnard College

52. Mirtes Zwierzynzki, original book page for *150 Artists Book, Connections Project/Conexus* on the theme of birth, 1986, paint on watercolor paper, 8 ¼ x 5 in. Photo Credit: Mirtes Zwierzynzki, Courtesy of Connections Project/Conexus Archive, Barnard College

53. Mimi Smith, original book page for *150 Artists Book, Connections Project/Conexus* on the theme of shelter, 1986, paint and pencil on watercolor paper, 8 ¼ x 5 in. Photo Credit: Mimi Smith, Courtesy of Connections Project/Conexus Archive, Barnard College

54. Emma Amos, original book page for *150 Artists Book, Connections Project/Conexus* on the theme of race, 1986, acrylic on watercolor paper, 8 ¼ x 5 in. Photo Credit: Emma Amos, Courtesy of Connections Project/Conexus Archive, Barnard College

55. Pamela Wye, original book page for *150 Artists Book, Connections Project/Conexus* on the theme of body, 1986, pencil and ink on watercolor paper, 8 ¼ x 5 in. Photo Credit: Pamela Wye, Courtesy of Connections Project/Conexus Archive, Barnard College

56. Faith Wilding, original book page for *150 Artists Book, Connections Project/Conexus* on the theme of environment, 1986, watercolor, ink, stamp, on paper, 8 ¼ x 5 in. Photo Credit: Faith Wilding, Courtesy of Connections Project/Conexus Archive, Barnard College

57. Laurabeatriz, original book page for *150 Artists Book, Connections Project/Conexus* on the theme of war/death, 1986, woodcut on watercolor paper, 8 ¼ x 5 in. Photo Credit: Laurabeatriz, Courtesy of Connections Project/Conexus Archive, Barnard College

58. Maria Lidia Magliani, original book page for *150 Artists Book, Connections Project/Conexus* on the theme of race, 1986, ink on watercolor paper, 8 ¼ x 5 in. Photo Credit: Maria Lidia Magliani/ Courtesy of Connections Project/Conexus Archive, Barnard College

59. Ida Applebroog, original book page for *150 Artists Book, Connections Project/Conexus* on the theme of war/death, 1986, lithograph on watercolor paper, 8 ¼ x 5 in. Photo Credit: Ida Applebroog/ Courtesy of Connections Project/Conexus Archive, Barnard College

60. *Conscientizado*, a three-part artists' book: 1. Freda Gutt-man 2. Sabra Moore 3. Barbara Lounder for three exhibits at Powerhouse Gallery and Articule in Montreal, Canada, sponsored by Guatemala Solidarity Project, 1986, photocopy, 4 ¼ x 11 in. Photo Credit: Courtesy of Sabra Moore

61. *Reconstruction Project*, installation at Powerhouse Gallery, Montreal, showing red wall, 1986, 35 mm slide. Left to right: Kate Correa, Kathy Grove, Linda Peer, and Kazuko. Photo Credit: Sabra Moore

62. *Reconstruction Project*, installation at Eye Level Gallery, Halifax, Nova Scotia, showing yellow wall, 1986, 35 mm slide. Left to right: Virginia Jaramillo and Sabra Moore with black wall around the corner. Photo Credit: Sabra Moore

63. Freda Guttman, *Guatemala: The Road to War*, installation at Powerhouse Gallery, Montreal, 1986, 35 mm slide. Photo Credit: Sabra Moore

64. *Reconstruction Project*, installation at Powerhouse Gallery, Montreal, showing black wall, 1986, 35 mm slide. Left to right: Chris Costan, Frankie Buschke, Josely Carvalho, and a view into Freda Guttman's companion show, *Guatemala: The Road to War*. Photo Credit: Sabra Moore

65. *Guatemala Solidaridad* card, 1987, offset, 4 ¼ x 6 in. Photo Credit: Courtesy of Sabra Moore New York City Women's Art Movement Archive, Barnard College

66. *No Aid to Guatemala*, Toronto Guatemala Solidarity Committee, requesting that suspension of bilateral aid to the government of Guatemala be upheld, 1986, color offset card, 6 x 4 in. Photo Credit: Collection of Sabra Moore

67. *Reconstruction Project*, Eye Level Gallery, Halifax, 1987, offset, 4 ¼ x 6 in. Photo Credit: Courtesy of Sabra Moore New York City Women's Art Movement Archive, Barnard College

68. *HOME*, curated by Faith Ringgold, Goddard Riverside Community Center, card folds into tiny house, 1987, card stock, 8 x 6 ¾ in. Photo Credit: Courtesy of Sabra Moore New York City Women's Art Movement Archive, Barnard College

69. Sabra Moore, *Elemental House (Earth/Air/Fire/Water)*, 1987, oil on gessoed paper with sticks, 26 x 20 ¾ x 36 in. Roger Mignon built the wooden cart based on Sabra's design, 1987, found wood with hemp rope and beads, 15 x 30 ½ x 35 in. Photo Credit: Sabra Moore

70. Sabra Moore, *Air House*, 1986, oil on gessoed paper, cloth, string, beads, sticks, 10 x 7 x 10 in. Photo Credit: Sabra Moore/ Private Collection

71. Willie Birch, *Song for Mother Earth*, 1992, mixed media on papier-mâché, 39 x 72 x 22 in. Photo Credit: Willie Birch

72. Pearl Street garden showing Manhattan Bridge arches, 1991, color snapshot. Photo Credit: Roger Mignon.

73. Pearl Street garden near Front Street corner with day lilies, 1991, color snapshot. Photo Credit: Roger Mignon.

74. Daddy Chess in Briggins Cemetery near Clarksville, Texas, circa 1983, black-and-white photo, 8 x10 in. Photo Credit: Roger Mignon.

75. Daddy Chess going into kitchen, circa 1986, black-and-white photo, 8 x10 in. Photo Credit: Sabra Moore/ print by Roger Mignon.

76. Picture of Mother Gladys in Briggins Cemetery near Clarksvllle, Texas, circa 1983, black-and-white photo, 8 x10 in. This is one of the photos Daddy Chess kept in the box and looked at with care after her death. Photo Credit: Roger Mignon.

77. Robin Michals, *Just Kidding*, paintings with open books of racial stereotypes blocking women's faces, 1989, Xerox books with oil painting, 24 x 60 in. Photo Credit: Robin Michals

78. Hannah Wilke, *Brushstrokes No. 6: January 19, 1992*, 1992, artist's hair on arches paper, 33 x 25 ½ in. Photo Credit: Courtesy of Donald and Helen Goddard and Ronald Feldman Fine Arts, New York/ Photo by Dennis Cowley

79. Lani Maestro, *Incision to Heal*, 1989, card for exhibit at Gallery Connexion, Fredericton, N.B., 1989, photo offset, 5 ¾ x 6 ¾ in. Photo Credit: Lani Maestro/ Courtesy of Sabra Moore New York City Women's Art Movement Archive, Barnard College

80.–81. *What Is Feminist Art?*, double page from *Heresies* issue #24: 12 Years, 1989, pages 26–27. Photo Credit: © 1989, *Heresies: A Feminist Publication on Art and Politics*

82. Anita Steckel, *New Mona on New York*, *Giant Woman* series, circa 1973, black-and-white photo collage and oil on paper, 3 x 4 in. Photo Credit: Estate of Anita Steckel

83. *What Is Feminist Art?*, third page from *Heresies* issue #24: 12 Years, 1989, page 28. Photo Credit: © 1989, *Heresies: A Feminist Publication on Art and Politics*

84. Sonya Rappaport, postcard response to question, *What Is Feminist Art?*, 1989, postcard collage, 4 x 6 in. Photo Credit: Estate of Sonya Rappaport/ Reprinted from *Heresies* issue # 24

85. *Reconstruction Project*, installation at Powerhouse Gallery, Montreal, 1987, 35 mm color slide. Artists (left to right) for white wall (north): Holly Zox, Sharon Gilbert, Jaune Quick-to-See Smith, and Nancy Spero. Photo Credit: Sabra Moore

86. Nancy Spero and Valerie Savilli, original book page for *150 Artists Book, Connections Project/Conexus* on the theme of body, 1986, woodcut on watercolor paper, 8 ¼ x 5 in. Photo Credit: Nancy Spero and Valerie Savilli/ Courtesy of Connections Project/ Conexus Archive, Barnard College

87. Nancy Spero, *Artaud Painting—Get Back Down in Your Grave God*, 1969, cut-and-pasted paper, gouache, and ink on paper, 25 x 19.75 in. Photo Credit: Art ©The Nancy Spero and Leon Golub Foundation for the Arts/ Licensed by VAGA, New York, NY

88.–89. *Heresies: Issues That Won't Go Away*, card for *Heresies* Tenth Anniversary Benefit Show honoring Lucy R. Lippard, PPOW Gallery, December 1987, designed by Sabra Moore and including 100 artists, 1987, photo offset, 5 ½ x 4 in., opens to 5 ½ x 8 in. Photo Credit: Courtesy of Sabra Moore New York City Women's Art Movement Archive, Barnard College

90. Susan Bee, *What is Feminist Art?*, postcard response to question, *What is Feminist Art?*, 1989, postcard collage, 6 x 4 in. Photo Credit: Susan Bee

91. Doorway into Mother Gladys's empty kitchen, circa 1986, black-and-white photo, 8 x 10 in. Photo Credit: Roger Mignon

92. Mother Gladys's empty dining room with *Last Supper* reproduction, circa 1986, black-and-white photo, 8 x 10 in. Photo Credit: Roger Mignon

93. Photographs of her three babies on Gladys's bedroom wall, undated snapshot. Uncle James Chester (Buddie) is on left and Sabra's mother Christine is on right with rectangular framed photo of Aunt Mary Jane in between the two oval portraits. Photo Credit: Courtesy of Sabra Moore

94. Lamidi Fakeye and Roger in front of *Oh Grandma. . .*, circa 1987, 35 mm color slide. Photo Credit: Sabra Moore

95. Lamidi Fakeye's photograph of dinner party for Lamidi in Sabra and Roger's Pearl Street loft, circa 1987, color snapshot. Left to right: Owen Levy, Fabio Salvatore, Obie Fisher, Maggie Rodgers, Sabra, Roger, and Marithelma Costa. Photo Credit: Courtesy of Sabra Moore

96. Carol Sun and Linda Peer at *Heresies* event listening as participants read statements for Lucy R. Lippard, 1987, black-and-white print, 8 x 10 in. Photo Credit: Roger Mignon

97. Participants getting slices of Carrie Cooperider's cake and taking rings from cake at *Heresies* party PPOW benefit part, 1987, black-and-white print, 8 x 10 in. Photo Credit: Roger Mignon

98. Ellen Lanyon is standing and reading a dedication to Lucy flanked by Emma Amos, Sabra is seated with her hands clasped on her knees in the crowded room, 1987, black-and-white print, 8 x 10 in. Photo Credit: Roger Mignon

99. Readers Avis Lang holding paper with Josely Carvalho, Sue Heinemann, and Marilyn Lanfear in line behind her, 1987, black-and-white print, 8 x 10 in. Photo Credit: Roger Mignon

100. Holly Zox, *Catch Me If You Can*, 1987, wood cutouts with chain and text, 9 x 15 x 2 ½ in. excluding chain. Photo Credit: Holly Zox/ Courtesy of Sabra Moore

101. BIOTA fashion performers, *Heresies* party PPOW benefit part, 1987, black-and-white print, 8 x 10 in. Photo Credit: Roger Mignon

Portfolio B

1. Frances Buschke, *Towards Me the Darkness Comes Rattling*, wall work created for black (north) wall, *Reconstruction Project*, Artists Space, 1984, rice paper, beads, string, feathers, gum Arabic, earth pigments, oil pastel, 21 ½ x 32 x 3 in. Photo Credit: Estate of Frances Buschke/ Collection of Linda McCloud, ©Goodman/ Van Riper Photography

2. Marina Gutierrez, *Untitled* (unveiled), wall work created for yellow (south) wall, *Reconstruction Project*, Artists Space, 1984, prints on paper, acrylic, corn husks, 3 x 7 ft. approximate size. Photo Credit: Marina Gutierrez

3. Helen Oji, *Untitled (Volcano Series #48)*, wall work created for black (north) wall, *Reconstruction Project*, Artists Space, 1984, charcoal, acrylic on paper, 3 x 7 ft. approximate size. Photo Credit: Helen Oji

4. Sabra Moore, *Renew*, wall work created for yellow (south) wall, *Reconstruction Project*, Artists Space, 1984, oil on gessoed paper with color Xerox cutouts, string, photo transfer, painted poles, 3 x 7 ft. Photo Credit: Sabra Moore

5. *Reconstructed Codex* double pages continue in sequence, 1984, 8 x 3 in. each.

Left to right, top row:

Colleen Cutschall, acrylic on watercolor paper. Photo Credit: Colleen Cutschall/ Courtesy of Sabra Moore New York City Women's Art Movement Archive, Barnard College

Sharon Gilbert, photocopy collage on watercolor paper. Photo Credit: Sharon Gilbert/ Courtesy of Sabra Moore New York City Women's Art Movement Archive, Barnard College

Chris Costan, acrylic on watercolor paper. Photo Credit: Chris Costan/ Courtesy of Sabra Moore New York City Women's Art Movement Archive, Barnard College

Left to right, middle row:

Catherine Correa, acrylic and earth pigments on watercolor paper. Photo Credit: Catherine Correa/ Courtesy of Sabra Moore New York City Women's Art Movement Archive, Barnard College

Holly Zox, ink on watercolor paper. Photo Credit: Holly Zox/ Courtesy of Sabra Moore New York City Women's Art Movement Archive, Barnard College

Jaune Quick-to-See Smith, acrylic and ink on watercolor paper. Photo Credit: Jaune Quick-to-See Smith/ Courtesy of Sabra Moore New York City Women's Art Movement Archive, Barnard College

Left to right, bottom row:

Catalina Parra, photo and newsprint collage on watercolor paper. Photo Credit: Catalina Parra/ Courtesy of Sabra Moore New York City Women's Art Movement Archive, Barnard College

Sabra Moore, oil on gessoed paper with laser transfer print and color Xerox cutouts. Photo Credit: Sabra Moore/ Courtesy of Sabra Moore New York City Women's Art Movement Archive, Barnard College

End pages, color Xerox edition, *Reconstructed Codex*, 1984, created by Sabra Moore. Photo Credit: Sabra Moore/ Courtesy of Sabra Moore New York City Women's Art Movement Archive, Barnard College

6. *Liliana Porter, Reconstruction, wall work created for yellow (south) wall, Reconstruction Project, Artists Space, 1984, lithograph and pencil, 3 x 7 ft. approximate size. Photo Credit: Liliana Porter*

7. Kazuko Miyamoto, *Untitled*, undated, watercolor drawing of a kimono on paper. Photo Credit: Kazuko Miyamoto

8. Sabra Moore, *Door*, 1986, oil on gessoed wood with fabric strips, sticks, string, and beads, 63 ½ x 36 x 7 ½ in. Photo Credit: Sabra Moore/ Rowan University Art Gallery, Sylvia Sleigh Collection

9. Sabra Moore, *Woodsman*, *Place/Displace* series, 1991, oil on gessoed paper with wood, beads, dried stems, cloth, Xerox transfer, 52 x 32 in. The text includes the story of Grandmother's murdered husband, Chester Bryant. Photo Credit: Sabra Moore

10. Sabra Moore, *Lillie's Peaks* with *Gypsy Baby Cart* emerging, *Place/Displace* series, 1988–1990, oil on gessoed paper and wood, Xerox transfer, cloth, found wood, cloth strips, beads, found tin, photographs, 73 x 40 x 36 in. *Gypsy Baby Cart*, oil on gessoed paper, found wood, string, 14 ½ x 18 x 31 in. Photo Credit: Sabra Moore

11. Sabra Moore, *Not a Civilian*, *Place/Displace* series, 1992, oil on gessoed wood, laser transfer print on cloth, chair, twigs, 37 x 24 x 23 in. The laser transfer print is from a rubbing of the tombstone of Dane Lewis, Sabra's great-grandfather, with his Union infantry regiment engraved in stone. Photo Credit: Sabra Moore

12. Original book page for *150 Artists Book, Connections Project/Conexus* on eight themes of social interest, 1986, various media on watercolor paper, 8 ¼ x 5 in.

Book pages, left to right, top row:
Vivian E. Browne, oil stick and paint on watercolor paper (environment). Photo Credit: Estate of Vivian E. Browne/ Courtesy of Adobe Krow Archives and *Connections Project/ Conexus Archive*, Barnard College

Michelle Stuart, rubbing on watercolor paper (spirit). Photo Credit: Michelle Stuart/ Courtesy of Connections Project/ Conexus Archive, Barnard College

Carolee Schneemann, self-print from impressings, monoprint on Arches watercolor paper (body). Photo Credit: Carolee Schneemann/ Courtesy of Connections Project/ Conexus Archive, Barnard College

Nancy Chunn, colored pencil of watercolor paper (race). Photo Credit: Nancy Chunn/Courtesy of Ronald Feldman Fine Arts, New York and *Connections Project/ Conexus Archive*, Barnard College

Book pages, left to right, middle row:
Sabra Moore, oil on gessoed paper, laser transfer print (shelter). Photo Credit: Sabra Moore/ Courtesy of Connections Project/ Conexus Archive, Barnard College

Charleen Touchette, paint on paper (race). Photo Credit: Charleen Touchette/ Courtesy of Connections Project/ Conexus Archive, Barnard College

Marina Moers, pencil of watercolor paper (spirit). Photo Credit: Marina Moers/ Courtesy of Connections Project/ Conexus Archive, Barnard College

Vida Hackman, pencil, paint, type on watercolor paper (environment). Photo Credit: Estate of Vida Hackman/ Courtesy of Adobe Krow Archives and *Connections Project/ Conexus Archive*, Barnard College

Book pages, left to right, bottom row:
Grace Graupe-Pillard, photo print of *The Man in Rags*, 1985, pastel cutout drawing (shelter). Photo Credit: Grace Graupe-Pillard/ Courtesy of Connections Project/ Conexus Archive, Barnard College

Pat Mercado, acrylic and mixed media with seeds on watercolor paper (food). Photo Credit: Pat Mercado/ Courtesy of Connections Project/ Conexus Archive, Barnard College

Katie van Scherpenberg, nylon hose, butterfly wings, mixed media on paper (war/death). Photo Credit: Katie van Scherpenberg/ Courtesy of Connections Project/ Conexus Archive, Barnard College

Howardena Pindell, collage on watercolor paper (environment). Photo Credit: Howardena Pindell/ Courtesy of Garth Greenan Gallery, New York and *Connections Project/ Conexus Archive*, Barnard College

13. *Sabra Moore, Shelter is Material, artwork on the theme of shelter for Connections Project/Conexus, MoCHA, 1986, oil on gessoed paper and wood with string, adobe fragment, found tin, straw, twigs, cloth ties, 82 ½ x 40 in. Photo Credit: Sabra Moore*

14. Marina Gutierrez, artwork on the theme of race for *Connections Project/Conexus*, MoCHA, 1986, acrylic and pencil on paper with rubbing/prints, paper veils, sticks, approximately 7 x 3 ft. Photo Credit: Marina Gutierrez

15. Mimi Smith, *Error 294*, artwork on the theme of shelter for *Connections Project/Conexus*, MoCHA, 1987, oil sticks, pencil and ink on canvas-backed paper, approximately 7 x 3 ft. Photo Credit: Mimi Smith

16. Catalina Parra, *Mortal Body*, artwork on the theme of for war/death, *Connections Project/Conexus*, MoCHA, 1987, feathers, leaves, plastic containers, and hospital tubing, tape, on vinyl curtain, metal hangers, approximately 7 x 3 ft. Photo Credit: Catalina Parra

17. Sabra Moore, *Preservation Work*, artwork for the Canadian venues of Powerhouse and Eye Level Gallery for yellow wall (south) *Reconstruction Project*, 1987, oil on gessoed paper and wood, painted sticks, cloth ties, with chair back rescued from Grandmother's thrown out possessions mounted above and tiny chair (not shown) mounted below, 7 x 42 in., chair back, 11 x 25 in. Text from Friar Diego de Landa printed on artwork reads: "Quite a distance away was a pyramid, so large and beautiful that even after it had been used to build a large part of the city they founded around it, I cannot say that it shows any sign of coming to an end."(Friar Diego de Landa, *Yucatan Before and After the Conquest*, Dover Publications Inc., New York, 1978, page 88.) Photo Credit: Sabra Moore

Chapter 9

1.–2. Arlene Raven and others look at unfurled *Reconstructed Codex* (photocopy version), 1984, during opening of *Committed to Print, Social and Political themes in recent American Art*, MoMA, 1988. The *Codex* was exhibited in the room devoted to War/Revolution, 1988, color snapshot (both). Photo Credit: Roger Mignon

3. Emma Amos, *Take One, 1985-87*, stencil, printed in color, 41 ½ x 29 ¼ in. Photo Credit: ©Emma Amos, Licensed by VAGA, New York, NY/photo by Becket Logan

4. *Committed To Print, Social and Political Themes in Recent American Art*, cover of catalogue, MoMA, 1988, photo offset, 9 x 9 ¾ in. Photo Credit: © 1988 The Museum of Modern Art, New York

5. *Heresies* issue #14: Women's Pages cover. Photo Credit: © 1985 *Heresies: A Feminist Publication on Art and Politics*

6. Sharon Gilbert talks to Liliana Porter at *Committed to Print* opening night at MoMA, with Kate Correa and Sabra chatting nearby, 1988, color snapshot. Photo Credit: Roger Mignon

7. Marilyn Lanfear, wearing a hat and glasses, is standing near Emma Amos, silhouetted to the right, in the room for the Economics/Class Struggle/The American Dream theme. Photo Credit: Roger Mignon

8. An installation view of the War/Revolution room with outstretched *Reconstructed Codex* (photocopy version) next to William Wiley's *El Salvador*, a woodcut with a guitar shape, 1988, black-and-white photo, 8 x 10 in. Photo Credit: Photograph by Kate Keller, Courtesy of The Museum of Modern Art, New York.

9. Marithelma Costa and Sabra at the *Committed to Print* opening near the *Codex*. Photo Credit: Roger Mignon

10. Sabra Moore, *Flowers #2* (series of three with grandparents walking into Briggins Cemetery), 1988, oil on gessoed found wood with Xerox transfer print, 15 ½ x 20 in. Photo Credit: Sabra Moore

11. Sabra Moore, *Leaves* (right side of two), based on a photo of Mother Gladys looking at a tombstone in Briggins Cemetery, 1988, oil on gessoed paper with Xerox transfer print, 6 ½ x 12 in. Photo Credit: Sabra Moore/Collection of Lucy R. Lippard

12. Josely Carvalho (right), Sabra (center on ladder), and art student Jayne Bissonette hanging artworks for the *Connections Project/Conexus* exhibit at Southeastern Massachusetts University Art Gallery, North Dartmouth in New Bedford, Connecticut. This photo appeared in an article by Richard Pacheco in *The Standard Times*, New Bedford, Massachusetts, March 30, 1988, B9. Photo Credit: *The Standard Times*, New Bedford, staff photo by Ron Rolo/ Courtesy of Connections Project/ Conexus Archive, Barnard College

13. Installation view of *Connections Project/Conexus* exhibit at Southeastern Massachusetts University Art Gallery showing the wall with artworks on the theme of war/death, 1988, black-and-white photo, 5 x 7 in. Left to right: Anésia Pacheco e Chaves, Ida Applebroog, and Ely Bueno; the platforms with pages of *150 Artists Book* are in the foreground. Photo Credit: Courtesy of Connections Project/ Conexus Archive, Barnard College

14.–15. Original book pages for *150 Artists Book*, *Connections Project/Conexus* on the theme of war/death, 1986, various media on watercolor paper, 8 ¼ x 5 in.

14. Cilia Colli, mixed media on watercolor paper. Photo Credit: Cilia Colli/Courtesy of Connections Project/ Conexus Archive, Barnard College

15. Maria Lucia Carneiro, ink on watercolor paper. Photo Credit: Maria Lucia Carneiro/Courtesy of Connections Project/ Conexus Archive, Barnard College

16. Overall view of *Connections Project* installation at Southeastern Massachusetts University Art Gallery, New Bedford, 1988, black-and-white photo, 5 x 7 in. Photo Credit: Courtesy of Connections Project/ Conexus Archive, Barnard College

17. Christy Rupp, *Humanitarian Aid*, 1987–1988, steel, oxidized metal, 6 x 9 ¼ x 9. This was reproduced on page 34 of *Heresies* issue #24: 12 Years. Photo Credit: Christy Rupp

18. Vanalyne Green, *Trick or Drink* performance, P.S.122, offset card, 6 ½ x 4 in. Photo Credit: Vanalyne Green/ Courtesy of Sabra Moore New York City Women's Art Movement Archive, Barnard College

19. Nancy Burson, *Cat Woman*, 1983, computer-generated photograph. This was reproduced on the inside back page of *Heresies* issue #24: 12 Years. Photo Credit: Nancy Burson

20. Sabra Moore, *Artifact/Artifice* (*AKIN* series), 1987, color Xerox covers, black-and-white interior, hand stamped, 44 pages, 6 ¼ x 5 ¾ in. This artist's book is based on childhood paper dolls cut out from the Sears catalogue and stored in a children's Bible book. Photo Credit: Sabra Moore

21. Sabra Moore, *4/TELLS #1* (*AKIN* series), set of four books with dark family stories (this one relates to Sabra's aunt Opal), 1989, black-and-white photocopy on archival paper with red covers and end papers, 46 pages, 6 ⅛ x 7 in. Photo Credit: Sabra Moore

22. Sabra Moore, *4/TELLS #4* (*AKIN* series), set of four books with dark family stories (this one relates to Sabra's grandmother Caroline), 1989, black-and-white photocopy on archival paper with blue covers, 22 double-sided accordion-folded pages, 7 x 11 ½ in. Photo Credit: Sabra Moore

23. *Heresies* issue #23: Coming of Age. Photo Credit ©1988 *Heresies: A Feminist Publication on Art and Politics*

24. Robin Michals, *Armed to the Teeth*, exhibit card, Buffalo Arts Studio, Buffalo, New York, 2003, color offset, 4 x 6 in. Photo credit: Robin Michals

25. 81 Pearl Street garden near loading bay, circa 1991, color snapshot. Photo Credit: Roger Mignon

26. Sabra in 81 Pearl Street loft near Roger Mignon painting, *Oh Grandma. . .*, circa 1989, color snapshot. Photo Credit: Roger Mignon

27. Golden light coming into the 81 Pearl Street loft under the bridge arches, circa 1989, color snapshot. Photo Credit: Roger Mignon

28. Sylvia's wisteria cutting growing in the garden at 81 Pearl Street and climbing up the strings that Sabra has hung from the sixth floor loft windows, circa 1990, color snapshot. Photo Credit: Roger Mignon

29. Gertrude Barnstone and Tobey Topek, *From a Silent Garden (Sculpture and Skins)*, exhibit card, Forty Walls Gallery, Houston, 1981, color offset on cardstock, 5 ½ x 8 ½ in. Photo Credit: Gertrude Barnstone

30. Roger at Tsankawi, Bandelier National Monument, New Mexico, circa 1989, color snapshot. Photo Credit: Sabra Moore

31. Sabra Moore, Journal drawings from Aztec Ruins, New Mexico, Book #40, 1985, black ink on paper, 9 ¾ x 7 ½ in. Photo credit: Sabra Moore

32. Sabra Moore, Journal drawings from Mesa Verde, New Mexico, Book #40, 1985, black ink on paper, 9 ¾ x 7 ½ in. Photo credit: Sabra Moore

33. Sabra with light from sunset near the Rio Grande Gorge above Taos, New Mexico, 1980s, color snapshot. Photo Credit: Roger Mignon

34. Storm clouds from Pearl Street loft windows, 1991, color snapshot. Photo Credit: Roger Mignon

35. Sabra walking around Stone Lions Shrine, Bandelier National Monument, New Mexico, 1985, black-and-white photo, 8 x 10 in. Photo Credit: Roger Mignon

36.–37. Sabra Moore, Journal drawings and notes at Stone Lions Shrine, Bandelier National Monument, New Mexico, Book #40, 1985, black ink on paper, 9 ¾ x 7 ½ in. Photo Credit: Sabra Moore

38.–41. Sabra Moore, Journal drawings, including painted cave at Bandelier National Monument and other petroglyph sites in New Mexico, Book #40, 1985, black ink on paper, 9 ¾ x 7 ½ in. Photo Credit: Sabra Moore

42. Sabra stands with Kate Correa in front of Kate and Lisa's adobe construction in Abiquiu, New Mexico, circa 1989, color snapshot. Photo Credit: Roger Mignon

43. White canyon on Plaza Blanca land, Abiquiu, New Mexico, circa 1989. Photo Credit: Roger Mignon

44. Sabra Moore, work in progress for *Lillie's Peaks* showing painted paper panels on both sides of right "peak" and the facing ends and stretched on studio wall for painting, 1988, oil on gessoed paper with Xerox transfer, single panel, 60 x 17 in. Photo Credit: Sabra Moore

45. Sabra Moore, *Lillie's Peaks*, *Place/Displace* series, side view with panels in place, open door, 1988–1990, oil on gessoed paper and wood, Xerox transfer, cloth, found wood, cloth strips, beads, found tin, photographs, 73 x 40 x 36 in. Photo Credit: Sabra Moore

46. Sabra Moore, *Gypsy Baby Cart*, *Place/Displace* series, detail, 1988–1990, oil on gessoed paper and wood, Xerox transfer, cloth, found wood, string, 14 ½ x 18 x 31 in. Photo Credit: Sabra Moore

47. *Heresies* issue #24:12 Years cover. Photo Credit ©1989 *Heresies: A Feminist Publication on Art and Politics*

48. *Heresies* issue #25: The Art of Education cover. Photo Credit ©1990 *Heresies: A Feminist Publication on Art and Politics*

49. *Women on Men* flier for submissions with a deadline of August 1, 1988, photocopy, 11 x 8 ½ in. This issue was never published. Photo Credit: Courtesy of Sabra Moore New York City Women's Art Movement Archive, Barnard College

50. *Heresies* issue #27: Latina cover. Photo Credit ©1993 *Heresies: A Feminist Publication on Art and Politics*

51. Ora Lerman in her studio with maquettes for painting. Photo Credit: Ora Lerman Charitable Trust/ photo by Malcolm Varon

52. Bea Kreloff and Edith Isaac Rose send greetings from Italy, undated, photo montage, 4 x 6 in. Photo Credit: Edith Isaac Rose and Bea Kreloff

53. Marilyn Lanfear, *Genie's Headpiece from Sleeping Beauty*, 1993, lead, wood, 23 x 9 x 10 in. Photo Credit: Marilyn Lanfear

54. Nancy Davidson, *Recent Works* cards for exhibit with Emily Chen and Fontaine Dunn, detail, A.I.R. Gallery, 1985. Photo Credit: Nancy Davidson/ Courtesy of Sabra Moore New York City Women's Art Movement Archive, Barnard College

55. Marilyn Lanfear, *Aunt Opal's Hat*, 1983, lead, wood, 23 x 10 x 10 in. Photo Credit: Marilyn Lanfear

56. Edith Isaac Rose, *We Are More Alike than Different, Similar/Dissimilar series (New Year's Greeting)*, 1992, color card, 4 x 6 in. Photo Credit: Edith Isaac Rose/ Courtesy

of Sabra Moore New York City Women's Art Movement Archive, Barnard College

57. *Connections Project/Conexus* show card, Museu de Arte Contemporânea, São Paulo, Brazil, 1989, photo offset, 5 x 7 in. Photo Credit: Courtesy of Connections Project/ Conexus Archive, Barnard College

58. Sabra Moore, *Shelter Is Material #2*, detail, 1989, oil on gessoed paper, laser transfer print, wood, clothespin, 84 x 36 x 5 in. This artwork was made to fold into a compact box for transport to the venue of *Connections Project/ Conexus* to the Museu de Arte Contemporânea in São Paulo, Brazil. Photo Credit: Sabra Moore

59. Sabra Moore, *Shelter is Material #2*, 1989, oil on gessoed paper, laser transfer print, wood, clothespin, 84 x 36 x 5 in. Photo Credit: Sabra Moore

60. Sabra Moore, Sketches for book page stands that Sabra sent in advance of the exhibition in Brazil for the construction of the stands for *150 Artists Book*. Photo Credit: Sabra Moore

Original book pages for *150 Artists Book, Connections Project/ Conexus* on eight themes of social interest, 1986, various media on watercolor paper, 8 ¼ x 5 in.

Book pages in caption order:

61. Vira and Hortensia Colorado, photocopy montage on paper (race). Photo Credit: Vira and Hortensia Colorado/ Courtesy of Connections Project/ Conexus Archive, Barnard College

62. Liora Mondlak, photo, ink drawing on watercolor paper (war/death). Photo Credit: Liora Mondlak/ Courtesy of Connections Project/ Conexus Archive, Barnard College

63. Marilyn Minter, mixed media prints on watercolor paper (spirit). Photo Credit: Marilyn Minter/ Courtesy of Connections Project/ Conexus Archive, Barnard College

64. Karen Shaw, collage on watercolor paper (war/death). Photo Credit: Karen Shaw/ Courtesy of Connections Project/ Conexus Archive, Barnard College

65. Betye Saar, cloth strips, print, paint, glue on paper (body). Photo Credit: Betye Saar/ Courtesy of Connections Project/ Conexus Archive, Barnard College

66. Kathie Brown, mixed media on paper (food). Photo Credit: Kathie Brown/ Courtesy of Connections Project/ Conexus Archive, Barnard College

67. Michiko Itatani, paint on watercolor paper (spirit). Photo Credit: Michiko Itatani/ Courtesy of Connections Project/ Conexus Archive, Barnard College

68. Mary Beth Edelson, lithograph (spirit). Photo Credit: Mary Beth Edelson/ Courtesy of Connections Project/ Conexus Archive, Barnard College

69. Judy Blum, woodcut on paper (war/death). Photo Credit: Judy Blum/ Courtesy of Connections Project/ Conexus Archive, Barnard College

70. Eva Cockcroft, paint on watercolor paper (race). Photo Credit: Estate of Eva Cockcroft/ Courtesy of Connections Project/ Conexus Archive, Barnard College

71. Leticia Parente, steel wool pad with paper cutout (race). Photo Credit: Leticia Parente/ Courtesy of Connections Project/ Conexus Archive, Barnard College

72. Marilyn Lanfear, ink on watercolor paper (food). Photo Credit: Marilyn Lanfear/ Courtesy of Connections Project/ Conexus Archive, Barnard College

73. Lygia Pape, paper strip on painted watercolor paper (environment). Photo Credit: Projecto Lygia Pape/ Courtesy of Connections Project/ Conexus Archive, Barnard College

74. Sharon Gilbert, press type letters, paint, on watercolor paper (environment). Photo Credit: Estate of Sharon Gilbert/ Courtesy of Connections Project/ Conexus Archive, Barnard College

75. Judith Miller, mixed media on watercolor paper (shelter). Photo Credit: Judith Miller/ Courtesy of Connections Project/ Conexus Archive, Barnard College

76. Erika Rothenberg, mixed media on watercolor paper (war/death). Photo Credit: Erika Rothenberg/ Courtesy of Connections Project/ Conexus Archive, Barnard College

77. Josie Talamantez, woodcut and press type on paper (race). Photo Credit: Josie Talamantez/ Courtesy of Connections Project/ Conexus Archive, Barnard College

78. Tomie Arai, lithograph on watercolor paper (race). Photo Credit: Tomie Arai/ Courtesy of Connections Project/ Conexus Archive, Barnard College

79. Susan Crowe, watercolor on paper (food). Photo Credit: Susan Crowe/ Courtesy of Connections Project/ Conexus Archive, Barnard College

80. Alice Brill, mixed media on paper (environment). Photo Credit: Alice Brill/ Courtesy of Connections Project/ Conexus Archive, Barnard College

81. Sophia Tassinari, ink on paper (race). Photo Credit: Sophia Tassinari/ Courtesy of Connections Project/ Conexus Archive, Barnard College

82. Jaune Quick-To-See Smith, oil stick, acrylic on paper (race). Photo Credit: Jaune Quick-To-See Smith/ Courtesy of Connections Project/ Conexus Archive, Barnard College

83. Maria do Carmo Secco, mixed media collage on paper (shelter). Photo Credit: Maria do Carmo Secco/ Courtesy of Connections Project/ Conexus Archive, Barnard College

84. Louise Neaderland, photocopy on paper (shelter). Photo Credit: Louise Neaderland/ Courtesy of Connections Project/ Conexus Archive, Barnard College

85. Angela Leite, woodcut on paper (environment). Photo Credit: Angela Leite/ Courtesy of Connections Project/ Conexus Archive, Barnard College

86. Sumiko Arimori, paint, burning on paper (environment). Photo Credit: Sumiko Arimori/ Courtesy of Connections Project/ Conexus Archive, Barnard College

87. Kathy Grove, stencils, paint on watercolor paper (race). Photo Credit: Kathy Grove/ Courtesy of Connections Project/ Conexus Archive, Barnard College

88. May Stevens, mixed media lithograph and photocopy on paper (spirit), Photo Credit: May Stevens, Courtesy of Ryan Lee Gallery, New York and *Connections Project/Conexus Archive*, Barnard College

89. Installation, *Connections Project/Conexus* exhibition at Mo-CHA, 1987, showing the wall with artworks on the theme of birth. Left: Josely Carvalho, *Rebirth*, from the *She is visited by birds and turtles* series, 1987, silkscreen on bark paper, raffia, branch eaten by beaver, burnt cheesecloth, ashes, turtles, size variable. Right: Liliana Porter, *Birth of the face, the pencil, the house, the journey*, 1987, acrylic, aluminum powder, assemblage on paper. Photo Credit: Courtesy of Connections Project/ Conexus Archive, Barnard College

90. A Brazilian television crew filming the installation of *Connections Project/Conexus* exhibition at Museum de Arte Contemporânea, Sao Paulo, Brazil, 1989, showing the wall on the theme of race. The filmmakers are blowing to raise one of the veils over the mixed media artwork of Marina Gutierrez. Photo Credit: Courtesy of Connections Project/ Conexus Archive, Barnard College

Original book pages for *150 Artists Book, Connections Project/ Conexus* on eight themes of social interest, 1986, various media on watercolor paper, 8 ¼ x 5 in.

Book pages in caption order:

91. Beatrice Leite, etching on watercolor paper (spirit). Photo Credit: Beatrice Leite/ Courtesy of Connections Project/ Conexus Archive, Barnard College

92. Faith Ringgold, photocopy, glue on watercolor paper (food). Photo Credit: Faith Ringgold/ Courtesy of Connections Project/ Conexus Archive, Barnard College

93. Jerri Allyn & The Waitresses, photograph (food). Photo Credit: ©The Waitresses – Jerri Allyn and Anne Gauldin/ Courtesy of Connections Project/ Conexus Archive, Barnard College

94. Sarah Swenson, watercolor on paper (spirit). Photo Credit: Sarah Swenson/ Courtesy of Connections Project/ Conexus Archive, Barnard College

95. Margot Lovejoy, montage on paper (birth). Photo Credit: Margot Lovejoy/ Courtesy of Connections Project/ Conexus Archive, Barnard College

96. *Documentation* booklet back cover, photocopy on paper based on envelopes from participating artists. Photo Credit: Courtesy of Sabra Moore New York City Women's Art movement Archive, Barnard College

97. Linda Herrit, pulverized marble chips, twigs, brass plate (death). Photo Credit: Linda Herrit/ Courtesy of Connections Project/ Conexus Archive, Barnard College

98. Rose Viggiano, cutouts, glue on paper (environment). Photo Credit: Rose Viggiano/ Courtesy of Connections Project/ Conexus Archive, Barnard College

99.–102. Sabra Moore, journal drawings, including trees and mountains near Rio de Janeiro, Brazil, Book #49, 1988–1989, ink on paper, 9 ¾ x 7 ½ in. Photo Credit: Sabra Moore

Original book pages for 150 Artists Book, Connections Project/ Conexus on eight themes of social interest, 1986, various media on watercolor paper, 8 ¼ x 5 in.

103. Josely Carvalho, silkscreen on paper (birth). Photo Credit: Josely Carvalho/ Courtesy of Connections Project/ Conexus Archive, Barnard College

104. Maurie Kerrigan, mixed media on watercolor paper (spirit). Photo Credit: Maurie Kerrigan/ Courtesy of Connections Project/ Conexus Archive, Barnard College

105. Aviva Rahmani, acrylic on paper (birth). Photo Credit: Aviva Rahmani/ Courtesy of Connections Project/ Conexus Archive, Barnard College

106. Glenna Park, acrylic on paper (shelter). Photo Credit: Glenna Park/ Courtesy of Connections Project/ Conexus Archive, Barnard College

107. Anésia Pacheco e Chaves, mixed media, ribbons, ink on paper (war/death). Photo Credit: Anésia Pacheco e Chaves/ Courtesy of Connections Project/ Conexus Archive, Barnard College

108. Caroline Stone, watercolor on paper (war/death). Photo Credit: Caroline Stone/ Courtesy of Connections Project/ Conexus Archive, Barnard College

109. Frances Buschke, mixed media, feathers, earth pigments, paint on paper (spirit). Photo Credit: Estate of Frances Buschke/ Courtesy of Connections Project/ Conexus Archive, Barnard College

110. Cecilia Vicuña, cutout photo of *Precario* (war/death). Photo Credit: Cecilia Vicuña/ Courtesy of Connections Project/ Conexus Archive, Barnard College

111. *Heresies* issue #24: 12 Years, double page, "Historias: Women Tinsmiths of New Mexico", article by Harmony Hammond, pages 38–39. Photo Credit: © 1989, *Heresies: A Feminist Publication on Art and Politics*

112. Sabra Moore, *Gladys Apron #2*, 1985, color Xerox mounted on archival cardstock, string, beads, gessoed chair part, morning glory vines cloth strips, 24 x 24 in. Photo Credit: Sabra Moore

113. Sabra Moore, detail from photocopier limited edition book *4/TELLS #4* (*AKIN* series) relating to Sabra's grandmother Caroline, 1989, black-and-white photocopy on archival paper with blue covers, 7 x 11 ½ in. Text reads: "If. . . her son were alive, it would be different. . ." Photo Credit: Sabra Moore

114. Sabra Moore, detail from photocopier limited edition book *4/TELLS #4* (*Akin* series) relating to Sabra's grandmother Caroline, 1989, black-and-white photocopy on archival paper with blue covers, 7 x 11 ½ in. Text reads: ". . .they had hit her for years ever since. . ." Photo Credit: Sabra Moore

115. Liliana Porter, book page for *150 Artists Book, Connections Project/Conexus* on the theme of birth, 1986,

collaged lithograph on watercolor paper, 8 ¼ x 5 in. Photo Credit: Liliana Porter/ Courtesy of Connections Project/ Conexus Archive, Barnard College

116. Installation wall, *Connections Project/Conexus*, on the theme of war/death, MoCHA, 1987, showing artworks by (left to right): Ely Bueno, Ida Applebroog, Anésia Pacheco e Chaves, and Catalina Parra. Photo Credit: Courtesy of Connections Project/ Conexus Archive, Barnard College

117. Ellen Lanyon, book page for *150 Artists Book*, *Connections Project/Conexus* on the theme of environment, 1986, watercolor drawing on watercolor paper, 8 ¼ x 5 in. Photo Credit: Estate of Ellen Lanyon/ Courtesy of Connections Project/ Conexus Archive, Barnard College

118. Josely Carvalho, *Turtle News*, Spectacolor lightboard, One Times Square, 1988, computer animation card, 5 x 7 in. Photo Credit: Josely Carvalho

119. Erika Rothenberg, *Is God Punishing Us?*, 1987–1988, acrylic on canvas, 40 x 54 in. Photo Credit: Erika Rothenberg

120. Theodora Skipitares, *Micropolis (Six Portraits & a Landscape)*, announcement card for performance, presented by La MaMa E.T.C., New York. Photo Credit: Theodora Skipitares

121. Bibi Lenĉek, *Endangered*, 1992, flashe on canvas, 50 x 74 in. Photo Credit: Bibi Lenĉek

122. Janet Culbertson, *Faces of the Peconic (Billboard* series), exhibit at East End Arts Council, circa 1987, color card, 5 ½ x 4 in. Photo credit: Janet Culbertson

123. Harmony Hammond, *Fan Ladies on the Edge*, 1982, oil on canvas with fabric, diptych, 71 ⅛ x 94 in. Photo Credit: Courtesy of Alexander Gray Associates. Art ©Harmony Hammond/ Licensed by VAGA, New York.

124. Artelia Court, *Aquifer* (front), 1984–1996, polychrome gypsum, 23 x 12 x 11 in. Photo Credit: Artelia Court

125. Ida Applebroog, *Two Women II (after de Kooning)*, 1985, oil on linen, 2 panels, each 72 x 74 in. Photo Credit: Ida Applebroog Courtesy of Hauser & Wirth Gallery

126. Artelia Court, *Aquifer* (back), 1984–1996, polychrome gypsum, 23 x 12 x 11 in. Photo Credit: Artelia Court

127. Announcement card for *4 Story House*, a performance by Interaction Arts: Jerri Allyn, Bill Gordh, Joe Lowry, and Debra Wanner at Franklin Furnace, New York, 1985. Photo Credit: Courtesy of Jerri Allyn and Sabra Moore New York City Women's Art Movement Archive, Barnard College

128. Joyce Kozloff, *Lobster and Croquembouche* (from *Pornament is Crime* series), 1988, watercolor on paper, 22 x 22 in. Included in *Heresies* issue #24: 12 Years. Photo Credit: Joyce Kozloff

129. Jerri Allyn and *The Waitresses*, performance, *American Dining: A Working Woman's Moment*, January 12, 1987, reading to accompany installation of artist-designed jukeboxes and placemats at Gefen's Dairy Restaurant, sponsored by New Museum of Contemporary Art, New York,

black-and-white photo, 8 x 10 in. Photo Credit: ©The Waitresses – Jerri Allyn and Anne Gauldin/ Courtesy of: The Woman's Building Image Bank at Otis College of Art and Design, Los Angeles, California, USA/ photo by Ellen Page Wilson

130.–131. Sabra Moore, *4/TELLS #1(AKIN* series), set of four books with dark family stories (this one relates to Sabra's aunt Opal), 1989, black-and-white photocopy on archival paper with red covers and end papers, 46 pages, 6 ⅛ x 7 in. Text from detail (130) reads: ". . .they had to cut away the tape. . ." and text from detail (131) reads: ". . .the trial all right. . ." Photo Credit: Sabra Moore

132. *On the Move* installation in the subway at 42nd Street and 6th Avenue, sponsored by NYC/WCA and Art for Transit Exhibition Program, 1989, announcement card, 4 ½ x 6 ⅛ in. Photo Credit: Courtesy of Sabra Moore

133. *Heresies* issue #24: 12 Years, double page organized and designed by Sylvia Sleigh, *The Male Nude: the gaze returned*, pages 46–47. Photo Credit: © 1989, *Heresies: A Feminist Publication on Art and Politics*

134. Sabra Moore, *Subject Matters*, artwork in response to the *Heresies* question, *What Is Feminist Art?*, 1989, oil on gessoed paper with string, 4 x 6 in. Photo Credit: Sabra Moore

135. *Vital signs: Artists Respond to the Environment*, exhibition card. Photo Credit: Sabra Moore New York City Women's Art Movement Archive, Barnard College

Chapter 10

1. Cerro Negro frames the newly built shed and tent site on our land in Plaza Blanca, Abiquiu, New Mexico, 1989, black-and-white photo, 8 x 10 in. Photo Credit: Roger Mignon

2. Sabra unpacks the camping gear to set up tent in the area that later became our house site, 1989, black-and-white photo, 8 x 10 in. Photo Credit: Roger Mignon

3. Looking into Madera Canyon from the mesa where we are camped as the water flows after a rain, 1989, black-and-white photo, 8 x 10 in. Photo Credit: Roger Mignon

4. Roger works to erect the first frame wall for the shed, 1989, color snapshot. Photo Credit: Sabra Moore

5. Sabra sits astraddle the shed roof nailing down the roofing tin 1989, color snapshot. Photo Credit: Roger Mignon

6. Sabra sits atop the finished shed roof with one shutter hanging, 1989, black-and-white photo, 8 x 10 in. Photo Credit: Roger Mignon

7.–10. Sabra Moore, drawings from Journal Book #52, showing the Abiquiu black-and-white shards found at various sites on the land, 1989, ink on paper, 9 ¾ x 7 ½ in. Photo Credit: Sabra Moore

11. Howardena Pindell, *Autoblography: The Search (Chrysalis/ Meditation, Positive/Negative)*, 1988–1989, mixed media on canvas, 72 x 112 in. Photo Credit: Howardena Pindell/Courtesy of Garth Greenan Gallery, New York

12. Vernita Nemec, *Surface Tensions*, a performance by Vernita with music by Lorin Roser, Snug Harbor Cultural Center, 1987, offset card, 5 ½ x 7 ¾ in. Photo Credit: Vernita Nemec

13. Sabra and Roger waiting with witness Marithelma Costa at Brooklyn City Hall to get married, 1989, color snapshot. Photo credit: Marithelma Costa

14. Photo for our wedding card, *Sabra and Roger Got Married*, showing us posed in front of the stud wall framing for our shed in Abiquiu, New Mexico, in front of the window that "fell through" Sabra, 1989, color snapshot. Photo Credit: Roger Mignon

15. Kazuko, *New Work*, show card, detail, 55 Mercer Street Gallery, 1999. Photo Credit: Courtesy of Kazuko Miyamoto, photo by Hisashi Okamoto

16. *Running Out of Time*, exhibit card with photo of Sabra's hands, childhood toys, and road in N'Zérékoré that led to the airport, 1989, photo offset, 7 x 4 ¼ in. Photo Credit: Sabra Moore

17. *Running Out of Time: 9 Women Artists Take a Planetary Turn to the 90s* list of participants, gallery onetwentyeight, New York. Photo Credit: Sabra Moore

18. *Running Out of Time* installation, gallery onetwentyeight; artwork by May Stevens is in the foreground. Photo Credit: Roger Mignon

19. Sabra Moore, *Running Out of Time: 13 House Count*, based on Aztec calendrical images, 1989–1990, mixed media, oil on gessoed paper and wood, various natural materials, 42 x 40 x 24 overall. Photo credit: Sabra Moore

20. Marina Gutierrez, *No Shelter*, artwork part of *Running Out of Time*, 1987, graphite and mixed media drawing on paper, 22 x 44 in. Photo Credit: Marina Gutierrez

21. Sabra working at gallery during installation of *Running Out of Time*, 1989, color snapshot. Photo Credit: Roger Mignon

22. Faith Wilding, *Godot's tree, the dream of eating leaves*, 1988, watercolor, ink, 12 x 9 in. Faith was one of the artists in *Running Out of Time*. Photo Credit: Faith Wilding

23. Mimi Smith, *Racing Against the Muck*, 1989, acrylic, Xerox, ink, computer print, on paper and clock, 70 x 28 in. installed. Photo credit: Mimi Smith

24. Mimi Smith, *Running Against the Muck*, installation view, foreground, *Running Out of Time* exhibit, gallery onetwentyeight, 1990. Photo Credit: Roger Mignon

25. May Stevens, *Fore River*, 1983, acrylic on canvas, 78 x 120 in. Photo Credit: May Stevens, Courtesy of Ryan Lee Gallery, New York

26.–29. Sabra Moore, *Running Out of Time: 13 House Count*, details (all), 1989, each house approximately 4 ¼ x 6 x 5 ½ in. 26. *Fire House*, oil on gessoed paper, sticks, cloth ties. 27. *Forest House*, oil on gessoed paper, sticks, cloth ties. 28. *Deer House*, oil on gessoed paper, stick, birch bark, cloth ties. 29. *Forest House*, oil on gessoed paper, sticks, cloth ties. Photo Credit: Sabra Moore

30. Sylvia Sleigh, *The Bride I (Lawrence Alloway)*, 1949, oil on canvas, 24 x 20 in. Photo Credit: Estate of Sylvia Sleigh/ Tate, London, Purchased with the support of the Estate of Sylvia Sleigh, 2015

31. Sylvia Sleigh, *Lawrence Alloway Tondo*, 1979, oil on canvas, 17 in. diameter. Photo Credit: Estate of Sylvia Sleigh/ Private collection, Chicago, IL

32. Sylvia Sleigh, *Lawrence Alloway with a Bowtie*, 1948, oil on canvas, 18 x 13 ¾ in. Photo Credit: Estate of Sylvia Sleigh

33. Sylvia Sleigh, *Lawrence in Bed (Ditching)*, 1959, oil on canvas, 24 x 36 in. Photo Credit: Estate of Sylvia Sleigh/ Private collection, England

34. Joan Semmel, *Self Portrait on the Couch*, 1983, oil on canvas, 68 x 72 in. Photo Credit: Courtesy Alexander Gray Associates, New York © 2015 Joan Semmel/Artists Rights Society (ARS), New York

35. Ora Lerman, *As the Sun Sets in Sidilkov, Eggs become Golden Suns*, 1986, hand-ground oil on canvas, 36 x 52 in. Photo Credit: Ora Lerman Charitable Trust/ photo by Malcolm Varon

36. Edith Isaac-Rose, *Milagros*, announcement card, Zeus-Trabia Gallery, 1987, photocopy, 4 ¾ x 7 in. Photo Credit: Courtesy of Edith Isaac-Rose

37. *Stars and Starlets*, *Heresies* performance and art raffle event card featuring women performance artists in upcoming issues #18: Mothers, Mags & Movie Stars and #19: Satire, Kamikaze, 1986, offset card, 6 x 4 ¼ in. Photo Credit: Sabra Moore New York City Women's Art Movement Archive, Barnard College

38. Photocopy of Nicole Hollander cartoon that Avis Lang solicited to support *Heresies*. Photo Credit: Sabra Moore New York City Women's Art Movement Archive, Barnard College

39. Flier advertising *Heresies* T-shirt with the graphic "H" design by Kathie Brown with the cutouts that Miriam Schapiro and Faith Wilding made for the cover of issue #24: 12 Years, 1989, photocopy, 11 x 8 ½ in. Photo Credit: Sabra Moore New York City Women's Art Movement Archive, Barnard College

40. *Heresies* issue #24: 12 Years back cover, with cutouts that Miriam Schapiro and Faith Wilding created for the cover. Photo Credit: ©1985 *Heresies: A Feminist Publication on Art and Politics*

41. Marina Gutierrez, *Biography*, 1988, acrylic on Masonite with suspended metal reliefs, 48 x 60 x 6 in. Photo Credit: Marina Gutierrez

42. Maria Magdalena Campos, *A Woman at the Border*, SOHO20 Gallery, exhibit card. Photo Credit: Maria Magdalena Campos

43. May Stevens, *The Second International*, one part of photo mural installation, *One Plus or Minus One*, New Museum, 1988, approximately 11 x 17 ft. Photo Credit: May Stevens, Courtesy of Ryan Lee Gallery, New York

44. May Stevens, *Eden Hotel*, one part of photo mural installation, *One Plus or Minus One*, New Museum, 1988, approximately 11 x 17 ft. Photo Credit: May Stevens, Courtesy of Ryan Lee Gallery, New York

45. *Bad Girls* show card, Aljira, Newark, 1990, cardstock, 4 x 9 ¼ in. Photo Credit: Sabra Moore New York City Women's Art Movement Archive, Barnard College

46. NYC/WCA newsletter illustration by Maria Carmen, *Asa Branca*, 1986, mixed media graphic for the theme "Shifting Power," 1990 WCA National Conference theme, Fall 1989. Photo Credit: © Fall 1989, New York City/ Women's Caucus for Art Newsletter

47. Brynhildur Thorgeirsdottir, *Hervör*, 1987, glass, silicon rubber, varnish, 40 x 36 x 20 in. Brynhildur states about *Hervör*: "a female, red and dangerous." Photo Credit: Brynhildur Thorgeirsdottir

48. *The All-Male Feminist Art Show*, curated by Robert Costa, New Waterfront Museum, Brooklyn, 1988, photocopy, 11 x 8 ½ in. Brynhildur Thorgeirsdottir is seated on the left with bow tie; Hannah Wilke is standing behind with hat and sunglasses. Photo Credit: Courtesy of Sabra Moore

49.–50. *Jumbo Dumbo* card, Brooklyn Waterfront Artists Coalition's 8th Annual Spring Show, 1987, photo offset, 7 x 5 each side. Photo Credit: Courtesy of Sabra Moore

51. View of Manhattan Bridge from sixth-floor loft fire escape, circa 1990, color snapshot. Photo Credit: Roger Mignon

52. Front Street building with rental signs in background, circa 1990, color snapshot. Photo Credit: Roger Mignon

53.–64. Sabra Moore, *This Is the Place Where the River Joins the Islands*, an installation in the East River at Jay Street sponsored by the Brooklyn Waterfront Artists (BWAC), 1990. The photos that follow document this installation; all are 35 mm color slides.

53. Roger holds web of Sabra's *Grass Rafts* near the wharf at Jay Street. Photo Credit: Sabra Moore

54. Roger tosses a *Grass Raft* into the East River. Photo Credit: Sabra Moore

55. Sabra working on web of *Grass Rafts* near trash at low tide, East River at Jay Street. Photo Credit: Roger Mignon

56. Close-up of *Grass Raft* lying on the cobblestone street. Photo Credit: Sabra Moore

57. Sabra tying ropes for *Grass Raft Web* near Con Edison plant. Photo Credit: Roger Mignon

58. Sabra stringing more of the *Grass Raft Web* from facing side near derelict building. Photo Credit: Roger Mignon

59. Sabra tying *Rope Bridge* near trash to suspend across the East River and above the *Grass Raft Web*. Photo Credit: Roger Mignon

60. *Rope Bridge* mirroring Manhattan Bridge is in place across the East River. Photo Credit: Roger Mignon

61. Sabra works to unfurling *Rope Bridge* from the other side of the wharf across from Con Edison. Photo Credit: Roger Mignon

62. Detail showing *Rope Bridge* floating across water. Photo Credit: Roger Mignon

63. Sabra Moore, *Documentation Blueprint*, documenting *This Is the Place Where the River Joins the Islands*, detail, 1990, laser transfer from blueprint onto cloth, includes wooden trim for top, 42 ½ x 44 in. Photo Credit: Sabra Moore

64. Close up of *Grass Raft* in East River. Photo Credit: Roger Mignon

65. Catalina Parra, *It's Incontestable Again* (series #1 of 10), 1992, mixed media collage, photograph, newspaper, red thread, white paper board. 28 x 22 in. Photo Credit: Catalina Parra

66. Howardena Pindell, *Autobiography: Africa (Buddha)*, 1986, mixed media on canvas, 51 x 91 in. Photo Credit: Howardena Pindell/ Courtesy of Garth Greenan Gallery, New York

67.–69. Pages from Sabra Moore's collective artist's book *Making/Making Art/Making Sex/Making Baby* for the *Carnival Knowledge* show at Franklin Furnace, New York City, 1984, color Xerox on archival paper, 8 ½ x 8 ½ in. each page.

67. Lucy R. Lippard, text written over Sue Maberry graphic with page composition by Sabra Moore. Photo Credit: Lucy R. Lippard with graphic by Sue Maberry/ Courtesy of Sabra Moore

68. Sabra Moore, page art with childhood dolls and doll clothes. Photo Credit: Sabra Moore

69. Graphic drawing by Nicky Lindeman with page composition by Sabra Moore. Photo Credit: Nicky Lindeman and Sabra Moore, Courtesy of Sabra Moore

70. Four watercolors (following) by Emma Amos, *The Gift*, 1990–1991, watercolor on paper, forty-four paintings, 26 x 20 in. each. 70. Joyce Kozloff 71. Camille Billops 72. Carol Sun 73. Sabra Moore. Photo Credit (all): ©Emma Amos, Licensed by VAGA, New York, NY/photo by Becket Logan

74. Manhattan Bridge from Sabra and Roger's 81 Pearl Street fire escape, circa 1990, color snapshot. Photo Credit: Roger Mignon

75. The fire escape view looking down Front Street from loft, circa 1990, color snapshot. Photo Credit: Roger Mignon

76. Buildings along Jay Street across from Sabra's studio windows, circa 1990, color snapshot. Photo Credit: Roger Mignon

77. Returning to camp in the shed with view of Madera Canyon in the distance, 1990, black-and-white photo, 8 x 10 in. Photo Credit: Roger Mignon

78. Roger and Sabra eating breakfast outside shed with Sunday Dog nearby, 1990, color snapshot. Photo Credit: Roger Mignon

79. Sabra talking with her mother (standing in red) inside the white canyon, 1990, color snapshot. Photo Credit: Roger Mignon

80. Sitting with Sunday Dog facing the white canyon, 1990, black-and-white photo, 8 x 10 in. Photo Credit: Roger Mignon
81. A chair and table set up for Sylvia Sleigh to paint a watercolor of Madera Canyon, 1990, color snapshot. Photo Credit: Roger Mignon
82. Sabra and Sylvia Sleigh in Pueblo de Abiquiu with a view of the fields along the Chama River, 1990, color snapshot. Photo Credit: Roger Mignon
83. Enjoying the flow of well water near the new well house, 1990, color snapshot. Photo Credit: Roger Mignon
84. Leaving the house site en route back to Pearl Street loft, 1990, color snapshot. Photo Credit: Roger Mignon

Chapter 11

1. Marina Gutierrez, *What Goes Around Comes Around*, Spectacolor lightboard, One Times Square, 1988, computer animation card, 5 x 7 in. Photo Credit: Marina Gutierrez/ Courtesy of Sabra Moore New York City Women's Art Movement Archive, Barnard College
2. Sharon Gilbert, *Hands/On*, exhibit card for *Neverland: Artist's Books and Electrographic Prints*, Barnett House, Poughkeepsie, New York, 1990, electrographic collage. Photo Credit: © Estate of Sharon Gilbert
3. Shirley Smith, *Tornado Watch*, exhibit card, *Recent Oil Paintings*, Aaron Gallery, Washington, DC, 1988, oil on canvas, 60 x 54. Photo Credit: Estate of Shirley Smith/ Courtesy of Sabra Moore New York City Women's Art Movement Archive, Barnard College
4.–7. Cindy Carr, *Adventures in Art & Politics*, each frame a detail from a cartoon page strip created as a subscription page for *Heresies* magazine. Photo Credit: Cindy Carr/ Courtesy of Sabra Moore New York City Women's Art Movement Archive, Barnard College
8. Flier for *Heresies* panel, *If you don't go to art school, can you still be a famous artist?*, symposium organized by Emma Amos and related to the upcoming *Heresies* issue # 25: The Art of Education, 1990, photocopy, 11 x 17 in. Photo Credit: Courtesy of Sabra Moore New York City Women's Art Movement Archive, Barnard College
9. Sabra Moore, *Dra- Raw- Wing*, for *Drawing Show* at gallery onetwentyeight, 1990, oil on gessoed paper and wood, laser transfer print, found sticks and cloth strips, waxed linen string, 14 ½ x 37 x 2 ½ in. Photo Credit: Sabra Moore
10.–11. Stages of the demolition of Jay Street buildings purchased by the Watchtower, across from the windows of Sabra's studio in Dumbo, 1990, black-and-white photograph, 8 x 10 each. Photo credit: Roger Mignon
12. *The Book as Vessel*, exhibit card, The Oregon Book Arts Guild, Oregon State Library, Salem, 1991, offset on card stock, 8 ½ x 5 ½ in. Photo Credit: Courtesy of Sabra

Moore New York City Women's Art Movement Archive, Barnard College
13. Sabra Moore, *It Won't Hold Water*, 1990, laser transfer print with oil and watercolor on gessoed paper, 9 x 10 ½ x 2 ½ in. each double page. One of two related artist's book works created for *The Book as Vessel* show. Photo Credit: Sabra Moore/ Artists Book Collection, Brooklyn Museum
14.–15 .Street installation of signs created for the *Lower Manhattan Sign Project*, organized by REPOhistory, 1992, two-sided silkscreen on metal, 24 x 18 in., installed on lamp posts at 36 sites in Lower Manhattan, (details, following 14 and 15). Photo Credit (both): Courtesy of REPOhistory
14. Tess Timoney and Mark O'Brien, *The Meal and Slave Market*, NE corner of Wall and Water Streets, *Lower Manhattan Sign Project*. Sign includes a seventeenth-century print depicting New Amsterdam with detail enlarged to reveal the presence of African slaves.
15. Greg Sholette, *The Other J.P. Morgan*, south side of Exchange Place between Nassau and William Street in front of J.P. Morgan corporate headquarters. Image is photo re-creation of anonymous soldier standing in front of Edward Steichen's portrait of Morgan. During the Civil War, J.P. Morgan hired a substitute to take his place in the Union army for a $300 fee.
16. Sabra Moore, sketch design for cloth tent, *Know Peace/ No Peace* installation, 1991. Photo Credit: Sabra Moore
17.–28. *Know Peace/No Peace* installation, 1991, gallery onetwentyeight, an exhibition organized by Kazuko and Sabra Moore in response to the Gulf War. The following photographs show various stages of the installation of the tent squares and of Kazuko's rope installation as well as the opening evening. All photos except where indicated are as follows: 1990, black-and-white photograph, 8 x 10 in. Photo Credit (17.–28.): Roger Mignon
17. Kazuko building branch and rope shelter.
18. Artists' names taped on ironed tent squares.
19. Sydney Hamburger's hand steadies her square from inside tent while Sabra laughs with Artelia Court (back of head).
20. Artelia Court sews square as Tak Inagaki films.
21. Amy Kalina installs *Know Peace/No Peace* artwork.
22. Unidentified artist holds his double square and sews from outside in while Amy Kalina works in the background.
23. Video stream of installation for Japanese television.
24. Participants Kazuko, Penny Josephides, Roger, and Sabra beside the tent.
25. Detail of many squares installed inside tent, 35 mm color slide.
26. Robin Michals and Sabra talk at opening inside partially completed tent.
27. Vyt Bakatis reads poetry near Kazuko's branch shelter; Marithelma Costa is to the left in white shirt.

28. Sabra performing *Oil Over Water* at opening evening with nieces Gina and Danielle Mignon (left to right) and Amy Kalina in upper right.

29.–36. Sabra Moore, drawings for *Bulfinch Mythology*, edited by Richard Martin, Harper Collins Publishers, New York, 1991 (all), 1990, black ink on paper, size varies and is indicated after each drawing. Photo Credit (29.–36.): Sabra Moore

29. Cadmus slaying a dragon from a black-figured Greek vase, 13 ½ x 11 in.

30. Thomas Bulfinch pictured inside a bronze mirror from Thebes, fifth century BC, 18 x 11 in.

31. Hercules bringing Hades's watchdog dog Cerberus to Eurystheus, king of Mycenae, from a Greek vase painting, 13 ½ x 11 in.

32. Cupid holding a dolphin, from a statue found in Pompeii, 13 ½ x 11 in.

33. Ceres, from a Roman terra-cotta bas-relief, 11 x 13 ½ in.

34. Celtic armor, the bronze shield is late first century object found in the Thames River; the helmet was also found in the river, near Waterloo Bridge, 13 ½ x 11 in.

35. An ensemble of divinities and mortals (left to right): Zeus, from a fifth century BC Greek vase painting; Hebe, from a fourth century Greek amphora; Ganymede, from a red-figured Greek vase; Diana, from a Roman statue known as the Goddess of Versailles; Atlas, from a fourth century BC Greek vase; and Goddess Eos, depicted on a Greek vase in the center, 18 x 24 in.

36. Virgil is seated holding *The Aeneid* between the muses of Epic and Tragedy, from a Tunisian mosaic, second–third century, 13 ½ x 11 in.

37. Cindy Carr, *Adventures in Art & Politics*, one frame from a cartoon page strip created as a subscription page for *Heresies* magazine. Photo Credit: Cindy Carr/ Courtesy of Sabra Moore New York City Women's Art Movement Archive, Barnard College

38. Cover, *Heresies* issue #26: Idioma, 1992. Photo Credit: © *Heresies: A Feminist Publication on Art and Politics*

39. Card for release of *Heresies* issue #26: Idioma, 1992, photo offset, 6 x 4 in. Photo Credit: Courtesy of Sabra Moore New York City Women's Art Movement Archive, Barnard College

40.–41 Sabra Moore, drawings for *Bulfinch Mythology* (all), 1990, black ink on paper, size varies and is indicated after each drawing. Photo Credit (40.–41.): Sabra Moore

40. Odysseus tied to mast as protection against the beauty of the sirens' songs, based on an attic red-figured pot, Vulci, 475–450 BC, 11 x 13 ½ in.

41. Bacchus playing lyre while satyrs dance, based on a Greek painting, 13 ½ x 11 in.

42. Sabra sitting near Avanyu petroglyphs in Madera Canyon below the house site in Abiquiu, New Mexico, 1991, color snapshot. Photo Credit: Roger Mignon

43. Sabra and Pat d'Andrea walking in Madera Canyon below the mesa with house site. 1991, black-and-white photograph, 8 x 10 in. Photo Credit: Roger Mignon

44.–47. Sabra Moore, Journal drawings, Books #40 and #43, including rock art en route to Chetro Ketl in Chaco Canyon (45.–47.) and the petroglyph site in Lyden, New Mexico (44.), 1985–1986, black ink on paper, 9 ¾ x 7 ½ in. Photo Credit: Sabra Moore

48.–49., 51. Three watercolors (following) by Emma Amos, *The Gift*, 1990–1991, watercolor on paper, forty-four paintings, 26 x 20 in. each. 48. Josely Carvalho 49. Marina Gutierrez 51. Lucy R. Lippard. Photo Credit (all): ©Emma Amos, Licensed by VAGA, New York, NY/photos by Becket Logan

50. *Heresies* issue # 27: Latina back cover. Photo Credit: © 1993 *Heresies: A Feminist Publication on Art and Politics*

52. Sabra Moore, Journal drawings, Book #40, the petroglyph site in Lyden, New Mexico, 1985, black ink on paper, 9 ¾ x 7 ½ in. Photo Credit: Sabra Moore

53. Sabra Moore, *Peace by Piece*, series made for *Group 90*, Vasarely Museum, Budapest, Hungary, 1991, photocopy cutouts on paper, watercolor, string, 8 ½ x 9 ¾ in. Photo Credit: Sabra Moore

54. Sylvia Sleigh, cover of *Ravishing*, from *Burning in Hell, a Project by Nancy Spero in Honor of the 15th Anniversary of Franklin Furnace*, 1991, color photocopied artist's book, 13 x 11 in. Photo Credit: Estate of Sylvia Sleigh

55.–56. Sabra Moore (both), *Woodsman*, 1997, multiple edition accordion-folded book, 40 double pages. *Woodsman* is based on photos of Grandmother Caroline's murdered husband Chester Bryant, circa 1910, and dedicated to her. 55. Cover, gessoed paper with oil and laser transfer print, watercolor edges, 6 ¾ x 4 ¾ in. 56. Double-page spread, photocopy on paper, 6 ¼ x 9 in. Photo Credit: Sabra Moore

57. Curtains hanging, *Place/Displace* installation, Puck Building, New York City, 1992, laser transfer on muslin, 35 mm color slide. Photo Credit: Sabra Moore, photo by Roger Mignon

58. Sabra Moore, close-up of *Directions*, *Place/Displace* series, 1990–1991, metal strips with beads, oil on gessoed beam with text, found padded stool, 3 ½ x 8 x 13 in., overall with stool: 25 ½ x 8 x 13 in. Text relates to the story of a murder of a female cousin by her husband in Clarksville, the person who gave directions to my mother as we searched for the road to Briggins Cemetery. Photo Credit: Sabra Moore

59. Sabra Moore, close-up of tent, part of *Woodsman* (floor), *Place/Displace* series, 1990–1991, muslin with laser transfer print, sticks, toy gun, beads, 11 ¼ x 11 ½ x 10 in. Photo Credit: Sabra Moore

60. Sabra Moore, *Arrowhead*, detail, *Place/Displace* series, 1990–1991, oil on gessoed drawer with text, sticks,

chair part, cement, 39 ½ x 26 x 26 in. Photo Credit: Sabra Moore

61. Sabra Moore, *Not a Civilian*, detail, *Place/Displace* series, 1990–1991, oil on gessoed wood, laser transfer print on cloth, chair, twigs, 37 x 24 x 23 in. The laser transfer print is from a rubbing of the tombstone of Winchester Dane Lewis, Sabra's great-grandfather, with his Co.1 63 Ohio Union infantry regiment engraved in stone. Photo Credit: Sabra Moore

62. Sabra Moore (both), *Peace by Piece #1*, series made for *Group 90*, Vasarely Museum, Budapest, Hungary, 1991, laser transfer cutout prints on paper, 8 ½ x 9 ¾ in. Photo Credit: Sabra Moore

63. *Peace by Piece #2*, series made for *Group 90*, Vasarely Museum, Budapest, Hungary, 1991, laser transfer cutout prints on paper, 8 ½ x 9 ¾ in. Photo Credit: Sabra Moore

64. Journal drawings of rock place where shards were found, black ink on paper, 9 ¾ x 7 ½ in. Photo Credit: Sabra Moore

65. Sabra Moore, *Grounded*, detail, showing feet on land, 1994, oil on gessoed paper, laser transfer prints, found metal, wire, beads, string, 72 x 76 in. Photo Credit: Sabra Moore

66. Flier for Viva Latina!, the earlier name for *Heresies* issue #27: Latina. Photo Credit: Courtesy of Sabra Moore New York City Women's Art Movement Archive, Barnard College

67. *Heresies* subscription flier, *Or Else*, circa 1992, photocopy, 11 x 8 ½ in. Photo Credit: Courtesy of Sabra Moore New York City Women's Art Movement Archive, Barnard College

68. Invitation to meeting to recruit new *Heresies* members at Josely's house. Photo Credit: Courtesy of Sabra Moore New York City Women's Art Movement Archive, Barnard College

69. Pink flier for *Heresies* meeting at Emma's house, 1991, photocopy, 11 x 8 ½ in. Photo Credit: Courtesy of Sabra Moore New York City Women's Art Movement Archive, Barnard College

70. Staking strings of house outline before digging stem wall, 1991, color snapshot. Photo Credit: Roger Mignon

71. Roger and Sabra inside start of concrete stem wall of house, Plaza Blanca mesa house site, Abiquiu, New Mexico, 1991, color snapshot. Photo Credit: Roger Mignon

72. Joe Gonzales and crew lay concrete block for stem wall, 1991, color snapshot. Photo Credit: Roger Mignon

73. Pouring concrete into stem wall near telephone poles, 1991, color snapshot. Photo Credit: Roger Mignon

74. Sabra raking and cleaning site of completed stem wall foundation, 1991, color snapshot. Photo Credit: Roger Mignon

75. A rainbow in front of Cerro Negro as seen from the house site, 1991, color snapshot. Photo Credit: Roger Mignon

76.–77. Sabra Moore (both), *Woodsman*, 1997, photocopy on paper, 6 ¼ x 9 in., 40 double pages, with cover, 6 ¾ x 4 ¾ in. Two double-page details of artist's book relating story of the murder of Grandmother's second husband. Photo Credit: Sabra Moore

Chapter 12:

1. Sabra Moore, drawing for *Place/Displace* installation, part of a series of installations for *Charting the Inner Terrain*, Pratt Manhattan Gallery, Puck Building, New York City, 1991, ink on paper, 11 x 17 in. Photo Credit: Sabra Moore

2. Sabra Moore, drawing for *Place/Displace* gates and curtain placement at the Puck Building, New York City, 1991, ink on paper, 11 x 17 in. Photo Credit: Sabra Moore

3. Sabra Moore, installation view of *Not a Civilian, Place/Displace* series, 1990–1991, oil on gessoed wood, laser transfer print on cloth, chair, twigs, 37 x 24 x 23 in. The text that encircles the rubbing reads as follows: "They didn't like him. But they spoke. His grandson eloped with their daughter. His granddaughter married their son, the second marriage. They said he married a doctor-bill. He made them put his Union infantry regiment on his tombstone, Co,1 63 Ohio Inf." Black-and-white photo, 10 x 8 in. Photo Credit: Sabra Moore/ photo by Roger Mignon

4. Sabra Moore, *Woodsman* (tent cloth), *Place/Displace* series, 1990–1991, muslin, laser transfer print, watercolor, wood, beads, toy gun, 32 x 52 in. The handwritten text reproduces a penciled text that Caroline Lewis had written on the back of a photograph of the murdered man, Chester Bryant. It reads as follows with spelling and punctuation kept as written: "Acworth Texas August 30 1912 T Some angry words were Spoken and then all most unaware Some unthinking angry lad and all of my weeping and my prayers can never make those false cruel words unsaid Come back to me Sweet heart and love me as before come back to me Sweet heart and Love forever more Loves bright pathway the Sun no longer shines come back to me and be no ones Sweet Heart but mine C Lewis." Photo Credit: Sabra Moore

5. Sabra Moore, *Arrowhead*, *Place/Displace* series, 1990–1991, oil on gessoed drawer with text, sticks, chair part, cement, 39 ½ x 26 x 26 in. Text inside drawer reads as follows: "You can find arrowheads. Somewhere near Briggins. We used to keep them in a box. The big ranch has the same name. Arrowhead bought her farm. They paid $1,500.00 for 35 acres, 2 barns, the house place, 2 sheds, a well. She got moved to town. They switched the road. It comes up across the pecan orchard. They cut the woods. They tore down the house. They kept the well." 35 mm color slide. Photo Credit: Sabra Moore

6.–7. *Place/Displace* installation (both) at the Pratt Manhattan Gallery, Puck Building in progress with Sabra making drawings of sticks on wall as another artist passes through, the string fence is visible in the foreground, 1992, black-and-white photo, 8 x 10 in. Photo Credit: Roger Mignon

8. Visitors stand near *Gate* with laser transfer *Curtain*, 1992, black-and-white print, 8 x 10 in. Text on curtain reads: "The lumber yard owns the woods now. They have the key for the road that leads to the cemetery." Photo Credit: Roger Mignon

9. Sabra Moore, *Woodsman* (wall), *Place/Displace* series, 1991, oil on gessoed paper with wood, beads, dried stems, cloth, Xerox transfer, 52 x 32 in. The text reads as follows: "He killed him. Maybe the gunman was her first husband or it was the first husband's brother. He rode up on horseback & shot him dead in the doorway. She was next door. Nothing happened after that. His family took the daughter. She buried him in Briggins. She knew I knew, not from her. One day, she showed me his pictures. 'A railroad man,' she said. 'Harry was good to me,' she said, 'he let me keep the pictures.' His stone is a woodsman stump, fallen over. Her day lilies grow nearby." Photo Credit: Sabra Moore

10. Close-up of Sabra drawing sticks on the walls, *Place/Displace* installation at the Pratt Manhattan Gallery, Puck Building, 1992, black-and-white photo, 10 x 8 in. Photo Credit: Roger Mignon

11. Sabra Moore, *Woodsman* (tent), *Place/Displace* series, 1991, wood, gessoed sticks with texts, oil, cloth, Xerox transfer, size varies. Text on sticks is from an inscription that Chester Bryant, the murdered man, wrote on the back of a photo: "He sends his picture form the tie camp. Inscription: I am the Boss in this camp C.F.B. C.E. Bryant fryes meat George Dec Keg makes bread C.E. Bryant washes dishes Billie the Rounder carrys wood and every boddy is the Boss in this camp this is the Durty Dozen the head knocker is the red Hon. C.E. Bryant." Photo Credit: Sabra Moore.

12. Sabra Moore, *Directions*, *Place/Displace* series, 1990– 1991, metal strips with beads, oil on gessoed beam with text, found padded stool, 3 ½ x 8 x 13 in., overall with stool: 25 ½ x 8 x 13 in. Text reads: "We drove almost to Red River, then doubled back. She went into the little store. & came back out with directions. A cousin, it seems. She knew the route to Briggins. The next year, she was dead. Her husband shot her. He shot her boyfriend. He spared the kids. They impounded his cows for bond. He'll get off for sure." Photo Credit: Sabra Moore:

13. Sabra Moore, *Arrowhead* (view into text box), *Place/Displace* series, 1990–1991, oil on gessoed drawer with text, sticks, chair part, cement, 39 ½ x 26 x 26 in. Black-and-white photo, 10 x 8 in. Photo Credit: Sabra Moore/ photo by Roger Mignon

14. Sabra Moore, completed installation, *Place/Displace* with *Lillie's Peaks* in center. Sabra Moore, *Lillie's Peaks* with *Gypsy Baby Cart* emerging, *Place/Displace* series, 1988– 1990, oil on gessoed paper and wood, Xerox transfer, cloth, found wood, cloth strips, beads, found tin, photographs, 73 x 40 x 36 in. *Gypsy Baby Cart*, oil on gessoed paper, found wood, string, 14 ½ x 18 x 31 in. Black-and-white print, 8 x 10 in. Photo Credit: Sabra Moore/ photo by Roger Mignon

Text for Lillie's Peaks printed on the inside of the peaks as follows:

"(river side) They wanted to bury her in town. It was muddy in the country, hard to get in. Lillie disagreed. She threatened to haunt them. Then she made the ranger promise he'd bulldoze the road for her. She had delivered him, She had delivered almost everyone back along the river. She got buried in Briggins as she wished.

"(wood side) The girls wished she'd curl her hair. Look at it, pulled back in a knot at her neck. She'd worn it the same way all their lives. And those little diamond studs on her ears. No one dressed like that now. Lillie refused. She kept her taste- print dress, sunbonnet when needed, socks. Her house was the same- photos of her kin from floor to ceiling, the truck of quilts in the side room. The daughters dressed her when she died. They cut her hair and gave her a permanent. She was dressed in style for her wake."

Text for Gypsy Baby:

"They used to come through back along the river. One year, the daughter died. The gypsy parents buried her in Briggins. Each year, they came & cleaned the grave, leaving ceramics- a china tea pot, a tiny high-heeled slipper. Once they built a metal fence. The last visit, they covered the top with wire. He knocked the fence down, that time he tried to clean the cemetery with a back hoe. The flowered shards remain, embedded in a grassy mound."

15. *Laser transfer Curtains frame window of Puck Building for Place/Displace installation, 1992, black-and-white print, 8 x 10 in. Photo Credit: Roger Mignon*

16. Faith Ringgold, show card for *Change: Painted Story Quilts*, Bernice Steinbaum Gallery, 1987, color offset card, 9 x 6 in. Photo Credit: Faith Ringgold/ Courtesy of Sabra Moore New York City Women's Art Movement Archive, Barnard College

17. Ayisha Abraham, *The Migration of Memory*, *Works Past/ Present*, The Brecht Forum, 1993, photocopy, card, 4 ¾ x 7 ¼ in. Photo Credit: Ayisha Abraham

18. Grace Williams, *Altar & Ceremonial Vessels*, curated by Chrystal Britton, Aaron Davis Hall at City College, 1994, photo offset card. Photo Credit: Grace Williams/ Courtesy of Sabra Moore New York City Women's Art Movement Archive, Barnard College

19. Women's Action Coalition (WAC) flier, Multicultural Coalition of Women and Women's Groups in Santa Fe, Railyard Performance Space, circa 1991, photocopy, 11 x 8 ½ in. Photo Credit: Courtesy of Sabra Moore New York City Women's Art Movement Archive, Barnard College

20. Card distributed at Women's Action Coalition (WAC) meetings with graphic from the National Clearinghouse on Marital and Date Rape, 1993, showing two heads under a veil and text: "In nearly 31 states, under many circumstances, it is legal for a husband to rape his wife." 1993, photo offset, 4 x 6 in. Photo Credit: Courtesy of Sabra Moore New York City Women's Art Movement Archive, Barnard College

21. *Domestic Violence: The Facts Are In*, group show at PS 122 Gallery presented in conjunction with *Combat Zone: Campaign Hq Against Domestic Violence*, 1996, photo offset, 6 x 4 in. Photo Credit: Courtesy of Sabra Moore New York City Women's Art Movement Archive, Barnard College

22. Su Friedrich, *The Ties That Bind*, film announcement with photo of Su (left) and her mother, 1984, a 54-minute documentary about Su's mother, Lore Friedrich, and her life growing up in Germany during the Second World War, photo offset card, 4 x 6 in. Photo Credit: Su Friedrich/ Courtesy of Sabra Moore New York City Women's Art Movement Archive, Barnard College

23. Guerrilla Girls book publication event announcement, New Museum of Contemporary Art, celebrating the publication of *Confessions of the Guerrilla Girls*, Harper Perennial, 1995, photo offset card, 4 ¼ x 6 in. Photo Credit: Courtesy of Guerrilla Girls

24.–25. Liliana Porter, *Two Mirrors* (diptych), 1990, acrylic, silkscreen, assemblage on canvas, shown at the exhibit *Fragments of the Journey*, Bronx Museum of the Arts, February 1992. Photo Credit: Liliana Porter

26. Zarina Hashmi, *House on Wheels*, 1991, cast and painted aluminum, 12 x 8 ½ x ¾ in., cover art for card, 1992 exhibit at Bronx Museum, *House with Four Walls: Sculptures and Etchings*, photo offset, two-fold card, 6 ¾ x 4 ¾ in. Photo Credit: Zarina Hashmi

27. Lenora Champagne, *From the Red Light District* performance with Kevin Duffy and Patricia Pretzinger, P.S. 122, photo offset card, 4 x 6 in. Photo Credit: Lenora Champagne, photo by Tina Freeman

28. Artelia Court, Halloween party invitation reads in part: "Outlandish & otherworldly/outfits or/ eccentric behavior/ will be zoot de riguer." circa 1991, photocopy, 8 ½ x 11 in. Photo Credit: Artelia Court/ Courtesy of Sabra Moore New York City Women's Art Movement Archive, Barnard College

29. Carole Byard, *The Perception of Presence: A Sculptural Installation in 2 Rooms*, 1992, Art in General, exploring the early deaths of black men and boys, two-fold exhibition card, photo offset, 5 x 8 in. Photo Credit: Carole Byard

30. Alison Saar, *Tattooed Lady*, 1985, mixed media collage/ drawing, 96 x 50 in., reproduced as the cover image for a group show organized by Howardena Pindell, *Autobiography: In Her Own Image*, Intar Latin American Gallery, 1988, photo offset card, 9 x 6 ½ in. Photo Credit: Alison Saar/ Courtesy of Sabra Moore New York City Women's Art Movement Archive, Barnard College

31. Theodora Skipitares, *Under the Knife III: A History of Medicine*, a theatrical production created, designed, and directed by Skipitares and presented by La MaMa E.T.C. and Skysaver productions, undated, offset two-fold color card, 5 ½ x 8 ½ in. Photo Credit: Theodora Skipitares

32. WAC ribbon, circa 1991, blue ribbon with WAC eye stamp 3 ¼ x 1 ½ in. Photo Credit: Courtesy of Sabra Moore

33. Catalina Parra, *Nubian Shield (Over Guns)*, undated, mixed media collage, X-Ray, black wool, white burlap thread, text, sterile gauze, acrylic, white card board. Photo Credit: Catalina Parra

34. *The June Wedding*, card for a benefit for WHAM! and Act Up, June 26, 1992. Photo Credit: Courtesy of Sabra Moore New York City Women's Art Movement Archive, Barnard College

35. *Happy Father's Day*, WAC action flier designed by Sabra Moore for June 19, 1992 action on Father's Day to highlight the thirty billion dollars in unpaid child support owed by American fathers to their families. Text on back reads: "June 19th s Emancipation Day/ Stop Economic Violence," 1992, two-fold photocopy, 8 ½ x 5 ½ in. Photo Credit: Courtesy of Sabra Moore New York City Women's Art Movement Archive, Barnard College

36. *Bea is 60*, flier to benefit *Kitchen Table: Women of Color Press* and honoring Bea Kreloff, photocopy, 11 x 8 ½ in. Photo Credit: Courtesy of Sabra Moore New York City Women's Art Movement Archive, Barnard College

37. Willie Birch, *Wake Up*, 1989, gouache on paper, 32 x 46 in. Cover image for exhibit card, *A Personal View of Urban America*, Exit Art Gallery, 1992, photo offset, 5 x 7 in. Photo Credit: Willie Birch

38.–40. Sabra Moore, *Running Out of Time: 13 House Count* (all), 1989, each house approximately 4 ¼ x 6 x 5 ½ in. and based on the Aztec calendar for thirteen-year periods or bundles of time. House and rabbit are two of the time symbols; Moore conceived of each house as a symbol of nature atop a snake-shaped table and our perilous relationship to the planet. 38. *Corn*, oil on gessoed paper with tied cornstalks and twigs. 39. *Cloud*, oil on gessoed paper with papier-mâché cloud. 40. *Deer*, oil on gesssoed paper with birch bark and wood. Photo Credit: Sabra Moore

41.–43. Sabra Moore, *Running Out of Time: 13 House Count* (all), 1989, each house approximately 4 ¼ x 6 x 5 ½ in. 41.–42. *Straw*, oil on gessoed paper with bundles of straw standing upright inside house. 43. *Continent*, oil on gessoed paper with gesso disk and wire. Photo Credit: Sabra Moore

44. Sylvia Sleigh, *Invitation to a Voyage: The Hudson River at Fishkill*, detail, *Riverside*, Panel 2 through 5, 1979–1999, oil on fourteen canvases, each 96 x 60 in. In Panel 2 (left), Susan Kaprov is seated; in Panel 4, Eileen Spikol is standing and gesturing; and in Panel 5, Lawrence is gallantly extending his arm to Sylvia Sleigh (in reality, at this point, Lawrence was partially paralyzed and in a wheelchair, but Sylvia painted him in this gently heroic pose). Photo Credit: Sylvia Sleigh/ Hudson River Museum, Yonkers, NY

45. WAC pink card mailed to Judge R. Benjamin Cohen concerning rape, circa 1991, photocopy, 5 x 7 in. Part of the text reads: "75% of women attacked know their rapists." Photo Credit: Courtesy of Sabra Moore New York City Women's Art Movement Archive, Barnard College

46. *Can We Get Along Here?*, Rodney King button. Photo Credit: Courtesy of Sabra Moore

47. Susanna Cuyler flier, *Patriarchy's Demolition: A Year of WACtion, What do you do with 98,648,000 angry women voters?*, mailer from TIT (Tell It True) fe/mail% post-wac, circa 1991, photocopy, 11 x 8 ½ in. Photo Credit: Courtesy of Sabra Moore New York City Women's Art Movement Archive, Barnard College

48. Sabra, Artelia Court, and Artelia's daughter India at WAC demonstration, color snapshot. Photo Credit: Courtesy of Artelia Court

49.–50. Brochure designed by Sabra Moore for WAC Mother's Day Action at Grand Central Station, May 8, 1992, 1992, photocopy, 8 ½ x 5 ½ in. Interior text includes a song that we sang with our drum core as agile activists managed to unveil a huge banner atop the wall of Grand Central Station: "Mother Dear, we're sorry/ You live in the U.S.A/ Of all developed countries/ Only this one won't pay/ For pre-natal care, or day-care/ Not to mention a living wage/ Child support is not enforced/ And we are in a RAGE!" Photo Credit: Courtesy of Sabra Moore New York City Women's Art Movement Archive, Barnard College

51. Todd Ayoung/Megan Pugh, *Choice Histories Chronology*, reprinted from *Choice Histories: Framing Abortion, An Artists Book by REPOhistory*, 1992, pages 22–23, photo offset, 11 x 8 ½ in. *Choice Histories: Framing Abortion* was also an exhibit at Artists Space, New York. Photo Credit: Courtesy of REPOhistory

52. Sarah Vogwill, *Chronology*, Flash Light, reprinted from *Choice Histories: Framing Abortion, An Artists Book by REPOhistory*, 1992, pages 38–39, photo offset, 11 x 8 ½ in. Photo Credit: Courtesy of REPOhistory

53. Sabra Moore, *Calendar*, artwork created for *Choice Histories: Framing Abortion* sponsored by REPOhistory, Artists Space, 1992, laser transfer print on muslin, cotton batting, safety pins, 12 pages, 13 ½ x 9 ¼ in. Imagery includes direct copies from desk calendar entries during

the twelve weeks in Guinea when Sabra sought to terminate an unintended pregnancy, interlaced with images from nineteenth-century slave sale ads. Photo Credit: Sabra Moore

54. Sabra Moore, *Hot Pads with Opal Story (left) Calendar (right)*, artworks created for *Choice Histories: Framing Abortion* sponsored by REPO history, Artists Space, 1992. *Hot Pads with Opal Story*, laser transfer and watercolor on gessoed paper cutouts in the form of hot pads, attached by string and beads, 12 x 7 ¾ in. each, string size varies. Photo Credit: Sabra Moore

55. *Kick Operation Rescue Out of NYC* call-to-action flier circulated at WAC meetings, July 11–18, 1992, photocopy, 14 x 8 ½ in. Photo Credit: Courtesy of Sabra Moore New York City Women's Art Movement Archive, Barnard College

56. WAC cloth banner for women's reproductive rights to be worn by fastening safety pins to one's shirt like a bib and could be used in the various pro-choice demonstrations during the spring of 1992, silkscreen on muslin, approximately 17 x 11 in. Photo Credit: Courtesy of Sabra Moore New York City Women's Art Movement Archive, Barnard College

57. *Homeplace* exhibit card, Mark O'Brien curator, including Sabra Moore, Marina Gutierrez, and others, Henry Street Settlement, New York, 1992, photo offset, 5 x 7 in. Photo Credit: Courtesy of Sabra Moore New York City Women's Art Movement Archive, Barnard College

58. Sandra Lee-Phipps, WAC demonstration, August 3, 1992, protesting the opening of the Downtown Guggenheim and honoring Ana Mendieta, 1992, black-and-white photo. A protestor wearing the Guerrilla Girls sack is in foreground with WAC signs beyond. Photo Credit: © 1992 Sandra Lee-Phipps

59.–60. Guerrilla Girls sack, printed on both sides of a white paper sack, 1992, approximately 17 x 11 in. Designed for the August 3, 1992 demonstration against the opening of the Downtown Guggenheim Museum protesting the exclusion of women artists and the inclusion of Carl Andre, who had been acquitted of the murder of his wife, artist Ana Mendieta. Sack reads in part: "What's new and happening at the Guggenheim for the discriminating art lover?" Photo Credit: Courtesy of Sabra Moore New York City Women's Art Movement Archive, Barnard College

61. Sandra Lee-Phipps, WAC demonstration, August 3, 1992 protesting the opening of the Downtown Guggenheim and honoring Ana Mendieta, 1992, black-and-white photo. The WAC silkscreen banner grieving Ana Mendieta is being carried behind the WAC drum corps. Photo Credit: © 1992 Sandra Lee-Phipps

62. Ana Mendieta, *El Laberinto de Venus (Labyrinth of Venus)*, 1982, acrylic on paper, 15 ¾ x 11 ½ in. Photo Credit: © The Estate of Ana Mendieta Collection, LLC/ Courtesy Galerie Lelong, New York

63. Sandra Lee-Phipps, WAC demonstration, August 3, 1992 protesting the opening of the Downtown Guggenheim and honoring Ana Mendieta, 1992, black-and-white photo. Photo Credit: © 1992 Sandra Lee-Phipps

64. *Lower Manhattan Sign Project*, parade, August 1992 with Ayisha Abraham (foreground) in orange and Sabra holding a fan slightly beyond, 35 mm color slide. Photo Credit: Roger Mignon

65.–66. Sabra Moore, *Origin of Pearl Street*, front and back view, sign created for the *Lower Manhattan Sign Project* sponsored by REPOhistory and installed on the south side of Pearl Street just west of Whitehall Street in Lower Manhattan, 1992-1993, silkscreen on metal, double-sided, 24 x 18 in. This was one of 39 signs created by various artists for this project and described how the name of Pearl Street had originated in the accumulation of sea shells that lined the banks of the East River, left from centuries of fishing by Native Americans at this site. Photo Credit: Sabra Moore/ Courtesy of Sabra Moore New York City Women's Art Movement Archive, Barnard College

67. Sabra Moore wearing a shell robe she created for the June 1992 parade celebrating the *Lower Manhattan Sign Project*, 35 mm color slide. Photo Credit: Roger Mignon

Epilogue

1. Sylvia Sleigh, *A.I.R. Group Portrait*, 1978, oil on canvas, 75 x 82 in. Photo Credit: Estate of Sylvia Sleigh

2. Frances Buschke, *Untitled*, circa 1978, mixed media on rice paper, feathers, gauze strips, oil pastel, earth pigments, gum Arabic, rocks, string, 21 ¼ x 12 ¼ in. Photo Credit: Estate of Frances Buschke/ Courtesy of Sabra Moore

3. Frances Buschke, *Untitled*, circa 1978, cloth, paper, feathers, string, earth pigments, gum Arabic, oil pastel, 3 ¾ x 3 ¼ in. Photo Credit: Estate of Frances Buschke/ Courtesy of Sabra Moore

4. Sabra Moore, *Palm Trees with Capitals*, 2000, laser transfer on cloth (trees), found metal, copper, wood-burned wood (capitals), each tree is approximately 76 x 11 in., six trees in overall installation. Sabra wrote 82 friends and asked each person to Xerox her palm print; she used these photocopies to create the laser transfer images. Photo Credit: Sabra Moore

5.–6. Sabra Moore, *Palm Trees*, detail (both), 2000–2006, aspen, cedar, and ponderosa poles, oil, wood-burning, materials for bases vary: cedar branches, wood, cast iron, each tree approximately 8 ft. high, base width varies, overall installation varies. Sabra wrote 82 friends and asked each person to Xerox her palm print; she used these photocopies to wood burn the palm prints into the poles of each palm.

7. Sabra installing *Three Boats*, comprised of (left to right) *Carreta Boat*, *Beaver Boat*, and *Trapper Boat*, Roundhouse, State Capital Building, Santa Fe, New Mexico, part of the 1999 exhibit *Animals of the Heart*, curated by Bobbe Besold, 1998–1999, *Carreta Boat*, wood, broken crockery, oil, wood-burning, wagon wheels, 102 x 57 x 54 in.; *Beaver Boat*, beaver-chewed wood, wood-burning, wire, 114 x 60 x 34 in.; and *Trapper Boat*, found iron, metal strips, oil, wood, wood-burning, 30 x 36 x 94 in. *Three Boats* relates to the history of beaver-trapper in the rivers of northern New Mexico. Photo Credit: Sabra Moore

8. Sabra Moore, *We Are All in the Same Boat*, 2002, metal strips, wire, found wood branches, candles, oil, 96 x 24 x 21 in. Photo Credit: Sabra Moore

9. Sabra working on *Carreta Boat* with *Beaver Boat* in the background, 1998. Photo Credit: Roger Mignon

10. Sabra Moore, *A Warhead Doesn't Have a Heart*, detail, 2003, salt cedar poles, oil, laser transfer print on gessoed paper, wire, copper, stone, cloth, 94 x 36 x 31 in. This artwork was made in response to the description of the bombs used in the Gulf War as "smart bombs," so Moore asked (and answered) the question: "If a warhead has a brain, does it have a heart?" The photo transfer images are taken from newspaper clippings the first week of the Gulf War and the salt cedar poles used in the core construction, also called tamarisk, are plants originating in Persia and seen as invasive, like us. Photo Credit: Sabra Moore

11. Sabra Moore and children from El Rito Elementary School, *Eagle/Bird Spirals*, one of two painted tile mosaics installed on the outer gymnasium wall of El Rito Elementary School, El Rito, New Mexico, 2012, painted clay tiles, approximately 84 x 84 x 2 in. each. *Eagle/Bird* was designed by Sabra Moore for an artist-in-the-schools project with fifth grade students. Photo Credit: Sabra Moore

12. Sabra Moore and children from El Rito Elementary School, *Eagle/ Bird Spirals*, detail showing Moore's red tile with hawk drawing. Photo Credit: Sabra Moore

13. Children looking at the *Leopard/Sunflower Mosaic* in the entry hallway of the newly constructed Alcalde Elementary School, 2013. *Leopard/Sunflower Mosaic*, 2013, painted clay tiles, approximately 116 x 116 x 2 in. This mosaic installation was designed by Sabra Moore for an artist-in-the-schools project; Sabra and children from all grades (kindergarten through sixth), the teachers, the principal, the librarian, and the custodians each created one painted clay tile with the image of a leopard for this mosaic while the school was in temporary portable buildings awaiting the move to a new building. Photo Credit: Sabra Moore

Illustration Index by Artist